Testimonio:
A Documentary History of the Mexican American Struggle for Civil Rights

D1558912

Testimonio:
A Documentary History of the Mexican American Struggle for Civil Rights

Edited by
F. Arturo Rosales

The Hispanic Civil Rights Series

Arte Público Press
Houston, Texas

I would like to thank the Arte Público Press staff,
especially Gabi Baeza Ventura for helping me
beyond what is expected from publishers.

This volume is made possible through grants from the Charles Stewart Mott
Foundation and The Rockefeller Foundation.

Recovering the past, creating the future

University of Houston
Arte Público Press
452 Cullen Performance Hall
Houston, Texas 77204-2004

Cover design by James F. Brisson
Document translations from Spanish to English by Gabriela Baeza Ventura

Rosales, Francisco A. (Francisco Arturo)
    Testimonio: a documentary history of the Mexican American Struggle
for civil rights / F. Arturo Rosales.
    p. cm.--(The Hispanic civil rights series)
    Includes index.
    ISBN 10: 1-55885-299-9 (alk. paper)
    ISBN 13: 978-1-55885-299-0
    1. Mexican Americans — Civil Rights — History — Sources.
2. Civil rights movements — United States — History — Sources.
3. United States — Ethnic relations — Sources. I. Title. II. Series.

E184.M5 R638 2000
973'.046872—dc21   00-024328

♾ The paper used in this publication meets the requirements of the American National
Standard for Information Sciences—Permanence of Paper for Printed Library
Materials, ANSI Z39.48-1984.

6 7 8 9 0 1 2 3 4 5   0 9 8 7 6 5 4 3 2

Para mi esposa, Graciela

Contents

Introduction   xv

I. Nineteenth-Century Mexicans in the Southwest and Civil Rights

Introduction   1

    Early Signs of Manifest Destiny   8

    The Treaty of Guadalupe Hidalgo   10

    The "Gadsden Purchase"   16

    Angelinos Resist   20

    Tejanos Lose Land   22

    Anglo Squatters in Arizona   23

    Maintaining Spanish   26

    Social Bandits   28

    Las Gorras Blancas   29

    The Legacy of the Vallejos   31

    An Old-timer in Phoenix   33

    Guadalupe Vallejo   37

    Catarino Garza   39

II. "The Brown Scare": The Mexican Revolution as a Source of Conflict

Introduction   42

    Ricardo Flores Magón   47

    "Low-Lifed Mexican"   51

    The "Brown Scare"   52

    "A Conspiracy Has Been Unearthed"   55

The Texas Rangers   61

El Plan de San Diego   63

"A Favor for an Old Mexican Rancher"   66

The Porvenir Massacre   68

Canales Testifies Against the Rangers   71

"Could Not Live with Them on Genial Terms" 73

The Dangerous Crossing   74

III. World War I and Massive Immigration in the 1920s

Introduction   **76**

"For the Most Part They Return"   82

Crossing the Border   84

"Far From Being Undesirables"   86

Waivers to the 1917 Act   88

"Gaining the Precious Genes of Nordics"   90

Alonso S. Perales and Mexican Immigration   91

The Race Question   93

"Give Their Places to Americans"   96

The 1929 Act   98

Mexican Americans Support Immigrants   100

"To Rid This Community of Mexicans"   101

IV. Immigrant Mobilization

Introduction   **103**

"The Spirit and Solidarity of Brotherhood"   107

Mexicanness and Racial Pride   108

The León Cárdenas Martínez Case   111

La Liga Protectora Latina   114

America for America   116

"An American . . . Who Loves Mexican People"   118

The Clemency Movements   120

Aurelio Pompa   122

Vida, Proceso, y Muerte de Aurelio Pompa—Corrido   123

Desegregation Success—Arizona   126

Desegregation Success—California 128

Desegregation Failure—Kansas 130

A Mexican *Colonia* During the Great Depression 132

V. Mexican Government and *El México de Afuera*

Introduction **134**

Mexicans on Death Row 139

The Draft Issue During World War I 141

Mistreatment and the Need for Mexican Labor 142

Documenting Mistreatment 144

The Comisiones Honoríficas Mexicanas and

Las Brigadas de la Cruz Azul Mexicanas 146

Mexican Study of Immigrant Conditions 149

The Mexican Government and Segregation 151

Police as Criminals 153

Mob Violence towards Mexicans 155

Lázaro Cárdenas and Mexican Immigration Policy 156

VI. Mexican American Mobilization

Introduction **157**

Early Mexican Americanism 164

League of United Latin American Citizens (LULAC) 165

Alonso S. Perales on the Ideals of Mexican Americans 167

A Pioneer in Mexican Americanism 168

Consoling Loyalty to the United States of America 170

The Social Security Classification 172

A Poignant Defense of the Whiteness of Mexicans 173

Faith in Americanization 174

Bert Corona and Mexican Americanism 176

World War II and Mexican Americans 178

A Veteran Returns to Mexico 180

Protesting Lack of Recognition During World War II 181

The Optimism of Returning Soldiers 183

El Club Chapultepec 185

The Citizen's Committee for Latin American Youth   187

The Spears Bill   192

Méndez v. Westminster   194

Judge Peña Remembers Desegregation Efforts   205

Mexican Americans and Ambiguity about Claiming Whiteness   207

Dolores Huerta on the Community Services Organization   211

Keeping in Touch with JFK   212

Mexican Americanism Becomes Militant   214

VII. Defense in the Workplace

Introduction   **216**

Daniel Venegas and the Workplace   223

Boss Violence in Track Work   224

Labor Competition and Violence   226

LULAC Defends White Worker Threats   228

"Black Lung" Disease   230

The Mammoth Tank Battle   231

"¡Solidaridad! ¡Solidaridad!"   232

The Bisbee Deportations   233

Workers' Demands in Clifton, Arizona—1918   236

Agricultural Workers in California   237

An Early Labor Society   238

Mainstream American Unions and Mexicans   239

Mexican Unions Emerge in the United States   241

Unionism in the Agricultural Fields   243

Radicals and Mexican Agricultural Workers in California   246

Emma Tenayuca   247

The Memorial Day Massacre   249

Luisa Moreno   258

The Empire Zinc Strike   259

Striving for Equal Opportunity   262

"On the Day They Were Defeated"   264

"If We Are Given the Opportunity . . ."   266

The Mine Mill   267

VIII. Catalysts of the Chicano Movement: Farm Worker Organizers and Land Grant Crusaders

Introduction	**269**
Chávez's Organizing: the Early Years	276
César Chávez on How It Began	282
Getting a Contract	285
MAPA Supports the Union	293
El Plan de Delano and the Chicano Student Movement	295
Boycott Strategy	296
The Texas Farm Worker Movement	298
Texas Rangers Suppress Farm Worker Organizing	300
The Farm Worker Union in Arizona	302
The Farm Worker Union Opposes Immigrant Workers	303
Young Organizers Meet in New Mexico	305
Poor People's March	306
Tijerina Speaks Out on Martin Luther King's Assassination	308
Tijerina Runs for Governor	321
A Government Agency Is Critical of Suppression	322
Protesting the El Paso Conference	325
Patsy Tijerina	327

IX. Chicanismo, Youth, and La Raza Unida Party

Introduction	**328**
Rodolfo "Corky" Gonzales Speaks Out	339
United Mexican American Students (UMAS)	348
Marcha de la Reconquista	350
Police Brutality	352
Blowouts!	353
The McKnight Letter	355
School Walkouts by the Crusade for Justice	360
The National Chicano Liberation Youth Conference	361
El Plan de Santa Bárbara	364
The Movimiento and the Catholic Church	370
Early Chicana Feminism	372

Mexican Americans Protest the Vietnam War   374

Rosalío Muñoz's Assessment of LAPD-Mexican American Relations   375

Arizona State University Chicano Students Awaken   377

Chicanos Por La Causa   379

La Caravana de la Reconquista   381

Formation of the Mexican American Youth Movement (MAYO)   383

MAYO Membership Requirements   385

Walkout Fever Spreads   386

Walkouts in Crystal City   387

La Raza Unida in Colorado   389

Chicanas and La Raza Unida Party   391

The August 29th Movement   394

Bilingual Education and MALDEF   400

LULAC Veers to the Left   404

Bibliography   **407**

Index   **413**

Photo Credits   **425**

Testimonio:
A Documentary History of the Mexican American Struggle for Civil Rights

Introduction

The idea for this anthology of historical documents on the struggle to obtain civil rights by Mexican people in the United States came about after I indicated to Nicolás Kanellos, the director of Arte Público Press, that in preparing my books, *Chicano!* and *¡Pobre Raza!*, I had amassed a treasure trove of primary documents pertinent to this topic. Professor Kanellos immediately suggested that we publish a documents history. We both felt that through the reading of original accounts, students, teachers, and lay people in general would obtain a better appreciation for the experience of Mexicans in the U.S as they struggled against rejection and repression. These records—personal letters, newspaper accounts, treaties, proclamations, government studies, diplomatic correspondence, family papers, founding papers of organizations, etc.—are contemporaneous to four eras in the overall history of civil rights and Mexican Americans. They reveal that the authors resorted to individual acts of resistance, to organizational efforts, and to appeals to the Mexican and U.S. governments to rectify problems of abuse. They fall under the rubrics of lost land identification, México Lindo nationalism, Mexican Americanism, and the Chicano Movement.

The documents appear in nine chapters organized around chronology and themes. Each section of primary sources is preceded by a short survey history for each era, which contextualizes the documents within a proper historical framework.

The Lost Land

The "Lost Land" era is chronicled in Chapter One. By the 1890s, railroads, outside capital, and outside entrepreneurs disrupted or eliminated the society forged by Hispanics and Anglos in the territories that the U.S. had acquired from Mexico in the mid-nineteenth century. Mexicans, native to the Southwest, felt as if they had lost their past and even their identity, ergo a "lost land" identity emerged. In this era, the southwest Mexican link to central Mexico was weak. Even early immigrants crossing the border from northern Mexico found more intimacy with the Hispanic Southwest's culture and people than if they had gone in the opposite direction to the interior of their country. As a consequence, they too felt a sense of loss when Anglo-American hegemony subordinated and made barrios out of former Mexican towns.

Consequently, the identity of this era rested on an idealized and romanticized view of life before Anglos wrought modernization. Ultimately, the loss of land, culture, and political self-determination created the rationale for the civil rights struggle. Try as Mexicans might, their political mobilization to stem these losses was unsuccessful.

But class differences abounded in the Mexican Southwest. Even after the Anglo takeover, some Hispanics amassed political and economic power within the total community, as well as a degree of prestige and respect. To establish economic and political links, the Mexican elite mixed and married with newcomer Anglos. While the elite did not necessarily assimilate—it was more likely that Anglos would Hispanicize—they did collaborate with the more powerful Anglo newcomers. In the process, they maintained their distance from the lower classes. The power accrued by the elite, however, did serve to provide relief to the lower classes in cases of violent hostility and injustices in the legal system.

México Lindo Generation

A *México Lindo* (pretty Mexico) identity emerged as large numbers of Mexican immigrants who arrived in the U.S. after 1900 and during the Mexican Revolution established colonias throughout the Southwest and the Midwest. Chapters Two to Five deal with this era. Anglo Americans measured the value of these immigrants mainly in the labor market. Border violence against Americans during the revolutionary upheaval provoked a resentment and fear of all Mexicans on this side of the border. Moreover, their barrios, which were segregated and subordinated, had little influence in shaping the image of the larger host communities. Survival and adaptation needs shaped political and defense strategies while their identity rested on an idealized and romanticized memory of the old country.

While *México Lindo* consciousness emerged in old Hispanic communities, such as San Antonio, it complemented a "Lost Land" source of identity in that city. Conversely, in Los Angeles, immigration was of such magnitude that the "Lost Land" ideal was inundated and hardly visible. In northern New Mexico, on the other hand, Hispano villagers until recently have maintained their "Lost Land" identity intact. But even in the new societies wrought by immigration, class differences existed and were promoted by the purveyors of *México Lindo,* who were mainly middle and upper class exiled conservatives from the Mexican Revolution. They adhered to an elegant *mexicanismo* and often looked with disdain at their uneducated poorer compatriots. No dignity and very little respect was attributed to their Spanish, their custom, their dress, etc.—these attitudes, of course, were class prejudices brought over from Mexico.

But when push came to shove, *México Lindo* nationalism prompted immigrant leaders to come to the aid of compatriots whose civil rights were violated. Immigrant leaders also organized mutual aid societies that, while not unions in the strict sense of the word, were designed to help working Mexicans. In addition, the Mexican government through its consular system, constantly vitalized *México Lindo* identity and served as a source of civil rights protection. Finally, during this era Mexicans unionized, especially in the mining districts of Arizona, relying to some degree on union traditions that they brought from northern Mexico.

Mexican Americanism

In Chapter Six, the rise of Mexican Americanism among second or third generation Mexicans is shown. This generation had a sense of permanency and a strong desire to live as the equals of other Americans within an Anglo American system. In urban Texas during the 1920s, the earliest large-scale manifestations of Mexican Americanism appeared when the state acquired the largest U.S.-born Mexican population in the country after 1910; from this base came a critical core that aspired to social mobility and equality. Geographically, Mexican Americanization occurred in a staggered order that waited for U.S.-born Mexicans to come of age. By the 1940s, there was no region in the U.S. where the process had not produced a large cohort group of individuals with a phenotypology and a cultural character of a Mexico, but to whom Mexico was a foreign country.

Mexican Americanization did not necessarily imply assimilation. Nonetheless, educated and more affluent Mexican Americans, who desired social mobility and the degree of assimilation required to achieve their dreams, adhered to many mainstream Anglo traditions. Middle class-aspiring Mexican Americans looked with disdain at their brothers and sisters who did not transcend working-class Mexicanness that persisted beyond the first generation. Significantly, the Mexican American middle classes applied the word chicano pejoratively to identify the lower classes.

In the process, many Mexican Americans promoted themselves as white Americans of Mexican ancestry. For the mainly mestizo Mexican population, however, such an assertion was nevertheless difficult to sustain. The claim constantly ran into racist, demeaning brick walls—a process witnessed by their children, many of whom became the promoters of a new Chicano identity. Nonetheless, racist obstacles hindered mobility; thus, Mexican American leaders launched an intensive civil rights struggle to tear down these barriers, especially, school segregation and job discrimination. In addition, all U.S.-born Mexicans, regardless of where they stood in the class hierarchy, resented mistreatment, such as police brutality or anti-Mexican violence. In the long run, these middle-class struggles benefited the children of the working classes who sought mobility.

More immediately, poorer Mexican Americans were more concerned with workplace conditions, which usually translated to a need for unions. This phenomenon, which is another manifestation of Mexican Americanism, is chronicled in Chapter Seven. Individuals from the Mexican American middle class made short-lived forays, such as the Socialist Congress of Spanish-Speaking People of the 1930s and 1940s and the Asociación Nacional México-Americana (AMMA, Mexican American National Association) in the 1950s, to broaden the civil rights agenda to include working-class issues. Because of the vigorous anti-socialist atmosphere in the U.S., these groups found it very difficult to survive.

Chicano Movement

Chapter Eight documents the farm worker movement of César Chávez in California and the land grant struggle of Reies López Tijerina in northern New Mexico. Because the Chicano Movement declared itself to be a radical grassroots crusade, different from its Mexican American predecessors, it appropriated these two movements, which struggled for the most dispossessed and marginalized Mexicans in the United States, as part of its initiative.

The final chapter of this book provides documents for the Chicano Movement. It arose during the youth rebellion of the 1960s, a time of protest against the war in Vietnam and "Black Pride" mobilization. The war provided Chicanos with one very important issue: stopping war casualties among young Mexican Americans. In Black Pride, which manifested itself through the promotion of self-esteem and the glamorizing of African history, Chicanos saw parallels to their own condition in the United States.

As a consequence, the Movement addressed the issue of identity and civil rights with a greater zeal than any other Mexican generation in the United States. The identity envisioned by *movimiento* leaders and bolstered by El Plan Espiritual de Aztlán had an impact everywhere the Chicano Movement was proclaimed. When dealing with the notion of denial, people saw a catharsis emerge that put an emphasis on the acceptance of being brown or mestizo and not being ashamed of it. The 1920s work of the Mexican philosopher José Vasconselos, *La raza cósmica* (The Cosmic Race), with its message of a new hemispheric bronze people, resonated. The concept of Aztlán, the homeland of the Aztecs alleged to be the present-day Southwest, gave the mestizo-Indian aesthetic, which Chicanos had been conditioned to see in negative terms, a heretofore unknown dignity. Cultural trappings and myths formulated at the 1969 Denver youth conference and in the Chicano design for higher education, the Plan de Santa Bárbara, fueled the nationalism necessary to commit to social struggle. Out of this effort came the rise and fall of La Raza Unida Party, the culmination of the Chicano Movement efforts.

Ultimately, these different generations served as building blocks to create what is today a vigilant framework of Mexican American civil rights organizations peopled by socially-minded activists. Within today's advocacy efforts, numerous traits have passed from the previous generations that struggled to deal with problems that they confronted in the era in which they lived. This book chronicles these struggles and the reader can see firsthand, the links that join the past with the present.

Chapter One

Nineteenth-Century Mexicans in the Southwest and Civil Rights

Mexico inherited the vast territory that today comprises the present states of Texas, New Mexico, Arizona, California, and parts of Nevada, Utah, Colorado, Oklahoma, and Kansas, when it acquired its independence from Spain in 1821. By 1853, however, after a series of confrontations, the United States had acquired this vast Mexican hinterland. Mexico's first land loss to the aggressive Anglo Americans came in 1836 after the Texas Rebellion. Stephen F. Austin planted the seeds of this severance, when in 1821 he signed an agreement with a newly independent Mexican nation to settle four hundred non-Hispanic Catholic families in a vast region known as *Tejas*. This contract became a wedge that allowed thousands of other Anglos to flock into the region in the ensuing decade.

With prodding from both Mexicans and Anglos in Texas and California, the Mexican Congress, in 1824, encouraged the immigration of even more non-Mexicans into other northern reaches of Mexico by passing a law that provided free and cheap land to Mexican settlers. By 1830, twenty thousand Anglos lived in the northernmost part of the state of Texas Coahuila. The outsiders never liked the arrangement, however, and were not shy about airing their grievances. For example, they complained that the Mexican government did not protect them from Comanche raids and that the Mexican legal code, based on Roman tradition, deprived them of rights to which they were accustomed under the more flexible English common law system. The location of the state legislature in Saltillo, Coahuila, hundreds of miles from the center of Anglo population, also antagonized the new settlers. Finally, Anglo and Mexican Texans declared their independence from Mexico in 1836, after strongman Antonio López de Santa Anna centralized power in Mexico City and then attempted to bring dissenting Texans under more rigid control. After defeating Mexican troops led into Texas by General Santa Anna himself, the rebels succeeded in subduing the uprising.

Mexican officials never accepted or recognized the Lone Star Republic and threatened the United States with war if it ever tried to annex the region. Suspecting that the United States had assisted the rebels in acquiring their independence, they remained antagonistic to further American inroads. In 1845, the United States Congress confirmed Mexico's worst fears when it ratified a treaty to annex Texas. Once the territory became part of the United States, President James Polk sent General Zachary Taylor across the Nueces River to enforce a dubious claim that the new acquisition extended all the way to the Rio Grande River. The Mexicans, relying on previous international agreements, maintained that Texas ended at the Nueces River, some two hundred miles to the north.

In reality, Anglo Americans wanted to fulfill a Manifest Destiny of expanding their country all the way to the Pacific coast. After the annexation, the ambitious President Polk, sent John Slidell, in November of 1845, to Mexico with an offer of twenty-five million dollars for New Mexico and California. Mexican officials refused to receive him. Polk then ordered General Zachary Taylor across the Nueces River to blockade the Rio Grande River by establishing a military garrison at its mouth in Port Isabel. When Mexicans retaliated on April 25, 1846, and inflicted casualties on the United States troops, Polk immediately obtained a declaration of war from Congress.

The United States' invasion proceeded from four different directions. General Taylor, with his troops already amassed along the Rio Grande, crossed into Northeastern Mexico, while General Stephen Watts Kearny took an army overland to New Mexico and then to California. From the sea, Commodore John C. Fremont inflicted another assault on Mexican California. Finally, General Winfield Scott ordered the U.S. Navy to bombard Veracruz and then, with a sizable force, he proceeded all the way to Mexico City, where his troops met the greatest resistance at Churubusco. Nonetheless, by September of 1847, the United States military occupied Mexico City. General Santa Anna, who had been president since December of 1846, personally conducted the war on the Mexican side, and in November of 1847, he resigned in disgrace because he failed to defend the homeland. Only after being thoroughly routed did the Mexicans agree to a peace treaty in the village of Guadalupe Hidalgo during February of 1848.

Under the terms of the treaty, the United States acquired the vast territories of New Mexico, Arizona, California, and parts of Nevada, Utah, and Colorado for fifteen million dollars. Crucially, the same treaty provided Mexicans who remained in what became U.S. territory, all the rights of citizens. Treaty provisions promised Southwest Mexicans protection of their property and the right to maintain religious and cultural integrity.

The Treaty of Guadalupe Hidalgo did not apply to Mexicans in Texas, but the 1836 constitution of the Texas Republic, which became the charter for statehood in 1845, required equal rights for Mexicans. The treaty signed at Guadalupe Hidalgo did not cede to the United States a region comprising today's southern Arizona and southern New Mexico, extending from present-day Yuma along the Gila River (twenty-five miles south of Phoenix) all the way to the Mesilla Valley in New Mexico. General Santa Anna sold this section to the United States when he returned to power in 1853 through the Gadsden Treaty. The provisions of this agreement gave Mexicans in the newly annexed territory similar rights to those offered in the Treaty of Guadalupe Hidalgo.

Anglo Americans did not accept Mexicans as equals and often the constitutional guarantees offered by the Treaty of Guadalupe Hidalgo were not honored. In the New Mexico Territory where the majority of the Hispanics resided, some sixty thousand, they forged a degree of political self-determination. But even there, the newly minted United States citizens encountered systematic discrimination. Outside of New Mexico, conditions were worse. In Texas, where the non-Indian population increased from 35,000 Anglos, black slaves, and Mexicans in 1836, to 140,000 persons in 1846 because of the rapid influx of Anglos, Mexicans numbered no more than 20,000. They became a deprived and disenfranchised minority. During the period of the Republic, many Mexicans who were deemed disloyal during the rebellion lost their citizenship rights and their property. White Texans also curbed the political involvement of Mexican Texans as well. Only one was elected as a delegate to the convention that created the new state constitution when Texas joined the Union in 1845. At that meeting, some convention delegates attempted to disenfranchise Mexicans of the vote, but failed. Nonetheless, intimidation often kept Texas Mexicans from voting. In the era of the Republic, only a few rich San Antonio Mexicans had obtained political influence. Juan Seguín was elected first mayor of San Antonio, but was forced out after the Anglo population increased. A bitter Seguín went to Mexico and fought the invading Americans during the Mexican-American War.

In Texas, few Mexicans participated in politics, either during the era of the Republic or after the United States annexed the territory. The state legislature of 1850, for example, did not have a single Tejano among its sixty-four members. Also, Tejano political ascendency was limited because local political bosses often influenced whom Mexicans voted for, irrespective of their interests. In addition, white-only primaries and grandfather clauses prevented Mexicans from casting the ballot, and since the Democratic party dominated in Texas, the elections were really decided in these primaries. The custom of charging a fee to vote, known as a poll tax, also deterred poor citizens from voting, a barrier

3

that included most Mexicans. These forms of disenfranchisement did not completely succeed in depriving Mexicans of all economic and political power, but they did violate the guarantees of the Treaty of Guadalupe Hidalgo. To avoid persecution, many Mexicans simply left Texas and crossed the border to resettle in Mexico.

Mexicans in California experienced less Anglo antipathy than their counterparts in Texas, but competition in the minefields during the Gold Rush resulted in violent conflict in the first decades after California entered the Union. California Mexicans participated in politics mainly during the early years of the United States takeover, before large numbers of gold seekers and other fortune hunters diluted the *californio* population. Even when participating, the *californios* only had minimal influence. For example, of the forty-eight delegates to the 1849 state constitutional convention, only eight were *californios.*

As in Texas, Mexicans in California were soon outnumbered. Fifteen percent of the population was Mexican in 1850; twenty years later that figure had dropped to only four percent. The economic and political influence of Mexicans declined first in the north, where thousands of Anglos had flocked to gold mining areas. Soon, Anglo politicians enacted legislation contrary to their interests. In 1851, inhabitants in the six southern counties, where most Mexicans resided, paid property taxes five times higher than did owners in northern counties, where the majority of Anglos lived. Then, clearly to suppress *californio* customs, in 1855 the state legislature enacted the so-called "greaser laws," which prohibited bullfights, bear fights, and cockfights. Many local governments also enacted vagrancy codes, which they mainly directed at Mexicans. The most onerous anti-Hispanic law was the 1850 Foreign Miners Tax. It levied a charge to stake out claims to anyone who was not a United States citizen. While many other foreigners were drawn to the lure of gold, Mexicans or South Americans, who possessed superior mining skills, comprised the bulk of the "foreigners." Consequently, the tax was seen as a blatant attempt to eliminate Hispanic competition in the gold diggings.

Economic and political participation was more extensive for Mexicans in New Mexico than in any other region because there, Hispanics maintained a numerical majority until the turn of the century. After the Mexican-American War, Anglos quickly dominated the southeastern part of the state, but Hispanics controlled the north from Albuquerque to Santa Fe. Essentially, Hispanics dominated most key political slots statewide and controlled the territorial legislature until the 1890s. In fact, one of the reasons it took so long for New Mexico to acquire statehood was because many members of the United States Congress objected to a new state dominated by Mexicans.

In Arizona, an area which remained part of the New Mexican territory until 1863, Mexicans conserved some political and economic power. This was especially true in the southern section of the state around Tucson, the area purchased with the Gadsden Treaty in 1853. After Arizona separated from New Mexico, Tucson became the territorial capital. This period saw significant Anglo and Mexican cooperation because economic activity depended greatly on trade through the Mexican state of Sonora. The building of railroads and the arrival of more Anglos in the 1880s, however, drastically reduced Mexican economic activities. This change resulted in Mexicans working mainly in brute labor sectors. Now Anglo elites did not have to cooperate with Mexican merchants, a factor that strained the once symbiotic relationship between both groups. Consequently, the little political power that Mexicans had amassed declined precipitously. The territorial seat shifted to Prescott in northern Arizona, away from Mexicans, and as Phoenix became more important, that city became the capitol.

Mexicans suffered an even greater loss in property rights. While the provisions in the Treaty of Guadalupe Hidalgo regarding the protection of the land and property were vague, the document contained definite commitments for protection. Large-scale Anglo immigration and subsequent economic development inflated land values, which fueled competition over property throughout the Southwest. Because land tenure systems differed considerably in Mexico from property record keeping in the United States, Southwest Mexicans were immediately burdened with proving land ownership through legal title.

To deal with the emerging land conflicts, Congress passed the California Land Act of 1851, ostensibly framed so that *californios* could legalize land they claimed prior to the takeover. California Hispanics, however, found that complying with the legislation sometimes took years. This saddled cash-strapped *rancheros* with large adjudication fees, which they paid with huge tracts of land. The 1862 Homestead Act, passed by Congress to allow squatters to settle and claim vacant lands in unsettled frontier areas, created even more burdens for Mexican landowners. To the dismay of the *californios*, thousands of Anglo settlers squatted on their lands, creating a morass of legal disputes, which the courts often settled in favor of the squatters. Land speculators took advantage of the confusion and used homesteaders as front men to obtain free lands, which they sold later for huge profits.

In 1854, Congress established the Surveyor of General Claims Office in the New Mexico Territory to resolve land disputes, a system that was even slower than the one in California. Settling just a few claims took decades, during which time speculators defrauded Mexicans of their land in grabs similar to the California schemes. In the 1890's, the building of the Santa Fe, Atchison, and

Topeka railroad from Kansas through the northern part of the territory inflated land values, and speculators, known as the "Santa Fe Ring," wrested farms and ranches from hundreds of Hispanic landowners. The establishment of state parks early in the twentieth century continued to erode the land holdings of Hispanics in New Mexico.

All in all, New Mexicans did not suffer the same degree of land usurpation as Hispanics in other parts of the Southwest, but the acreage held by Hispanics prior to the Mexican War declined considerably. In the final analysis, while the Treaty of Guadalupe Hidalgo did not precisely define the rights of Mexican Americans, it is clear that most of the guarantees were not upheld. As a result, the economic and political fortunes of Mexican Americans of the Southwest languished because of Anglo domination.

The United States justice system also discriminated against Southwest Mexicans. During the 1880s, in Texas border communities where Mexicans maintained influence, local court proceedings were allowed to be conducted in Spanish, and Mexican Americans who did not speak English served on juries. In the rest of Texas, however, an 1856 law prohibiting Spanish in the courts was vigorously enforced. This was the case in other areas where juries, judges, and law enforcers applied the law to Mexicans in a discriminatory fashion. In Arizona's infamous territorial prison, more than half of the convicts were Mexican in 1890.

Criminal violations against Mexicans by Anglos almost always went unpunished. Lynching parties commonly targeted Mexicans; in California, they were commonplace during the Gold Rush years in the 1850s. In Texas, the intensity of this kind of violence increased during and immediately after the Civil War and did not abate until the end of the century. It was not just minorities who suffered the illegal reprisals, but they were applied to them more frequently and with greater ferocity.

Ultimately, tension and resentment among Mexicans built up, and they struck back through violence and criminality against their perceived oppressors. In New Mexico during the 1890s, hundreds of New Mexicans organized into bands of hooded night riders known as Las Gorras Blancas (The White Caps) and rode out at night to tear down fences and derail trains, hoping to stem the encroachment of Anglo land development and railroad building. Nineteenth-century Texas, with the largest Mexican population and the longest border with Mexico, experienced the greatest ethnic discord, stemming mainly from border conflict and property competition. From the time of Texas's independence in 1836, the region between the Nueces and the Rio Grande rivers was plagued by warfare between marauding Mexican and Anglo livestock raiders. Mexican brigands easily crossed the Rio Grande to Mexico if conditions became "too

6

hot" because of retaliatory Anglo rampages. The most famous and cited example of this activity is that of Juan "Nepomuseno" Cortina, a landowner in the Brownsville area. He precipitated years of warfare and brigandage between Mexicans and Anglos in 1859 when he killed a Brownsville deputy sheriff for mistreating a Mexican vagrant. Texas Rangers zealously suppressed local bandits and Mexicans who struck from across the Rio Grande.

In spite of the atmosphere of animosity that existed in the pre-immigrant era, by the turn of the century Mexicans who were born in the Southwest acquired methods of defending themselves that did not leave them as vulnerable to Anglo aggression and the dual standard of applying justice. Court records in New Mexico, for example, show native Hispanics litigating land and business issues in the courts, often holding their own. In contrast, records for states where Mexican immigrants prevailed over native Hispanos—California, Arizona, and Texas—the legal proceedings have more to do with criminal cases and less with civil. In conclusion, where Mexicans kept political power in the nineteenth-century Southwest, they were able to use the legal system more effectively, and although the litany of abuses is extensive, there is also evidence of ability to provide community defense by maintaining political influence.

Early Signs of Manifest Destiny

The ideology of Manifest Destiny, aptly expressed in an editorial by John O'Sullivan in the *New York Sun* during 1847, indicated that "the [Mexican] race is perfectly accustomed to being conquered, and the only new lesson we shall teach is that our victories will give liberty, safety, and prosperity to the vanquished, if they know enough to profit by the appearances of our stars." A much earlier indication of "Manifest Destiny" is in an account by William Shaler, a ship captain who traded with *californios* for otter skins, who wrote in his journal in 1804 that California would be better off under the Americans.

Foreigners in their Native Land: The Historical Roots of Mexican Americans

California "would fall without an effort" by William Shaler, 1808.

The Spanish population of California is very considerable; by the best information I could obtain, it exceeds 3,000 souls, including the garrison. With the exception of the officers, there are very few white people: it principally consists of a mixed breed. They are of an indolent, harmless disposition, and are fond of spirituous liquors. That they should not be industrious is not surprising; their government does not encourage industry. For several years past, the American trading ships have frequented this coast in search of furs, for which they have left in the country about 25,000 dollars annually, in specie and merchandise. The government has used all their endeavors to prevent this intercourse, but without effect, and the consequences have been a great increase in wealth and industry among the inhabitants. The missionaries are the principal monopolizers of the fur trade, but this intercourse has enabled the inhabitants to take part in it. At present, a person acquainted with the coast may always produce abundant supplies of provisions. All these circumstances prove that under a good government, the Californians would soon rise to ease and affluence.

....

The mutual jealousies and selfish policies of the great European powers have been the causes that some of the most beautiful regions of the universe have long languished under the degrading shackles of ignorance and superstition; and the Spanish monarchy has for so long been the quiet enjoyment of the finest part of the new world, that they have been at full liberty to extend their conquests there in every direction, without any other obstacle than the feeble opposition of the native savages. Any of the great maritime powers that should determine to give independence to New Spain, or wrest it from the Spanish dominion, would naturally seek to establish themselves in California, from whence, as a place of arms, they might carry on their operations against the defenseless kingdom with a certainty of success. This the Spaniards have doubtless foreseen, and been before hand in occupying it, with a view of forming barrier to those possessions. The foregoing shows that what they have yet done has had a directly contrary effect. They have, at a great expense and considerable industry, removed every obstacle out of the way of an invading enemy; they have stocked the country with such multitudes of cattle, horses, and other useful animals, they have no longer the power to remove or destroy them; they have taught the Indians many of the useful arts, and accustomed them to agriculture and civilization; and they have spread a number of defenseless inhabitants over the country, whom they never could induce to act as enemies to those who should treat them well, by securing to them the enjoyments of liberty, property, and free trade, which would almost instantaneously quadruple the value of their actual possessions: in a word, they have done everything that could be done to render California an object worthy of the attention of the great maritime powers; they have placed it in a situation to want nothing but a good government to rise rapidly to wealth and importance.

The conquest of this country would be absolutely nothing; it would fall without an effort to the most inconsiderable force; and as the greatest effort that the Spanish government would be capable of making towards its recovery would be from the shores of New Spain, opposite the peninsula, a military post, established at the bay of Angles, and that of San Diego fortified and defended by a component body of troops, would render such an attempt ineffectual. The Spaniards have few ships or seamen in this part of the world; the arsenal of San Blas would be their only resource on such an occasion, and that might be very easily destroyed. But, admitting that the inactivity of the invaders should permit them to transport troops over to the peninsula, those that come from New Spain could not be very formidable, either in point of numbers or courage, and they would have to penetrate through Lower California, where they would not find even water in their march; all the other resources of that desolate country could be easily removed out of their way. They could not march round the head of the gulf. The natural obstacles of such an expedition would be very numerous; and they must besides force their way through many warlike nations of savages.

An expedition by sea to Upper California would be equally difficult for them; the bad weather they must encounter in winter, and the great length of the passage in summer, on account of the prevailing northwest winds, would render it a very precarious undertaking. In a word, it would be easy to keep California in spite of the Spaniards, as it would be to wrest it from them in the first instance.

In David Weber, *Foreigners In Their Native Land: The Historical Roots of Mexican Americans* (University of New Mexico Press, 1973), pp. 65-68.

The Treaty of Guadalupe Hidalgo

After the Mexican-American War, Mexicans who lived in the territories annexed by the United States were given guarantees under provisions of the Treaty of Guadalupe Hidalgo, which was signed on February 2, 1848. Articles eight and nine impinged the most on the Mexicans left in what became U.S. territory.

Treaty of Guadalupe Hidalgo, 1848

IN THE NAME OF ALMIGHTY GOD:

The United States of America and the United Mexican States, animated by a sincere desire to put an end to the calamities of the war which unhappily exists between the two Republics, and to establish upon a solid basis relations of peace and friendship, which confer reciprocal benefits upon the citizens of both, and assure the concord, harmony, and mutual confidence wherein the two peoples should live, as good neighbours, have for that purpose appointed their respective plenipotentiaries, that is to say:

The President of the United States has appointed Nicholas P. Trist, a citizen of the United States, and the President of the Mexican Republic has appointed Don Luis Gonzaga Cuevas, Don Bernardo Couto, and Don Miguel Atristain, citizens of the said Republic;

Who, after a reciprocal communication of their respective full powers, have, under the protection of Almighty God, the author of peace, arranged, agreed upon, and signed the following Treaty of Peace, Friendship, Limits, and Settlement between the United States of America and the Mexican Republic.

ARTICLE I
There shall be firm and universal peace between the United States of America and the Mexican Republic, and between their respective countries, territories, cities, towns, and people, without exception of places or persons.

ARTICLE II
Immediately upon the signature of this treaty, a convention shall be entered into between a commissioner or commissioners appointed by the General-in-chief of the forces of the United States, and such as may be appointed by the Mexican Government, to the end that a provisional suspension of hostilities shall take place, and that, in the places occupied by the said forces, constitutional order may be re-established, as regards the political, administrative, and judicial branches, so far as this shall be permitted by the circumstances of military occupation.

ARTICLE III
[Stricken out]

ARTICLE IV
[Stricken out]

ARTICLE V

The boundary line between the two Republics shall commence in the Gulf of Mexico, three leagues from land, opposite the mouth of the Río Grande, otherwise called Río Bravo del Norte, or opposite the mouth of its deepest branch, if it should have more than one branch emptying directly into the sea; from thence up the middle of that river, following the deepest channel, where it has more than one, to the point where it strikes the southern boundary of New Mexico; thence, westwardly, along the whole southern boundary of New Mexico (which runs north of the town called Paso) to its western termination; thence, northward, along the western line of New Mexico, until it intersects the first branch of the river Gila; (or it should not intersect any branch of that river, then to the point on the said line nearest to such branch, and thence in a direct line to the same); thence down the middle of the said branch and of the said river, until it empties into the Río Colorado; thence across the Río Colorado, following the division line between Upper and Lower Calfornia, to the Pacific Ocean.

The southern and western limits of New Mexico, mentioned in this article, are those laid down in the map entitled *"Map of the United Mexican States, as organized and defined by various acts of the Congress of said republic, and constructed according to the best authorities. Revised edition, Published at New York, in 1847, by J. Disturnell,"* of which map a copy is added to this treaty, bearing the signatures and seals of the undersigned Plenipotentiaries. And, in order to preclude all difficulty in tracing upon the ground the limit separating Upper from Lower California, it is agreed that the said limit shall consist of a straight line drawn from the middle of the Río Gila, where it unites with the Colorado, to a point on the coast of the Pacific Ocean, distant one marine league due south of southermost point of the port of San Diego, according to the plan of said port made in the year 1782 by Don Juan Pantoja, second sailing-master of the Spanish fleet, and published at Madrid in the year 1802, in the atlas to the voyage of the schooners Sutil and Mexicana, of which plan a copy is hereunto added, signed and sealed by the respective Plenipotentiaries.

In order to designate the boundary line with due precision, upon authorative maps and to establish upon the ground landmarks that shall show the limits of both republics, as described in the present article, the two Governments shall each appoint a commissioner and a surveyor, who, before the expiration of one year from the date of the exchange of ratifications of this treaty, shall meet at the point of San Diego, and proceed to run and mark said boundary in its whole course to the mouth of the Río Bravo del Norte. They shall keep journals and make out plans of their operations; and the result agreed upon by them shall be deemed a part of this treaty, and shall have the same force as if it were inserted therein. The two Governments will amicably agree regarding what may be necessary to these persons, and also as to their respective escorts, should such be necessary.

The boundary line established by this article shall be religiously respected by each of the two republics, and no change shall ever be made therein, except by the express and free consent of both nations, lawfully given by the General Government of each, in conformity with its own constitution.

ARTICLE VI

The vessels and citizens of the United States shall, in all time, have a free and uninterrupted passage by the Gulf of California, and by the river Colorado below its confluence with the Gila, to and from their possessions situated north of the boundary line defined in the preceding article, it being understood that this passage is to be by navigating the Gulf of California and the river Colorado, and not by land, without the express consent of the Mexican Government.

If, by the examinations which may be made, it should be ascertained to be practicable and advantageous to construct a road, canal, or railway, which should in whole or in part run upon the river Gila, or upon its right or its left bank, within the space of one marine league from either margin of the river, the Governments of both republics will form an agreement regarding its construction, in order that it may serve equally for the use and advantage of both countries.

ARTICLE VIII

Mexicans now established in territories previously belonging to Mexico, and which remain for the future within the limits of the United States, as defined by the present treaty, shall be free to continue where they now reside, or to remove at anytime to the Mexican Republic, retaining the property which they possess in the said territories, or disposing thereof, and removing the proceeds wherever they please, without their being subjected, on this account, to any contribution, tax, or charge whatever.

Those who shall prefer to remain in the said territories may either retain the title and rights of Mexican citizens, or acquire those of citizens of the United States. But they shall be under the obligation to make their election within one year from the date of the exchange of ratifications of this treaty; and those who shall remain in the said territories after the expiration of that year, without having declared their intention to retain the character of Mexicans, shall be considered to have elected to become citizens of the United States.

In the said territories, property of every kind, now belonging to Mexicans not established there, shall be inviolably respected. The present owners, the heirs of these, and all Mexicans who may hereafter acquire said property by contract, shall enjoy with respect to it guarantees equally ample as if the same belonged to citizens of the United States.

ARTICLE IX

The Mexicans who, in the territories aforesaid, shall not preserve the character of citizens of the Mexican Republic, conformably with what is stipulated in the preceding article, shall be incorporated into the Union of the United States, and be admitted at the proper time (to be judged of by the Congress of the United States) to the enjoyment of all the rights of citizens of the United States, according to the principles of the Constitution; and in the meantime, shall be maintained and protected in the free enjoyment of their liberty and property, and secured in the free exercise of their religion without restriction.

ARTICLE X
[Stricken out]

ARTICLE XI
Considering that a great part of the territories, which, by the present treaty, are to be comprehended for the future within the limits of the United States, is now occupied by savage tribes, who will hereafter be under the exclusive control of the Government of the United States, and whose incursions within the territory of Mexico would be prejudicial in the extreme, it is solemnly agreed that all such incursions shall be forcibly restrained by the Government of the United States whensoever this may be necessary; and that when they cannot be prevented, they shall be punished by the said government, and satisfaction for the same shall be exacted—all in the same way, and with equal diligence and energy, as if the same incursions were meditated or committed within its own territory, against its own citizens.

It shall not be lawful, under any pretext whatever, for any inhabitant of the United States to purchase or acquire any Mexican, or any foreigner residing in Mexico, who may have been captured by Indians inhabiting the territory of either of the two republics nor to purchase or acquire horses, mules, cattle, or property of any kind, stolen within Mexican territory by such Indians.

And in the event of any person or persons, captured within Mexican territory by Indians, being carried into the territory of the United States, the Government of the latter engages and binds itself, in the most solemn manner, so soon as it shall know of such captives being within its territory, and shall be able so to do, through the faithful exercise of its influence and power, to rescue them and return them to their country, or deliver them to the agent or representative of the Mexican Government. The Mexican authorities will, as far as practicable, give to the Government of the United States notice of such captures; and its agents shall pay the expenses incurred in the maintenance and transmission of the rescued captives, who, in the meantime, shall be treated with utmost hospitality by the American authorities at the place where they may be. But if the Government of the United States, before receiving such notice from Mexico, should obtain intelligence, through any other channel, of the existence of Mexican captives within its territory, it will proceed forthwith to effect their release and delivery to the Mexican agent, as above stipulated.

For the purpose of giving to these stipulations the fullest possible efficacy, thereby affording the security and redress demanded by their true spirit and intent, the Government of the United States will now and hereafter pass, without unnecessary delay, and always vigilantly enforce, such laws as the nature of the subject may require. And, finally, the sacredness of this obligation shall never be lost sight of by the said Government, when providing for the removal of the Indians from any portion of the said territories, or for its being settled by citizens of the United States; but, on the contrary, special care shall then be taken not to place its Indian occupants under the necessity of seeking new homes, by committing those invasions that the United States have solemnly obliged themselves to restrain.

ARTICLE XII

In consideration of the extension acquired by the boundaries of the United States, as defined in the fifth article of the present treaty, the Government of the United States engages to pay to that of the Mexican Republic the sum of fifteen millions of dollars.

Immediately after this treaty shall have been duly ratified by the Government of the Mexican Republic, the sum of three millions of dollars shall be paid to the said Government by that of the United States, at the city of Mexico, in the gold or silver coin of Mexico. The remaining twelve millions of dollars shall be paid at the same place, and in the same coin, in annual installments of three millions of dollars each, together with interest on the same at the rate of six per centum per annum. This interest shall begin to run upon the whole sum of twelve millions from the day of the ratification of the present treaty by the Mexican Government, and the first of the installments shall be paid at the expiration of one year from the same day. Together with each annual installment, as it falls due, the whole interest accruing on such installment from the beginning shall also be paid.

ARTICLE XIII

The United States engage, moreover, to assume and pay to the claimants all the amounts now due them, and those hereafter to become due, by reason of the claims already liquidated and decided against the Mexican Republic, under the conventions between the two republics severally concluded on the eleventh day of April, eighteen hundred and thirty-nine, and on the thirtieth day of January, eighteen hundred and forty-three; so that the Mexican Republic shall be absolutely exempt, for the future, from all expense whatever on account of the said claims.

ARTICLE XIV

The United States do furthermore discharge the Mexican Republic from all claims of citizens of the United States, not heretofore decided against the Mexican Government, which may have arisen previously to the date of the signature of this treaty, which discharge shall be final and perpetual, whether the said claims be rejected or be allowed by the board of commissioners provided for in the following article, and whatever shall be the total amount of those allowed.

ARTICLE XV

The United States, exonerating Mexico from all demands on account of the claims of their citizens mentioned in the preceding article, and considering them entirely and forever cancelled, whatever their amount may be, undertake to make satisfaction for the same, to an amount not exceeding three and one-quarter millions of dollars. To ascertain the validity and amount of those claims, a board of commissioners shall be established by the Government of the United States, whose awards shall be final and conclusive, provided that, in deciding upon the validity of each claim, the board shall be guided and governed by the principles and rules of decision prescribed by the first and fifth articles of the unratified convention, concluded at the city of Mexico on the twentieth day of November, one thousand eight hundred and forty-three; and in no case shall an award be made in favour of any claim not embraced by these principles and rules.

If, in the opinion of the said board of commissioners or of the claimants, any books, records, or documents, in the possession or power of the Government of the Mexican Republic, shall be deemed necessary to the just decision of any claim, the commissioners, or the claimants through them, shall, within such period as Congress may designate, make an application in writing for the same, addressed to the Mexican Minister for Foreign Affairs, to be transmitted by the Secretary of State of the United States; and the Mexican Government engages, at the earliest possible moment after the receipt of such demand, to cause any of the books, records, or documents so specified, which shall be in their possession or power, (or authenticated copies or extracts of the same,) to be transmitted to the Secretary of State, who shall immediately deliver them over to the said board of commissioners, provided that no such application shall be made by or at the instance of any claimant, until the facts that it is expected to prove by such books, records, or documents, shall have been stated under oath or affirmation.

ARTICLE XXIII

This treaty shall be ratified by the President of the United States of America, by and with the advice and consent of the Senate thereof; and by the President of the Mexican Republic, with the previous approbation of its general Congress; and the ratifications shall be exchanged in the city of Washington, or at the seat of Government of Mexico, in four months from the date of the signature hereof, or sooner if practicable.

In faith whereof we, the respective Plenipotentiaries, have signed this treaty of peace, friendship, limits, and settlement, and have hereunto affixed our seals respectively. Done in quintuplicate, at the city of Guadalupe Hidalgo, on the second day of February, in the year of our Lord one thousand eight hundred and forty-eight.

(SEAL.) N. P. TRIST.
(SEAL.) LUIS G. CUEVAS.
(SEAL.) BERNARDO COUTO.
(SEAL.) MIGL. ATRISTAIN.

The "Gadsden Purchase"

Five years after the signing of the Treaty of Guadalupe Hidalgo, Americans again acquired territory from Mexico in an agreement that has become known as the "Gadsden Purchase." The plain language of the treaty indicates clearly the use to which this territory would be put. The protection assigned in the Treaty of Guadalupe Hidalgo to Mexicans living in the territory acquired in that agreement would also apply in this treaty.

Gadsden Treaty, 1853

IN THE NAME OF ALMIGHTY GOD:

The Republic of Mexico and the United States of America, desiring to remove every cause of disagreement which might interfere in any manner with the better friendship and intercourse between the two countries, and especially in respect to the true limits which should be established, when, notwithstanding what was covenanted in the Treaty of Guadalupe Hidalgo in the year 1848, opposite interpretations have been urged, which might give occasion to questions of serious moment: To avoid these, and to strengthen and more firmly maintain the peace that happily prevails between the two republics, the President of the United States has, for this purpose, appointed James Gadsden, Envoy Extraordinary and Minister Plenipotentiary of the same near the Mexican Government, and the President of Mexico has appointed as Plenipotentiary *ad hoc* his excellency Don Manuel Diez de Bonilla, Cavalier Grand Cross of the National and Distinguished Order of Guadalupe, and Secretary of State and of the office of Foreign Relations, and Don José Salazar Ylarregui and General Mariano Monterde, as scientific commissioners, invested with full powers for this negotiation; who, having communicated their respective full powers, and finding them in due and proper form, have agreed upon the articles following:

ARTICLE I

The Mexican Republic agrees to designate the following as her true limits with the United States for the future: Retaining the same dividing line between the two Californias as already defined and established, according to the 5th article of the Treaty of Guadalupe Hidalgo, the limits between the two republics shall be as follows: Beginning in the Gulf of Mexico, three leagues from land, opposite the mouth of the Río Grande, as provided in the fifth article of the treaty of Guadalupe Hidalgo; thence, as defined in the said article up the middle of that river to the point where the parallel of 31° 47' north latitude crosses the same; thence due west one hundred miles; thence south to the parallel of 31° 20' north latitude; thence along the said parallel of 31° 20' to the 111th meridian of longitude west of Greenwich; thence in a straight line to a point on the Colorado River twenty English miles below the junction of the Gila and Colorado Rivers; thence up the middle of the said river Colorado until it intersects the present line between the United States and Mexico.

For the performance of this portion of the treaty, each of the two Governments shall nominate one commissioner, to the end that, by common consent, the two thus nominated, having met in the city of Paso del Norte, three months after the exchange of the ratifications of this treaty, may proceed to survey and mark out upon the land the dividing line stipulated by this article, where it shall not have already been surveyed and established by the mixed commission, according to the Treaty of Guadalupe, keeping a journal and making proper plans of their operations. For this purpose, if they should judge it necessary, the contracting parties shall be at liberty each to unite to its respective commissioner scientific or other assistants, such as astronomers and surveyors, whose concurrence shall not be considered necessary for the settlement and ratification of a true line of division between the two republics; that line shall be alone established upon which the commissioners may fix, their consent in this particular being considered decisive and an integral part of this treaty, without necessity of ulterior ratification or approval, and without room for interpretation of any kind by either of the parties contracting.

The dividing line thus established shall, in all time, be faithfully respected by the two Governments, without any variation therein, unless of the express and free consent of the two, given in conformity to the principles of the law of nations, and in accordance with the constitution of each country, respectively.

In consequence, the stipulation in the 5th article of the Treaty of Guadalupe upon the boundary line therein described is no longer of any force, wherein it may conflict with that here established the said line being considered annulled and abolished wherever it may not coincide with the present, and in the same manner remaining in full force where in accordance with the same.

ARTICLE II

The Government of Mexico hereby releases the United States from all liability on account of the obligations contained in the eleventh article of the Treaty of Guadalupe Hidalgo; and the said article and the thirty-third article of the treaty of amity, commerce, and navigation between the United States of America and the United Mexican States, concluded at Mexico on the fifth day of April, 1831, are hereby abrogated.

ARTICLE III

In consideration of the foregoing stipulations, the Government of the United States agrees to pay to the Government of Mexico, in the city of New York, the sum of ten millions of dollars, of which seven millions shall be paid immediately upon the exchange of ratifications of this treaty, and the remaining three millions as soon as the boundary line shall be surveyed, marked, and established.

ARTICLE IV

The provisions of the 6th and 7th articles of the Treaty of Guadalupe Hidalgo having been rendered nugatory for the most part by the cession of territory granted in the first article of this treaty, the said articles are hereby abrogated and annulled, and the provisions as herein expressed substituted therefore. The vessels and citizens of the United States shall, in all time, have free and uninterrupted passage through the Gulf of California, to and from their possessions situated north of the boundary line of the two countries. It being understood that this passage is to be by navigating the Gulf of California and the river Colorado, and not by land without the express consent of the Mexican Government; and precisely the same provisions, stipulations, and restrictions, in all respects, are hereby agreed upon and adopted, and shall be scrupulously observed and enforced, by the two contracting Governments, in reference to the Río Colorado, so far and for such distance as the middle of that river is made their common boundary line by the first article of this treaty.

The several provisions, stipulations, and restrictions contained in the 7th article of the Treaty of Guadalupe Hidalgo shall remain in force only so far as regards the Río Bravo del Norte, below the initial of the said boundary provided in the first article of this treaty; that is to say, below the intersection of the 31° 47' 30" parallel of latitude, with the boundary line established by the late treaty dividing said river from its mouth upwards, according to the 5th article of the treaty of Guadalupe.

ARTICLE V

All the provisions of the eighth and ninth, sixteenth and seventeenth articles of the Treaty of Guadalupe Hidalgo, shall apply to the territory ceded by the Mexican Republic in the first article of the present treaty, and to all the rights of persons and property, both civil and ecclesiastical, within the same, as fully and as effectually as if the said articles were herein again recited and set forth.

ARTICLE VI

No grants of land within the territory ceded by the first article of this treaty bearing date subsequent to the day—twenty-fifth of September—when the Minister and subscriber to this treaty on the part of the United States proposed to the Government of Mexico to terminate the question of boundary, will be considered valid or be recognized by the United States, or will any grants made previously be respected or be considered as obligatory which have not been located and duly recorded in the archives of Mexico.

ARTICLE VII

Should there at any future period (which God forbid) occur any disagreement between the two nations which might lead to a rupture of their relations and reciprocal peace, they bind themselves in like manner to procure by every possible method the adjustment of every difference; and should they still in this manner not succeed, never will they proceed to a declaration of war without having previously paid attention to what has been set forth in article 21 of the Treaty of Guadalupe for similar cases; which article, as well as the 22nd, is here re-affirmed.

ARTICLE VIII

The Mexican Government having on the 5th of February, 1853, authorized the early construction of a plank and rail road across the Isthmus of Tehuantepec, and, to secure the stable benefits of said transit way to the persons and merchandise of the citizens of Mexico and the United States, it is stipulated that neither Government will interpose any obstacle to the transit of persons and merchandise of both nations; and at no time shall higher charges be made on the transit of persons and property of citizens of the United States than may be made on the persons and property of other foreign nations, nor shall any interest in said transit way, nor in the proceeds thereof, be transferred to any foreign government.

The United States, by its agents, shall have the right to transport across the isthmus, in closed bags, the mails of the United States not intended for distribution along the line of communication; also the effects of the United States Government and its citizens, which may be intended for transit, and not for distribution on the isthmus, free of custom-house or other charges by the Mexican Government. Neither passports nor letters of security will be required of persons crossing the isthmus and not remaining in the country.

When the construction of the railroad shall be completed, the Mexican Government agrees to open a port of entry in addition to the port of Vera Cruz, at or near the terminus of said road on the Gulf of Mexico.

The two Governments will enter into arrangements for the prompt transit of troops and munitions of the United States, which that Government may have occasion to send from one part of its territory to another, lying on opposite sides of the continent.

The Mexican Government having agreed to protect with its whole power the prosecution, preservation, and security of the work, the United States may extend its protection as it shall judge wise to it when it may feel sanctioned and warranted by the public or international law.

ARTICLE IX

This treaty shall be ratified, and the respective ratifications shall be exchanged at the city of Washington within the exact period of six months from the date of its signature, or sooner if possible.

In testimony whereof we, the Plenipotentiaries of the contracting parties, have hereunto affixed our hands and seals at Mexico, the thirtieth (30th) day of December, in the year of our Lord one thousand eight hundred and fifty-three, in the thirty-third year of the Independence of the Mexican Republic, and the seventy-eighth of that of the United States.

(SEAL.) JAMES GADSDEN.
(SEAL.) MANUEL DIEZ DE BONILLA.
(SEAL.) JOSE SALAZAR YLARREGUI.
(SEAL.) J. MARIANO MONTERDE.

Angelinos Resist

In September of 1846, Los Angeles Mexicans resisted takeover by Commodore Stockton's troops. Under the leadership of Sérvulo Varela and Leonardo Cota, four-hundred men signed a petition condemning the occupation by Anglo American soldiers.

Pronunciamento de Varela y otros de California contra los americanos

Citizens: For a month and a half, due to a pitiful misfortune, the result of cowardice and incompetence of the primary authorities of the area, we have been subjugated and oppressed by a measly force of adventurers from the United States, who, placing us in a situation worse than that of slaves, are dictating despotic and arbitrary laws to us by which they charge us with fees and onerous taxes, being that they wish to destroy our industries and our agriculture and force us to abandon our properties so that they may take them over and divide them amongst themselves. Should we remain subjugated and silently accept the heavy burden of slavery? Perhaps we should lose the land inherited from our fathers which cost them so much blood? Should we then let our families fall victim to the most cruel servitude? Should we wait until we see our women raped and our innocent children beaten with the American whip, our properties plundered, our temples profaned, and ourselves submerged in a life of embarrassment and disgrace? No! A thousand times no! Compatriots, better dead than that! Which one of you does not feel your heart beat and your blood boil when you contemplate our situation? Who will be the Mexican who will not be infuriated and raise his weapons to put an end to our oppressor? We believe that there will not be one so vile and cowardly. Therefore, the majority of the inhabitants of this district, justly angered with these tyrants, raise our cry for war and with weapons in our hands, we swear to support the following articles:

1. We, all the citizens of California, as members of the great Mexican Nation, declare that our wish is and has been to belong only to her, free and independent.
2. Therefore, we declare useless and inoperative the authorities designated by the North American invading forces.
3. We swear not to rest until we see all North Americans who have humiliated Mexico expelled from our land.
4. Every Mexican citizen between the ages of fifteen and sixty who does not seize weapons to support this plan is declared a traitor, under the penalty of death.
5. Any Mexican or foreigner who directly or indirectly aids Mexico's enemies will be punished in the same manner.
6. All property of North American residents that may have been taken directly or indirectly, belonging to those who may have aided Mexico's enemies, will be confiscated and used to cover all the costs of war, and its citizens will be sent to the Republic's provinces.

7. All who may oppose the present plan will be executed.
8. All the citizens of Santa Barbara and of the north district will immediately be invited to join this plan.

A camp near Los Angeles, September 24, 1846. Sérvulo Varela, Leonardo Cota, and three-hundred more.

Pronunciamento de Varela y otros de California contra los Americanos, 24 de septiembre, 1846, MS, Bancroft Library, University of California.

Tejanos Lose Land

In Texas, embittered Anglos, who wanted the property of the outnumbered Mexicans or who resented their presence, forced them off their property, sometimes claiming the Mexicans had been disloyal. In 1853, the Mexican Consul in Brownsville provided his home government with examples of this process.

Secretaría de Relaciones al Ministro de México en Washington, December 28, 1853

Your Excellency:

On the 8th of the current month, I stated the following to the General Consul of the Republic in the United States of America: "During the last few days, it has been said that neighbors of Matagorda County in the State of Texas, who united in an assembly, decided to expel the Mexican population residing in the same county. Several reasons are attributed for such an extraordinary and illegal measure, and until it is truly revealed what has taken place, I will limit myself to give Your Excellency knowledge of this, following this letter with a copy of a paragraph, that with this date I have addressed to Mr. Kingsbury, a member of the State Legislature, asking for reports on the already mentioned matter. It states: I have been notified of a cruel and illegal act committed by the citizens of Matagorda County; it appears that those citizens, despising all duty of justice and humanity, have determined to expel their neighbors of Mexican descent. I am unaware of the reasons that have prompted such resolution made at a public meeting. Therefore, I would truly appreciate it if you would communicate to me what took place in this matter, as well as tell me if the Mexicans, so brutally treated, are or are not naturalized according to the laws of the United States of America. I should warn that, if they are still citizens of Mexico, I will make the news available to our Embassy residing in Washington. As soon as I receive the report I requested, I will proceed accordingly, and I will inform Your Excellency appropriately."

Secretaría de Relaciones al Ministro de México en Washington, December 28, 1853, Archivo Histórico de la Secretaría de Relaciones Exteriores, 1-C-R1.F. 433-435 in Angela Moyano Pahissa (ed.) *Protección Consular a Mexicanos en los Estados Unidos* (Mexico City: SRE, 1849-1900), pp. 127-128.

Anglo Squatters in Arizona

The majority of Mexicans lost land and economic power in a less dramatic fashion than just simply being thrown off their land. Squatters often compromised the land claims of Mexicans. Historians have often recounted this process as it happened in California, New Mexico, and Texas. The document shown here, sent in 1878 by M. Escalante, the Mexican consul in Tucson, to the Mexican foreign minister, describes the process in southern Arizona.

M. Escalante, Mexican Consul in Tucson, Arizona, to Mexican Secretary of the Foreign Ministry

One of the matters that most seriously affects the interests of Mexican citizens in Arizona is one that is related to the execution of the treaties by virtue of which part of the Mexican territory passed into United States control.

According to those treaties, the American government solemnly agreed to respect and protect the property of Mexicans included in the limits of the ceded territory. In 1854, they declared as valid the articles that with the same purpose had been assigned to the Treaty of Guadalupe Hidalgo in 1848.

And what is it that the government of the United States has done to carry out the obligations that this treaty imposed? Which state currently safeguards this serious and important business?

As a result of the extraordinary size of immigration that the discovery of gold attracted to California, in 1851, the Congress issued a law, organizing a commission to examine and decide the validity of existing title deeds within the limits of that state.

Later in 1854, the Congress of the United States dictated a law for the examination and assessment of title deeds in New Mexico, but instead of creating a new special commission as in California, the General Surveyor of the territory was responsible for receiving the mentioned titles and annually issuing a report on them; the Congress thus reserved to itself the right to revise and grant a final decision in each case.

During that time, Arizona was part of New Mexico's territory, and after its separation was decreed and once it was established as an independent territory, Congress applied to Arizona the already mentioned law of 1854.

Twenty-four years have elapsed and experience has evidently proved day after day that the law involved is completely useless in achieving the objective the treaties had proposed.

Thus, it is obviously urgent that this law be revised as soon as possible because it has only served to hinder and delay the right that Mexicans have, according to the context of the treaties, to be respected and protected in their properties.

In the history of this serious business, Arizona has undergone the worst part. Because as it has been stated, in California a commission was established for reviewing and resolving Mexican deeds and, no matter what their procedures were, the commission carried out the assignment, and the pending claims of that state were judged and almost all of them have been definitively resolved.

In New Mexico, another system was established and, although it was defective and impossible to execute, it produced some sort of result.

But in the Arizona territory, not one step has been taken toward executing the mentioned law, because if the government extended it to here, it did not allocate in the expenditure budget any amount for the essential costs that the surveyor should incur while fulfilling his commission.

Countless Mexican residents here and in the state of Sonora own many properties with legitimate titles in Arizona, some of them issued by the colonial government and others by the government of the Republic.

Landowners in Arizona cannot call themselves proprietors, much less possessors of what legally belongs to them. Their condition could not be more precarious and, as time goes by, it worsens to a positively inconceivable degree.

In the passing of so many years and especially since the United States carried out the pacification of wild tribes that inhabited these regions, adventurers called squatters have been occupying the richest portions, the immense titled lands, and their owners cannot protest against such usurpation because their titles are not honored nor confirmed, being that they are inadmissible and do not have any legal value.

But this is not all, Mexican owners undergo an even more unjustifiable offense. While the acknowledgment and decision on the titles is delayed indefinitely, while a remedy against the invasions of the squatter adventurers is lacking, and the Mexican owner does not possess nor enjoy anything, the College of Assessors, in other words, the Quoting Councils, include in the tax lists the properties at issue, and they levy them with exorbitant taxes that their so-called owners should pay.

This is horrendous and unfair, for they are only considered owners when it concerns taxes, without an exchange for those obligations in which they may enjoy the guarantee and right to the taxed properties. To add mockery to the injustice, the same usurpers, squatters who cultivate and benefit from the land, do not pay anything and are exempt from any fees. The process is repeated year after year, until the taxpayer, tired of paying uselessly, unable at other times to cover his debts, and always losing the hope that his titles will one day be recognized and confirmed, sells his property at any price or else loses it in a financial auction.

That is how gradually and progressively the rights of many Mexicans who owned immense and rich lands are disappearing and, if a quick and efficient remedy is not applied to such serious evils, if Mexico does not raise its voice and make vigorous demands before the Washington Cabinet, so that the Treaty of 1848 can finally be executed, the property of our citizens in this territory will be lost forever.

I think it is suitable to go into detail on the same considerations regarding the land matter in the state of California because the history of the cases processed by the Commission there offer a precedent of much importance to Mexico when demanding from the United States a loyal execution of the treaties.

The 1851 law that ostensibly had as its purpose the observance of the Treaty of Guadalupe Hidalgo was in reality expedited out of necessity and convenience to the American nation during the exceptional circumstances in which California became a state. This law produced immense evils for Mexican owners.

The commission was always ready to dispute Mexican titles, no matter how perfect and respectable they were; the law would force them to undergo such high costs that were equivalent to depriving Mexican owners of their properties. This forced them to place liens, mortgage, or sell them. Often dealing with all these obstacles, few reached the triumph of their rights after so many years awaiting an uncertain final judgment, while some are still engaged in litigation.

A better definition of the nature of this law and its practical effects could not be better than that given by Hoffman, District Court Judge in the state of California, when determining on September 4, 1876, the judgment of the United States against Benjamin Flint and others over the validity of a Mexican title.

This law states, although dictated with good intentions, in its practice it has imposed costly obligations (perhaps inevitable) on the holders of Mexican titles these have been submitted to great costs and delayed judgments that at the end of twenty-five years it can hardly be said that they have been settled.

Whatever critical judgment may be formulated about the law of 1851, it has not jeopardized in the least the interests of the United States.

The opinion of this magistrate, so notable for his knowledge, is of great weight. He has presided over the court of appeals on all judgments over property titles in California. It can be deduced from what has been expressed that the government of the United States, when issuing the law of 1851, was not motivated to exercise the duties contracted by the Treaty of 1848, and it may be assumed that its intention was to protect at any costs its own interests.

The principal idea in this serious business, on behalf of the American government, has truthfully not been to honor its vehement faith in Guadalupe Hidalgo. Far from this, instead of adjusting to the spirit and the context of the stipulations, admitting in general theory that all Mexican titles were valid, it established as a fixed foundation the unjustifiable principle that *they were all false.*

Mexican owners were forced to prove in a judgment the unquestionable authenticity of their titles. Thousands of difficulties and increased expenses in the business proceedings were created, and the door almost closed on them before they could achieve the triumph of their lawful right.

Such was the case that some landowners did not even appear before the commission, because they saw that their property did not even represent half the value that the expenses would amount to.

M. Escalante, Mexican Consul in Tucson, Arizona, to Mexican Sectetary of the Foreign Ministry, August 6, 1878, Archivo Histórico de la Secretaría de Relaciones Exteriores, 11-2-106, in Angela Moyano Pahissa, ed. *Protección consular a mexicanos en los Estados Unidos, pp. 28-30.*

Maintaining Spanish

Mexicans keeping their language in the United States territory longer than most other non-English-speaking ethnic groups is partially due to continuous Mexican immigration and because of resistance to Anglo domination. After the Anglo conquest, Southwest Mexicans continued to speak their language, regardless of political and cultural domination. And they published hundreds of Spanish language newspapers to cover not only news and advertising, but also to support their own ideas, language, and culture. Below are two articles that appeared on November 1 and on March 8, 1856, in the Los Angeles newspaper, *El Clamor Público*. The first is an editorial by the newspaper's publisher, Francisco Ramírez, which laments the lack of Spanish instruction for Hispanic children in Los Angeles schools. The second demonstrates a strong desire to establish schools for local Hispanics that would maintain Spanish and develop a bilingual tradition.

Schools

We have seen a petition addressed to the Mayor and City Council, signed by a respectable number of our Spanish community. They asked that a salary be given to the director of schools for Spanish children in this city. This school is attended by a certain number of needy children who are not responsible for monthly fees; at the present time, they have thirty-five children in their school, from whom they receive $21 monthly.

The object of this petition is that an equal distribution of the funds for support be made between them and the schools where students are taught in Spanish. Many parents do not send their children to public schools because they only teach them in English and, for that reason, we hope that the petition cited will receive the City Council's attention.

Truly, nothing would give parents more joy and pleasure than to take advantage of a privilege granted for them like their neighbors, out of the hope that they may be able to educate their children in their native language.

Since a great number of the Spanish population have families and have contributed in the common funds for schools, we flatter ourselves in believing that our petition will receive some consideration.

Catholic School
for
Young Men and Women

We have the pleasure of announcing to parents, as well as any other Spanish person, that next MONDAY, March 10, a new Learning Establishment will open at D. Luis Vigne's home next to EL CLAMOR PÚBLICO.

The following courses will be taught:

SPELLING,	READING,
GEOGRAPHY,	WRITING,
ARITHMETICS,	GRAMMAR,
ENGLISH,	DRAWING.

An establishment of this house must be granted protection by the children of this country, particularly by those who wish to be educated in their native language, as well as those who want to learn English correctly.

Parents who wish to take advantage of this Establishment will be satisfied, in that the Director will do all possible to further the students in the various courses mentioned above as well as in their ethics and good manners.

Teaching hours will be from 9 to 12 and from 2 to 4 in the afternoon.

The cost of teaching: two *pesos* per month for each student.

Social Bandits

Mexican resistance to Anglo rule was manifested in various ways. The most dramatic was through banditry against Anglos. Below, the Tejano Juan A. "Nepomuceno" Cortina and the Californio Tiburcio Vásquez, two "social bandits" whom Anglos considered just plain criminals and whom Mexicans saw as heroes, explain why they engaged in violence.

Juan Nepomuceno Cortina issued this proclamation on a broadside on November 23, 1859, in which he eloquently expressed the complaints of Texas Mexicans against discrimination, oppression, and expropriation of lands and rights:

"Mexicans! When the state of Texas began to receive the new organization which its sovereignty required as an integral part of the Union, flocks of vampires, in the guise of men, came and scattered themselves in the settlements, without any capital except a corrupt heart and the most perverse intentions. Some, brimful of laws, pledged to us their protection against the attacks of the rest, while others, abusing our united confidence when we entrusted them with our titles, that secured the future of our families, refused to return them under false and frivolous pretexts. Many of you have been robbed of your property, incarcerated, chased, murdered, and hunted like wild beasts, because your labor was fruitful, and because your industry excited the vile avarice which led them.

"Mexicans! My part is done; the voice of revelation whispers to me that I am entrusted with the work of breaking the chains of your slavery."

* * *

Tiburcio Vásquez, the famous California "bandit" or social rebel, gave these reasons for striking out at the Anglo population: "My career grew out of the circumstances by which I was surrounded as I grew into manhood. I was in the habit of attending balls and parties given by the native Californians, into which the Americans, then beginning to become numerous, would force themselves and shove the native-born men aside, monopolizing the dances and the women. This was about 1852.

"A spirit of hatred and revenge took possession of me. I had numerous fights in defense of what I believed to be my rights and those of my countrymen. The officers were continuously in pursuit of me. I believe that we were unjustly and wrongfully deprived of the social rights which belonged to us. So perpetually was I involved in these difficulties that I at length determined to leave the thickly-settled portion of the country, and did so."

Las Gorras Blancas

The political platform of Las Gorras Blancas (The White Caps), the hooded night riders who rode out at night to tear down fences and derail trains stem Anglo encroachment during the 1890s in New Mexico left no doubt that their purpose was to counter the loss of land to unscrupulous speculators. Juan José Herrera, one of the leaders of the group, issued this platform in 1890.

Our Platform

Not wishing to be misunderstood, we hereby make this our declaration.

Our purpose is to protect the rights and interests of the people in general, especially those of the helpless classes.

We want the Las Vegas Grant settled to the benefit of all concerned, and this we hold is the entire community within the grant.

We want no "land grabbers" or obstructionists of any sort to interfere. We will watch them.

We are not down on lawyers as a class, but the usual knavery and unfair treatment of the people must be stopped.

Our judiciary hereafter must understand that we will sustain it only when "Justice" is its watchword.

The practice of "double-dealing" must cease.

There is a wide difference between New Mexico's "law" and "justice." And justice is God's law, and that we must have at all hazards.

We are down on race issues, and will watch race agitators. We are all human brethren, under the same glorious flag.

We favor irrigation enterprises, but will fight any scheme whose purpose is to monopolize the supply of water courses to the detriment of residents living on lands watered by the same streams.

We favor all enterprises, but object to corrupt methods to further the same.

We do not care how much you get as long as you do it fairly and honestly.

The People are suffering from the effects of partisan "bossism," and these bosses had better quietly hold their peace. The people have been persecuted and hacked about in every which way to satisfy their caprice. If they persist in their usual methods, retribution will be their reward.

We are watching "political informers."

We have no grudge against any person in particular, but we are the enemies of bulldozers and tyrants.

We must have a free ballot and a fair count, and the will of the majority shall be respected.

Intimidation and the "indictment" plan have no further fears for us. If the old system should continue, death would be a relief to our sufferings. And for our rights, our lives are the least we can pledge.

If the fact that we are law-abiding citizens is questioned, come to our homes and see the hunger and desolation we are suffering; and "this" is the result of the deceitful and corrupt methods of "bossism."

Be fair and just and we are with you; do otherwise and take the consequences.

The White Caps, 1,500 Strong and Growing Daily

"Platform of Las Gorras Blancas issued by Juan José Herrera in 1890," in Prince Papers, New Mexico State Records Center and Archives.

The Legacy of the Vallejos

In 1914, with practically all of the family wealth exhausted, Dr. Platón M.G. Vallejo, the scion of the Vallejo family of Sonoma, California, recounted in a newspaper how family lands and fortune were swallowed up in suits against squatters.

The latter half of the year 1846 was not a pleasant one for Californians. But the resistance forced by the Bear Flag revolt was easily crushed. On March 8, 1847, General Kearney, military governor of California, was able to say this in his report to the Secretary of War at Washington:

"The Californians are now quiet, and I will endeavor to keep them so by mild and gentle treatment. Had they received this treatment from the first, I believe there would have been no resistance. But they were cruelly and shamefully abused by our own people, both here and on the Sacramento, by our own irregular volunteers. Had they not resisted, they would have been unworthy the name of men."

Of course, there were still rumors of uprisings, mostly inspired by interested motives, just as we have rumors of foreign wars today to help the sale of armor plate and guns. But the truth is, California was never more undisturbed than during the year just preceding the discovery of gold.

No one was better pleased than my father when the news came of the Treaty of Querétaro, whereby California became forever a part of the United States. Under the rule of Mexico, he knew that the case was hopeless. Here was a fulfillment of all his hopes. He set himself at once abreast with the forward movement and was thenceforward the most enthusiastic Yankee of them all.

* * *

Then came the mighty gold rush. It swept over California like a tidal wave, under which the native people were submerged. A more experienced race might well have staggered and gone down with the shock. Of the Californians, many, knowing little more than children of the big moving world and its ways, came to the end of their rope, then acquired the wild habits of the day, and often parted for a trifle with land that later came to be of immense value. But still it was surprising how many kept their heads, hanging on to their possessions with tenacity and shrewdness.

Better results might have followed had a quick settlement of land titles been arranged. The Treaty of Querétaro confirmed Californians in all the rights and land grants made by the government of Mexico. But some of the grants were most indefinitely described. Also, some grants were issued by Pío Pico after he had been deposed as Governor and were fraudulently antedated. All were subject to survey and final confirmation. Had my father's warning to the government of Mexico been heeded, to make an instrumental survey of each rancho or grant, and place monuments on the corners, all this later confusion would have been avoided. As it was, "squatters" settled on nearly every grant, vast sums were spent in litigation, titles of the most important lands were clouded for more than a generation, and, in the end, everyone was broke—except the lawyers. Those who began a legal fight very seldom finished it. The fight, and the property, passed into other hands. Even today, after sixty-five years, echoes from the old Spanish land-grant lawsuits are still heard, indicating that they are not yet exactly dead. A large portion of my father's great fortune was swallowed up in the vast cost of defending many suits.

Platón M. G. Vallejo, "Memoirs of the Vallejos," *San Francisco Evening Bulletin,* February 13, 1914, California State Library, Sacramento.

An Old-timer in Phoenix

Most accounts by Mexicans who lived in the nineteenth-century Southwest are from the perspective of the elites, such as the Vallejos. In 1938, Ernest F. Mendivil, a Federal Writer's Project writer, interviewed his uncle, Pedro Pérez, a working-class old-timer who was born in 1860 and who came to the Salt River Valley of Arizona from Sonora in the 1870s. He recalled the lynchings of Mexicans and how Henry Garfías, another Mexican and the first Marshal of Phoenix, helped him get citizenship and a job.

Early Mexican Pioneer of Arizona

Related life story of Pedro Pérez, now residing at 711 S. 13th Ave., Phoenix, Arizona, as taken by Ernest F. Mendivil, on August 7th, 1938.

I, Pedro Pérez, was born on January 31st of 1860 in Pitiquito, District of Alta, Sonora, Mexico. My father's name was Justodio Pérez, and my mother's name was Aniseta Vásquez.

We were living at that time in Pitiquito, the family of ours which was composed of the following brothers and sisters: the oldest was Lemerenciana, a daughter, and next to her followed Carmen, and the brothers, Pedro, Gamesindo, Rafael, and José.

We all came over to what is now known as Phoenix, but at that time was known as EL SALADO, said name was adopted from the Río Salado (Salt River), which is still applied to the river south of Phoenix now. Our first visit to the Salado was in 1870. In coming here, we followed the route then known as the Guajaro, which trail went through Casa Grande then. As we parted from Pitiquito, we hit on the route following rancherías, as they were then called, now ranch colonies. First, we hit the Ranchería called Cabolta, then Tecolote, Uitaxl Ijotoba. In some of these Rancherías, especially the first ones, the inhabitants were Yaquis, and then when we came to the Ranchería del Tecolote, from there on we traveled among Papago Indians, who were rather friendly with the travelers. Since at that time quite a few of these small towns such as Chandler and Gilbert were not in existence, we might have passed through the actual locations where they are now established. One town that is really old and was very old at that time is Tempe, through which we passed when we traveled, until we finally came to the end of our journey by settling in EL SALADO (THE SALTY) now called Phoenix. We lived in El Salado approximately 11 months and then we returned back to Pitiquito, through the same route that we came.

We forgot the idea of traveling for a while, and then in 1875, I myself decided to come back. So then I left Pitiquito for a second time, this occasion I made up my mind to stay and make a living some way, so I took the same route as before and again hit Phoenix, but I did not stay here long, for there was quite a bit of enthusiasm in Gold around Volcho (Vulture). As I left Phoenix and went to Volcho (Vulture), and there I made a living and lots of money for a year and four months, and then I decided to go back to my folks at Pitiquito. In 1877, for the last time we all left Pitiquito, never to return. We again traveled through the same route, and we established ourselves in EL SALADO (THE SALTY) on a ranch owned at that time by a Mr. Henshaw who had owned lots of land at that time.

From 1875 to 1880, lots of people were hanged for small steals of any kind, and lots of them were framed in horse stealing, cattle. In 1875, there was quite a stir over the case of a certain young man of fine reputation and a very good family, but the young man made the mistake of getting one drink too many, and he got the notion to steal a cow from a big rancher and a very mean Tejano (Anglo Texan). The young man's name was Mariano Tisnado, and he was well liked by all the town, and above all he was wealthy. But then he happened to be infatuated with a certain woman in town, and he made the mistake of following the wrong advice, thus causing him the loss of his life. Mr. Grey and a few other Tejanos got together and captured Mariano Tisnado, and they made a necktie party out of the case. When this happened, most of the early Mexican families besides ours that were residing here left town, and for awhile it looked like the future of the town was done for. But after quite a while the people began to come back.

There was at that time too, a famous bandit and outlaw called Jack Suelar. He was a Texan, and he had as a companion a Mexican bandit whose name was José Durán. They were living in town and they used to rob left and right, although with the poor people, they were rather generous with their loots, from the Stage and Express robberies that they made. They used to bury their loots, which up till now is not known where to be found.

In spite of the fact that they lived right in town, they would not have opposition in gunfire, but they were so daring and expert shooters that nobody dared to combat against them. They thrived from the year 1865 till 1880 when they decided to retire from the life that they were in, and as Congress was adopting laws to be enforced in the West, the law of the guns was being cut out. So Jack Suelar retired to his ranch that he bought in Agua Fría (Cold Water), and years after, he was arrested for murders and robberies that he had committed previously, and he died an old man in the Yuma prison. Leaving all that he had in property in Agua Fría towards Cañón Negro (Black Canyon). Don José Durán was not caught because he had left some time before to Old Mexico, taking with him lots of money, and it was never known definitely where he lived or died. During that period, this State had around 10,000 inhabitants, it was not Arizona then, it was all Nuevo México (New Mexico). Of this quantity, 4,000 were Indians of the different tribes that predominate in all the state, and 6000 were composed of Caucasians such as Mexicans and Anglo-Saxons, etc.

In 1873, we got acquainted with Mr. Carlos Hayden, Sr. (Carl Hayden) in Tempe, who is father of Carlos Hayden (Carl Hayden, Jr.), now Arizona National State Senator. In that period, Mr. Carlos Hayden was already operating the only flour mill in the State, and as the main product of the Valle Salado was wheat and food products, it naturally flourished in importance of business standing. When we knew Carlos Hayden Sr. (his son Carlos Hayden Jr., used to go to school on horseback a *pata a raíz* bare footed), the Hayden family was always well liked by the community for their liberality and usefulness to their community and the public in general. The flour mill, which now makes the brand of Estrella Rosa (Star Rose) flour, is still located in the same place where it was originally constructed. The Hayden Canal, which is still running through Tempe, is still in the same old place. The Hayden Flour Mill and the Hayden Canal are approximately 80 years old.

We used to have Apaches around this town as in other parts of the state, but this town was not attacked by the Apaches, because the Indian tribes living around Phoenix, such as the Maricopas, Pimas, Yumas, were more industrious and were very friendly with the people that would settle here. And since this tribe did not believe in warfaring, they were good fighters, and they knew how to fight the Apaches, so the Apache tribes did not bother this Valle Salado at all.

In 1880, I was married to a young Señorita Anita Ortega, in EL SALADO. We had quite a celebration on account of my wedding in the ranch which was then called the Balz Ranch. There was a Mexican orchestra, lots of food was served, and plenty of dance till the early hour of the following day.

The location of the Balz Ranch was at 14th Street and Henshaw Wood. From there on I separated from my folks and lived the best I knew how, for the next eighteen years. I was in the line of farming and ranching. My four sons and daughters were born during this period: Arnulfo, Adela, Teodora, who were born in the Balz Ranch, and Pedro Jr., was born in a government ranch on the other side of the Salt River.

In 1890, I received my United States citizenship papers. Immediately, I began to exercise my rights as a citizen by voting by the Señal Cruz (Cross Sign), as I did not know how to read and write at that time. Although quite a few years later, a new law deprived me of voting because I could not read or write.

I sold my ranch on the other side of the Rio Salado (Salt River) in 1895 and moved into town and settled in a house number 524 S. 35th Ave., which does not exist anymore. We lived there two years. From this house I moved with the family to a house on Jackson and 5th Avenue, more or less the present location of the Union Depot of the Southern Pacific Railroad Company. This happened in 1900, when I went into the business of freighting for the next nine years. My son Arnulfo and my daughter Adela were married previously to 1906, so in 1907 my daughter Adela, now residing at 1144 W. Sherman Street, Phoenix, brought to this world her first baby, whose name was Ernest Mendevil, now residing at 807 S. 2nd Avenue thus I began to have grandsons from there on from all my children. My son-in-law, then an amateur in photography, is Rafael A. Mendivil, who now resides in 1144 West Sherman, and now has a studio shop at 216 W. Washington Street.

Going back to 1900, I happened to go in the business of freight when the Roosevelt Dam was begun. I had a couple of Studebaker heavy-duty wagons, which were the best in old times. And they were very expensive too, but they were worth the money because they were rugged for the kind of treatment the roads had to give them, very especially the Old Apache Trail, where you had to be a real Teamster driver or else you could not stay on the road. With the canyons so deep and high and rugged, if anybody rolled off, it would be too bad. Up till today when you drive the new-styled cars, you can still see part of the old trail when you travel toward Miami and Globe and so on till you reach the dam, and then you may verify what I have just admitted. But in spite of all this danger, I, as well as other old-timers dared this, and so for nine years I made good money until I quit about a year before the Roosevelt Dam was completed, which was in 1910.

In 1910, we moved from the house on 5th Avenue and Jackson Street, because Mr. John Bayori sold a big tract of land to the Southern Pacific Railroad Co., for the purpose of constructing a new depot, which was not constructed immediately, but quite a few years later. So then I moved to 918 W. Grant Street, retired from business, but I did not stay long idling, I went to work as a cowboy and cattleman in the mountains for five years under my boss by the name of Mr. Snyder of Bumble Bee, and seven years I worked in the same line of activity with different bosses such as Don Julio Rodríguez, Charles Garret, Bill Cook, and Mr. Mitchell. Then I quit this strenuous activity.

In 1922, till 1924, I worked in the city of Phoenix, under the Municipal Government in outdoor work. In 1925, my wife Anita Ortega Pérez died after 42 years of companionship. By 1925, all my children married, and I had lot of grandsons and granddaughters. Three of my children are now living in Phoenix, Adela Mendivil, Teodora Pérez, Pedro Pérez Jr., and Arnulfo Pérez is in Los Angeles, California.

Since 1926, I have been taking it easy because I am too old now, but I feel very strong yet. My eyesight is good, and I still possess my original set of teeth, and I am well satisfied since I am receiving a small pension which helps me to a certain extent. Although, a little more would be more justified because us old-timers have a hard time to get the cooperation of our children, because most of our children have their own problems to contend with.

I should have mentioned before my appreciation for a certain man that did quite a bit of good to this old-time communities; his name is Enrique Garfias a Mexican Marshall Deputy, an official at that time, in 1890 when the Gavillas of Tejanos (Gangs of Texan Bandits) used to romp and raise hell, and make trouble here. They used to rob and throw the town in disorder. The stages would not be left alone. The law of the gun was not yet forgotten by some people.

During this period, Enrique Garfias was a very desperate and strong supporter of law and order, but these Tejanos would come in town often and make trouble. Enrique Garfias was a very good shot, cool, and, above all, very brave. He used to rout and follow any bandit, and he would defend with life and soul his town people and the community from such bandits. He used to go after these Texans (*Tejanos*), and he would get them allright in fact, he finished most of them. And the other *Tejanos* and other Bandits on the side used to dodge him, because he would get his man that he went after. Sometimes he would engage entire gangs, and they would quit on him. So through his actions and his sincerity in law and order, he gained the sympathy of the people. He used to help everybody in solving their everyday problems. I, for one, appreciate the fact that he helped me to get my business of citizenship solved, and I now see that my efforts were not ill spent. Because now as an old-timer, I am getting benefit of that affair.

"Related Life Story of Pedro Pérez," interview typescript by Ernest F. Mendivil, on August 7, 1938, steel file biographies, Arizona Department of Library, Archives and Public Records, Phoenix.

Guadalupe Vallejo

Anglo Americans often commented on the bitter fate of Southwest Mexicans. In 1890, a San Francisco reporter sought out Guadalupe Vallejo, niece of Mariano Guadalupe Vallejo, who had written a nostalgic article on life in Mexican California. The journalist interviewed her after finding her living modestly in Oakland. In this lengthy account, the writer, Knapp relates Guadalupe Vallejo's memories of the coming of the Americans to northern California during the invasion of 1848.

We younger ones were terribly afraid of the Americans then. "Those terrible Americans" was the manner in which we thought of them. I will never forget my first experience with them. My uncle General Vallejo was confined in the jail of Sacramento. He managed to procure a pencil and wrote on a lot of cigarette paper a message of warning to my father that the Americans were coming on our way and would capture him if he did not flee at once. This note he made into a wad and threw it at one of our countrymen who waited under his window, and who at once brought it to my father. We were then living at what is now the town of Niles, but was then only known as Vallejo's Mills. We had a house there, as well as at the Mission. My father deemed it wise to heed the General's warning and resolved to take a company of Indians and go to the forest for safety, while the women of the family should go on to the present town of Haywards, where lived the Castros, who were relatives of my mother. Well, the men would need much food in the forest, and therefore, great fires were built in the huge oven and an enormous quantity of the finest bread was baked for them to take with them. Other provisions were also made ready, and the party was nearly equipped to start when the dreaded Americans themselves arrived upon the scene. Of course, no explanation was made as to why such great quantities of food had been prepared, and I suppose they must have concluded it was the regular Spanish style of doing things, and I thought they were good enough for it just then, for they had been making long, hard marches but with scant provisions, and were dearly famished. So they fell upon and in a very short time completely made way with the food, which they had expected would last my father and his Indians for many days in the forest. This band had no orders to arrest my father, but they desired to enter and search the house for arms and ammunition, as it was their policy to disarm all the Spanish residents. Of course, all the readily available arms had been safely hidden, but my father was deeply incensed at the idea of his house being searched, and sitting down beside his door, he said to the officer in command: You may go in, if you will, but you will not come out.

It was very XXX of my father to take this tone with the soldier, but he was deeply indignant at another little thing that occurred just then, and he could not forget that he was a Spanish gentleman and entirely within his own rights. The little incident I refer to was in connection with myself. I was but a wee child then, and I stood gazing in awe at the idea of being touched by one of the awe-inspiring conquerors and ran back. The coals with which the great oven had been heated had been raked out and were still glowing red on the hearth. So great was my terror of the American who essayed to touch me that, deeming my doom sealed anyway, I ran to the pile of coals and would have thrown myself on them, in my fright, had not my father's barber put out his arm and saved me. Seeing my alarm made my father angry, and as he was usually a brave man, he lost sight of the possible danger to himself in his determination to defend his home.

And so you say the old house at the Mission is still standing? It must be badly fallen into decay. It was an unusually fine structure for those days. There were other two-story adobes at Monterey, but none in our section, all the Mission structures being one story in height.

Save for the little cluster of houses about the Mission, there were very few buildings between us and the bay, and I remember with what interest we children used to climb the brown sides of Mission Peak and look off across the level to note whether any new buildings were going up. The smallest but seen in the distance, if new, was an event; that served us for a theme of conversation and speculation for a long time. The scene from the peak now is very different. I can assure you.

Vallejo Family File, *San Francisco Morning Call*, December 14, 1890, microfilm at California State Library, Sacramento.

Catarino Garza

Catarino Garza, an immigrant from Tamaulipas, a Mexican state bordering Texas, became a firebrand politician in South Texas and once led a campaign to oust Porfirio Díaz by crossing the border from Zapata County with a band of followers. Garza had been previously involved in a shootout with an Anglo lawman in Rio Grande, Texas, who was accused of killing Mexicans indiscriminately. In a rambling manuscript that explains his political formation, he also reveals the mistreatment that Mexicans had to endure in Texas at the hands of Anglo Americans.

Well then, with two or three months left before the electoral battle, serenades, public meetings, speeches, shouts, punches, walks through main avenues begin. To the disgrace of our country, the tri-colored banner is seen just as the Mexican national anthem is played. People dress up in gold and blue, and many times they kill each other while they defend their candidates. The candidates have fun during the political quarrels; they walk together and drink without showing the least enmity, while the Mexican community constantly creates incredible scandals, and I have noticed that many times there are divisions within the families in the communities. Young ladies will appear at dances wearing big colorful ribbons that represent their party, and they do not allow ladies from opposing parties to participate for any reason. As I mentioned before, a few days before the election, the County's or District Secretaries' offices are filled with unhappy Mexicans who are led by other speculators into politics. They go to these offices to make their statement of citizenship in the most degradable and ridiculous manner that is ever seen, since most of them, if not all, do not know what that sham entails. The citizenship law in the State has the following requirements: that a person who wishes to become a citizen of this country prove that he has lived one year in this State and six months in the County. Second, he must declare his intention before the District and County Secretary by swearing to a solemn pledge, which must be translated if they do not understand the country's language. Third, before they can consider themselves citizens, after their declaration of citizenship, they must live in this country for five years without leaving, and they must submit an application to the Supreme Government, which will grant a certificate or credential that justifies the recognition. All this is a dead deed in the State of Texas and primarily in bordering populations where abuses and infractions to the law are the only items recorded.

Here in Texas, the only thing that a Mexican needs is to do away with his shame, approach the Secretary, and swear that he has lived in the State for a year, even though he just crossed the Rio Grande or deserted the Mexican military. He can then proceed to pledge in English. The oath states the following, "Do you pledge and swear in the name of God to defend the flag of the United States of America in case of war with any nation, especially with yours (Mexico)?" To which they reply, "Yes, sir," because that is what they have been advised to do by the shameless election agents (it is understood that some of them are Mexican). Many times after the degrading ceremony, electoral agents take up to fifty Mexicans to the bar, where they previously mixed whiskey with alcohol so that when the Mexicans leave, they are ready to fight blues or reds, depending on what party they belong to.

These maneuvers are very strange. I remember that in the year in reference, a servant of Don José de García, a wealthy rancher from Santa Rosalía in Cameron County, came to the establishment in which I worked. A few minutes after he had been buying some things there, one of the many petty politicians approached him and told him, "I want you to come with me so you can check yourself in to vote in the following election and you will also receive protection as an American citizen." That miserable man did not make a plea, but he wanted to know what that man who had invited him to vote was talking about. He approached me and asked, "Could you tell me if I will be penalized when they check me because I have two packets of cigarette tobacco?" The reader can just imagine the intellectual level of most of the Mexicans who serve as tools to their own executioners. That unfortunate servant thought that they would literally check him, and since the cigarettes he had were prohibited in this country, the novice thought that he could be accused of smuggling when they would look in his pockets and find the corpus delicti.

I have been a witness to similar cases that inspire more laughter than indignation. For example, the day before the elections, political parties call general meetings; speeches begin in such a clear language that they reek of clarity. They are so barbaric because they are synonymous to nonsense, and the Mexican national anthem is played with its corresponding beating of the drums. Directors will try to extend their sessions to 4:00 a.m. of the next day. They will then give out whiskey to everyone so that by the time election booths are installed, they can take the raffle of drunks in the carriages that petty politicians have set up, and the drunks *freely* vote, as it is cynically said. In the booths, electoral agents vulgarly argue over the ownership of the leaflets; in other words, it is such a disaster that we are embarrassed to admit that such men are from Mexico.

* * *

An American lawyer by the name of Russell was quite angry because several people wanted to lift the quarantine. He said, "Sirs, it is assured that Matamoros has had several cases of yellow fever. Consequently, it is not advisable to lift the quarantine for any of the reasons espoused. If the working community is harmed or if they die of hunger, it does not matter to us. We need to see that the yellow fever does not invade us because a white man might die, and a white man is worth more than ten Mexicans. That is why I oppose the idea of lifting the quarantine."

Personally, I have been informed that a lawyer of this city by the name of Russell stated that, he protested against the idea of lifting the quarantine, claiming that the city could suffer a few disasters as a result of the yellow fever that was already in Matamoros, and that if Mexican people died of hunger due to lack of work, it did not matter. What needed to be addressed was that whenever the quarantine was lifted, the city would easily be infected and that one or two Americans could die and that the life of "one white was worth more than ten Mexicans etc., etc." This and other nonsense spilt out of the mouth of a man who appears to be educated, but with due respect, I must tell your Excellency, Mr. Editor, that men such as he do not deserve to be included in any intellectual society because they violate courtesy, tactfulness, and respect.

This white lawyer should know that he vilely lies in assuring that an American is worth more than ten Mexicans. In Mr. Bloomberg & Raphael's residence lives a Mexican, who is not black, and he can prove to you, in any land you would like, that he is worth as much as any of your coreligionists. That man must also understand that being someone who expresses himself in such manner immediately reveals that he does not possess common sense etc., etc."

Catarino Garza, *La lógica de los hechos, o sea observaciones sobre las circunstancias de los mexicanos en Texas desde el año 1877 hasta 1889,* (Unpublished ms., 1890) pp. 34, 43-44.

Chapter Two

"The Brown Scare": The Mexican Revolution as a Source of Conflict

Francisco I. Madero's El Plan de San Luis Potosí, which called for an uprising for November 20th, 1910, precipitated the Mexican Revolution, a bloody struggle that lasted twenty years. As regimes fell in and out of power, exiles from whatever faction was losing fled to the United States. But even those who had no stake in the conflict found that fleeing as refugees was the only solution to surviving economically and in peace. The upheaval forced across the border Mexicans from all walks of life, creating early in the century a rich and heterogeneous immigrant society in the United States.

The Revolution also brought to the fore underlying tensions that had characterized U.S.-Mexico relationships, both official and informal. Before the insurrection broke out, American efforts to shore up the border led to stringent measures to curtail smuggling and to enforce immigration laws. Such zeal transformed Mexican immigrants, accustomed to casual migration and trade, into criminals and undesirables. The Mexican Revolution, however, demonstrated that the idea of a border was more fragile than previously imagined. The uprising spilled out into United States border areas, foiling the efforts the United States had made to establish a clear line of demarcation. Warfare and border violence received prominent coverage in newspapers, popular magazines, and in the emerging cinema, provoking an Anglo backlash against Mexicans in the United States and Mexico. This phenomenon, dubbed the "Brown Scare" by historian Ricardo Romo, affected relationships between Anglos and U.S. Mexicans not involved in political intrigue or in revolutionary activity.

Madero's call for an uprising eventually succeeded in ousting the dictator Porfirio Díaz, who had ruled Mexico for more than thirty years. Although Madero enjoyed support from influential Texas Anglos disenchanted with Díaz, most Americans resented Mexicans hatching plots on U.S. soil. After two years of chaotic rule, General Victoriano Huerta ousted and murdered the idealistic

President Madero. The ouster had the blessing of U.S. Ambassador Henry Lane Wilson. President Woodrow Wilson, inaugurated in February of 1913, the same month Madero was murdered, recalled Ambassador Wilson. Because he did not approve of Huerta, the U.S. president attempted to destabilize Huerta's new government. Huerta retaliated by orchestrating propaganda campaigns and anti-American demonstrations. This intensified American antipathy toward Mexico, and Mexican immigrants continued to be objects of Anglo-American antagonism and fear.

An agricultural recession put thousands of Mexicans out of work in the Southwest during the spring of 1914. President Wilson directed U.S. troops to occupy Veracruz in April, purportedly to end political chaos; both events exacerbated existing tensions. Fearful that angry Mexicans and Mexican Americans might launch reprisals, American government officials put enforcement agencies on red alert, a move that exaggerated the threat posed by Mexicans on the American side of the border.

The most violent attacks on Mexicans in the United States occurred in retaliation to the Texas-based Plan de San Diego in 1915. The Plan called for revolution and the separation of Texas from the Union. Texas Mexicans, angry over mistreatment, reportedly concocted the Plan and invited other racial minorities to join in driving Anglos out of the Southwest. The declaration, which called for the execution of all Anglo males over sixteen years of age, was irreverently designed to coincide with Washington's birthday on February 20. In anticipating the raids, Texas Rangers and volunteers summarily executed hundreds of Mexicans in the Rio Grande Valley and forced thousands across the border.

The invasion of Veracruz helped revolutionary allies of the murdered Madero defeat Huerta, but the rebel leaders Francisco "Pancho" Villa and Venustiano Carranza soon split and engaged in an internecine struggle known as the "War of the Winners." Early in 1915, Villa was courting favor with Americans, hoping with U.S. help to prevail in the war against Carranza, whose forces meted out defeat after defeat against his army. After President Wilson extended de facto recognition to Carranza in October, Villa then turned against the United States. In November, Carranza's forces, with official permission from the U.S. government, were transported by railroad on American soil from El Paso to Agua Prieta. This town, to which Villa had laid siege, was strategically placed on the Arizona-Sonora border. The *villistas* had not expected such large forces and were almost annihilated. With the defeat, Villa's bitterness towards Americans increased.

To avenge what Villa considered a betrayal and to sabotage Carranza's relations with the United States, during January of 1916, Villa's men killed seventeen American mining engineers after dragging them from a train at Santa Ysabel, Chihuahua. The American mining company which had employed the technicians brought back the bodies from Chihuahua through El Paso in coffins draped with American flags. After witnessing this procession, enraged Anglo civilians and soldiers rampaged in the Mexican parts of El Paso, attacking every Mexican man they could lay their hands on.

Villista attacks on a number of border communities along the Big Bend region of Texas only fueled animosity towards Mexicans. The most infamous raid was the March 9 predawn invasion of Columbus, New Mexico. Villa's men killed twenty-two American soldiers and civilians and wounded many others, while Villa's forces suffered more than two hundred casualties. President Wilson immediately deployed U.S. troops led by General John Pershing to pursue Villa into Chihuahua. This foray became known as the "Punitive Expedition."

The raids had corroded U.S.-Carranza relations just as Villa had expected, but Pershing's army vacated Mexico on February 5, 1917, as Americans prepared to enter the war in Europe. But Anglo Americans did not easily forgive, and Mexicans in turn resented the violation of their sovereignty. Reportedly, outraged Mexicans of diverse loyalties considered returning from the United States to defend Mexico against the Pershing expedition. In the meantime, American officials jailed hundreds of Mexicans suspected of subversion.

Xenophobia induced by World War I increased the fear already felt towards Mexicans, prompting even more doubt about the loyalty of those living in the United States. In the spring of 1914, even before the United States entered the war, American newspapers sensationally reported that the U.S. Navy had confiscated German arms bound for Huerta in a ship called the Yripanga. German collusion with some Mexicans did in fact exist. Huerta had languished in Spanish exile after his 1914 ouster, but in 1915, he attempted a return to power with German support. His plans were foiled on the Texas border, where he was arrested trying to enter Mexico. The Plan de San Diego uprising discussed above was also seen as a German provocation, an assertion that was also partially correct.

In 1917, U.S. officials in El Paso investigated reports that German agents in Mexico and American draft evaders had inspired bandit raids on the border. After the United States entered the war in April, 1917, the fear of Mexico allying itself with Axis powers heightened, but the business of sending troops to Europe left very little time for further intervention in Mexican affairs. Border violence affecting Americans continued during the short time U.S. troops were in Europe. After the Armistice was signed, the clamor for an invasion of Mexico intensified. The Association for Rights of Americans in Mexico, a group made up of U.S. politicians and businessmen with interests in Mexico, issued a report in July, 1919, that listed 317 Americans killed in Mexico between 1910 and 1919. Americans also doubted Carranza's loyalty during the war and, because he had resisted American efforts to influence Mexico's economy, many U.S. politicians and businessmen demanded his removal.

Relations improved somewhat when a tentative peace returned to Mexico after Carranza's enemies assassinated him in 1920, and Álvaro Obregón came to power. But another diplomatic crisis ensued when in 1926, President Plutarco Elías Calles repressed the Catholic Church, provoking a Catholic rebellion known as *La Cristiada*, and promised to enforce Mexican subsoil rights, an act that threatened foreign oil interests. At this point, the U.S. Secretary of State and his ambassador in Mexico resumed the bashing again. Militant Catholics welcomed American criticism and potential intervention, but Mexican nationalists and the Mexican press reacted bitterly. A recession in the United States coincided with this negative propaganda towards Mexico, and feelings towards Mexican immigrants again worsened.

Other sources of conflict along the border also caused intense anti-Mexican feelings. One of these was smuggling. This established way of life on the border, which continues into the present day, acquired vibrancy during the Mexican Revolution, when gun-running attracted thousands of adherents. With the increase in immigration during the first three decades of the twentieth century, human contraband became the most common form of smuggling. Ferrying "illegal aliens" across the Rio Grande became a lucrative trade after Congress passed restrictive immigration laws in 1917 and tightened up requirements even more in 1921 and again in 1924. These laws, aimed more at Eastern and Southern Europeans and Asians, forced these groups to try to enter through the Mexican border clandestinely, creating even more opportunities for runners.

The 1924 act, which imposed a quota on Europeans and totally banned Asians, excluded the western hemisphere from any of these restrictions. Hemispheric immigrants still paid a head tax and a visa fee totaling eighteen dollars, a requirement that many could not afford. The potential immigrants also had to comply with the literacy requirements written into all three congressional bills.

Mexicans were not immediately targeted for compliance. When the need for their labor was great, immigrant agents often ignored their illegal entry. In addition, Mexicans who chose to work in agriculture and on railroads were often provided with temporary waivers from complying with the literacy requirements of all of these bills. But as labor markets became saturated, the Mexicans also became unwanted, and immigrant agents now aimed more vigilance at Mexicans. As harassment heightened in 1926, the Mexican Chamber of Deputies passed a law requiring the government to extend protection to emigrants.

Large-scale illicit entry of liquor and drugs from Mexico originated early in this century as well. To force abstention on U.S. soldiers, Congress passed the War Prohibited Act in 1918, which created dry zones along the length of the border. Along the Texas border, this provoked the smuggling of a cheap but potent moonshine called *sotol*. When the 1919 Volstead Act ushered in full prohibition, extensive contraband rings emerged. In addition, drugs, such as cocaine, morphine, and opium, found ready markets in the United States, further propelling the illegal trade.

Anglo Americans, Middle Easterners, Chinese and Mexican merchants ran the large operations, but ground troops known as "mules" were recruited from the working-class barrios of border towns. Because of the border evils, Americans cast a critical eye towards Mexicans, assuming that all Mexicans reflected these values. Most Anglos and their representatives of justice did not discriminate between Mexicans and Mexican Americans; to them, they were one and the same. Eventually, an outcry of public indignation, which blamed Mexico for border evils, demanded an end to smuggling and pressured politicians to act. The result was repression of both Mexican immigrants and Mexican Americans.

During the decade of the Revolution and its aftermath, more antipathy towards Mexicans was generated than what had built up in the hundred years since Mexicans and Americans had first made direct contact. Just as the persistence of apartheid after the abolition of slavery fueled the civil rights movement for blacks, for Mexican Americans the antipathy generated during this era provided an important part of the foundation for their civil rights movement.

Ricardo Flores Magón

Precursor plots by Mexican *revoltosos* (insurgents) on U.S. territory rankled Americans even before the Revolution began. U.S. authorities reserved the most zeal for pursuing the Flores Magón brothers and other members of the Partido Liberal Mexicano (PLM), who were exiled by President Díaz immediately before the Revolution. The press followed their activities closely, and eventually officials jailed PLM members for violating U.S. neutrality laws. In 1921, after languishing in prison for years, Ricardo Flores Magón, one of the founders of the PLM, tells firsthand the troubles that he encountered in the United States in a long letter to his lawyer, Harry Weinberger.

Sembradores: Ricardo Flores Magón y El Partido Liberal Mexicano

After years, many years, of an unequal struggle in the press and the political clubs of the City of México against the cruel despotism of Porfirio Díaz; after having suffered repeated incarcerations for my political beliefs ever since I was 17 years old, and having almost miraculously escaped death at the hands of hired assassins on several occasions in that dark period of the Mexican history when the practice of the government was to silence truth's voice with the firing squad, or the dagger, or the poison; after the judiciary, by judicial decree of June 30, 1903, forbade me not only to write for my own journals but to contribute for theirs as well, having my printing plants successively sequestrated by the government and my life being in peril, I decided to come to this country, which I knew to be the land of the free and the home of the brave, to resume my work of enlightment of the Mexican masses.

The 11th day of January, 1904, saw me set my foot on this land, almost penniless, for all that I had possessed had been sequestrated by the Mexican Government, but rich in illusion and hopes of social and political justice. *Regeneración* made its reappearance on American soil in November, 1904. On the following December, a ruffian sent by Díaz entered my domicile, and would have stabbed me in the back had it not been for the quick intervention of my brother, Enrique, who happened to be nearby. Enrique threw the ruffian out of the house, and showing that this brutal assault on my person had been prepared by certain authorities, and the possible failure of the ruffian's attempt foreseen, at the falling of the latter on the sidewalk a swarm of agents of the public invaded the premises. Enrique was made a prisoner and jailed, and finally condemned to pay a fine for disturbing the peace. Emboldened by the protection he enjoyed, the ruffian again forced his entrance into my house. This time I telephoned the police; the man was arrested, and I was summoned to appear in court the following day early in the morning. When I arrived at the police court, the man had already been released.

Being my life was so lightly regarded by those who claim to have been empowered with authority to safeguard human interests and life, I decided to move southward, and in February, 1905, *Regeneración* resumed publication at St. Louis, Missouri. In October the same year, trouble broke loose against me. A Mexican Government official by the name of Manuel Esperón y de la Flor, who maintained the worst type of slavery in the district under his command, for he used to kill men, women, and children as feudal lords used to do, was chosen by Díaz to come and file against me a complaint for what he deemed to be a slanderous article which had been printed in *Regeneración*, dealing with the despotism he displayed on the unfortunate inhabitants of the district under his control. A charge of criminal libel was preferred, and I was thrown into jail with my brother Enrique and Juan Sarabia. Everything in the newspaper office was sequestrated—printing plant, typewriter machines, books, furniture, and so on—and sold before a trial had taken place.

A detail that illustrates the connivance between the Mexican and American authorities to persecute me, may be seen in the fact that the postmaster at St. Louis called me to his office with the apparent purpose of getting from me some information as to the financial status of the newspaper, but in reality to let a Pinkerton detective see me, that he might identify me later. The detective was already in the postmaster's office when I arrived there in compliance to his summons. This same detective led the officers who arrested me. After months of languishing in a cell, I got released on bail to find that the second-class privilege of *Regeneración* had been canceled by the Postmaster General on the flimsy pretext that more than half of the regular issues of the newspaper circulated in Mexico, and that extradition papers were being prepared in Mexico to ask my delivery to the Mexican authorities. I paid my bondsman the amount on my bail, and on March, 1905, I took refuge in Canada, for I was certain that death awaited me in Mexico. At that time, the mere asking by Díaz for a man he wanted was enough to spirit a man across the line to be shot. While in Toronto, Ontario, *Regeneración* was being published in St. Louis. The Díaz agents found at least my whereabouts. I was informed of their intentions and evaded arrest by moving to Montreal, Quebec. Few hours after my having left Toronto, the police called at my abandoned domicile. I ignore until today how Díaz could throw the Canadian authorities against me.

While in Montreal, my Mexican comrades in Mexico were planning an uprising to overthrow the savage despotism of Porfirio Díaz. I secretly moved to the Mexican frontier on September, 1906, to participate in the generous movement. My presence in El Paso, Texas, though kept strictly unknown, was discovered by American and Mexican sleuths, who on the 20th of October, same year, assaulted the room where I had to confer with some of my comrades. Antonio I. Villarreal, now Minister of Agriculture in Obregón's cabinet, and Juan Sarabia, were arrested. I escaped. A price was put on my head. A $25,000 reward was offered for my capture, and hundreds of thousands of leaflets bearing my picture and a description of my personal features were circulated throughout the Southwest and fixed in post offices and conspicuous places with the temptive reward. I succeeded, however, in evading arrest until August 23, 1907, when, with Librado Rivera and Antonio I. Villarreal, I was made prisoner in Los Angeles, Cal., without the formality of a warrant.

The intention of the persecutors was to send us across the border, this being the reason of their actions without a warrant, as they had done on Manuel Sarabia on June of the same year. Sarabia was one of my associates. Without a warrant, he was arrested at

Douglas, Ariz., by American authorities, and in the dead of night delivered to Mexican *rurales*, who took him to the Mexican side.

Charge after charge was preferred against us, ranging in importance from resisting an officer to robbery and murder. All these charges were successfully fought by Harriman, but in the meantime our persecutors were forging documents, training witnesses, and so forth, until at length they finally charged us with having broken the neutrality laws by giving material assistance to patriots to rise in arms against Porfirio Díaz. The forged documents and trained witnesses were examined by the United States Commissioner at Los Angeles, and as a result, after more than 20 months' incarceration in the county jail, we were sent to Tombstone, Ariz., to be tried. The mere reading of the depositions made by the government witnesses before the United States Commissioner at Los Angeles, and then before the judge of our trial at Tombstone, shows that they committed perjury in either place, or in both. Experts for the defense proved that the exhibited documents were gross forgeries. We were, however, sentenced to 18 months' imprisonment, which we served in Yuma and Florence, Ariz., being released on August 1, 1910, after three years spent behind prison bars.

Regeneración appeared again in September of the same year, this time in Los Angeles, Cal. On June, 1911, I was arrested with my brother, Enrique, Librado Rivera, and Anselmo L. Figueroa, charged with having violated the neutrality laws by sending men, arms, and ammunition to those fighting in Mexico against that form of chattel slavery known as peonage, which has been the curse of four-fifths of the Mexican population, as everyone knows. Jack Mosby, one of the prospected witnesses for the prosecution, said on the stand that the United States District Attorney had promised him all kinds of benefits if he perjured against us. Fake testimony was introduced by the prosecution, as proven by affidavits sworn by its witnesses after the trial was over, affidavits that must be on file in the Department of Justice, as they were sent there in 1912. In June, 1912, after a year of fighting the case, we were sent to McNeil Island to serve the 23 months' imprisonment to which we were condemned, having been released on January 19, 1914. Figueroa died shortly afterward as a result of his imprisonment.

On February 18, 1917, I was arrested with my brother Enrique, for having published in *Regeneración* articles against the treachery committed by Carranza, then President of Mexico, against the workers, and for having written that the Mexicans who at the time were being assassinated by Texas Rangers deserved justice rather than bullets. I got a sentence of one year and one day, for I was expected to live only a few more months, having been taken from a hospital bed to be tried. Enrique got three years. We appealed and finally succeeded in getting bond, under which we were released pending the appeal.

On the 21st of March, 1918, I was arrested with Rivera for having published in *Regeneración* the Manifesto for which I was given 20 years' imprisonment and Rivera, 15. The wording and meaning of the Manifesto were construed as seditious by the prosecution, that is, as aiming at the insubordination and revolt of the military and naval forces of the United States. Any sensible person who happened to read the Manifesto would not draw such a conclusion, for in reality the Manifesto is only an exposition of facts and a fair warning to all mankind of the evils those facts might produce. In one of its paragraphs, it is clearly stated that no one can make a revolution, on account of it being a social phenomenon. The Manifesto was aimed at the prevention of the evils a revolution carries itself—the revolution being regarded from a scientific standpoint as a world-wide inevitable result of the unsettled conditions of the world. The Manifesto does not refer in the least to the policies of the American Government in the last war, nor gives aid and comfort to its enemies. It is neither pro-Germany nor pro-Ally, and does not single out the United States in its brief review of the world conditions. It was enough, however, to secure for me a life term behind prison bars. The persecution, this time, was exceedingly severe. My poor wife, María, was incarcerated for five months and is now free on bond, awaiting trial for having notified my friends of my arrest, that they should assist me in my legal defense.

After reading this extremely long and dreadfully tedious statement of facts, how could any person believe that I have rightfully been prosecuted and in no way persecuted? In each case, and in defiance of the law, bail has been fixed at enormous rates so as to prevent me making use of the privilege. As to the veracity of my assertion, my honor as a life-long fighter for justice is hereby solemnly pledged.

Juan Gómez Quiñones, *Sembradores: Ricardo Flores Magón y El Partido Liberal Mexicano: a Eulogy and a Critique* (Los Angeles: Chicano Studies Center, University of California, 1977), pp. 142-147.

"Low-Lifed Mexican"

On November 2, 1910, enraged townspeople in Rock Springs, Texas, burned Antonio Rodríguez at the stake for killing a white woman named Mrs. Clem Anderson. Widely publicized in the Mexican press, the outrage provoked violent anti-American demonstrations in Mexico City and in Guadalajara. The demonstrations, misreported in the American press, provoked a heated backlash against Mexicans in the U.S., especially those living in Texas. This deep-seated prejudice is seen in a letter penned by F.W. Meyer, a haberdasher from Bonney, Texas, who wrote to President Taft to complain about the disturbances in Mexico City and Guadalajara.

F. W. Meyer to William Taft, President of the U.S.

F.W. Meyer, Brazoria County
Bonney, Tex. Nov. 10, 1910

Mr. Wm. Taft, President, U.S.A.

Dear Sir:

Something MUST be done to protect Americans in Mexico. Because Antonio Rodríguez, an admitted low-lifed mexican Criminal, who murdered a Texas Woman and destroyed an American HOME, the Mexicans murder good Americans because said greaser got his just dues from the People of Texas. They are also destroying property of Americans who do a legal business in Mexico.

Besides otherwise insulting the foremost Nation on this Globe, such occurrences come too often. They MUST be stopped. It will require very radical action from the U.S. to forever stop this murdering habit of the greasers.

I will propose a plan here: Every time an American gets murdered in Mexico, by Mexicans, let this Gov. collect, besides other indemnification, one million dollars for every American life so lost and take one million of acres off of Mexico, adjacent Texas. Then open this million acres immediately for Homesteads for Americans only.

Do this, and do it at once. There is no intelligent American Citizen who will doubt the efficiency of this plan.

This plan is also just and right. The life of an American Citizen is worth more than a million dollars. The million acres of land is a practical safeguard against further repetitions.

F.W. Meyer to William Taft, Pres. of U.S., Nov. 10, 1910, National Archives, U.S. Department of State, Record Group (RG) 59, 311.122R61.

The "Brown Scare"

Newspapers ignited "Brown Scare" emotions among Americans. The article below, printed in 1913, portrays the California Mexico border as dangerous and Mexicans as potential invaders. Sensationalist reporting sold newspapers, and publishers allowed exaggerated stories to appear, regardless of the unwarranted backlash that these reports inspired among Anglos against Mexicans.

Mexicans Await Pretext to Raid Across Border

Caches of Arms Are Said to Indicate a Plot to Loot American Cities.

Banditti. Having Devastated Their Own Land, Now Seek a Motive to Invade Their Neighbors' Country. Carranza's Warning to Wilson Timed With a Threat to Attack Mexicali.

(BY DIRECT WIRE TO THE TIMES)

SAN DIEGO (Cal.) Nov. 14. [Exclusive Dispatch.] Agents of the United States government came into possession of the startling information today that Mexicans have made caches of arms and ammunition along the Coast and border for prospective raids on the cities of San Diego, El Paso, Eagle Pass, and other exposed border cities in case of eventualities between the United States and Mexico.

The mere fact that Mexicans have deposited weapons and ammunition at convenient places to raid border cities is taken as a symbol of a temperament on the part of the Mexicans that may be easily aroused to commit acts of violence on the slightest provocation. Any act on the part of the United States that could be interpreted as hostile may become the signal of a reign of terror, according to information in the hands of government agents. Any act on the part of the Mexican government, or either, or any, of the warring factions in Mexico that could be interpreted as a call to arms on the part of Mexicans everywhere, is likely to cause a rush to the caches and a raid into American cities and towns.

The situation is said to be so acute that the government agents have taken extraordinary measures to prevent news of the location of the caches leaking out lest it inflame public opinion, but in the zeal to conceal the facts, they have been revealed.

Fear Intervention

For some time, the rebels and their sympathizers along the border have been obsessed by the notion that the United States means to intervene in Mexico and annex border states, and they have interpreted the efforts of President Wilson to oust Huerta and to prevent the meeting of the newly elected Mexican Congress as proof that the

United States intends to intervene. The acts of Wilson have inspired the rebels on the border, with whom the administration in Washington of late has professed open sympathy, with a hatred akin to that which is said to prevail in Mexico City on the part of Huerta and his adherents against the American government. Instead of making friends of the rebels and their sympathizers, it appears from careful investigations made by official and unofficial agencies that the American government has engendered in them a hatred that is likely to burst forth in terrible acts at any moment. Indeed, the rebels and their sympathizers may be said to be frantic for a desire to loot and pillage. They have run through, in one or the other of the numerous revolutions in Mexico in recent years, nearly every city in Northern Mexico worthwhile, and there is nothing left in them to loot and carry away. So, filled with the war spirit and either misunderstanding, or purposely misinterpreting the purposes of the American government, the border Mexicans are eager for a brush with the United States authorities, as that would give them what they would call a "reasonable motive" to pillage and plunder the rich and prosperous American cities, towns, farms, ranches, and other properties along the border, properties of Americans located in some instances in Mexico, but in thousandfold more cases located on this side of the border.

Carranza Defiant

A telegram was received tonight from Nogales in which Gen. Carranza is quoted to have said even worse things of President Wilson's peace plans than Gen. Huerta in Mexico City has yet deigned to say.

"We shall accept neither the transactions nor the interference of any nation to regulate the internal affairs of Mexico," Carranza, leader of the rebel Constitutionalists, is reported to have said.

Both the followers and the sympathizers of Carranza have already interpreted this to mean that President Wilson is undertaking to meddle in the internal affairs of Mexico, and the temper of Mexicans is such that an overt act on the part of men who have gone so far already as to hide away the arms and ammunition for the terrible day may be expected at any time.

Plunder Motive Strong

The plunder motive is strong with border Mexicans just now. It has been cultivated so long in numerous rebellions that it has come to be second nature. Looking across the imaginary geographic line called the "border," the plunder bond of Mexicans sees rich valleys, wealthy cities, immense ranches well worked and well tilled, prosperous homes, banks with real money in them in contrast with those in Northern Mexico carrying flat money of this or that rebellion, and they are itching for a chance to get at it all.

The threat of Rodolfo Gallego to attack Mexicali, the Mexican border town just across the line from Calexico, Cal., either tomorrow or next day is generally interpreted here by Americans, whose fears are fully aroused, as bearing out the findings that the border Mexicans have hidden away arms for the awaited day to invade American city and country and pillage and plunder money bags and vaults in a way never before heard of in Mexico. Gallego is alleged to have warned of his forthcoming attack to enable American citizens in Mexico to get across the line and out of harm's way, but those who know Gallego and the three or four hundred freebooters in his train well know that they would suffer no pangs of conscience if, drunk with some success, they should mistake an American home or bank for Mexican property or mistake an American miss for a Mexican maid.

Los Angeles Times, November 15, 1913.

"A Conspiracy Has Been Unearthed"

Even after Huerta's ouster in July of 1914, border tension and suspicions remained high. In August, the *Arizona Republican* revealed a plot brewing in the Salt River Valley. Nine conspirators were jailed after police tracked them for two months. According to this incredulous story, Maricopa County officers uncovered the conspiracy in which Mexicans and Arizona Indians plotted to loot Phoenix businesses and the National Guard armory. The story appeared during the recession of 1914, a period of great unemployment and labor strife in Arizona, which many Americans saw as problems stemming from unchecked immigration.

Red Flaggers Would Loot Phoenix—Kill and Divide Spoils

Nine Conspirators Now in Jail and Dragnet Out for More of the Gang—Two Months' Work is Rewarded

HAD PLAN TO GET INDIANS UP IN ARMS

Were Getting Munitions Together for Armed Assault—Dynamite, Rifles, Reloading Machines and Letters in Evidence.

Through the activity of Sheriff Jeff D. Adams, Constable Jim Murray, Chief of Police George O. Brisbois, and the men operating under their instructions, a conspiracy has been unearthed in this county that had for its object the capture of the city of Phoenix by hordes of banditi, the rifling of the stores and banks, and the gradual spread of the conditions of anarchy into other portions of the state, together with an armed attempt by a combined force of Indians and Mexicans against the government of the United States, starting from this section. Nine men are now in the county and city jail charged with complicity in the offense, and more arrests are being made hourly.

The meat of the conspiracy was to obtain sufficient arms and ammunition and dynamite to make such force as the conspirators could gather together formidably, and with this, to raid all the food stores of the city, following this with a raid on the banks, and after this to go after such of the stores and business houses of the city as the conspirators might then think would give them anything that could be used in further and more extensive operations. Gradually, the conspirators were gathering together their arms and cashing them; providing for ammunition after the first issue was expended by making more themselves—reloading instruments having been obtained and augmenting this punitive provision by making dynamite bombs of the usual Mexican sort of tomato cans, loaded with dynamite caps and iron or steel slugs, and bits of nails. Enough dynamite would be placed in these bombs to almost wreck a modern building.

Coming upon the trail of this conspiracy by chance, the officers of the county and city had been working upon it for nearly two months. Finally within the last three weeks they got it into such shape as to be able to scoop up many of the ringleaders and land them in durance vile and put some of those in custody through a course of cross examination that has led to the intimate knowledge of the plot now possessed by Sheriff Adams and his deputies and Chief Brisbois and his officers. When it was found that the conspiracy was against the government of the United States, and involved as well the wards on the United States, the Indians on the Sacaton reservation, the case was turned over to the United States district attorney, and Hon. Wiley Jones has been working since then in the strictest confidence with the local officers.

Since the beginning of the unearthing of the conspiracy some two months ago, the reporters of *The Republican* having been working in strict secrecy and co-operation with the peace officers of the city and county, well aware that any premature publication of the endeavors of the officers would result in the men that were most wanted getting away. Not until the majority of the leaders were securely locked in the city and county jail was this paper willing to tell the story of the serious condition from which Phoenix had been rescued by the activity and sagacity of Sheriff Adams, Constable Murphy, Chief Brisbois, and their men. No movement has been made in connection with the apprehension operations of the officers with which this paper has not been cognizant and of which it has not heartily approved.

The Conspiracy

Elaborate plans were laid in connection with the organization of the conspiracy, and in the course of them a line of dispatch carriers was established from Phoenix all the way to Bisbee. Juntas in every little village of importance between here and that city looked after passing the word along. In addition to the large number of men who were expected to rally in this city as soon as the standard of the "red flaggers" was raised, almost the entire Yaqui village of Guadalupe was promised for assistance, and one of the ringleaders went so far as to promise five hundred Sacaton Indians to the cause.

Miguel Ortíz, or Mike Ortíz, was responsible for this portion of the conspiracy. He was not only promised the assistance of the Yaquis, but also the help of the Sacaton Indians, and he has been assiduously at work to deliver the goods ever since. At present he is still at large, although the loyal Indian police at the reservation are on the lookout for him and other officers are expected to pick him up. Ortíz transferred the information of the alleged disaffected Indians to the local *Junta,* who thereupon wrote the following letters to them, which are in themselves self-explanatory.

* * *

Tempe, Guadalupe, August 1, 1914.

Mr. Juan Moroyoque,

My very appreciable and dear friend - Well, it is with much pleasure I reply to your very fine letter, under date of the ninth of the month just passed.

Well, my friend, we find ourselves well in health and if you are enjoying perfect health, then accept salutations from us with the receipt of this manifesto.

Friend, my family, neither of one or of the other is there anything new.

(Here follow some unintelligible words, apparently conveying in cipher or code the meat of the instructions. As nearly as possible, the translator renders them as in the original:)

yutama nebutia jaisa tua machi humania y Miki—pues A'man hala Gualúpepo tule: cayta tequil macheane cate qui panoa. Pues jaegosa el A man pael yaloabae, honse pues gehul y nia be loqui yn tebotey hen bituaeau.

(Then without pause or punctuation, the missive leaps into that flowery Spanish ending:)

without more! Good by (good by).

reply to me as soon as you can.

Without more, your very affectionate and (Here some more code:) atto. S. S. S.

Feliciano Garcías

* * *

Phoenix, Arizona, July 20, 1914.

Señor Miguel Ortíz.

Companion, your health.

We received today your letter and that of the governors, and in reply to them we will say the following: That we are ready, as always, to second the movement which according to the letter of the governor's, you wish to carry to an end. Already you are acquainted with our attitude, and we only await your resolution to draw near when you are disposed to do it, so much do we wish that you will see them to the end that they may say on what date we ought to expect them. And you send us to give notice, or, well, if you cannot do it very quickly, and if they want us to have a conference over this matter, you send them to speak as your own self.

But we give you notice that we prefer that in place of having a conference, it is better that they send us to speak as you told us, for the guard can be here ready for the insurrection and we are in waiting.

Also, see that this business is had on Saturday, if it is possible.

Yours, for land and liberty S.

T.N. Córdoba

V. Alfaro

L.L. Badillo

* * *

The following letter signed by the revolutionary committee was sent to various Indians on the reservation:

Phoenix, July 20, 1914.

Mr. Choosen:

Dear Fellow:

We have received two letters, one from Mike Ortíz, and the other from you to Mike Ortíz. We have learned from your letter that you are prepared to rise in arms against the government, capital, and the American people, compelled by the abuses committed upon you by them; and in answer to your letter, we will tell you that we are in the same condition, and we must heartily support your revolutionary movement.

Now: We want to know when you intend to make the attack to this city, or if you will carry your movement to another place.

But, if you expect to attack this city soon, please let us know by anticipated note in order to get ready to co-operate with you.

We are willing that this event take place the next Saturday if possible. Mike may inform you about this matter.

T. Córdoba
S.L. Badillo
V. Alfaro

Identical letters were sent by the "committee," to Mr. Luis and Mr. Chon Jus. Chon Jus' American name is John Hays, of Sacaton Flats, and Mr. Luis is Lewis Jackson, a Black-water Indian. A similar letter was sent to Antonio Azul, a son of the famous old chief and himself a kind of a chief.

* * *

One of these letters fell into the hands of Agent Thackeray, and he promptly instituted a search for the others, with the result that a whole number of letters were obtained, and upon their discovery a few days ago the arrests began. Arrests have been made nearly every day since, and to date the following men are in jail awaiting preliminary examination: S. L. Badilla, T.N. Córdova, José María Flores, Francisco Méndez, J. M. Lugo, José Encinas, Tomás Calderón, Juan Moroyoqui, and José Franco. The cache with the arms has not yet been discovered, but quantities of dynamite, the reloading apparatus, and the plans of the conspiracy have been unearthed.

Too much cannot be said in commendation of the fine work of Officer Alberto López in this case. As a special policeman, as a regular member of the force, and as a deputy sheriff, he has worked faithfully and well and intelligently upon the case for two months. He has shadowed the conspirators at all times, oftentimes in disguise attending their meetings. He has worked at times for as many as seventy-two hours at a stretch in order that no phase of the conspiracy might escape him. The final corroboration of his reports enabling the arrests to be made came when the letters were discovered. At night López has lain outside the meeting places of the conspirators and learned more of their plans and more of the men engaged in them. He now has a knowledge of the whole affair that is invaluable and which will doubtless lead to the early capture of the rest of the "*jefes*" of the proposed storm.

As is usual in cases of this kind, one of the men confessed. The confession was made on Thursday evening in the sheriff's office in the presence of a number of officers and a representative of the Republican. This man told of meetings in the south part of town, at Guadalupe, in Tempe, in Mesa, and even in the I.W.W. hall in this city. It appears that the first meeting was held in the I.W.W. hall, but the growth of the movement became too swift and too savage even for that organization, and the men who were once identified with the beginnings of the agitation quietly dropped out, the hall was closed against the others, and the meetings were then held in the houses of Mexicans on the south side.

The First Arrest

Having pursued his investigations sufficiently far enough to warrant an arrest, Officer López "pulled" one of the members of the local Mexican colony for being a suspicious character. This was five or six weeks ago. At a conference held then in the sheriff's office between the officers and the man, it was decided that the charge would not be pressed against him if he would go to work and assist in unearthing the conspiracy. This he did, and faithfully, adding still further evidence to the accumulating pile, bringing in the then unbelievable story of the contemplated attack on the Ezra Thayer hardware store, and of the underground telegraph to the villages south. He alleged that an emissary of Ricardo Flores Magón of Los Angeles, the Mexican anarchist, has visited Phoenix and added his word of wisdom to the council, advising that all the Mexicans take up arms against the United States and the present condition of affairs. This man is said to be Teodoro Gaytán, whom it was planned to make a "*jefe*," although according to the man that Thursday confessed there were to be "no generals, all being *compañeros.*"

The Wicked Flee

José María Torres, now hotfooting it to Mexico with all unseemly haste, considering he has no money and no mule, was the secretary of the "*junta*," and kept the full lists of names of the conspirators. Still another conspirator with a likely name for such goings on is that of "Zapata," whose present whereabouts is unknown. His relationship, if any, with the rebel Zapata is unknown also. A man, Salazar, said now to reside at Clifton, who also has a name with a twang to it to those who have followed Mexican conspiracies, is also at large, as is Viviano Alfaro. The net is out, however, for all of them, and they may be brought in at any time. They are a number of local "*compañeros*" still at large for whom the drag net is out and who will be apprehended in the very near future.

The Plan Outlined

The man that confessed Thursday night said that he had gotten quite innocently into the conspiracy, but that once in, he was willing to "go through to the end with it." He considered it no crime to take up arms against the United States and the people of this valley, especially since he had been without work for five months and had a *"familia"* consisting of *"una esposa,"* only one wife, to depend on him for support. He had lived in the United States, he said, for thirty-six years, but was not a citizen and did not want to be one.

He said the plan was to get the *"compañeros"* together at Tempe, capture the militia rifles, and make a descent on Phoenix, taking first the stores with provisions in them, then the banks, and then the moneyed stores other than the *"tiendas abarrotes."* In making the descent, they were to use rifles and grenades composed of homemade dynamite bombs, and they proposed to kill all and sundry who came in their way. As far as he knew, they had no further plans after the capture of Phoenix, expecting *"mucho otros"* to join the "red flag." When the loot should have been obtained, a division was to be made. The date for this was not definitely set.

It is evident that agitators have been working upon the ignorance of the Mexicans in this country for some time, telling them that all that was necessary to establish a millennium and to obtain an equal division of wealth was to start a general ruction of rapine and plunder headed by these men whose grievances were either real or imaginary. At some of the meetings held, as many as a hundred men were present. At these, delegates would often appear from the other *"juntas,"* giving the message of aid and good cheer. Miguel Ortíz was a frequent visitor to them, and emissaries from Los Angeles were often present.

Up to the present time, three statements have been obtained by the officers, each sustaining the other, and these, with the evidence of Officer López, the sheriff and his men, and Constable Murphy, to say nothing of the letter now in the hands of Assistant District Attorney Jones, make out a very strong case against the conspirators. It is not known when the examining trial of the men will be held, but it is thought not until more of them are in "quod."

Arizona Republican, August 8, 1914.

The Texas Rangers

The Texas Rangers were held in high regard throughout the United States, primarily because Americans believed Mexicans were uniformly villainous. In 1914, a laudatory article in the *New York Times*, aptly titled "Texas Rangers Who Ride, Shoot and Dare," not only heaped praise on the Rangers but in the process related numerous anecdotes that were anti-Mexican and stereotypical of Mexican criminality.

Sir Gilbert Parker has made the fame of the Royal Northwest Mounted Police of Canada secure in English-speaking countries and most of the other civilized lands where stories of grit and daring and coolness in the face of great dangers are appreciated. But there is another body of picturesque men, whose organization is older, whose history teems with brilliant exploits and hair-raising rides and charges, whose horsemanship and marksmanship are superb, but whose daring is yet to be recounted by a man gifted as is the English narrator of the deeds of the Northwest Police.

The organization referred to is that of the Texas Rangers, whose word is law on the Texas side of the Rio Grande, and the very mention of whose name is sufficient to cow into submission the most desperate Mexican renegade who now and then crosses the border to steal, and even at times to murder.

Nearly everyone knows that such an organization is in Texas and that the men are charged with the protection of life and property. But few people outside of Texas know much about the history of the Texas Rangers, the reasons that caused the Texas Legislature to authorize their organization shortly after the close of the Mexican War, the kind of men they are, what they look like, where they operate, and who their commanders are.

First of all—what is the organization known as the Ranger Force of Texas?

The act providing for the organization, as passed by the Legislature of Texas, states that it is "a Ranger force for the protection of the frontier against marauding and thieving parties and for the suppression of lawlessness and crime throughout the state." It is an organization of four companies, each commanded by a captain and each made up of one sergeant, one quartermaster, and twenty enlisted privates. Thus, the maximum strength of the Texas Rangers is 92 men.

The law confers on the Rangers all the powers and authority of peace officers and they are permitted to operate in any part of the state. But there are also restrictions, and the Rangers must keep within the law; they must not use abusive language nor be "unnecessarily harsh" with those with whom they come in contact "in the line of duty." They act under the direct orders of the Governor, when it is possible to communicate with that official. When not possible they use their best discretion, and "best discretion," has been the procedure in most of the cases in which they have figured during the past seventy years.

As originally organized, the Rangers were intended not for service along the Rio Grande, as so many people think, but for service along the northern border of the state for the protection of the people of northeastern Texas from the raiding bands of Indians, who in the old days were in the habit of swooping down from the Indian Territory to steal and commit other depredations. In those days the force numbered about 400 men, and of this number less than fifty were assigned to duty along the Mexican border. Mexico, so far as the United States was concerned, was a fairly peaceful community at that time.

New York Times, March 15, 1914.

El Plan de San Diego

The Plan de San Diego, signed by Luis de la Rosa and Aniceto Pizaña, was in itself a remarkable document, albeit somewhat vague on how all of its tenets would be implemented. Texas Mexicans, angry over mistreatment, reportedly concocted the Plan, which proclaims a revolution and a separation of the Southwest from the Union. The degree of animosity that the writers had towards Anglo Americans is seen in the section that called for execution of all Anglo males over sixteen years of age.

We, who in turn sign our names, assembled in the revolutionary plot of San Diego, Texas, solemnly promise each other on our word of honor that we will fulfill and cause to be fulfilled and complied with, all the clauses and provisions stipulated in this document and execute the orders and the wishes emanating from the provisional directorate of this movement and recognize as military chief of the same Mr. ———, guaranteeing with our lives the faithful accomplishment what is here agreed upon.

1. On the 20th day of February, 1915, at 2 o'clock in the morning, we will rise in arms against the Government and country of the United States and North America, one as all and all as one, proclaiming the liberty of the individuals of the black race and its independence of Yankee tyranny, which has held us in iniquitous slavery since remote times; and at the same time and in the same manner we will proclaim the independence and segregation of the States bordering on the Mexican nation, which are: Texas, New Mexico, Arizona, Colorado, and Upper California, of which States the Republic of Mexico was robbed in a most perfidious manner by North American imperialism.
2. In order to render the foregoing clause effective, the necessary army corps will be formed under the immediate command of military leaders named by the supreme revolutionary congress of San Diego, Texas, which shall have full power to designate a supreme chief who shall be at the head of said army. The banner which shall guide us in this enterprise shall be red, with a white diagonal fringe, and bearing the following inscription: "Equality and Independence," and none of the subordinate leaders or subalterns shall use any other flag (except only the white for signals). The aforesaid army shall be known by the name of "Liberating Army for Races and Peoples."
3. Each one of the chiefs will do his utmost by whatever means possible, to get possession of the arms and funds of the cities which he has beforehand been designated to capture in order that our cause may be provided with resources to continue the fight with better success, the said leaders each being required to render an account of everything to his superiors, in order that the latter may dispose of it in the proper manner.
4. The leader who may take a city must immediately name and appoint municipal authorities, in order that they may preserve order and assist in every way possible

the revolutionary movement. In case the capital of any State which we are endeavoring to liberate be captured, there will be named in the same manner superior municipal authorities for the same purpose.

5. It is strictly forbidden to hold prisoners, either special prisoners (civilians) or soldiers; and the only time that should be spent in dealing with them is that which is absolutely necessary to demand funds (loans) of them; and whether these demands be successful or not, they shall be shot immediately, without any pretext.

6. Every stranger who shall be found armed and who cannot prove his right to carry arms, shall be summarily executed, regardless of race or nationality.

7. Every North American over 16 years of age shall be put to death, and only the aged men, the women, and children shall be respected. And on no account shall the traitors to our race be respected or spared.

8. The Apaches of Arizona, as well as the Indians (redskins) of the territory, shall be given every guarantee, and their lands which have been taken from them shall be returned to them, to the end that they may assist us in the cause which we defend.

9. All appointments and grades in our army which are exercised by subordinate officers (subalterns) shall be examined (recognized) by the superior officers. There shall likewise be recognized the grades of leaders of other complots which may not be connected with this, and who may wish to co-operate with us—also those who may affiliate with us later.

10. The movement having gathered force, and once having possessed ourselves of the States above alluded to, we shall proclaim them an independent republic, later requesting, if it be thought expedient, annexation to Mexico without concerning ourselves at that time about the form of government which may control the destinies of the common mother country.

11. When we shall have obtained independence for the Negroes, we shall grant them a banner which they themselves shall be permitted to select, and we shall aid them in obtaining six States of the American Union, which States border upon those already mentioned, and they may from these six States form a republic, and they may therefore be independent.

12. None of the leaders shall have the power to make terms with the enemy without first communicating with the superior officers of the army, bearing in mind that this is a war without quarter, nor shall any leader enroll in his ranks any stranger unless said stranger belongs to the Latin, the Negro, or the Japanese race.

13. It is understood that none of the members of this complot (or anyone who may come in later) shall upon the definite triumph of the cause which we defend, fail to recognize their superiors, nor shall they aid others who with bastard designs may endeavor to destroy what has been accomplished with such great work.

14. As soon as possible each local society (junta) shall nominate delegates, who shall meet at a time and place beforehand designated, for the purpose of nominating a permanent directorate of the revolutionary movement. At this meeting shall be determined and worked out in detail the powers and duties of the permanent directorate, and this revolutionary plan may be revised or amended.

15. It is understood among those who may follow this movement that we will carry as a singing voice the independence of the Negroes, placing obligations upon both races, and that on no account shall we accept aid, either moral or pecuniary, from the government of Mexico, and it need not consider itself under any obligations in this, our movement.

EQUALITY AND INDEPENDENCE.

Translated copy of Plan de San Diego in National Archives, RG59, 812.00/1583.

"A Favor for an Old Mexican Rancher"

During the height of the Plan de San Diego uprising in August, 1915, a group of Rangers led by Captain Tom McKee lay an ambush at the ranch of Cenobio Rivas, a farmer near Hondo, Texas, after the officials accused him of harboring Plan de San Diego insurgents. When some Mexican grubbers appeared asking for water, the Rangers shot indiscriminately into the ranch house, wounding the Mexican workers and Rivas' teenaged daughter. Many years later, a young Mexican American soldier in the U.S. Army attempted to obtain compensation for Rivas' losses and wrote to Governor Dan Moody. The letter recounted the tragic chain of events that followed after Rivas was accused.

The writer desires to ask a favor for an old Mexican rancher, whose name is Cenobio Rivas, residing in Los Marranos Ranch, relative to the death of a daughter and wounding of a son, during the bandit troubles of 1926 [re. 1915]. The death of the girl was due to the shooting of his home in the Charco Hondo Ranch, by a party of State Rangers, about eight or ten in number.

About eleven o'clock one night, in 1915 during the height of the bandit troubles, a party of Rangers called at this Mexican's house, just as he was returning from the fields, and asked him what he was doing, where he had been, etc., and the man replied "Am just returning from my work in the fields, where I have been all day." Then the leader of the Rangers told him to get into the house, put out all the lights, and remain there, as they were watching and waiting for some bandits to make their appearance at that particular place, as they had been told by some parties in Brownsville, that he (Cenobio Rivas) was in the habit of sheltering bandits at his Ranch, and they wanted to investigate and make sure. About eleven o'clock, two Mexican laborers, from a grubbing camp in Los Cuates Ranch, stopped there on their way home, and asked for some water to drink. Immediately on their stopping there and knocking, the Rangers started shooting, thereby hitting these two laborers. After they had fallen, they continued shooting at the house where the family was asleep, killing his daughter Martina Rivas, and wounding his son George Rivas. The girl was fifteen years of age at the time she died, and the boy was ten years. The boy recovered from his wound, which was not extremely serious, but nevertheless, kept him in a sick bed for about two months. The shot that killed his daughter, entered her back below the left shoulder, as she was lying on her right side in bed, piercing the heart. Another bullet hit his son George, also in the same bed. It hit him on top of the head, making a line from his forehead to the top of his head. This was a slight wound, but due to their inability and lack of knowledge of hygiene, it became a bad sore, thereby putting this boy in bed for a considerable length of time, and depriving the father of his services in the field.

The following named parties were present at the funeral of this man's daughter, and saw the place where the bullet entered the body and also where it came out. They are: Mr. and Mrs. Marcos Arredondo, of the Huisache Ranch, and their son Esteban Arredondo; Santos Meza of Matamoros Mexico, (formerly of the Agua Negra Ranch) and his step-son Martin. The Rangers themselves sent the last two named to help this man bury his girl, the day after the shooting.

The morning following the shooting, the Rangers conversed with the two wounded laborers, and ascertained from them who they were, where they worked, and also ascertained that they were not bandits, but law-abiding laborers going to their camp. Immediately after, other people came to this man's house, and took notations of all that had happened, stating at the time that they would see that immediate settlement would be made for the death of the girl. J. T. Canales, Ira Webster, and Frank Pierce, all three of them being Attorneys here in Brownsville, undertook to collect damages for all persons residing in the Ranches around Brownsville that had suffered casualties at the hands of the Rangers, this man's case being one of them. However, they never called him for anything, and the matter has been at a standstill since then.

The writer has recently interviewed Attorney Webster relative to this man's case, and he has promised to look thoroughly into the matter, but since he has not done anything, the claimant has asked me to write direct to you, asking your permission, or asking you just how to go about obtaining permission to sue the State of Texas for the damages. He is now and has been since the girl's death, in destitute circumstances, being afflicted with a disease that causes him to shake continually, thereby preventing him from working to properly maintain his family. His wife is in the same condition, both also suffering from the heart, including the son George, due to the shock caused by the death of the girl. This man is now 70 years of age and his wife 50. They are at present endeavoring to trap animals and catch snakes for their living, but, of course, this is not sufficient to satisfy their needs.

At the time that this happened, the man possessed over one hundred and thirty chickens, three ranch houses, thirty or forty bee-hives, and about one hundred and forty animal traps. Everything was destroyed after he left the ranch, as he was afraid to remain there after what had happened. He immediately came to Brownsville, staying at Snake King's for about three or four months, until things quieted down enough so that he could return to his former home. When arriving there, he found that everything had been destroyed, thereby completely destroying his means of making a living for himself and the family.

I would very much appreciate your attentions in this matter, and would appreciate your reply as to how to go about this matter for this old gentleman.

Thanking you in advance for your reply, and assuring you that any favors shown, will be highly appreciated, I beg to remain,

Very respectfully,
P.C. Alamía, Pvt.
Co. "M" 357th Inf., E. R. C.,
Brownsville, Texas
P.S. You may address your reply to my home address 714 Adams St.

P. C. Alamía to Moody, November 15, 1927, Texas State Archive, Record Group 301, Box 56.

The Porvenir Massacre

On January 28, 1918, about thirty Texas Rangers, accompanied by Anglo ranchers and twelve U.S. Army soldiers went to Porvenir, an isolated community in the Big Bend region of Texas, to arrest supposed outlaws. The soldiers stayed on the outskirts, but the accompanying Anglo vigilantes took fifteen Mexican small farmers and stock owners a mile out of town, executed them, and mutilated their bodies with knives. Henry Warren, an Anglo school teacher in Porvenir, married to the daughter of one of the victims, left behind this bitter account, dated January 28, 1918.

The Porvenir Massacre in Presidio

On Saturday, Jan. 26, 1918, the State Rangers visited the small village of Porvenir in Presidio County and arrested the men folks and boys there, standing them up in a row before day in the bitter cold January morning and searching them for arms; they also roughly and unceremoniously entered the houses, turning over beds, and forcibly looking into trunks and boxes searching for arms. They found only two arms in this peaceful hard-working village of one hundred and forty souls: only a pistol belonging to John Baily, the only white man living at Porvenir, which John kept in his house hanging over his cot and the other was a Winchester of a special make belonging to Rosendo Mesa. Both men were married and had families, Baily being a native-born citizen of the U.S. Both arms were taken and neither ever returned. At that time the Rangers arrested three men and took them away with them: Manuel Fierro, who lived at Pilares, seven miles below on the River, Eutimio Gonzales, and Román Nieves. These men the Rangers took up to their camp at the old railroad tunnel in the hills about ten miles off, and kept them under arrest till late in the day of the next day and then turned them loose. The men then, it being late in the day, went to Pilares, which was Manuel Fierro's home, and stayed all night. The next day, being Monday, Jan. 28, the two other men, Eutimio Gonzales and Roman Nieves, came back to Porvenir to their families where they lived and farmed. That day—the fatal Jan. 28, 1918, some time in the night the Rangers again made their appearance at Porvenir accompanied by four ranchmen, Buck Pool, John Pool, Tom Snyder, and Raymond Fitzgerald and twelve U.S. soldiers under their Captain Anderson, Troop G, 8th Calvary from Camp Evetts, about four miles off.

Capt. Anderson threw a cordon of U.S. soldiers around the houses while the Rangers went in and took the men and boys out of their warm beds, they making no resistance whatever.

Having the men and boys in their possession, the Rangers started off down the river road, the soldiers accompanying them a part of the way to where the solders' trail left the main road leading back up to Camp Evetts. After the soldiers left them, it was only a few minutes before the latter heard a fusillade of shots. One of the soldiers rode back and seeing what the Rangers had done, (the moon was shining nearly as bright as day) cursed them, and told them "what a nice piece of work you have done tonight."

The killed were fifteen, as follows:

1. Macedonio Huertas. Aged about 30. His wife named Rita Jáquez. His children, Filomeno, boy about 6 yrs.; Eligio, boy about 3 yrs.; Francisco, boy about 2 yrs.; Matilde, girl about 1 year or less.
2. Alberto García. About 35. Wife Victoria Jiménez. Left 3 children.
3. Ambrosio Hernández. Wife Eulalia Gonzales, Child Victorio, b. less than one year old.
4. Severiano Herrera. About 15 yrs. old. Grandchild of Severiano Morales. Had been there only about 10 days. Came from the Pecos country.
5. Zarapio Jiménez, about 25.
6. Pedro Jiménez, about 27, Unmarried.
7. Antonio Castamudo, Son-in-law of Juan Mendes. Left wife and maybe children. Had been there only about 10 days; came from the Pecos country.
8. Román Nieves. Wife Alejandra Children: Ventura, g. about 14; Margarito, b. about 18; Matilde, g. about 8; Francisco, b. about 5; Casimiro, b. about 4; Ynéz, b. about 3 and a post-humous child born in April 1918 about 3 months after Román's death = 7 children.
9. Viviano Herrera. Unmarried. About 23. Grandson of Severiano Morales. Had been there only about 10 days; came from the Pecos country.
10. Longino Flores. Aged about 44. Wife Juana Bonilla. Children: Mrs. Rosindo Mesa (Benita by name who had one child and was pregnant at the time of the murder of her father), Narcisco, b. aged about 15; Juan, b. aged about 11.
11. Pedro Guerra. Aged about 25. Grandson of Severiano Morales. Had been there only about 4 (four) days. Came from the Pecos country.
12. Juan Jiménez, a boy aged about 16. Son of Pabla Jiménez.
13. Manuel Morales. Aged about 47. Wife Francisca Hernández. Children: Leandro, b. about 13; Eustacio, b. about 10; Jesús, b. about 4; Manuelita, g. about 3; Juanita, about 2; and a little girl born on the very night her father was murdered, viz on Jan. 28, 1918; and Jovita, a stepdaughter aged about 12.
14. Tiburcio Jáquez, aged about 50. Wife Librada Montoya. Children: Mrs. Juliana Warren; María, g. about 17; Cecilia, g. about 15; José, b. about 14; Marcelo, about 13; Alberto, about 10; Ezequiel, g. about 6.
15. Eutimio Gonzales, about 37. Wife Concepción Carrasco. Children: Mrs. Eulalia Hernández, about 18; Francisco, b. about 19; Pedro, b. about 16; Santos, g. about 12; Refugia, g. about 11; Luisiana, g. about 6; Gerónima, g. about 4; Blasa, about 5; and a little girl less than a year old = 9.

All the bodies were found lying together, side and side. Some were partly lying upon others about a hundred or so yards from the road by a little rock bluff. I saw the bodies on the early morning of Jan. 29.

The assassins spared several old Mexicans: Cesario Huertas, Eulogio Gonzales, Gorgonio Hernández, old man Jiménez, and one other (name forgotten).

Juan Mendes escaped death because he was absent that night. Rosendo Mesa and one of the Jiménez boys were absent, had gone to Van Horn to buy some provisions. Francisco Hernández and Francisco González escaped death because they had gone up to Neville's ranch about three miles up the river. John Baily, the only white man living on the ranch within this village of one hundred and forty men, women, and children, mostly women and children, was spared.

The women and children then ran to the Mexican side of the river to desert country where there wasn't a sign of habitation, without a canopy to shield them against the pitiless winds of January and without a change of clothing and without a morsel to eat. There they stayed and the quiet little village of Porvenir with its peaceful farms and happy homes was no more! The Rangers and four cow-men made 42 orphans that night.

Now what was the cause of this wholesale destruction of these Mexicans, these peaceful farmers, and small-stock raisers?

Tom Snyder had, unknown to the Mexicans, rounded up their mares and colts and taken them to Valentine and shipped them off and sold them some weeks before, and for fear of prosecution he schemed to have the Mexicans killed so there would be no witnesses against him. So he told the Rangers that the Porvenir Mexicans had assisted in the raid on Brite's Ranch. Now the truth is that the Mexicans were at Porvenir Xmas day, 1917, and Brite's Ranch was 40 miles away, and there was no road, not even a trail between the two places, but several wire fences between. The Rangers believing or affecting to believe this story, embodied to the extent of about 30 and started out accompanied by the four ranchmen aforesaid. They belonged to Capt. M. Fox's Co.

When the truth finally reached the Adj. General Harley of the State Rangers at Austin, he discharged all the Rangers who were connected with this most infamous affair and forced Capt. Fox to resign.

Henry Warren, "The Porvenir Massacre in Presidio County, Texas, on January 28, 1918," typescript in Henry Warren Collection, Box 4, folder 88, Archives of the Big Bend, Sul Ross State University.

Canales Testifies Against the Rangers

In 1919, at special hearings in the Texas legislature motivated by the severity of Ranger brutality, the Porvenir Massacre being foremost, numerous Texas officials, including Legislator José T. Canales, called for curtailment of Ranger authority. Canales was born in Brownsville, Texas, and became a state legislator from that district. In the 1920s, Canales became a judge and a founder of the League of United Latin American Citizens.

The effect was that immediately every relative of that Mexican would go to Mexico with his tale of woe, and it aroused a strong feeling between them and the bandits. That feeling increased to the extent that practically the Mexican border on the other side was at war with us, sympathizing with the relatives of these men that had been wrongfully killed, taken out of their homes at night after the Rangers had said, "If you surrender your arms, we can protect you." Yet after they surrendered their arms, the Rangers would go into their homes afterward and shoot them at night. Ten men were killed right near San Benito, right near the house of the father of Miss Janes, my stenographer.

Now, matters got very bad, until it culminated in the wreck of the train October 18, 1915. I was in constant touch with the situation, and I co-operated with the military authorities there and furnished evidence to them. Sheriff Vann, who had been only elected shortly before and didn't know the Mexican character very well, was adverse to putting in Mexican deputies. I insisted to Captain Vann to put in Mexican deputies, because they could get in touch with those other Mexican bandits and thereby trap them easily. After the wreck, he realized that the condition was serious. General Nafarrate was openly co-operating with the bandits and helped them with money and ammunition. We knew that. I then suggested the means of establishing Mexican scouts to co-operate with the military authorities that had camps every five miles. I told him it was necessary to get the Mexicans that lived in there and had been farmers and tenants along that border to give out information and to act as guides. The suggestion was taken up by Captain Vann and endorsed by him.

I then went to Colonel E. P. Blockson, gave him my plan, and he endorsed it. He gave me a short letter, giving orders to every commanding officer along the border to admit into full confidence any Mexican that I would recommend to him. Those scouts were unarmed: they were not to arrest anybody; they were merely to give information and serve as guides for the soldiers in order to trap those bandits. They were organized about three days after the railroad wreck. I spent three months organizing, guiding, and supervising this system of scouts. They were especially to watch at night while the soldiers were in camp, and they were instructed how to come at night into the camp without any risk to their lives. The first bandits connected with the wreck of the train were arrested at San Pedro Ranch on information given by my scouts. Major M. C. Butler, who was afterward murdered at Alpine, was in command at that time. I have his own letter stating that since the organization of the Mexican scouts, not a single band of Mexican bandits crossed through his line through the efficient information given by these scouts.

71

I also had on the other side of the border men whom I had represented and who were in close touch and would give me information. I would furnish that immediately to the authorities on this side.

In December 1915, by the time the raids had been minimized, General Carranza came to Matamoros, and I was a member of the committee who called upon him. We requested of him the removal of General Nafarrate because we had information and evidence that he was assisting the bandits. He soon gave us his word he would relieve him, and he sent his own nephew, General Ricant, who was stationed there, and from that time we had no further trouble with the bandits.

But the Rangers had established a precedent—that is, whenever a suspect was arrested they would unceremoniously execute him on the road to Brownsville or to the jail, without giving him any opportunity. Frequently we would find dead bodies, and the ranches burned. Relatives were intimidated to the extent that they would not even bury their own relatives. That condition existed until it was nauseating, nauseating. It was terrible. I wrote to Governor Ferguson and told him what Captain Ransom and his men were doing. I received no information or reply from him.

Testimony given in 1919. *Proceedings of the Joint Committee of the Senate and the House in the Investigation of the Texas State Ranger Force* (Austin, Texas, 1919), pp. 856-874.

"Could Not Live with Them on Genial Terms"

U rging against waiving immigration laws to allow entry of Mexican workers in 1920, Texas congressman John C. Box summed up the attitude that Mexicans were dangerous because of their experience in the Mexican Revolution and because of their nature.

The people whom it is proposed to import are a mixture of Spaniard, Indian, and Negro, crossed and living under adverse conditions for many generations. Americans found they could not live with them on genial terms in Texas 80 years ago. In a contest that arose when the Mexican showed both his inferiority and savage nature, the same traits which prevailed with them in the days of the Alamo and Goliad show themselves in the dealings with each other and with the Americans now. I could go on indefinitely for the story has no end. Villa, Huerta, Orozco, Carranza, and their bands and the conditions of Mexico now are exhibits of Mexican character.

During President Jackson's administration more than eighty years ago, he wrote a message to Congress on the unsettled conditions of the Mexican people and the Mexican nation, and if some dates and local coloring were eliminated, it would fit into the message of President Taft or President Wilson during any of the last 12 years, for he describes conditions almost identical with those existing now, and those conditions have been the prevailing characteristics of Mexican life.

U.S. Congress. House. Committee on Immigration and Naturalization, *Hearings on Temporary Admission of Illiterate Laborers from Mexico. 66th Congress, 2nd Session* (Washington, D.C.: Government Printing Office, 1921), p. 303.

The Dangerous Crossing

Border crossings for immigrants not involved in smuggling or banditry became a danger-ous event during the Revolution, and during the 1920s they continued to be perilous. The report below is from a study of the Mexican Claims Commission, which adjudicated claims from both sides of the border, regarding loss of property, injuries, or loss of life during the 1910-1930 period.

The Same: The Teodoro García Case

The most interesting of these cases is the Teodoro García Case. Several members of a Mexican family, none of whom carried firearms, were engaged in crossing the Rio Grande on a raft at a place where crossing was unlawful. A troop of American soldiers under the command of an officer saw the raft, and thinking the persons on it were engaged in smuggling, fired in order to bring the raft to a halt. A bullet that ricocheted from the water killed a little child, whose parents were the claimants before the Commission. The officer who ordered the firing had been court-martialed for disobeying army regulations that provided that "firing on unarmed persons supposed to be engaged in smuggling or crossing the river at unauthorized places, is not authorized." The court-martial's decision was reversed by the President of the United States on the ground that these regulations should be interpreted to authorize firing where the officer has reason-able grounds for assuming that the delinquents are armed, the presumption being in favor of their carrying arms. The Commission stated that no denial of justice had been committed by the United States.

"In order to assume such a denial, there should be convincing evidence that, put to the test of international standards, the disapproval of the sentence of the court-martial by the President acting in his judicial capacity amounted to an outrage, to bad faith, to willful neglect of duty, or to an insufficiency of governmental action so far short of international standards that every reasonable and impartial man would readily recognize its insufficiency. None of these deficiencies appears from the record."

Nevertheless, in spite of the lack of a denial of justice and in spite of the fact that in view of the President's decision the shooting was proper under the army regulations, the Commission granted an award. Its reasoning was as follows:

"The only problem before this Commission is whether, *under international law,* the American officer was entitled to shoot in the direction of the raft in the way he did. . .

"The Commission makes its conception of international law in this respect depend-ent upon the answer to the question, whether there exists among civilized nations any international standards concerning the taking of human life. The Commission not only holds that there exists one, but also that it is necessary to state and acknowledge its exis-tence because of the fact that there are parts of the world and specific circumstances in which human practice apparently is inclined to fall below this standard. . .

"If this international standard of appraising human life exists, it is the duty not only of municipal authorities but of international tribunals as well to obviate the use of firearms. . .

"In order to consider shooting on the border by armed officials of either Government (soldiers, river guards, custom guards) justified, a combination of four requirements would seem to be necessary: (a) the act of firing, always dangerous in itself, should not be indulged in unless the delinquency is sufficiently well stated; (b) it should not be indulged in unless the importance of preventing or repressing the delinquency by firing is in reasonable proportion to the danger arising from it to the lives of the culprits and other persons in their neighborhood; (c) it should not be indulged in whenever other practicable ways of preventing or repressing the delinquency might be available; (d) it should be done with sufficient precaution not to create unnecessary danger, unless it be the official's intention to hit, wound, or kill. In no manner can the Commission endorse the conception that a use of firearms with distressing results is sufficiently excused by the fact that there exist prohibitive laws, that enforcement of these laws is necessary, and that the men who are instructed to enforce them are furnished with firearms."

These are fine words, but how can such talk by a transitory international "obviate" the use of firearms? The Commission seems to have been misled by its excellent humanitarian impulses. Surely, it is not the business of such a tribunal to attempt to lay down detailed rules for such a situation. If we look through this veil of words, it is apparent that what the tribunal really held was that the American army regulations, as interpreted by the President, were below the international standard. The American Commissioner (Nielsen) saw this quite clearly, and he urged that Mexico be required to show this by a comparison to the laws of other countries. The failure of the Commission to do this is perhaps explainable by a very understandable desire to render an award in favor of the bereaved parents and by a reluctance to be forced into a position of stating boldly that the regulations were below the international standard.

Abraham Feller, *The Mexican Claims Commission*, 1923-1924 (New York: The Macmillan Co., 1935), p. 138.

Chapter Three

World War I and Massive Immigration in the 1920s

After Francisco I. Madero initiated his revolt in November of 1910, hundreds of thousands of refugees poured across the border. The violence of the struggle deteriorated the already desperate situation in which Mexicans lived. As a consequence, poverty, lack of resources, and not knowing what to expect north of the border combined to make Mexicans who crossed the border during this time among the most vulnerable immigrants to ever come to the United States. Their forced and hasty exodus prevented them from preparing adequately for their sojourn across the border. Between 1910 and 1930, the number of Mexican nationals living in the United States increased from 219,000 to close to one million. This huge influx came after years of border violence had provoked in Anglo Americans intense feelings of hostility towards Mexicans (see Chapter Two). Anglo Americans easily marginalized the newly arrived, vulnerable Mexicans.

Migration during the 1910s fluctuated because the destruction caused by the war at times blocked transportation routes northward. Coinciding with difficulty in traveling to the border was a sluggish Southwest economy. In 1914, farm prices dropped drastically, and thousands of Mexicans wanted to return but were without funds. Texas, with the longest border, contained the largest number of indigent and destitute immigrants. The Mexican Labor Ministry in April considered supplying henequen producers in Yucatan with unemployed Mexican repatriates from Texas. Recovery came quickly, however, spurred by the United States serving to supply the Allies in World War I, which broke out in 1914. Irrigation projects financed through the Newlands Reclamation Act of 1903 served to prepare southwestern farmers for the war-borne opportunity. Farmers planted lettuce on irrigated acreage in the Salt River Valley of Arizona and in California's Imperial Valley in 1915; along with cotton, lettuce was responsible for the most important economic activity in both areas.

When a relative peace came to revolution-torn Mexico after 1917, normal migration resumed. A food crisis prompted Mexicans to respond to the needs of a now-accelerating economy in the United States during World War I. Thousands of U.S. workers were conscripted into military service when the United States became directly involved in the struggle, creating labor shortages in agriculture, mining, basic industry, and transportation. Mexico seemed the logical source for replacements.

Obstacles to this source soon emerged. Responding to a restrictionist mood, bolstered by wartime xenophobia, Congress enacted in February of 1917 an immigration act that imposed a literacy requirement and an eight-dollar head tax on all immigrants. The framers did not consider the potential manpower shortages of a wartime economy in this bill, which they enacted before the United States had entered the war. Although the bill targeted an "undesirable" influx from Southern and Eastern Europe, where illiteracy rates were as high as 75 percent, it presented Mexicans with difficulty because of their own low rates of literacy. With the impending summer harvests, agricultural interests pressured Congress to waive the law for Mexicans, and in June, Congress complied.

Passage of the Selective Service Act in May presented yet another threat to the flow of Mexicans into the United States. Only naturalized immigrants, or those in the process of naturalizing, could be drafted, but all immigrants were required to register regardless of status. Wary Mexican immigrants returned home en masse, however, when local boards conscripted compatriots who were not eligible. Consequently, the consuls spent much time and energy trying to obtain discharges for Mexican nationals who were drafted illegally or who were jailed for draft evasion. This reverse migration caused anxiety among American employers who depended on Mexican labor for economic expansion. Both governments joined in a widespread campaign to assure fearful Mexicans they would not be drafted. Eventually, this collaboration resolved the conscription problem, and Mexican immigration resumed a normal flow.

During 1918, American companies dispatched Mexican American contractors (*enganchistas*) into Mexico to recruit in areas where railroads offered easy transportation to the border. Often *enganchistas* exploited the vulnerability of their charges by not paying full wages or by overcharging for food and lodging. Once at the border, contractors often abandoned boys under sixteen or those workers stricken with diseases because they did not meet entry requirements.

Congress, on June 16, 1918, allowed the waivers to apply to all industries that needed Mexican labor. When the warring nations signed the Armistice in December of 1918, the Department of Labor officials anticipated a surge of returning veterans and voided the waiver to prevent a backlash from American workers who resented the presence of Mexicans. Consequently, "illegal aliens" were enthusiastically rounded up and dumped on the other side of the border.

Before 1915, Mexicans had labored primarily in border-area agriculture, railroads, and mining. During the war era, automobile factories in Detroit, the stockyards in Chicago, the steel mills of Indiana, and other sectors employed large numbers of Mexicans. According to one estimate, as many as 35,000 Mexican laborers resided outside the southwestern states in 1918, mostly in the Midwest. Wartime conditions hastened their entry into labor sectors that were previously the exclusive domain of U.S. citizens, even in the Southwest. The oil fields of west Texas and the chemical industry in Freeport, a town near Houston, Texas, previously the bailiwick of white workers, for example, came to employ thousands of Mexican workers in this era. More than 400,000 Mexican nationals lived in the United States by 1920. Increasingly, they constituted an integral part of the economy rather than just serving as a temporary expedient. But as definite signs of a postwar depression appeared early in 1921, the desirability of Mexican immigrant labor waned. As happened in downturns in 1908 and 1914, Mexican immigrants became vulnerable to the usual privations suffered during periods of unemployment. The destitution that affected Mexicans disproportionately during economic plunges magnified their presence to Americans, who perceived their situation as a "Mexican problem." Deportations by the U.S. government increased during 1921 as thousands of Mexican workers were rounded up throughout the country.

Employers once again sought Mexican labor as the recession eased after 1923. In 1924, the Department of Labor announced that more Mexicans had entered the United States during the fiscal year ending in June than in any other year in history. The passage of even more restrictive legislation in 1921 and 1924 further curbed European immigration, sustaining the demand for Mexican labor throughout the United States. The 1924 Immigration Quota Act proved to be the most exclusionary. It barred nonwhite immigrants from Asia and restricted southern and eastern Europeans, and added a ten-dollar visa fee to the already existing eight-dollar head tax.

Massive recruitment by labor-hungry industries followed, especially in West Central Mexico, where the wages in the United States seemed like a tremendous improvement over the few *centavos* that workers could earn at home. Because of this relentless recruitment, the markets in the United States filled up with surpluses in spite of the seemingly unlimited need for workers.

In 1926, zealous recruitment by American employers combined with push factors in the ailing Mexican economy to create even greater pressures for Mexicans to emigrate. By summer, even U.S. employers looked askance at the saturated labor markets; deportations soon followed. That fall, because the cotton yield in Texas and Arizona fell severely below expectations, the need for Mexicans was reduced even further.

With the labor market replete, the Department of Labor added new requirements to existing immigration regulations, which already barred applicants with a history of vice violations. Persons living in common-law liaisons, for example, were barred, and single women not accompanied by husbands were required to have two character reference letters. In addition, the immigration service no longer ignored illegal entries as they had during periods of labor shortage; it stepped up efforts to stop the U.S. illegal entries of Mexicans— sometimes violently.

Oblivious to changing attitudes, thousands of Mexicans entered the United States illegally. This provided Americans with a rationale for marginalizing and deporting Mexicans, many of whom could not understand why they were not barred outright from entering, as were Asians.

Anti-Mexican attitudes increased in 1926 when President Plutarco Elías Calles threatened to enforce provisions established in the 1917 Mexican Constitution banning private ownership of subsoil rights. Because the measure would threaten American oil interests in Mexico, Secretary of State Frank Kellogg and the U.S. Ambassador to Mexico, James Sheffield, publicly reprimanded Calles in the American press. That same year Calles had decided to persecute Catholics *(cristeros),* an initiative that American Catholics used to demonize the Mexican government. With Mexico in disfavor, Texas Representative John C. Box, the archetypical immigration foe, tried to pass legislation to halt Mexican immigration. Atrocities against Mexicans, accompanied by stepped-up deportations, increased during this period of intense anti-Mexico sentiment.

Congress passed the 1929 immigration act when it became obvious the economy did not have a chance of recovery. For John C. Box and other nativists who had pressed for a specific Mexican immigration ban throughout the 1920s, the legislation served as a partial victory. Although the provisions targeted undocumented immigrants from all countries, it became the most restrictive legislation for Mexicans up to this point. According to the law, those caught without documents a second time could be imprisoned for one year and fined one thousand dollars. William Doak, named Secretary of Labor in 1930 by President Herbert Hoover, decided to reduce the Mexican population by employing the new act. In cooperation with local law enforcement officials, Department of Labor agents zealously pursued Mexican undocumented immigrants throughout the country.

In the 1930s, the collapsed economy of the Great Depression left millions homeless or without jobs. The lives of Americans from all walks of life were disrupted, but the upheaval created the greatest challenge to Mexican immigrants. Their enclaves in industrial cities like Detroit, where unemployment in

1932 soared as high as 75 percent, fared the worse. Transient camps filled with the unemployed ringed every city in the country by 1932. The inhabitants sought sustenance in charity soup kitchens or in garbage dumps. The evolution of the Mexican *colonias* (Mexican immigrant communities) changed, owing to this terrible ordeal as well. Desirable as workers in the previous decade, employers discharged Mexicans by the thousands, who were then pressured to leave the country by community authorities. Six hundred thousand Mexican nationals and their children, many of them U.S. citizens, about one-third of those in the United States, returned to Mexico between 1929 and 1936. While most Mexican immigrants wanted to return home because of unemployment and the inability to obtain adequate shelter and food, they resented the view held by many Americans that they had no right to be in the United States.

Because Los Angeles contained the largest concentration of Mexican immigrants, repatriation affected Mexicans the most in that city. Los Angeles officials found in the 1929 restrictions another weapon to get rid of Mexicans. Federal agents sent to Los Angeles by Secretary of Labor Doak worked hand in hand with Charles P. Visel, Los Angeles County coordinator for unemployment relief, and with local Los Angeles police to arrest as many undocumented Mexicans as possible.

Officials knew that it would be impossible to corral all of the undocumented Mexicans, even with beefed up police manpower. So they devised a strategy to intimidate aliens into leaving on their own by coordinating well-publicized raids and rounding up hundreds of Mexicans, regardless of whether or not they carried documents. They discovered that only a small percentage of the Mexicans were undocumented. The next step was to coordinate the voluntary repatriation of southern California Mexicans—i.e., those who were not deportable under the 1929 act. In 1931, Charles P. Visel traveled to Mexico, hoping to arrange with Mexican officials a policy that would allow the homeland to absorb thousands of Mexicans whom county officials and Visel hoped to repatriate.

Various repatriation groups in the United States, including Visel's program in Los Angeles County, found the Mexican government cooperative. An arrangement was agreed upon in which American groups would raise funds to send Mexicans to the border, at which point Mexico promised to take responsibility for the repatriates once they crossed. Repatriation on the American side, however, was more efficient than the measures taken south of the border. Bottlenecks resulted, which left thousands of Mexicans marooned in border towns with little to eat and nowhere to sleep.

The repatriation effort, with its zeal and quickness, demonstrated that many Americans saw undocumented or destitute Mexicans as a commodity that could be thrown out once their labor was no longer needed. The promises made by Mexican officials to help those returning home did not materialize. In the early 1930s, the Mexican government had become more conservative. Social reform, such as land redistribution and concessions to labor, had slowed down. The Mexican federal government put the burden of helping these economic refugees on state governments or on private charities in Mexico, and aid in general turned out to be woefully inadequate.

"For the Most Part They Return"

A November 1926 editorial in the *New York Times* warned about dangers stemming from unregulated inflow. It stated that there were two kinds of Mexicans in the United States: the old stock with more Spanish blood, thus desirable by American standards, and newer immigrants, more visibly Indian. Fortunately, said the *Times*, these latter tended to return to Mexico.

The Southwest's Immigration Problem

The Los Angeles Chamber of Commerce is disturbed over the large number of Mexicans in California and elsewhere in the Southwest. It states that there are more Mexicans in Los Angeles than in any city in Mexico with the exception of the capital and Guadalajara. It would have Congress pass a law compelling the registration of aliens.

At first glance, this plaint is like that often made here in the East. We have been told how such and such an Eastern city has more Lithuanians than the capital of Lithuania, or more Hungarians than Budapest, or more Irishmen than Dublin. But there is a distinct difference between these two cases. The gates have been closed against the immigration that formerly flooded the East, whereas the Southwest is open to virtually unrestricted immigration. Nor can it defend itself against a large volume of "bootlegged" immigration, inasmuch as its long desert borders are easily crossed and can be patrolled only with difficulty.

No complete census has recently been made of the Mexicans in the Southwest. There are two classes of them—the older stock which has lived there for generations and the recent wave of transient laborers. The former are American citizens. Many of them have inherited their lands from ancestors who settled there when the country was still ruled by the King of Spain. In parts of Texas and Arizona, and particularly in New Mexico, these "old-timers" are numerous. Spanish is as much the official language of the New Mexican Legislature as is English. It is commonly asserted that this older stock is almost pure Spanish, whereas the newer working element that has drifted across the border and gone even as far north as Kansas City is largely Indian in blood.

This immigrant invasion across the Southern border was foreseen as inevitable when the immigration restriction laws were passed with no provisions to keep out natives of the American Continent. Their work is largely manual. The railways use them in construction; they work on the roads and to some extent as laborers on farms. The shortage of this type of labor caused by shutting off the supply of Europeans inevitably drew them northward. For the most part they return to their old homes as soon as they have laid by a few hundred dollars.

Whether these people should be excluded as are the Europeans will soon have to be decided. In the meantime, Mexico herself is beginning to try experiments in restricting immigration. She is reported not only to have decided permanently to exclude Negroes, but also to have stiffened passport regulations for tourists as well as for possible future settlers entering Mexico, whether from abroad or from the United States. The primary purpose appears to be to check the entrance of "undesirable" persons. Mexico is learning from us. It remains to be seen whether she will copy our mistakes as well as our wiser policies.

New York Times, November 10, 1926.

Crossing the Border

During 1918, Mexican American contractors (*enganchistas*), hired by American companies, entered Mexico and recruited in areas where railroads offered easy transportation to the border. Since this was the first emigration for most workers, *enganchistas* many times exploited their vulnerability. In October of 1919, Rafael de la Fuente, a Mexican railroad official, sent this dismal report to his superiors in Mexico City after the governor of Nuevo León suggested that he see firsthand the conditions of arriving *braceros* at Nuevo Laredo.

On the night of November 26, I headed for that city (Monterrey), in which, after all investigations for the case had been made, I obtained the following information from the authorities as well as from private sources:

All Mexican laborers who in search of work make their way to the neighboring Republic, due to either negligence or lack of funds, do not go to the State Capital to which they belong to obtain the corresponding passport that would allow them to cross without difficulty. As a result, when they arrive at the ports and because they lack this prerequisite, they cannot cross in a legal manner, since there are no authorized employees to expedite passports there.

The lack of passports forces laborers to look for another way of getting across, usually through some ford on the river and, with this, it turns out that they have to be smuggled in. In both cities (Mexican and American) there is an infinite number of persons whose only business consists of smuggling these laborers, and starting from that moment, the exploitation of the laborers becomes too expensive and, in many cases, fatal. Many of the laborers who returned told me that because they were lacking resources to tend to their subsistence, as well as the fear of being punished by authorities, they have had to divide themselves into small groups and in the confusion decided to take to the mountains where they have been abandoned. And some who are not familiar with the land get lost, and it has been the case that several of them have starved to death.

The persons dedicated to this business of speculation do it in the following manner: Every day they look for all laborers who arrive here wanting to cross to American territory without passports. They assemble them in groups of a minimum of fifteen or twenty (what they call a *BONCHE*), charging each one from four to five dollars to smuggle them in, telling them that once they are on the other side, they will have people contacted who for a moderate price will drive them in trucks to the city of San Antonio, Texas, which is where everybody goes when they are looking for work. There they have labor contracting offices for the majority of the United States, and they contract whomever best fits their needs.

After paying the set fee, the smuggling is carried out at night, and instead of meeting on the American side with the person who would take them to San Antonio, according to the agreement, they find three or four armed individuals who are probably in on the agreement. They wait for them and, calling themselves American employees and showing them badges that prove it, the innocent laborers do not know who they are. They scare them by telling them that they will take them to court for having been smuggled in, therefore accusing them of breaking the law. After intimidating them, they propose that since they are ignorant, the mistake will be forgiven as long as each one gives them three to four dollars, minimum. (This fee always depends on the conscience of these business opportunists.) After this second speculation has ended, one of the unknown employees entrusts himself to drive them with a friend in their trucks to San Antonio. Once the agreement has been settled, they are conducted to the outskirts of the city, and there, they encounter another accomplice who will let them rest the remainder of the night at his house. He tells them that first thing in the morning, they will set out on their trip. At dawn, the owner of the house appears and makes a new agreement with them; he will drive them to their destination if each one pays him four to five dollars more. This person drives them fifteen to twenty miles and with the mere excuse of stopping at a certain town to eat, hides from them. This allows another employee from the same town to come and arrest them and take them to a makeshift court. Moments later, the employee appears and threatens, as previously done, and without listening to their pleas, takes them back to the truck, allowing the person who brought them there to return.

After the employee walks around for a while, he becomes compassionate and, claiming that they are compatriots, asks for four or five dollars from each one, and he lets them go free. In this way, the laborers continue their long Journey of the Cross until they run out of money.

As a result of this, they begin to stay in towns they find along their journey, while others take to the mountains in small groups of three or four in order to free themselves of these speculators as they try to arrive at their final destination.

On their return, they come back with savings from six to eight months with hopes of buying a little farm for their family or to rest for three or four months, while the winter season lasts, to return once again in the spring. It turns out that when they arrive at the border, they are once again the object of speculations that, even though they are less serious, they are nonetheless harmful.

From the moment they get off the train, they are confronted by speculators in this business who tell them that the American money they have cannot be taken to the Mexican side because it will be taken away or it will not circulate. They are told they have to exchange it for Mexican currency; they offer to take them to some exchange house where they are charged from five to eight, even ten percent by the fleecer.

From there the cabby, the owner of the lodging house, and even the loader will double and triple their respective rates, and on their journey home they also fall victims to some unscrupulous employee who will recheck their luggage, charging them duties on items that have already been checked, which happen to be for personal use and should not be taxed.

By what has been expressed above, you will see what needs to be studied in order to correct those abuses that are being committed daily, since emigration and return migration are almost constant. So, in my humble opinion, I believe that if the Government could only protect the immigrants' interests, it would help laborers immensely.

Departamento de Salubridad Pública to Secretaría de Industria y Trabajo, January 16, 1920, report to "Al Agente Sanitario Inspector de Guardia Ferrocarril, October 20, 1919," Archivo General de la Nación, Ramo Secretaría de Industria y Trabajo, 228-2.

"Far From Being Undesirables"

The Southwestern economy needed Mexican labor to such a degree that employers and their associations concocted a stereotype of Mexicans as childlike, inoffensive creatures who were satisfied with very little and did not want to stay in the United States. Charles Teague, a large landowner in California and an activist in agricultural and booster associations in the state, published the following powerful statement shown below in 1928. Ironically, restrictionists put forth negative stereotypes that saw Mexicans as menacing and threatening, while supporters of Mexican immigration posited stereotypes with benign but negative characteristics.

Mexican laborers who would be chiefly affected by the projected exclusion measure are so far from being undesirables that the Southwest would experience great difficulty in getting along without them. Most of the great development work of this area has been accomplished and is maintained by Mexican labor. The great industries of the Southwest—agricultural, horticultural, viticultural, mining, stock raising, and so on—are to a very large extent dependent upon the Mexican labor which this law would bar out. This region's railways were built and their roadways are maintained by Mexicans.

If, as it is claimed, the city of Los Angeles is devoting much of its charitable funds to Mexican relief, it is probable that the funds are not as carefully handled as they should be, as it is a significant fact that El Paso, with a Mexican population of from 60 to 70 percent, devoted but 6 percent of its charitable budget to Mexican relief in 1926. Los Angeles' Mexican population, as stated above, is but 5 percent of the total.

Dr. George P. Clements, manager of the agricultural department of the Los Angeles Chamber of Commerce and a close student of the Mexican both in Mexico and California, says that misguided and unconsidered charity makes an habitual indigent of the Mexican. As long as he is "being taken care of by the Government"—the Mexican's primitive conception of food-and-clothes dole—he need not work. He won't work, consequently.

Congressman John N. Garner, of Texas, in a statement before the House Committee on Immigration, in 1926, said: "My observation is, living right there on the border, or within fifty miles of it, that 80 percent of the Mexicans that come over for temporary work go back."

Observations by California farm advisers, labor agents, and large employers of Mexican casual labor confirm this statement.

There is little evidence anywhere in rural California of a Mexican disposition to acquire land and make permanent settlement. There is no large body of Mexicans on the soil as citizens and landholders such as the solid units of Europeans in the Northern Middle West.

There are around 136,000 farmers in California. Of these, 100,000 have holdings under 100 acres; 83,000, farm tracts under forty acres. With these small farmers, their project is a one-man affair until harvesting period is reached, then they need ten, twenty or fifty hired hands to get their crop off and into market. Fluid, casual labor is for them a factor determining profits or ruin. Specialized agriculture has reached its greatest development in California. The more specialized our agriculture has become, the greater has grown the need for a fluid labor supply to handle the cropping.

Mexican casual labor fills the requirement of the California farm as no other labor has done in the past. The Mexican withstands the high temperatures of the Imperial and San Joaquin valleys. He is adapted to field conditions. He moves from one locality to another as the rotation of the seasonal crops progresses. He does heavy field work—particularly in the so-called "stoop crops" and "knee crops" of vegetable and cantaloupe production—which white labor refuses to do and is constitutionally unsuited to perform.

W.E. Goodspeed, superintendent of the California Orchard Company in the Salinas Valley, says: "Our peak harvest demands run from 400 to 500 employees as against a normal labor demand of from 75 to 100. We have tried out every form of transient labor except the Negro, with the result that we have found it necessary to confine our surplus as nearly as possible to Mexicans." This statement is typical of growers' experience on both large and small properties. Farm advisers, labor agencies, and ranch managers in the San Joaquin Valley, in the citrus and walnut districts south of Tehachapi, and the irrigated districts of the Coachella and Imperial valleys agree that at present Mexican casual labor constitutes between 70 and 80 percent of the total of that class.

California agriculture is not wedded to Mexican labor because it is cheap labor. According to statistics of the United States Department of Agriculture, California paid the highest farm wage—ninety dollars—in the country in 1926. Where white labor is available it works with Mexican and at the same wage. According to the same statistics, the average United States farm wage is fifty dollars. It has been increasingly demonstrated that in certain production areas, notably in the growing cotton acreages of the San Joaquin Valley, white casual labor refuses to work at these jobs. Of 2000 whites from Oklahoma who came to the San Joaquin cotton areas two years ago, less than 2 percent finished the season.

If, as some claim, there is some social problem connected with the immigration of Mexicans, those who are proposing the closing of the door to them will bring to the Southwestern states a much more serious one by forcing the agriculturists to bring Puerto Rican Negroes or Filipinos—which they certainly will do as a matter of self-preservation before they will let their industries perish—and certainly no one can maintain that either of the races mentioned would be as desirable as the Mexican. A large percentage of the Mexicans return to Mexico after the harvests are over. The most of the balance are alien and could be reported should any serious problem arise. On the other hand, if either of the other races mentioned are brought here in numbers, they would have to be supported through the periods when there is no work to do.

Charles Teague, "A Statement on Mexican Immigration," *Saturday Evening Post,* Vol. 107 (March 10, 1928), pp. 45-46.

Waivers to the 1917 Act

In 1920, Congressman Albert Johnson chaired hearings to determine if Congress would continue giving waivers to Mexicans to the literacy provisions of the 1917 immigration act so that they would continue to enter the country and work temporarily in agriculture. The testimony of various witnesses demonstrates how Americans were divided on the issue of Mexican immigration. Two schools of opinions can be discerned: those that stated that Mexican labor was essential and did not threaten the integrity of American culture primarily because Mexicans returned to Mexico and those who saw Mexican labor as a threat to the American workingman, to Anglo culture, and to racial purity. Here, Arizona Congressman Carl Hayden argues for a continuation of the waivers.

It was represented to the Department of Labor during the war that the Arizona cotton growers were producing an article essential to the needs of the country, and the Secretary of Labor was induced to suspend the restrictions as to the head tax, contract labor, and illiteracy, so as to permit the temporary admission into the Salt River Valley of agricultural laborers from Mexico for the cultivation of Egyptian cotton.

Last year the Salt River Valley produced crops of a total value of approximately $40,000,000, of which about $25,000,000 was cotton, and the representation made to me by the cotton growers there is that unless they can secure seasonal labor from Mexico, the production of long-staple cotton must be greatly reduced.

I have made every effort to see whether such labor could not be obtained from other sources. I have taken the matter up with the United States Employment Service and other Government bureaus in order to ascertain whether cotton pickers could not be sent to Arizona from other parts of the United States, but without success. I thought it might be possible to obtain additional labor during the picking season from the Indian tribes in Arizona and New Mexico. In the beginning the Cotton Grower's Association was comparatively successful in inducing a considerable number of Indians of the Pima Tribe to work in the cotton fields. But the Indians are now growing Egyptian cotton themselves where they have water for irrigation, and are actually employing labor to pick it. The industry in the meantime grew by leaps and bounds, until all the Indian labor obtainable is insufficient.

In 1854, my father went to Tucson, Ariz., then a small Mexican town. Everybody spoke Spanish, and Mexican manners and customs were observed. Today there are in Arizona ten times as many people of Mexican blood as there were at the time of the Gadsden purchase. Yet they constitute but about one-seventh of our population, because so many thousand Americans have settled in my State. The American people make the laws, but there has been no discrimination against the people of the Mexican race who reside in Arizona.

Mr. Sabath. Was this labor beneficial to your section of the country—in general, aside from the farmers who got it?

Mr. Hayden. I had an interesting conversation with a skilled laborer in Phoenix, Ariz., about that. He is a carpenter who is now getting $10 a day for his work. The town has been very prosperous on account of the production of Egyptian cotton and the high prices received for that commodity. He said that he believed the importation of the Mexicans which brought about this agricultural prosperity had redounded to the benefit of all the skilled laborers in that section, because the people generally had more money, were building more houses and improving their property; so that skilled laborers in Phoenix had benefited from having unskilled Mexican labor admitted, and that he personally had no objection to the suspension of the immigration law as a temporary measure.

Mr. Sabath. Did you have any trouble with those Mexicans who came in? Did they breed any strife?

Mr. Hayden. No. The agricultural labor which is imported from Sonora comes from the farms and small villages, and is usually law-abiding. The principal difficulties we have had have been with Mexicans imported some years ago by the mining companies, from the old silver mining districts in the heart of Mexico. They seem to me to be a different type of men—more quarrelsome and much more inclined to crimes of violence than the ordinary farm laborers from the State of Sonora.

U.S. Congress. House. Committee on Immigration and Naturalization, *Hearings on Temporary Admission of Illiterate Laborers from Mexico*. 66th Congress, 1st Session (Washington, D.C.: United States, GPO, 1921), pp. 264-273.

"Gaining the Precious Genes of Nordics"

In January of 1930, Congress again held hearings on the question of Mexican immigration. At issue here was whether or not to put Mexicans on the quota. Representative John Garner of Texas submitted a letter from a restrictionist group in support of his clear and succinct statements on why Mexicans were undesirable.

Anonymous threatening letters that were mailed to this commission because it advocates a quota against Mexico have, until now, gravitated to the wastebasket. One now comes, however, with a collection of newspaper clippings that help one to understand the mentality of the Amerind (American-Indian) peon, of his hopes of gaining for his children the precious genes of Nordics, that the latter may become mestizo.

One clipping pictures a Negro and an American, another a Korean and American marriage. The bride in every case is a white girl. This threatening letter includes a boast that the hybrid children of such marriages will constitute the American citizenry of the tomorrows. Is this perhaps nearly true? Does our failure to restrict Mexican immigration spell the downfall of our Republic, with all its hopes of betterment for all humanity? Athens could not maintain the brilliancy of the Golden Age of Pericles when hybridization of her citizenry began. Rome fell when the old patrician families lost their race consciousness and interbred with servile stocks.

Ought not legislation be hastened to place Latin America, itself already pathetically hybridized, under the same quota we maintain against Europe?

U.S. Congress. House. *Immigration from Countries of the Western Hemisphere: Hearings.* 2nd Session (Washington, D.C.: Government Printing Office, 1921), p. 165.

Alonso S. Perales and Mexican Immigration

Alonso S. Perales, a founder of the League of United Latin American Citizens (LULAC), testified in the 1930s hearings on immigration. Perales was a native of Texas, a World War I veteran, and had served in a diplomatic mission to Central America. His message, that he was offended about the racist characterizations permeating the congressional hearings, resonated in almost every instance of his comments.

Mr. Perales: At the outset, Mr. Chairman and members of the committee, I want to state that I am not here to oppose the Box bill or the Johnson bill or any other bill, but to promote the welfare of Texas—of the American people. Therefore I am not going to discuss the economic phases of this problem.

However, I do wish to refer to the statements made by some sponsors of this quota bill, to the effect that the Mexican people is an inferior and degenerate race. Being a Mexican by blood, and being just as proud of my racial extraction as I am of my American citizenship, I feel it my duty to deny most emphatically that the Mexican race is inferior to any other race, and I have quoted authorities here in support of my statement.

The charge is also made that Mexicans ought to be restricted because they do not become American citizens. I am one of the founders of what is known in Texas as the League of United Latin-American Citizens.

Mr. Canales, the gentleman who preceded me, is also one of the founders, and foremost leaders, of this organization. The main objects of this organization are to develop within the members of our race the best, purest, and most perfect type of a true and loyal citizen of the United States of America; and to define with absolute and unmistakable clearness our unquestionable loyalty to the ideals, principles, and citizenship of the United States of America.

The acquisition of the English language, which is the official language of our country, being necessary for the enjoyment of our rights and privileges, we declare it to be the official language of this organization, and we pledge ourselves to learn, and speak, and teach the same to our children.

We shall oppose any radical and violent demonstration which may tend to create conflicts and disturb the peace and tranquility of our country.

Now, gentlemen, the question is also asked that, if we are not an inferior race, why is it that we have not produced outstanding men? Well, if I may answer that in a general way, I will say that we have, despite our handicap as a race, produced a few outstanding men. I will quote, for instance, Doctor Maca, one of the outstanding statesmen of the world.

I will also refer to another Mexican, who is now in Europe, an outstanding European lawyer, now serving as umpire on several international claims commissions.

Why have we not produced outstanding men in Texas? Gentlemen, the problem in Texas has been mostly one of racial prejudice, with us. We have received very little encouragement to forge ahead and become useful American citizens. On the other hand, attempts have been made to keep us down. Therefore, our effort here to organize ourselves into this organization known as the League of United Latin American Citizens, to the end that we may become better citizens, seems to me to be all the more commendable.

That is all I wish to say, and I will be very glad to answer any questions.

Mr. Green: I would like to ask the gentleman if he believes we should have any restrictions on immigration from Mexico into the United States?

Mr. Perales: Yes, if you can prove that these Mexicans come in here to compete with American citizens.

Mr. Green: Then do you believe in restricted immigration? You are an American citizen?

Mr. Perales: I am an American citizen.

Mr. Green: A member of the bar?

Mr. Perales: Yes.

Mr. Green: From your statement, you have the interests of our country at heart?

Mr. Perales: Yes.

Mr. Green: Would it not be better, then, for us to thoroughly Americanize all the foreign strains which we have in our land now, rather than to permit others to come in? We must first look to America, not to the country of our nativity—I mean the country of our ancestors.

Mr. Perales: As to the method of doing it, I do not care to answer one way or the other. I believe I have made myself very clear—that I am for any measure that will tend to promote the welfare and happiness of the American people; and therefore, if the sponsors of this bill or any other bill can prove that the Mexicans—that is those from Mexico—are a menace to the American workingmen, because they come here and work for lower wages, then I say all right; good luck to you; more power to you.

U.S. Congress. House. *Immigration from Countries of the Western Hemisphere: Hearings.* 2nd Session (Washington, D.C.: Government Printing Office, 1921), pp. 180-182.

The Race Question

Roy Garis, professor of economics at Vanderbilt University and a proponent of eugenics, the pseudo-scientific theory that racial minorities were inferior to whites, supported putting Mexicans on the quota because of their alleged inferiority. After demonstrating that Mexicanization of the Southwest was proceeding at an alarming rate, Professor Garis explained why this was such a threat to the well-being of the nation.

Logically, a continuation of such conditions means but one thing: the abandonment of this section of the country by the white population, for white Americans cannot live in competition with peons trained by 400 years of Spanish oppression and political and economic exploitation, to live on next to nothing in the way of subsistence and shelter.

The above facts indicate clearly that Mexican immigration is now a national problem rather than the problem of the Southwest. Indeed, the border States are now to a very large extent merely stepping-stones to the interior of the country where this Mexican labor is in demand by industries and agricultural interests which seek cheap labor, regardless of the ultimate cost in terms of American welfare and progress. The restriction of European immigration has made this invasion from the South an increasingly important factor in our communities and industries, so that at the present time we must reckon with it or be engulfed by it. We cannot postpone the erection of an adequate barrier any longer, for it is an invasion, even more serious than if it were military.

Indeed, the Mexicans have come in such large numbers during the last few years as almost to reverse the essential consequences of the Mexican War. Today Mexican immigrants are making a reconquest of the Southwest more certainly, if we consider the matter of time, than America made the conquest in 1845, 1848, and 1853—while the outposts of their invasion extend far into the interior.

The greatest possible contrast has existed in the building up of the population of Mexico and that of the United States. The native Indian population that lived in the present area of the United States was generally sparse or was concentrated in special districts. The Europeans who came to this country were settlers who introduced their own civilization, who very rarely interbred with the Indian, and who came in such a continuous and substantial volume that it required but a short time for the population of European stock to equal and presently to outnumber the Indian stock, so that today the pure Indian stock and the white stock having Indian intermixture is relatively and numerically insignificant.

At every point the Mexican development is in contrast. When the white man arrived, the native stocks were highly populous and inhabited the best lands of the country. Since the Spanish invaders sought gold and not homes, very few of their women ever went to Mexico. Indeed, many of the men returned to Spain after a time. Immigrants from the other countries of Europe have been conspicuous by their absence. Indeed, but few European immigrants have gone to Mexico in the century since the Mexican population achieved independence from Spain. Today, therefore, the population of pure Indian blood or of mixed Indian blood outnumbers very greatly the pure European stock.

The few Spanish women in Mexico became the mothers of the pure creole stock, which has never been very large. Beyond doubt the most frequent unions of the Spanish men were with Indian women. The result was presently the beginning of a new race of mixed Indian and white blood, called by the Spanish name of mestizo. Since Spaniards from all parts of Spain mingled with Indian women of many tribes having distinctive ethnological traits, some differences of type resulted. By further intermarriage of Spaniards with Indians during the past century, or of mestizo with Indian, the mixed-breed population has still further increased, and throughout the centuries there has been much intermarriage of mestizo with mestizo.

Still other than Spanish or Indian elements have been present in Mexico. During a period of about two centuries prior to 1817, there was some importation of Negroes to be used as slaves. They were largely males, a part of whom subsequently united with Indian women. So far as the Negro stock persists today it is in the so-called zambos, the offspring of crosses between Indian and black, and it tends to be unrecognizably absorbed into the race stock of the country. Likewise, a considerable tide of oriental immigration has added to the color scheme.

It is evident, however, from what has been written that the stock of the Mexican people is principally of mixed Indian blood. Since the process of fusion is still going on, the stock is likely to become even more characteristically one of mixed blood than it has been. It is entirely fitting, therefore, to call this stock Mexican. However, if a color designation is used, it is plainly a mistake to continue the common practice of speaking of the stock as white, for its basis is more copper than white.

In industry in Mexico, the Indians occupy the lowest places. They are farm hands, unskilled laborers, mule drivers, factory hands, workers in the mines, sometimes servants—"human beasts of burden." They seem to be men of few wants, apathetic, without ambition, not concerned with the future. Rarely do they own land. They are improvident and prefer to work intermittently, getting into debt with their employers, who thereby are enabled to hold them to their estates. They are much given to drinking pulque, an intoxicating liquor.

The mestizos resemble the pure Indian in many respects. Most are of the peon or labor class, but, like the white class above them, they often scorn manual labor. They, too, are given to drinking pulque. They are clannish, their lives being largely determined by custom. It is evident from these traits that we should expect to find a high rate of illiteracy, a condition which characterizes the population of Mexico. According to their last census, only 3,000,000 persons in a population of 15,000,000 could both read and write, while over 7,000,000 Mexicans, 12 years of age or over, could neither read nor write. We can search in vain throughout the countries of Europe—the source of white immigration—for biological, economic, and social conditions fraught with a fraction of the danger inherent in the immigration of Mexicans into the United States.

According to every test as to the desirability of this immigration, including the assumed economic demand of peonage or common labor, there can be but one answer— it must be restricted. Its restriction is as inevitable as it is necessary if we are to protect our national welfare and reap any permanent value from the restriction of European and the exclusion of oriental immigration. For much more powerful than the claims of neighborhood are the blood ties between the people of the United States and those of Europe, for in blood the people of this country are mainly European and white. In blood the people of Latin American and the West Indies are mainly Asiatic (Indian) or African, mainly brown or black. The vast majority of them are not white and certainly not Caucasian. Now it is a fact known to all that the Supreme Court of the United States has held that only "white" persons are eligible for citizenship. Likewise, the court has held in recent years that white means "Caucasian." It is thus that not only persons of the colored races are ineligible for citizenship but even certain persons properly designated as "white"—including the Hindu—may not become citizens, unless they belong to the Caucasian branch of the white race.

U.S. Congress. House. *Immigration from Countries of the Western Hemisphere: Hearings.* 2nd Session (Washington, D.C.: Government Printing Office, 1921), pp. 424-428.

"Give Their Places to Americans"

With the advent of the Great Depression, immigrants, Mexicans in particular, became unwanted, and soon politicians and government officials began to make pronouncements to create programs to get rid of Mexicans. Secretary of Labor William Doak was particularly zealous in his efforts to rid the country of foreigners. Doak targeted Mexicans in the cities where they predominated, especially in Los Angeles and in the Chicago area.

Spurred by the unemployment existing among native-born citizens of the United States, Secretary of Labor Doak has ordered a "nonspectacular but thorough" drive to deport approximately 400,000 aliens said to be illegal residents of the country.

"I'm going after every evader of our alien laws, regardless of nationality, creed or color, because I hold to the belief that persons who have no right to be here should give their places to Americans," Secretary Doak declared today.

"My men are out in full force, particularly in the large industrial centers, and they are making good headway in a difficult task. I am informed that many of those deported recently left vacant jobs for worthy citizens in need of employment.

"Some may say to deport these people is inhuman, but my answer is that the government should protect its own citizens against illegal invaders. This I propose to do with every weapon in my power. Law is law, and I intend to enforce it as long as I hold my office."

Mr. Doak disclosed that more than 1100 aliens have been deported from New York City alone since the middle of January. More than half of these deportations created jobs for unemployed Americans. Twenty-five inspectors attached to the New York immigration office and a score of picked agents from the department here are waging the crusade in New York City.

"We are not directing a campaign against the Communists or any other special class," Secretary Doak emphasized. "We are aiming only at undesirable aliens as a general group, without regard to classification according to radical beliefs and sundry doctrines. If any alien is in this country illegally, he may expect no favors from the Department of Labor."

BORDERS WATCHED

The Labor Secretary said that extreme vigilance is being maintained at the ports and borders to prevent surreptitious entry of more aliens. Despite the precautions, he said, smugglers succeed in slipping by the blockade.

"Why, they're even using planes for alien smuggling," Mr. Doak said. "We have to watch land, sea, and air to detect all the ramifications of the smuggling ring. It is this group of aliens against which we are bringing to bear the provisions of the deportation laws.

"We are not deporting anyone without careful study of all phases of the individual case. Not until I am certain our action will stand the test of the courts do I issue the necessary warrant. To obtain proper evidence, it often is necessary to devote considerable time to investigation, tending to slow up the final action."

Nearly 17,000 aliens were deported last year and Secretary Doak hopes to rid the country of some 20,000 more during the present year, it is understood. Aliens who have resided in this country for five years are not deportable.

Los Angeles Times, April 11, 1931.

The 1929 Act

With passage of the 1929 Immigration Act, the jailing of Mexicans increased because entering the country illegally became a felony. Enrique Santibáñez, a journalist, historian, and consul who served in various posts in the United States, including San Antonio, lamented this situation in a book he wrote on Mexicans in the United States just after this law was passed.

Mexico's citizens have the tendency to consider a crime that damage which is done to society or to a neighbor, irreparable many times to its property, its honor, or its life. And we consider a violation, an act which does not cause damage but is censurable. Regarding the act of crossing a border without respecting the law, we, Mexicans do not think that we are committing a crime which must be paid for in a penitentiary next to someone who has robbed or killed. But the law is the law, and the foreigner must subject himself to the laws of that country, laws that it has created as an exercise of its sovereignty.

But that foreigner does have the right to ask that if he is found guilty, that a punishment without ill treatment be applied. The Border Patrol, in other words, the Immigration Service Agents who are in charge of chasing down those who break laws of that particular branch, are individuals who treat unfortunate Mexicans who come into this country illegally, as though they were perverse criminals and assassins, and that is why they interrogate them and treat them roughly. They handcuff them, and there have been confirmed cases in which they have been mistreated. Also, that foreigner has the right to ask that in jail he be treated with dignity, and that he, at least, be given a piece of earth where he can rest and sleep. The County of Hidalgo, Texas, has failed in all of these humane precepts, and it is certain that when the Department of Labor becomes aware of this flaw, it will see to it that it does not repeat itself in honor of the great American Nation.

A law has been passed so that women and children are not incarcerated, but rather placed under the custody of the Mexican Blue Cross, which has one of its brigades in McAllen, and that the Edingburg jail begin to decrease its number of inmates. It had three times more than its natural capacity.

The October 10, 1929, issue of San Antonio's *La Prensa* (it could not have been more recent), stated that an agent of the Department of Labor who is in charge of finding employment for those who do not have any, found in a Texas County some 300 Mexicans imprisoned, accused of vagrancy; he immediately tried to free them. We have already explained in another chapter that Mexican people usually do not find year-long employment in this country and they have to migrate from county to county, and even from State to State, in order to find work. Under those conditions they are not vagrants who wander along the roads, but men whose only fortune has not been favorable enough for them to work a daily and constant job in one place.

The immigration agents and officers do not have the power to free or deport those who have been arrested under the suspicion of having broken a law. That decree comes from the Department of Labor in Washington, to whom an individual report of each detainee is sent. Or it is assigned to a federal judicial authority when a circumstance that increases the seriousness of the crime is found in the case. A month and many days can go by before orders of the Department of Labor on deportation arrive in Texas; that is why detainees overflow jails that were built to fulfill the common necessities, but are useless in extraordinary circumstances such as the present one. And since the orders are processed individually and the Border Patrol traps in its network families who represent three generations—the elderly, middle-aged people, and children who await the decision on their cases—they are usually deported separately. Sometimes the husband is deported before his wife or vice-versa; at other times, the elderly grandmother or the younger daughter, and these unfortunate women arrive in Mexican territory without resources and without someone who can aid them, since their relatives are left in jail.

In cases in which there are aggravating circumstances—like the recurrence of smuggling, the Order of the Federal Court which judges and a Federal Court or Court which sentences—punishments are imposed that must be carried out in a penitentiary, and since there are no federal establishments of this kind in Texas, Mexicans are sent to Atlanta, in the State of Georgia, so that they can serve their time. In addition to the months or years, there are fines of $200 and $300, and since the prisoners never have money, another 200 or 300 days are added. The indicted wait four to five months in jail in order to be tried because juries meet only twice a year.

Washington authorities should be blamed for the evils that are the outcome of proceedings that could have been considered when formulating the laws, proceedings that have been known and that will undoubtedly be amended. (Our predictions have proven true. Previous to the publication of this article, the severity with which the law was practiced has been disappearing. It became more humane along the lines that I had hoped.)

Enrique Santibáñez, *Ensayo acerca de la inmigración mexicana en los Estados Unidos* (San Antonio: The Clegg Co., 1930), pp. 68-70.

Mexican Americans Support Immigrants

The document shown here, penned by Alonso S. Perales, the Texas lawyer and founder of LULAC, demonstrates that many leaders of the Mexican American generation sympathized with the plight of immigrants and advocated their fair treatment. Here, Perales writes his congressman, John Garner, in May of 1929, protesting the inhumane jailing of "illegal aliens" and their families.

I have been informed by *La Prensa* of San Antonio, Texas, that a great number of Mexicans residing here, including many women and children, have been accused of having entered illegally into the United States and are confined to common jails, next to presumed ordinary criminals. Without discussing the merits of the immigration law by virtue of which such arrests have been made, I address myself to you, to ask that you have the kindness to use your good positions to persuade the federal authorities in charge to obey the mentioned law and adopt the following procedure:

1) That they be kind to women and children, allowing them to remain in their homes in those cases in which the male head of household is in jail, accused of having entered the country illegally. If it cannot be allowed that women and children remain in their home, that they be accommodated in an appropriate detention home while they prove their right to reside in the United States.
2) That in those cases in which the male head of household has the right to reside in the United States but not his family, that the family be placed in a home for the appropriate detention while they prove their right to live in this country.
3) That women and children, who do not have a male head of household and who are accused of having entered illegally into the United States, be lodged in a home for adequate detention while they prove their right to reside in this country.

Be certain that the undersigned and all Mexican people will be quite grateful for any step you take in remedying this unfortunate situation.

Alonso S. Perales, *En defensa de mi raza*, Vol. I (San Antonio: Artes Gráficas, 1936), pp. 44-45.

"To Rid This Community of Mexicans"

Members of the American Legion in East Chicago, Indiana, organized a campaign to repatriate Mexicans during the Great Depression. The following letter written by Paul Kelly, who took the lead in this effort, to Secretary of Labor William Doak, indicates why the group, made up of World War I veterans, took this action.

This community, in the heart of the great industrial region in northwestern Indiana, has a problem, which if settled, would solve many questions vitally affecting each and every one of us here. We have a population, at present, of about 3500 Mexican nationals here in East Chicago comprising some seven hundred odd families. Our social service (charitable) organizations are now caring for the bulk of this Mexican population, few of them now being self-supporting. There are now about 1500 of these aliens willing and ready to go back to old Mexico, but lack the funds necessary for transporting them to the border. Our charitable organizations face an exhaustion of funds with which to feed, house, clothe, and care for indigents and do not have any funds available now for the transportation of aliens to the borders of our country. Prospects for funds in the near future to carry on this charitable work look very dim—the county is faced with a money shortage; in fact, many of the bills for poor relief are paid with "script" payable at tax collecting time in May and November, 1935. Our cities also face a shortage of money, partly due to the immense drain on their resources and partly due to funds tied up in closed banking institutions. Our existing charitable organizations likewise must depend on subscriptions raised from those of us who are fortunate enough to be employed, and receiving pay, and also from subscriptions and donations by the industries of this city.

Here is our problem—to rid this community of Mexicans. The solution, as we understand it, can be had for those who have been here less than three years and are willing to sign an affidavit, or statement, that they will never return to the United States, but we would still have a great many of them remaining here. We also understand that the Mexican government has deported vast numbers of Chinese from Mexico and is endeavoring to populate the areas from which the Chinese are being deported with Mexican nationals who return from other countries so that there would be no diplomatic entanglements to complicate our problem. We understand that the Mexican government is anxious to repatriate all Mexicans who desire to return to their native country and will provide transportation from the border to the place of colonization in Mexico. There are perhaps a thousand Mexicans here who could be deported by that method. To deport the remainder of them is another story.

Our theory is that those railroads who were given their rights-of-way by the United States government when their railroads were built, might be willing to concede a point and run a solid train of these Mexicans to the border, or if need be, several solid trains of them to the border. Certainly some arrangements could be made to feed them on their trip to the Rio Grande by agencies here, but the problem of railroad fare is the momentous one to us, and the latter problem is one that we cannot solve, hence our appeal to you.

If we were able to transport all of the Mexicans who are willing to return to their native country, there would be few, if any remaining here. They cannot withstand the rigors of our severe winter seasons, many of them are afflicted with syphilis, more of them are afflicted with tuberculosis, and they certainly present a difficult social problem.

Many of the Mexicans who are now residing here work two or three days a week, some of them more, many of them less, and if an opportunity was given these folks to return to Mexico, they most certainly would grasp that opportunity. By them leaving, our unemployment problem here in this city, and in fact of almost the entire of Lake County, would be solved.

Paul Kelly to William P. Doak, Secretary of Labor, March 4, 1932, American Legion Repatriation File, East Chicago Historical Society.

Chapter Four

Immigrant Mobilization

Large-scale Mexican immigration to the United States after 1900 provided the impetus for the emergence of Mexican immigrant enclaves throughout the Southwest and Midwest. Accompanying the formation of these "Little Mexicos" was the creation of a *México Lindo* identity that consisted of a desire to return to the homeland as soon as possible, a desire to maintain Mexican citizenship and culture, and to idealize and romanticize memories of the old country. Exile nationalism spread quickly throughout the United States by means of an extensive inter-immigrant network made up of businessmen, leaders of mutual aid societies, editors of newspapers, and Mexican consulates.

When it came to civil rights, Mexican immigrants accepted an outsider role in American society. They mainly wanted to be treated with dignity and to make their temporary home in the United States tolerable. Nonetheless, Anglo American racism, rejection, and outright violent hostility toward them thwarted this simple wish.

Because the Mexican diplomatic service did not give much priority to immigrant protection during the Mexican Revolution, expatriate Mexicans found it difficult to depend on consuls. Necessity obliged immigrant societies—normally oriented towards mutual aid, patriotism, and recreation—to add protection to their agenda.

Immigrant activists were persistent. Mistreatment only galvanized their desire to prevail against blatant injustices. The organizing in Laredo of El Primer Congreso Mexicanista (The First Mexicanist Congress) during 1911 became one of the first major attempts to organize Mexican immigrants on a statewide basis. Nicasio Idar, the influential editor of Laredo's *La Crónica,* spearheaded this pioneering civil rights effort, and hundreds of Texas Mexican journalists, schoolteachers, and mutual aid society representatives joined with Idar to try and make the meeting a success. The major issues on the agenda were land ownership, segregation in schools, lynchings, police brutality, and capital punishment. It is unclear if the lot of Texas Mexicans changed because of this historic meeting, but certainly it became a building block for future mobilization. Houston's Mexican immigrant population increased five-fold from 1910 to the mid-twenties. And as happened in other areas with intense immigration, the reception from the police was often hostile. The need to defend against abuses emerged as a result, prompting the formation of the Asamblea Mexicana (Mexican Assembly) in 1924 by Fernando Salas, a merchant, and Frank Gibler, a former U.S. consul to Guadalajara who was married to a Mexican woman. Helping immigrants who had been jailed unjustly became one of its prime objectives.

Arizona, like Texas, absorbed the initial immigration waves from Mexico in the late nineteenth century. In order to ameliorate police mistreatment in the 1880s, Mexicans in Tucson led by newspaperman Carlos Velasco began El Centro Radical Mexicano (The Mexican Radical Center). Thousands of Mexicans were immigrating to southern Arizona to work in the laying of track for the Southern Pacific Railroad and for industries stimulated by the trains themselves, such as mining. During 1894, Mexicans in Tucson organized La Alianza Hispano Americana (Hispanic American Alliance) as a mutual aid society and political organization. It soon spread throughout the Southwest and by the 1920s had accumulated a respectable record in protecting civil rights for Mexicans.

La Liga Protectora Latina (Latin Protective League) was organized during 1914 in Phoenix to deal with violations of civil rights and labor abuse. One of its successful major issues was opposition to legislation that threatened to prohibit non-English speakers from working in the Arizona mines. La Liga's priorities also extended to defending Mexicans in the justice system.

Between 1915 and 1925, Los Angeles experienced the most rapid increase of Mexicans. As in other areas with large *colonias,* defense organizations quickly appeared. La Liga Protectora Mexicana (The Mexican Protective League) and La Confederación de Sociedades Mexicanas (The Federation of Mexican Societies), for example, pursued immigrants' legal rights, even keeping lawyers on retainer for that purpose. In the 1920s, California had the most disproportionate sentencing of Mexicans to the gallows anywhere in the country, and immigrant groups soon manifested intense opposition to capital punishment.

Urban enclaves of Mexicans in the industrial Midwest—in Kansas, Missouri, Northwest Indiana, Illinois, and Michigan—formed after those in the Southwest, primarily after 1915. As a consequence they had a disproportionate number of young single men whose lifestyles invited contact with the police, who often administered justice without regards to civil rights. The majority of the newly arrived inhabitants were from central Mexico, and they lacked experience with the American judicial system, its laws and ordinances. The youthfulness of these immigrant men resulted in leadership vacuums and the belated appearance of immigrant institutions.

But adversity itself forced immigrant leaders to act. For example, because the Mexican arrest rate in Chicago during the 1920s was higher than in southwestern communities, intensive crusades to help compatriots in trouble with the law emerged. An umbrella organization for thirty-five Chicago mutual aid societies, La Confederación de Sociedades Mexicanas de los Estados Unidos de América (The Federation of Mexican Societies in USA) was founded in Chicago on March 30, 1925. Finding jobs, temporary shelter, and offering protection from the police emerged as the core objectives of this ambitous undertaking.

Immigrants gained crucial experience in fighting against other kinds of abuses when they defended Mexicans arrested for political activity, a frequent occurrence in this era. Revolutionaries and other activists were regularly arrested by U.S. officials for violating neutrality laws, for border banditry, for smuggling arms into Mexico, and for labor union activity. Even before the outbreak of the Revolution, members of El Partido Liberal Mexicano (The Mexican Liberal Party) were the most persecuted activists. Organizations initially established to assure that compatriots arrested for political crimes would be treated justly were turned to deal with more general violations. The discriminatory sentencing of Mexicans to capital punishment greatly concerned the immigrant community. Saving Mexicans from the gallows became an emotionally charged issue that provoked U.S. Mexicans to organize widespread campaigns for the raising of defense funds and the lodging of official protests.

To curtail school segregation, immigrant leaders and the Mexican consuls lodged challenges either through the courts or through direct confrontation with school boards and administrators. Initially, Mexicans accepted the rationale given by school officials for separating Mexican children because they did not know English. That argument wore thin, however, when bilingual children were still being separated in the 1920s. Nonetheless, immigrant communities were not ready to mount effective desegregation efforts until their communities were stable and had a sense of permanency. Obviously, the longer the Mexican immigrants lived in the United States, the more important a quality education for their children became. This concern was an early sign of Mexican Americanization.

After thousands of Mexicans lost their jobs throughout the United States during the Great Depression, they either returned to Mexico voluntarily or were coerced to repatriate. About two-thirds of the Mexicans living in the United States remained in place, however, to ride out the economic storm as best they could. But the privations of the Depression forced many immigrant organizations to close their doors or more narrowly channel assistance to the destitute and to those wishing repatriation to the homeland.

Unfortunately, the repatriation of unemployed Mexicans to Mexico in the early 1930s resulted in depopulating of communities and weakening of their organizations. This was occurring at precisely the time that a distinct Mexican-American (not Mexican national) ideological thrust was growing. The emergence of the League of United Latin American Citizens, one of the longest lasting and most powerful civil rights organizations, in Texas during 1929, was a sure sign that Mexican Americanization was well under way in Mexican communities by the end of the 1920s.

"The Spirit and Solidarity of Brotherhood"

The establishment of a *México Lindo* ideology depended on the formation of mutual aid societies by the workers themselves. The founding statement of the Sociedad Mutualista "Benito Juárez," issued on May 25, 1919, vividly demonstrates how and why the society in Houston, Texas, was organized. The emphasis on naming the organization after the Indian, Benito Juárez, Mexico's most revered political leader, illustrates the emphasis the group put on expatriate nationalism as well as a pride in their Indian past.

On the eve of May 25, 1919, neighboring Mexicans of Magnolia Park were standing vigil for the wife of a Mexican man. The people present acknowledged the misfortune and helplessness in which many of our compatriots encounter death. They were so impressed that they decided to organize a Mutual Benefit Society in order to tend to the necessities of those members who may find themselves in such a distressing situation.

The preliminary meeting took place the 18th of May in Mr. Pablo Saenz's home. Mr. Manuel Varela addressed the meeting and was followed by Mr. Adolfo S. Morales and Mr. Miguel Olvera. The aforementioned presented useful and spirited ideas supporting mutualism, and those present decided to second the project of creating a society of that nature, and with that purpose they called a meeting where the Society would be organized.

The meeting was held at Mr. Marín Magallanes' home the 5th of May in the morning. Discussion was open in order to determine the basis of the Society and once they were established, they proceeded to choose a name and a motto. "Benito Juárez" was the name proposed and accepted by unanimous applause. Everyone admitted that the Mexican heart has a passion for improvement and that the example of a true Indian, who by his civic virtues and self-worth rose to the first place among his compatriots and became a national Mexican symbol, was the name for their society. As a motto they chose "Union and Progress." The following people were chosen to the board of directors: Mr. Elías Ramírez, President; Anastacio Moreno, Vice-President; Luciano M. Rodríguez, Health President; Genovevo García and Wenselao Espinoza, Vocals.

The participants of this meeting ended their labor organization quite satisfied in having accomplished an admirable and commendable act, because the new society would facilitate the unity of Mexican citizens and would revive the spirit of aid and fraternity so useful everywhere, but even more so, among people who reside away from their homeland.

"Acta Primordial de la Sociedad Mutualista 'Benito Juárez'" in Houston, Texas, May 25, 1919, Signed by Elías Ramírez, President, and Manuel Varela, Secretary, (Small collection), Houston Metropolitan Research Center, Houston Public Library.

Mexicanness and Racial Pride

Essays in Houston's *La Gaceta Mexicana* demonstrate the degree to which Mexican immigrants felt Mexican culture should be maintained in the United States and the reverence that they paid to their Indian past. The first one, entitled "Eduquemos a nuestros hijos" (Educating Our Children), regards the proper education Mexican children in the United States should receive; it appeared anonymously. The second one, "Nosotros los indios" (We, Indians), on the pride of having Indian blood, is by Houston jeweler Emilio Ypiña.

Educating Our Children

Mexican parents who, for whatever circumstances, reside in the United States are responsible for everything involved in the education of their children. It may be possible that they may be twice more responsible than parents who live and educate their children in their homeland.

Over there, it is only necessary to teach them to be good citizens and to earn their living in an honest manner, while here, education must be the same, but with a delicate feature that many parents do not wholly comprehend and, as a result, children grow up with an education quite different from what they are supposed to receive. Here, they must learn their own language correctly as well as the official language of this country for business matters. They must have a clear notion of their obligation to respect the laws of the country that hosts them, while at the same time they must continue respecting their own country and honoring their parents through acts which may grant respect to their native homeland. This will render an absolute change in the criteria that many North Americans have of Mexico and its citizens.

It is distressing and deplorable that Mexican parents who build their homes in this country and raise children here, either out of vanity or negligence, believe that they satisfactorily fulfill their duty toward their children by educating them in North American schools, by teaching them English and United States history.

The country of origin must never be forgotten. Italian, Spanish, and German colonies prove to be successful because they have incorporated into the education of their youth the teaching of their own language, the practice of traditional customs, and their highest goal is that when their children become men, they will nonetheless be American as a result of the laws, but they will still love and honor their country of origin.

Obtaining a different citizenship will not change the characteristic features of a race, and no matter how much we, Mexicans, Americanize ourselves, we will always be Mexican to the children of the United States. We will always be worthy of their disdain if we do not learn to make ourselves deserving of their consideration through careful education in which we respect our forefathers' country. Stating that we are Mexican should not be a cause for humiliation, because our true Mexican race is not composed of those citizens who have forgotten to honor their country and commit shameful acts, as it is believed by many. The majority of delinquents within our people are individuals born to Mexican parents in this country. They have not been taught to love and honor

Mexico and their race, a fundamental necessity in ennobling them before outsiders and their own.

Therefore, the duty of Mexican parents who have children here or who brought them when young is to make sure that they first learn Castilian Spanish to perfection; this will certify that they are educated and will facilitate the learning of English. Later in life this will allow them to succeed and earn the respect of U.S. citizens and of their racial brothers because their erudition and dignity will be the factors that will finally bring respect and consideration to all Mexicans, who will continue to be Mexican before the eyes of the North American. But they will no longer be the uncivilized nor the law violators; they will be law-abiding Mexicans of the United States who protect the name of their forefathers' country.

La Gaceta Mexicana, April 15, 1928.

We, Indians

The article that makes reference to Benito Juárez, our great national hero in the *Spanish Encyclopedic Dictionary "La Fuente,"* edited by Sovena Publishing House, states that, "He was Indian, BUT of great intelligence and conviction."

Do these encyclopedians ignore the fact that our fathers, our Indians, bequeathed their marvelous Sun Stone to Science, that they knew how to sculpt without chiseling with iron, that they molded gold as you would a soft wax without using a hearth, that they knew how to carve diamonds, that they were explorers, and that their melodious language was carried over to beautiful poetry and music compositions? Do they not know that our precious Anáhuac is sown with marvelous ruins and palaces which bare witness to its arduousness and art? Or do they believe that we, their children, without exception, need a "but" in order to be considered intelligent or men of good will?

Nowadays, there is a belief that an Indian, a Negro, or an oriental person cannot be as prepared, as familiar with progress and morality as a European or his children would. And if we now live in the Age of Enlightenment, of Science, and the Century of the "last war" where such ideas are fostered by scholars, what could be expected of the days of the Great Admiral? And what of the time of Hernán Cortés?

....

And if the Spanish monopoly drowned in us the spiritual intention, if the uncertainty that our properties would be respected made us lose trust, if the eternal governing by foreigners in our country made us want to occupy the best public positions, if they made us weak with their methods, why is it that now, after having a Father Hidalgo, do we not become the Aztec community, the most civilized and virile of North America? Why do we not forgive the conquerors' mistakes, disregard their adventurers' examples and practice all the good that their honorable men taught us and, above all, exercise that which has come from men like Fray Bartolomé? Let us fight; everything is possible for people who battle.

Will the white man always be white? Will the Indian always be the Indian, the unredeemed?

Whoever tells us that God or Nature created us with the eternal intention that the North would always be North and the South forever South, let us reply that the Universe does not acknowledge the center thus; it does not have North nor South.

Emilio R. Ypiña,
Houston, Tex., Sept. 15 de 1928.

La Gaceta Mexicana, September 15, 1928.

The León Cárdenas Martínez Case

The questionable death sentence in Pecos City, Texas, of the teenager León Cárdenas Martínez, for killing a white woman, had occurred just a few months before The First Mexicanist Congress that convened in Laredo in 1911. Since lynchings and unjust sentencing were major items on the agenda, the León Cárdenas issue fueled the resolve of the participants. Notwithstanding collective action, the relatives of these purported victims often took the lead in crusades to save their kin. Here, the condemned boy's father, León Cárdenas Martínez, Sr., relates to the Mexican ambassador in Washington a story of mistreatment after his son's sentencing.

The undersigned, of legal age, married and a native of Mapimi, in the State of Durango, Mexico, and residing at present in El Paso, Texas, in the United States of America, very respectfully represents:

That as a Mexican citizen who came to the United States about five years ago, and as the father of León Cárdenas Martínez, Jr., who is a minor of the age of fifteen years, and who at the present time is confined in the County Jail of Midland County, State of Texas, where he was transferred from the jail of Pecos City, Reeves County, Texas, and who has been sentenced to the death penalty for the crime of homicide, I beg leave to give you in detail the facts relative to the case, the proceedings in the trial thereof, and other data in connection therewith.

As my main object is to save my aforesaid son from the execution of an inhuman sentence, it behooves me in behalf of his defense and in honor of the truth to show the facts as they have taken place in such a fearful tragedy, viz:

On July 23rd, 1911, my son León C. Martínez, who is 15 years, 1 month, and 13 days old, was arrested at the old town of Saragosa in Reeves County, Texas, by two officers from the sheriff's office, under suspicion of being guilty of the crime under investigation. Immediately on being arrested he was taken to the place where the crime was committed (three miles out of town), and on arriving there, the officers told him to say if he was the guilty party, under the assurance that they would protect him from the wrath of a band of ranchers who wanted to lynch him. Under such pressure León was compelled to answer in the affirmative. At this particular time, Jim Mayfield appeared on the ground and, placing a double-barreled shot-gun against his head, threatened to kill him unless he gave all the particulars in connection with the killing of Miss Emma Brown. I do not know if my son is really the slayer of Miss Brown. They produced no evidence through witnesses to prove it at his trial, except the confession he was compelled to make, and it must be taken into consideration that he was forced to do this to save his life.

While this was going on, the sheriff of the County did all in his power to control the fury of the maddened mob and took my son away from them by escaping with him through the desert and confining him in the Pecos jail. Shortly afterwards the jail was assaulted, the jailor overpowered, and it cannot be explained as yet why the lynching was averted. Then, at midnight of the 24th, the sheriff was compelled (without the knowledge of the populace) to take him to Midland, where he remained until the 27th when he was taken back to the original place for trial. On the 28th his trial took place. The jury impaneled to try him was composed in the main of men under the influence of passion and with a formed opinion. The attorneys for the defense tried their best to prove my son's age, his mother and myself testifying under our oaths the exact year, month, and day in which he was born, having filed with the Clerk our marriage certificate to better prove his age. But instead of listening to this testimony, the Court called in other witnesses for them to determine by guessing the age of the defendant, who erroneously estimated the same at 18 and 19 years. As a matter of fact, a simple guess cannot prevail against positive proof. The result of the trial, without allowing the motion for the presentation of the certificate of birth and baptism of the accused, and ignoring the efforts of his counsel, was the death penalty, and the day for the execution of the sentence was fixed by the Court to be September 1st, 1911. The defendant was removed then to the Midland jail, where he is confined at present.

Now, it seems to me that the manner in which these proceedings were had makes them unjust and unfair for the following reasons:

1st. That no proof was adduced, no testimony taken to prove the guilt of my son, except his own confession, which he was forced to make through threats of violence against his life;

2nd. That in the investigation of my son's age, the testimony of his parents who are in a position to know what it is, was not considered, nor was the motion asking for time for the producing of legal evidence through certificates to prove it; and that the guessing as to his age by witnesses biased against him was taken as proper evidence by the Court.

3rd. That everything in connection with the trial was done in great haste, as it only took six days in which to fix up all matters connected with it.

4th. That the jurors were not impartial men, without a fixed opinion in the case to be tried by them; but on the contrary, some of the said jurors on being qualified said that they had formed an opinion and knew who the guilty party was, meaning the defendant.

5th. That the jury trying the case, as well as the attorneys for the prosecution, witnesses, and even public opinion, were under the influence of a most marked indignation, aided by the exciting threats of a mob composed of ranchmen, who were crying for revenge, all this showing the injustice of a speedy trial, when they ought to have had it when the public mind had cooled off and was susceptible of being controlled by reason.

6th. That all persons, including the attorneys for the defense, who showed or attempted to show any sympathy for my son or for myself, either directly or indirectly, were immediately threatened with the loss of their lives if they made any effort to assist us in our trouble in any way or form, going so far as to prevent people from talking to us.

The statements made above are true in every particular and justify themselves to annul the proceedings they had, there being sufficient cause for a new trial of the case within the terms of the law.

Based on these facts I do not hesitate to say that the judgment was rendered without due attention being given to legal forms, and this is the expressed opinion of all cool-headed persons who frankly state that all the proceedings were carried through under the influence of the most barefaced prejudice, which under the semblance of a legal trial, if the sentence is carried out, will be simply an assassination in the sight of human justice.

In corroboration of the deductions hereof and to further show the threatening attitude of the people in charge of the prosecution, I will simply state what they did to me, my family, and my property.

At 9 p.m. when my son was arrested and the family, having no idea of what was going on, about twenty Americans, well armed and on horseback, went to the Meat Market, my place of business, and informed me that León had been arrested and that they gave me two hours' time in which to leave the town, otherwise that I would suffer the consequences of their indignation. Among my assailants I recognized Pink A. Harbert, sheriff of the town, who was the one who gave me the order to leave; Messrs. Honaker, Lee Harbert, Taylor and John Conger; the others I did not know as they kept in the dark. Having before me the initiative of an attempt against my own life and the menacing attitude of my assailants, I thought proper and I was advised by others to leave my place of business immediately. I went home, a distance of about 1/4 of a mile, and among the most heated excitement from everything around me, I made preparations to obey the order in great haste. Half an hour afterwards, Taylor, John Conger, and Edward Bardy (the last named acting as interpreter) came to my house to tell me to leave right away, warning me not to go to any near towns, but to somewhere 25 miles distant and through the open desert.

At 12 o'clock that night I left my home with my wife who had been sick for over four months. The excitement of the situation increased with an old lady 60 years old, and my four children ranging from two to twelve years of age. Fearing the results of a trip through the desert, which I was ordered to make, it being a dark, rainy night, I thought proper to go to a place called Brogado, six miles from my home, when all of a sudden Taylor and John Conger reassaulted me. In a threatening manner they prevented me from following the road I was taking, compelling me by force to follow the road that they and the others had ordered me to take, without allowing me even to provide myself with water for my family.

León Cárdenas Martínez, Sr., to Mexican Ambassador, August 3, 1911, National Archives, Record Group 59, 311.1221/7.

La Liga Protectora Latina

La Liga Protectora Latina (The Latin Protective League), formed in Arizona in 1915 by Mexicans with long U.S. residence, became a pioneer in pursuing civil rights protection for the Hispanic community, a main item on its agenda. Article Four of their incorporation papers also demonstrates that besides providing traditional mutual aid benefits, protecting civil rights figured as a crucial objective.

First chapter. Denomination, address, objective, and principles.

Art. 1. This Society was called "Liga Protectora Latina" (Latin Protective League) when it was created and will continue to bear the same name.

Art. 2. This Society was organized in Phoenix, Arizona, on February 10, 1915, where it was incorporated and legally authorized to exercise its duties according to the laws of that state on August 30, 1915.

Art. 3. Its legal address and primary branch of business will be Phoenix, Arizona, under the government of the Supreme Board of Directors, which will execute its authority over the Branches established or those that will be set up in the State of Arizona, in other states of the American Union, and Latin-American countries where its extension and development will be pursued.

Art. 4. The Latin Protective League is a POLITICAL, FRATERNAL, AND EDUCATIONAL Corporation whose objective is to:

I. Pursue unity and development of brotherhood between Latinos regardless of nationality.

II. Aid members in need in case of illness and if they should die, attend their funerals, and offer a pecuniary death benefit to the member so that it is received according to the ordinances.

III. Pay attention to the Legislatures and other departments within the State of Arizona and everywhere else so that laws or dispositions are not issued whose objectives might deprive Latinos of their privileges and rights as citizens or of their individual guarantees sanctioned by the Constitution of the United States and present treaties.

IV. Try to defend members of the Institution and people of Latin descent before all officials or courts so that they receive the same treatment and law enforcement as individuals of other races.

V. Encourage Latino voters to exercise their political rights by guiding and unifying their vote toward the interests of our race during general elections in order to help citizens of Latin descent or those who are not hostile toward our race obtain positions in the Executive, Legislative, and Judicial Branches.

VI. Promote intellectual, moral, and economic improvement of Latinos through proper educational systems, English and Spanish classes, by establishing Cooperatives, Savings Banks, and other similar methods.

VII. Harmonize the interests of the diverse economic elements by establishing mutual agreement and respect for individual rights, by abstaining from the use of violence and class struggle, and by trying to solve conflicts that may appear with the settlement of the principles of conciliation and arbitrage.

Art. 5. PROTECTION, EQUALITY, AND JUSTICE are the principles that the Latin Protective League adopts, and condensed in them you will find the objectives that they pursue as they are listed in the previous article.

Art. 6. The "Protection" principle forces all League members to wait and help all individuals of the race, especially their comrades in all situations in which that protection is necessary. The manner and cases in which it is necessary to provide protection for the Society will be arranged by the ordinances and regulations.

Art. 7. The "Equality" principle indicates that the Latin Protective League advocates the exercise of political rights, including carrying out public tasks of popular election and jury duty by Latinos, as well as the identical treatment in labor fields, political and private fields, and the abolition of laws and practices that try to establish race distinctions which prejudice Latinos or residents of the same origin in the United States.

Art. 8. When the Latin Protective League proclaims the "Justice" principle, it intends to obtain for its members, and Latinos in general, unbiased and just decisions in civil trials and the granting of all guarantees that the laws concede a defendant in criminal liability cases.

Art. 9. All banners, emblems, badges, correspondence, stamps, and other objects of the Supreme Court and its Branches will have the name of the Corporation inscribed and next to it the following words, "PROTECTION, EQUALITY, JUSTICE" or its initials "P.E.J." which will be used as the formal closing on the Society's official and private correspondence as well as between its members.

Second chapter. Motto, coat of arms, and the use of social badges.

Art. 10. The motto of the Latin Protective League is "One for all. All for one." It represents the mutual aid and brotherly love as the basis of our Institution. They should also be inscribed in the objectives addressed in the previous article.

Art. 11. The Society's coat of arms will have the shape, allegory, and emblem that are drawn here:

All for one. One for all.

"Estatutos de la Liga Protectora Latina, Phoenix, Arizona, Reformados Por la Cuarta Convención Reunida en Tucson, Arizona, Del 11 al 14 de septiembre, 1920" Chicano Research Collection (CRC), Hayden Library, Arizona State University Library.

America for America

Immigrant leaders routinely objected to racist literature and negative journalism. Former Texas Governor James E. Ferguson penned a particularly vitriolic broadside in the *Ferguson Forum* in November, 1920, in which he charged Mexicans were inferior to Negroes and that Mexico had contributed nothing to civilization. The former governor lived in Temple, the heart of Texas nativism and conservative populism. Reprinted below is part of his invective.

America for America, when brought home, means Texas for Texans. It should mean more. It should mean that we are going to have less Mexicans swarming across the border into Texas.

―――――――――

Now when the war is over, here they come back, demanding one-third of our cotton for picking and murdering our citizens because somebody objects to the damn greasers riding in a coach with white people. I have been traveling quite a great deal lately, and I have observed how bold these Mexicans are.

―――――――――

We have a separate coach law to separate white and black, and to keep down trouble, the Mexican must be separated too. We are not going to give more privilege to the Mexican than we do to the Negro, who is far superior to the Mexican in every attribute that goes to make a good citizen. I dare the incoming legislature to ignore this situation.

―――――――――

The Mexican people have not improved one bit in civilization, and they are more blood thirsty than ever. They are not disposed to and have no desire to become real Americans and never will be.

They come to the United States for one purpose and for one cause only. They want our money, and they have been spoiled by being paid more for one day's labor here than they could get for a whole week's work in their own country.

California has a great danger of their state being overrun with the Japanese, who are replacing American labor and acquiring an alarming amount of land.

I had rather have a hundred Japs than a dozen Mexicans in Texas. But I don't want either. I would stop both from coming.

―――――――――

The farming interests don't need the Mexicans, because no money can be made by farming with hired labor. Absentee land lords ought not want and should not be permitted to import a Mexican population to occupy Texas to the exclusion of or even in competition with red-blooded Americans.

The railroads should not be permitted to continue to bring thousands of these Mexicans into this country and take the place of native Americans who need the money and who have no other intention but to be a good citizen, loyal and true to the stars and stripes.

If you are a Texas land owner, you now know to your sorrow that the most unprofitable farming you can undertake is to hire Mexican labor to chop and pick your cotton, charging you always three times what it's worth.

If we fail or falter in this, the spirits of our ancestors will haunt us and the ghosts of Texas heroes will walk in the night to reprove us.

JAS. E. FERGUSON

The Ferguson Forum, December 16, 1920.

"An American . . . Who Loves Mexican People"

Alonso S. Perales, the Texas lawyer and a founder of the league of United Latin American Citizens, wrote Ferguson to denounce his diatribe, saying he defended Texas Mexicans and immigrants alike. *El Imparcial de Texas,* in publishing Perales' letter on January 7, 1921, characterized him as an "American who understands and loves Mexican people."

Protest Against What was Stated by James E. Ferguson

Mr. Alonso S. Perales has written to former governor Ferguson from Washington, D.C., informing him that everything that he has stated in his newspaper is simply groundless accusations, since Mexicans who come to the United States are loyal and honest workers, a true and efficient benefit to the agricultural and industrial sectors, therefore, they are essential to the community.

Mr. Perales sends a translation of the letter he sent to former governor Ferguson to *La Prensa.* We gladly reproduce it in its entirety:

I have before me a copy of an article published by you in an issue of the *Ferguson Forum* dating, December 16, 1920, which, in part, states the following, "During the war, when Mexicans were needed here so that they could help in farming the land, most of them hurried back to Mexico; now that the war is over, they have returned demanding a third of our cotton because they harvested it, and they are also killing our citizens because someone is opposed to 'damn greasers' riding in the same car with white people."

"We have a law that separates black and white people. In order to avoid difficulties, Mexicans should also be segregated. We will not grant more privileges to Mexicans than what are given to the Negro, who is by far above the Mexican in all attributes that comprise a good citizen."

"Mexicans have not improved in the least with regards to civilization and they are more blood-thirsty than ever."

"They (Mexicans) come to the United States with a sole purpose, for one reason only. They want our money and they have gotten spoiled here due to the fact that they are paid more for one day's worth of work here, than a week's work in their country."

"Let's proclaim before the world that we are not willing to recognize Mexicans as our equals, not socially, nor in any other manner."

My belief in justice inspires me to write to you with the sole and exclusive purpose of condemning your attitude and to refute, in the most emphatic manner, the statements asserted by you with regards to the true merit of the Mexican race. The U.S.-born American citizen who writes this letter knows Mexicans perfectly well. I am therefore capable of proving to you that you made errors in your article and, if you would like, I can explain in detail.

Even when the event that took place on a Missouri, Kansas & Texas train; near Granger, is truly pitiful, this case is truly exceptional and should not be used as the basis for which you falsely accuse the honorable Mexican race. You should understand that individuals of a weak nature have always been present, not only in the Mexican community, but in all countries of the world.

The collective segregation of the Mexican race, as you propose, is an injustice. Sometimes it is necessary to distinguish between people according to their behavior and customs; but even then, the distinction should be applicable to individuals and not to the community. Mexicans do not come to kill our citizens; they come to work and the truth is that they have helped Texas towns a lot in the harvesting of their crops. In that regard, they have contributed greatly in the development of the State. I am certain that the majority of Texas residents will agree with me when I say that the Mexican laborer, far from being blood-thirsty hordes, as you say, are loyal and honest workers.

In regards to the degree of civilization and culture obtained by Mexicans, fortunately for them, the entire world is more aware than you on this matter and they will ignore the unjust false accusations hurled by you. I accept the fact that the majority of Mexicans have not had the good fortune of obtaining an education but this is due to the lack of opportunities and not because they are incapable of learning. The positions occupied by prominent Mexicans such as Felipe Ángeles, whose deeds are well known throughout the world, as well as the triumphs of Lic. Francisco León de la Barra, who was recently named president of the Franco-Austrian arbitration commission established by the Saint Germaine Treaty, have demonstrated the intellectual capability that the modern Mexican race possesses. In addition to these two gentlemen, there are thousands of Mexicans who, in the present, honor Mexico on foreign lands.

In proclaiming before the world that we do not want Mexicans to be seen as our equals, neither socially nor in any other way, you should use the singular pronoun "I" and not the plural "we." Even though there is no doubt that a few individuals, just like you, hate Mexicans, the truth is that you cannot rely on the support of the majority of good and sensible citizens. Therefore, you lack the authority necessary to proclaim, in a collective sense, the feelings of this great American nation.

It is a true shame that while worthy organizations, such as the Pan-American Union, the Pan-American Round Table, the Pan-American Federation of Labor, and the Business Bureaus of the United States, strive in establishing friendship bonds that unite both republics and consolidate good understanding between the two communities, you would find pleasure in opposing such a noble cause by insulting Mexicans in your newspaper.

Respectfully,
ALONSO S. PERALES

Washington, D.C.
January 3, 1921

Alonso S. Perales, *En defensa de mi raza*, Vol. I, (San Antonio: Artes Gráficas, 1936), pp. 5-8.

The Clemency Movements

Even if Mexican immigrants lost a crusade to save compatriots from the gallows, the mere forcing of officials to pay attention to their plight provided a sense of empowerment and affirmed their right to live in the United States. When they succeeded, this affirmation achieved even greater prominence. The article below, from San Antonio's *La Prensa*, April 9, 1914, announced the formation of committees to defend León Cárdenas Martínez.

A committee for the defense of Cárdenas Martínez has organized itself in Waco, Texas.

We have received the following important document that proves that, as to be expected, our compatriots have taken an interest in saving the life of the young man, León Cárdenas Martínez.

I have the honor of chairing the "Defense Committee," and during the organizing session it was agreed to send you a copy of their certificate of uniformity, which states the following:

On March 29, 1914, in Waco, Texas, the undersigned women met at 10:00 p.m. at Mrs. Dolores G. de López's home with the purpose of uniting forces to lend moral, collective, and financial aid to the defense of León Cárdenas Martínez. He is the young man incarcerated in the Pecos prison in the County of Reeves, Texas, and sentenced to receive the death penalty. The women agreed to unite, as it is mentioned above. They proceeded to name the board of directors, which was established in the following manner: President Mrs. Wenceslao de Méndez, Treasurer Mrs. Dolores G. de López, Secretary Mrs. Rosaura S. de Loza, Vice-president Mrs. Concepción de Herrera, Subtreasurer Mrs. María F. de Flores, and Pro-Secretary Mrs. Eduviges Vega. Everyone accepted the nominations promising to execute them faithfully. By unanimous decision, they then agreed to call the new body DEFENSE COMMITTEE. In order to extend the directing committee, it was agreed to have a meeting the following April 4 without redressing to verify who was necessary to tend to labor defenses. The resolutions that follow were immediately adopted: to completely support the EXCITATIVE launched by the parents of the Cárdenas Martínez boy, which is included in the committee's documentation, and to that effect, it is arranged to send a copy of this certificate to newspaper editors who had previously received the EXPOSITION published in the last issue of *El Internacional*, and to representatives of the Mexican government offering our moral aid in raising the funds that such a case requires, to send a petition letter to the Governor of Texas asking for the suspension of the sentence, and finally to carry out all tasks necessary in saving our defendant from the gallows. We have made extensive petitions in local neighborhoods asking that this Certificate be included in the next issue of *El Internacional*, advising our readers to offer their timely and efficient aid in the defense. This document concluded with the signatures of the board of directors present: Wenceslao de Méndez, President; Dolores G. de López, Treasurer; Rosaura S. de Loza, Secretary;

Concepción de Herrera, Vice-president; María F. de Flores, Sub-Treasurer; and Eduwiges Vega, Pro-Secretary.

I have the honor of presenting this certificate to you, thus fulfilling the aforementioned and stressing the need for your cooperation in the pertinent manner.

We protest special consideration,

Waco, Texas, April 1, 1914.

Rosaura Sierra de Loza, Secretary

Wenceslao de Méndez, President.

Aurelio Pompa

The most well-known effort to save a Mexican from execution was the campaign for Aurelio Pompa's life. In April of 1923, Pompa was convicted of first-degree murder and sentenced to death. During the trial, the prosecution contended William McCue had struck Pompa after an argument at work and that Pompa had gone home, obtained a pistol, returned to the work site, and then shot the carpenter. The Mexican community believed that Pompa tried to defend himself after the abusive carpenter threatened him with a hammer. Pompa was hanged, nonetheless. The mothers of condemned men could wield much influence among those who lined up for the defense in these cases. Here, Aurelio's mother appealed to Mexico's President Álvaro Obregón.

I take the liberty of writing this letter to you because I feel I am authorized since you so kindly offered to help my unfortunate son, Aurelio Pompa, with your worthy influence.

After having exhausted all legal resources to save my son from the terrible death penalty to which he is sentenced, the only thing left is being negotiated before the State Governor by Mr. Frank Domínguez, the defense counsel, and that is to ask for forgiveness.

The sentence is to be executed the seventh of next month if the plea for mercy for my unfortunate son is not granted.

The story regarding his judgment is well known, and for that reason I will not go into details again.

Above all, I am a mother. My only love on earth is my son, and before the possibility of losing him, my soul is appalled by the grief of such horrible pains that even though I feel it, I could not possibly describe it to you.

But in the immense darkness of my grief, I see grace for my son as a ray of hope. That forgiveness, which is being negotiated, should it be enriched with your most valuable intercession, Mr. President, the Governor of the State of California who is the only person authorized to grant it, would most certainly spare the life of my poor son. I still have the honorable telegram in which you offered your support, the support that I appeal from you Sir as head of Government, certain that you will find it in your generosity to grant it to me as a mother and as a Mexican woman.

Esther Ibarra, Vda. de Pompa to Álvaro Obregón, January 5, 1924, Archivo General de la Nación, Ramo Presidentes, Obregón-Calles 811-P-64.

Vida, Proceso, y Muerte de Aurelio Pompa—Corrido

A play and a *corrido* (ballad) were written about the Aurelio Pompa case, and his name became a household word in Mexican immigrant homes throughout the nation. The following is one version of the corrido.

VIDA, PROCESO, Y MUERTE DE AURELIO POMPA

Voy a contarles la triste historia
de un mexicano que allá emigró
Aurelio Pompa, así se llamaba,
el compatriota que allí murió.

Allá en Caborca, que es de Sonora,
el pueblo humilde donde nació,
"Vámonos, madre," le dijo un día
que allá no existe revolución.

"Adiós, amigos, adiós, María,"
dijo a la novia con gran dolor,
yo te prometo que pronto vuelvo,
para casarnos, mediante Dios.

Adiós, Aurelio, dijo la novia,
que sollozando se fue a rezar,
cuídalo mucho, Virgen María,
que yo presiento no volverá.

El señor cura y sus amigos,
junto a la novia fueron a hablar,
a suplicarle al pobre Aurelio
que no dejara el pueblo natal.

Fueron inútiles tantos consejos
también los ruegos de su mamá
vámonos, madre, que allá está el *dollar*
y mucho, juro, que he de ganar.

El mes de mayo de hace cuatro años
a California fueron los dos
y por desgracia en la misma fecha
en una cárcel allá murió.

LIFE, TRIAL, AND DEATH OF AURELIO POMPA

I'll tell you the sad story
of a Mexican who emigrated there–
Aurelio Pompa, so he was called,
our compatriot who died there.

Out there in Caborca, in Sonora,
the humble village where he was born,
"Come on, mother," he said one day,
"Over there, there are no revolutions."

"Goodbye, friends; goodbye, María,"
he said to his betrothed very sadly.
"I promise you that I will return soon,
So we can get married, God willing."

"Goodbye, Aurelio," said the girl,
and she went sobbing to pray.
"Look after him, Virgin Mary,
I have a foreboding he'll not come back."

The priest and his friends
along with this sweetheart
talked and begged poor Aurelio
not to leave his native village.

Such advice was useless,
so were his mother's pleas.
"Let's go, mother, over there is the dollar,
I swear I'll earn a lot of them."

Four years ago in the month of May
the two of them went to California
and on the very same date
died there in prison through misfortune.

Un carpintero que era muy fuerte,
al pobre joven muy cruel golpeó,
y Aurelio Pompa juró vengarse
de aquellos golpes que recibió.

Lleno de rabia contó a la madre
y la pobre anciana le aconsejó
"por Dios, olvida, hijo querido,"
y el buen Aurelio le perdonó.

Pero una tarde, que trabajaba,
con tres amigos en la estación
el carpintero pasó burlando
y al pobre Pompa le provocó.

Los tres amigos le aconsejaban
que lo dejara y fuera con Dios
y el carpintero, con un martillo
muy injurioso lo amenazó.

Entonces Pompa, viendo el peligro,
en su defensa le disparó
con un revólver y cara a cara,
como los hombres él lo mató.

Vino la causa, llegó el jurado
y el pueblo Yanqui lo sentenció.
"Pena de muerte" pidieron todos,
y el abogado no protestó.

Veinte mil firmas de compatriotas
perdón pidieron al gobernador
toda la prensa también pedía
y hasta un mensaje mandó Obregón.

Todo fue inútil, las sociedades,
todas unidas pedían perdón.
La pobre madre, ya casi muerta,
también fue a ver al gobernador.

"Adiós, amigos, adiós, mi pueblo,
Querida madre, no llores más,
díle a mi raza que ya no venga
que aquí se sufre que no hay piedad."

A carpenter who was very strong
struck the poor young fellow cruelly.
Aurelio Pompa swore to be revenged
for those blows he had received.

Filled with rage he told his mother about it.
The poor old woman advised him,
"*Por Dios,* forget it, dear son."
And good Aurelio forgave him.

But one afternoon, while working
with three friends at the railroad station
The carpenter came to mock him
and aroused poor Pompa.

The three friends advised him
to leave him alone and go his way,
but the carpenter, with a hammer,
very offensively threatened him.

Then Pompa, seeing the danger,
fired in self-defense
with a revolver and face to face
as a man he killed him.

The case in court, the jury arrived,
and the Yankee people sentenced him.
"The death penalty," they all demanded,
and the lawyer did not object.

Twenty thousand signatures
asked the Governor for pardon,
all the newspapers asked for it too,
and even Obregón sent a message.

All was useless; the societies,
all united, asked his pardon.
His poor mother, half-dead already,
also went to see the Governor.

"Farewell, my friends, farewell, my village.
Dear mother, cry no more.
Tell my race not to come here.
For they will suffer here; there's no pity here.

El carcelero le preguntaba;
"¿español eres?" y él contestó
"soy mexicano y orgullo serlo
aunque me nieguen a mí el perdón."

Esta es la historia de un compatriota
que hace cuatro años allí llegó
y por desgracia en la misma fecha
en una cárcel muy mal murió.

The jailer asked him:
"Were you Spanish?" And he answered,
"I'm Mexican and proud of it,
although they deny me a pardon."

This is the story of a compatriot,
who four years ago arrived there,
unfortunately on the same date
died dreadfully in prison.

Manuel Gamio, *Mexican Immigration to the United States: A Study of Human Migration and Adjustment* (Chicago: University of Chicago Press, 1930), p. 104.

Desegregation Success—Arizona

The first successful desegregation court case of Mexicans took place in Tempe, Arizona, in 1925. Mexican families, whose ancestors helped found the city in the 1870s, succeeded in overturning a segregation policy in effect since 1915. Unfortunately, segregation continued for children of the recently arrived or from poorer families until the 1940s. Reproduced below are portions of the court records in this case.

THE COURT: This is an action brought by the plaintiff Adolfo Romo against the Board of Trustees and Superintendent of School District No. 3 of Maricopa County, comprising the town of Tempe wherein he prays for a writ of mandamus requiring the defendants to admit his four children to the public schools of said district upon equal terms with all other children of school age residing within said school district. The plaintiff in his complaint says that he and his children are of "Spanish-Mexican" descent; that the defendants Trustees of School District No. 3 have entered into an agreement with the Board of Education of the Tempe Normal School of the State of Arizona, whereby one of the two school buildings of School District No. 3, known as the "Eighth Street School" has been set apart, designated and declared to be a "Normal Training School" and its use, insofar as it relates to "Primary or elemental education," shall be restricted to "Spanish-American" or "Mexican-American" children; that the children required to attend said Eighth Street School pursuant to said agreement are taught exclusively by "student teachers"; that the plaintiff presented his four children to the defendant Superintendent of School District No. 3 on September 14th, 1925, and requested their admission to the public schools of School District No. 3, but that said defendant, acting under the orders and directions of defendants Board of Trustees of School District No. 3, refused and still refuses to admit said children to the public schools of said School District No. 3 but required and directed them to report to the authorities of the said Normal Training School pursuant to said agreement; that by reason of the said acts of defendants the children of plaintiff, as well as all other Spanish-American and Mexican-American children entitled to be admitted to the public schools of School District No. 3, are, on account of their race or descent, and without regard to their age, advancement or convenience, segregated, excluded and compelled to attend the Eighth Street School taught exclusively by student teachers of the Normal Training School of the Tempe State Teacher's College.

An alternative writ was issued and the defendants filed their return to the writ and answer to plaintiff's complaint, admitting that plaintiff's children are entitled to admission to the public schools of School District No. 3, if they reside with him in said district, but deny that said children have been refused admission to said schools; alleging that for purposes of convenience and advantage to the children of Spanish-American and Mexican-American extraction and descent, all such children, including the children of plaintiff, admitted to the first six grades of elemental education were located in what is commonly called the Eighth Street School and taught by teachers able to speak and understand the Spanish language; that the course of education in said Eight Street

School is the same in every respect and the same character of, surroundings, advantages and equipment prevail therein, as is maintained by the defendants in any other school in said district, and that teachers of the same grade in ability are employed in said Eighth Street School as are employed in said Tenth Street School.

* * *

This action having come on for trial upon the complaint of the plaintiff herein, the return and answer of the defendant thereto, and having been tried by the court sitting without a jury, and the court having filed its findings of fact herein, and the court having determined as conclusions of law, that the relator is entitled to a permanent peremptory writ of mandamus, as prayed for in the complaint.

NOW, upon motion of Edward B. Goodwin and Harold J. Janson, attorneys for said plaintiff.

IT IS ORDERED, ADJUDGED AND DECREED, that the said Adolfo Romo, plaintiff herein, have a permanent peremptory writ of mandamus, and that the same do issue forthwith directed to and commanding the said defendants, William E. Laird, J.H. Daniel and I.F. Waterhouse, as members of, and constituting the Board of Trustees of Tempe School District No. 3, and G. W. Persons, Superintendent of Tempe School District No. 3, Maricopa County, Arizona, upon the pain and peril that shall fall thereon for refusal, that they and each one of them, shall admit the children of Adolpho Romo, namely, Antonio Romo, age fifteen; Henry Romo, age fourteen; Alice Romo, age eleven; and Charles Romo, age seven, on the same terms and conditions to the public schools of said Tempe School District No. 3, Maricopa County, Arizona, as children of other nationalities are now admitted.

Done in open court this 5th day of October, A.D. 1925.
Joseph S. Jenckes,
Judge.

In the Superior Court of the State of Arizona in and for the County of Maricopa, Adolfo Romo, Plaintiff vs. William E. Laird, J.H. Daniel and I.F. Waterhouse as members of and constituting the Board of Trustees of Tempe School District No. 3 and G.W. Persons, Superintendent of Tempe School District No. 3, Defendants. No. 21617, Judgment and Findings of Fact and Order, October 5, 1925.

Desegregation Success—California

Amore sweeping success was the 1930 undertaking in Lemon Grove, California, a community near San Diego, where Mexican parents successfully sued to end segregation of their children in the local schools. The anthropologist Robert Álvarez, whose father was the plaintiff in this case, was able to research this incident in part by interviewing his grandmother, Ramona Castellanos. As a member of the Los Vecinos de Lemon Grove (The Lemon Grove Neighbors), the organization that pressed the desegregation suit, she had kept numerous records of the incident. The final judgment was considered one of the most important victories in obtaining civil rights for Mexicans.

The petition of Roberto Álvarez, a minor, by Juan M. González, his guardian *ad litem,* having been presented and filed herein for a Writ of Mandate, and said minor and guardian ad litem, appearing by their attorneys Fred Noon and Charles A. Brinkley, and it appearing to the Court from reading said petition, this said minor is beneficially interested herein and acting in his own behalf and for the benefit of numerous other minor children of Mexican parentage, beneficially interested herein, and that it is impracticable to bring them all before the Court, and that it appears from said petition that said pupils have been excluded and prevented from attending the elementary school or the district school of Lemon Grove, County of San Diego, State of California, by the section of the Board of Trustees of said school district, consisting of E. L. Owen, Anna E. Wight and Henry A. Anderson, members thereof, and Jerome J. Green, Principal of said school, acting under instruction of said Board of School Trustees, and it appears further from said petition that said Roberto Álvarez, petitioner herein, and about seventy-four other pupils in the public school at the District School of Lemon Grove, beneficially interested, have been excluded and prevented from attending public school in the five-room school building at Lemon Grove, where they attended prior to the fifth day of January, 1931, because of their Mexican parentage and nationality, and that said children are not now permitted to attend said school and receive instruction on a basis of equality with other children of said school district; and it further appears that an attempt is being made by you and each of you to segregate the petitioner and all other children of Mexican parentage, attending the public school in said district in a separate and distinct school apart from children of American, European and Japanese parentage, and that said children of Mexican parentage are not now attending the public school as required by law, and have not attended school since the fifth day of January, 1931, and that there is not a plain, speedy and adequate remedy in the ordinary course of law; and it appearing that there is good cause for issuing an alternative Writ of Mandate directed to said respondents and each of them to admit and receive said petitioner and other children of Mexican parentage and nationality into said public school where they attended and received instruction prior to the fifth day of January, 1931, or show cause why said petition should not be granted and said Writ of Mandate issued by this Court.

THEREFORE, it is ordered and adjusted that an Alternative Writ of Mandate be issued out of this Court, and the Clerk of this Court is hereby directed to issue an Alternative Writ of Mandate directed to E. L. Owen, Anna E. Wight and Henry A. Anderson, members of and constituting the Board of Trustees of Lemon Grove School District, County of San Diego, California, and E. L. Owen, Anna E. Wight and Henry A. Anderson, individually, and Jerome J. Green, commanding them and each of them immediately after the recent of said Writ, to admit and receive Roberto Alvarez, petitioner herein, and all other pupils of Mexican parentage and nationality of said school district, beneficially interested herein, into the five-room school building, the same being the public school in the School District of Lemon Grove, County of San Diego, State of California, where said children of Mexican parentage and nationality attended school and received instruction prior to the fifth day of January, 1931, on a basis of equality with other children of said school district, and without separation or segregation in a separate school, because of race or nationality, or that said respondents appear and show cause before this Court before the Honorable judge thereof, presiding over Department No. 4 in the Court House in the City of San Diego, County of San Diego, California, why they have not done so, and that said alternative Writ of Mandate be made returnable on this 14th day of February 1931, at 10 o'clock a.m.

In the Superior Court of the State of California, in and for the County of San Diego, Roberto Álvarez vs. E.L. Owen, et.al. Order for Alternative Writ of Mandate, February 14, 1931.

Desegregation Failure—Kansas

During 1924, Mexican parents, mainly from Guanajuato, and the Mexican consul protested when white parents vociferously opposed Mexican students attending the Argentine, Kansas, high school. The Mexican students had graduated from segregated elementary schools. The school board refused to expel the Mexican children, but the threats were so severe from white parents that Mexican parents did not send their children to school. The story is told in the words of M.E. Pearson, Superintendent of Schools of Kansas City, Kansas.

Q. Now Mr. Pearson, I would like to have you state the facts in connection with the Mexican school children attending the new Major Hudson School or any other school that may be involved in this matter.

A. The matter of the separation of the Mexican children from the native children in separate rooms and buildings was urged upon the Board of Education by patrons of the Emerson School in the Argentine district several years ago. The children in the lower grades were placed in separate rooms of the Emerson building. This separation continued for about four years when there was a general movement in the Argentine district, among the patrons, insisting that the Board of Education build a separate building for the Mexicans. A three-room building, now known as the Clara Barton School, was built in north Argentine and has since been maintained as a Mexican school.

After the separation of the Mexican pupils in the Argentine district, the people of Armourdale sent several delegations before the Board of Education demanding that the pupils be separated in the John J. Ingalls School. The pupils in the lower grades were placed in separate rooms. After three or four years the Board was asked to provide a separate building. They refused to do this for about two years until the demand became so persistent that they provided a three-room building in the yard of the John J. Ingalls School. There are four teachers in this building at the present time, one being an assistant kindergarten teacher. There is one additional room in the basement of the main building.

When the new Major Hudson School was completed in the spring of 1924, the patrons of that district were very emphatic and very persistent in their demand that no Mexican children be allowed to attend. The Board of Education provided room for the lower grades in the old Major Hudson building. Four boys of the upper grades attended at the main building until the close of the school year. When the school opened the following September, these four boys enrolled again in the Major Hudson School with the native children. In the afternoon, on the day of their enrollment in the morning, about 200 patrons of the district surrounded the building and made a great demonstration against the Mexican children attending, and they called for their own children to leave the building, which they did. The threats, from the crowd, of bodily injury to the Mexican children were such that police officers were asked to take the Mexican children to their homes in safety. The following day, only a very few native children returned to school. Public meetings were held and members of the Board of Education did their best to quiet the feeling in the neighborhood. The Mexican children never returned to the Major Hudson School. The Board made no order keeping them out of school. They were not advised to stay away from the school by the Board. Their parents reported that they were afraid to return.

The old Major Hudson School was opened at the beginning of the school year, September 1924. Seven Mexican children enrolled. The records show that about 53 should have enrolled. Nothing was done to force these Mexican children into school until the latter part of 1924 and the early part of 1925 when action was brought in Judge McCombs' court, Kansas City, Kansas, to force the children in school. This action was taken under the Compulsory Attendance Law. The whole matter was dropped on the advice of Judge McCombs that a decision from the Federal Government be received before action be taken. Since then a great many of the Mexican children have enrolled in the Major Hudson district. At the present time there are 31 Mexican children enrolled in the old Major Hudson School building.

Q. How many should be enrolled?

A. I cannot state that. There are many children now enrolled in Parochial schools and some of them have moved from the district. It is my opinion that there are no Mexican children of school age who are not attending school somewhere.

At the close of school in May, 1925, four Mexican children graduated from the eighth grade of the Clara Barton School. They were given the regular diploma which admitted them to high school at the beginning of school in September. These four Mexican children enrolled in the Argentine High School and were received and placed in their proper classes with the native children. One week later a delegation appeared before the Board of Education in regular session and asked the Board of Education in very emphatic terms, to remove these children from the Argentine High School. This, the Board of Education refused to do. Several meetings, some public and some private, were held in Argentine, and the feeling and opposition grew to such an extent that the parents of the Mexican children were afraid that violence would be done to their children. On the advice of a friend, they took the children out of school. They have not attended the school since.

Q. Do they attend any school?

A. I don't know.

The Board of Education, through the Superintendent of Schools, authorized the securing of a room and the employment of a special teacher for the four children. The room was secured, the teacher engaged, but the parents did not allow the children to attend. It was ascertained that they would be allowed to enroll in one of the high schools of Kansas City, Missouri.

Interview with M.E. Pearson, Superintendent of Schools, Kansas City, Kansas, by W.C. Ralston, Assistant Attorney General of Kansas, October 21, 1925, National Archives, Record Group 59, 311.1225, Kansas City.

A Mexican *Colonia* During the Great Depression

The letter below describes conditions of life and work for Mexicans living in Douglas, Arizona, when the Great Depression affected production in this mining-smelter city. It was penned by Red Cross worker F.T. Wright to L.W. Douglas, an Arizona Congressman proposing repatriation of Mexicans.

The only industries of this city are, as you know, the copper smelters of the Phelps Dodge Corporation, and the Calumet & Arizona Mining Company. When the depression in the copper industry began to manifest itself, the production of these smelters began to be cut down, and during the year 1930 the production was practically cut in half. This led to the discharge of a large number of employees, of whom the greater number were Mexicans. On January 1st, 1930, the number of Mexicans employed was about 800. April 1st, 1931, this number had decreased to about 300. Almost the entire number of those who lost their jobs were obliged to remain in Douglas because the general industrial condition of the state offered them no employment elsewhere. For several months their financial condition was not acute owing to the fact that they had some small resources saved up, or were being assisted by friends who still had employment, but commencing about December 1st, 1930, it was necessary to begin to assist them for charity funds. From December 1st up to the present time, the amount necessary to furnish assistance to these Mexicans has steadily increased. In April the amount furnished was considerably over $1,200.00. These funds were at first supplied by the local chapter of the Red Cross, later from contributions by the citizens of Douglas.

The general condition of these unemployed Mexicans is rapidly becoming worse. Aside from the fact that they are receiving barely enough in the way of food to keep soul and body together, they have no means to pay rent, water bills, or to provide themselves with clothing and other small necessities. It is inevitable that their physical condition will deteriorate, especially that of the children, and the general morale of that portion of the community must suffer severely.

For the existing conditions thus outlined, there is no immediate relief in sight. It is well understood that the copper situation cannot possibly be corrected for several months. These unemployed have no hope of obtaining employment elsewhere. They must remain as a burden on a community which already has the responsibility of affording relief to its own unemployed citizens.

It has occurred to me that some measure of relief could be attained if some of these unemployed Mexicans could be returned to their native country. Many of them, as I have learned by inquiry, have friends or relatives in the interior of Mexico with whom they could live; others would be willing to return if there were reasonable assurances of being able to make a living when they got there.

You may think it advisable to have representations made to the Mexican Government stating the facts as above outlined, and asking if they are prepared to assist us in repatriating some of their needy countrymen. This could be done by either:

1. Providing transportation to their interior of Mexico for those who are wiling to go there, and/or
2. Making some provision whereby those who wish to return would be reasonably assured of a place and means to make a living however precarious.

If the Mexican Government were to find itself sympathetic to this proposition, the details could be worked out rather easily. I am sure that the Mexican Consul in Douglas would give us all the assistance in his power, and proper safeguards could be thrown about the proceeding so that none of the advantages would be abused.

I may say that through my association with the Red Cross, which has had the care of looking after these destitute Mexicans, I am able to speak with a considerable amount of certainty in regard to the present conditions and future prospects.

I will thank you to give this matter your careful consideration, and to take such action as you may think proper.

I may add that at the present time we are giving assistance to approximately 1000 persons. Even if only a small percentage of these were to return to Mexico, the situation would be considerably relieved.

F.T. Wright to L.W. Douglas, United States Representative to Congress from Arizona, May 23, 1931, National Archives Record Group 59 311.1215/22.

Chapter Five

Mexican Government and *El México de Afuera*

Because of the severe mistreatment of its expatriates, Mexico was forced to intervene extensively on their behalf during most of this century. The U.S. government made it difficult for efforts to be effective because it mostly assumed a defensive posture when confronted with grievances from the Mexican government. Consuls also served as sources of legal assistance for immigrants who ran afoul of the law, especially during the initial formation of the *colonias* when immigrant institutions were barely forming. Unfortunately, owing to turmoil in Mexico, instability often plagued the diplomatic corps. Mexican consuls consistently tried to protect their compatriots; evidence of consular defense dates to the California Gold Rush. For example, the Mexican consul in San Francisco submitted protests when in 1850 the U.S. Congress allowed a foreign miners' tax to keep Mexicans and other Latin Americans out of the gold fields. By the nineteenth-century, however, increased emigration required a more defined and elaborate expatriate policy, but such a policy was retarded in developing because of instability in Mexico.

The Mexican government expected its consuls to maintain *mexicanidad* among immigrants, hence loyalty to the homeland. Benito Juárez's government in the 1860s ordered San Francisco consuls to organize *juntas patrióticas* (patriotic committees) to support republicanism at a time when Mexico had been invaded by the French.

During the late nineteenth century, Porfirio Díaz's efforts to modernize Mexico required the fostering of economic and political unity, a process aided by efforts to enhance nationalism through symbol manipulation. Once established, nationalistic sentiments traveled with immigration across the border. As the number of Mexicans in the United States increased, Porfirian diplomats blended their program of assisting destitute compatriots and intervening in the justice system on their behalf with instilling Mexican patriotism. As early as 1903, the Mexican consulate in Los Angeles, for example, had a special fund for assisting Mexicans who encountered difficulties with the legal system. As leaders of the expatriate community, consuls led *juntas patrióticas* in swearing allegiance to Mexico and, by extension, the Díaz administration.

After Francisco I. Madero ousted Porfirio Díaz in 1911, many exiled supporters of the toppled dictator, as well as other immigrants, complained that consular services had deteriorated. But Madero was more concerned with political survival. From his inauguration as president in the fall of 1911, to when General Victoriano Huerta ordered his assassination in February of 1913, endless plots to overthrow Madero were hatched both in and outside of Mexico. With Huerta as president, the consular system continued to spy on exiled enemies and to try to gain the support of expatriate Mexicans. After the civil war broke out a greater outflow of migrants enlarged the scope of mistreatment of Mexicans by Anglo Americans. Because the large number of expatriates in the United States depleted consular resources, the Foreign Ministry under Huerta considered restricting emigration by imposing a fine on anyone caught recruiting workers. But Venustiano Carranza's initiative to oust Huerta resulted in the destruction of railroads, bridges, and rolling stock, paralyzing transportation and emigration. As happened during the Madero years, Huerta's consuls turned to unabashed full-time propagandizing at the expense of helping the expatriates in the United States. The American invasion of Veracruz in 1914 helped Venustiano Carranza oust Huerta. Carranza's government then implemented a more vigorous policy of expatriate support. It included underwriting Spanish-language publications and establishing an elaborate network of agents who even tried to provoke racial unrest in the United States.

The Mexican Foreign Ministry began a program of trying to reform the consular corps after the United States recognized Carranza at the end of 1916. Although Carranza's administration appointed a large number of new consuls, these were transferred with dizzying regularity, thus creating voids detrimental to immigrants. Under Carranza, the Foreign Ministry had more time to establish policy in defense of the immigrants. During World War I, for example, local draft boards obliged Mexican immigrants to register, albeit they were not subject to the draft. To avoid problems, consuls organized meetings to explain draft rules to Mexicans who feared winding up in the European war and helped them fill out registration forms. The consuls also obtained releases for immigrants jailed for not registering and secured discharges for those mistakenly drafted into the Army.

When World War I ended, many American investors worried that a revolutionary Mexican government was putting their investments in Mexico at risk. Article 27 of the new constitution implemented in 1917 under Carranza called for Mexican control of subsoil rights, such as oil, which were in the hands of

American and British companies. Moreover, border banditry seemed to rage uncontrollably, a phenomenon that many Americans felt should have been prevented by Carranza. Because of the deterioration of relations, the United States made plans to invade Mexico, and in 1919, consuls throughout the Southwest asked expatriates to prepare for war.

In his message to the opening session of the Mexican Congress on September 1, 1919, Venustiano Carranza devoted a large portion of his speech, a vociferous attack on U.S. policy towards Mexico, to alleged injustices committed against Mexican workers in the United States. These included such incidents as lynchings, indiscriminate murders in which law officials participated or did not investigate, the drafting of Mexican nationals into the U.S. Army, and overt discrimination, especially in Texas. Carranza was not exaggerating. Mexicans felt so completely marginalized that many thought that owning property required citizenship. Like his predecessors, Carranza used the diplomatic service for political survival more than for helping the immigrants.

Assassinated in 1920, Carranza was succeeded by Álvaro Obregón, who had the Foreign Ministry make more resources available to expatriates. In 1920, only fifty-one consulates existed to assist close to one million Mexicans living throughout the United States. The load was somewhat eased, however, because the Foreign Ministry added personnel and funds to these. The 1921 recession severely tested the ability of the service to help Mexicans in the United States who were becoming destitute by the thousands. The Mexican government formed the Department of Repatriation in order to relocate some 400,000 workers who were being threatened with deportation or wanted to return to Mexico voluntarily.

President Obregón's diplomatic problems differed from those of Carranza. Recognition of his government by the United States hinged on assurances that his government would not tamper with foreign-owned oil properties. In addition, because of the record number of Mexicans in the United States, the immigrant problems that had worried the governments in the previous decade had quadrupled. According to a report in 1920 by the Mexican consul in El Paso, 391 compatriots were killed by Americans, primarily the police, between 1910 and 1911. These atrocities continued during Obregón's administration. During the recession, record unemployment brought on white-worker resentment against workers from Mexico. Anti-Mexican riots, some extremely violent, ensued as a result. These incidents reached such a crisis level that Obregón's government created, in July, 1921, a cabinet-level agency within the Secretaría de Industria y Trabajo (Secretariat of Industry and Labor) to investigate migration causes, to prevent emigration, and to deal with repressive treatment of Mexicans in the United States.

That year, the consuls decided at a conference in San Antonio to create the Comisiones Honoríficas Mexicanas (Honorary Mexican Committees). The first one was established in San Marcos, Texas, and then a spate of others followed that same year in San Antonio, Dallas, Austin, Los Angeles, and other cities. By the end of the decade they had spread throughout the nation. The main purpose of these organizations was to assist Mexicans during the 1921 recession. Concurrently, the Brigadas de la Cruz Azul Mexicana (Mexican Blue Cross Brigades), made up of immigrant women, were formed to provide medical help and food relief to needy immigrants. The difficulties facing consuls became insurmountable, however, and the Mexican government decided to use the commissions to help repatriate jobless workers. In a related move that same year, the Foreign Ministry directed its consular service to more aggressively ameliorate *atropellos* (aggressions against Mexicans). This policy helped immigrants through the depression-related surge of lynchings and anti-Mexican riots.

After the United States recovered from the 1921 downturn, a dramatic outflow alarmed Mexican officials, who feared another recession that would again leave Mexicans stranded in the United States. The Mexican Ministry of Industry and Commerce warned the governors of Guanajuato, Jalisco, Michoacán, and San Luis Potosí, states where most immigrants originated, to discourage recruiter propaganda. Indeed, during 1926, economic downturns racked the Southwest and demands for repatriation increased.

As had occurred to other presidents before him, it became important to President Plutarco Elías Calles to keep as much of the immigrant population in his camp to offset propaganda against his government distributed by Catholic militants in exile during the Cristero War. Moisés Saenz, a Protestant minister, as Sub-Secretary of Education in 1926, initiated a campaign in Mexico and the United States to combat rural backwardness among Mexican children. Basically, the revolutionary elites wanted to modernize Mexico, and they blamed the Catholic Church for fostering superstitions and submissiveness. Among the immigrants, the consuls established *escuelitas* (little schools) to maintain the new Mexicanness among children.

How the expatriates measured the success of the consuls in the 1920s was often contradictory because they did not know the limitations of consuls or because uncaring or incompetent consuls ignored their mandates. Generally, most consuls did their best. The consuls mostly hired Anglo lawyers to help Mexicans in trouble with the law, either because of their availability or because they knew that juries were prejudiced against Mexican American lawyers. Nonetheless, Mexican Americans who were often the only bilingual attorneys available, defended immigrants frequently, and many went on to become civil rights leaders in the Mexican American era.

Mexican envoys worked diligently, sometimes effectively, to help compatriots during the Great Depression of the 1930s. In Los Angeles, Consul Rafael de la Colina often lodged protests against the raids by the police who rounded up and jailed Mexicans by the hundreds before it was decided if they had entered the country illegally. Immigrants often complained about consular effectiveness during this period, but the emissaries were probably at their best in assisting Mexicans in the exodus. For the *colonias*, a side effect of repatriation was a more stable social atmosphere because the exodus had pared down the disproportionate population of young single males and produced a more normal demographic pattern with proportionately more women, young children, and older people. In the 1930s, Mexico reduced the number of consuls in the United States as Depression-related problems declined, because the most vulnerable compatriots had returned home during the massive repatriation. Nonetheless, they continued to pursue their usual efforts to protect immigrants and continued to intervene in labor disputes, especially in California.

General Manuel Ávila Camacho, whom Mexicans elected to replace Lázaro Cárdenas in 1940, was a moderate who decided to ally with the United States during World War II. Agreeing to the Bracero Program, which provided badly needed workers recruited by the U.S. Department of Labor in Mexico for a war-fueled economy, became the most significant pillar of this support. However, the guest workers experienced so much prejudice in the United States, especially in Texas, that Mexico blacklisted that state from receiving *braceros* until officials implemented measures that would reduce mistreatment.

The demand for Mexican immigrant labor diminished after World War II, but the Korean War in the early 1950s expanded the market. After the Korean War, the desirability of Mexican workers again declined because a recession followed this latest international altercation. In 1954, Immigration and Naturalization Service officers rounded up thousands of undocumented workers and deported them to Mexico during the so-called "Operation Wetback."

Mexicans on Death Row

In 1915, twelve men awaited execution on death row in Arizona—seven Americans (one was a black) and five Mexicans. Francisco Rodríguez, Eduardo Pérez, N.B. Chávez, Miguel Peralta, and Ramón Villalobos were to hang for unrelated crimes on the same day in May. Preventing this mass execution became one of the first issues of the newly organized La Liga Protectora Latina (Latin Protective League) and the Mexican revolutionary factions, despite their being at odds with one another in Mexico. Enough pressure was placed upon Governor George P. Hunt of Arizona that he conveyed the following message to the state legislature on May 27, asking for a clemency resolution not out of humanitarian concerns but because of the possible reprisals on American citizens living in Mexico. The five condemned men received delays, but in the end, four hanged. Only Pérez, who had killed another Mexican, received a commutation. In contrast, the Board of Pardons and Paroles commuted the sentences of the seven Americans on death row in 1915.

Gentlemen:

It becomes my duty to transmit herewith copies of telegrams received at the Executive Office from Hon. Wm. J. Bryan, Secretary of State of the United States, General Francisco Villa of the Republic of Mexico, and Hon. José M. Maytorena, Governor of Sonora, Mexico, relative to the five condemned men whose executions are scheduled to occur at the Arizona State Prison tomorrow, May 28th. It should, furthermore, be added, with reference to the telegram received from the Honorable Secretary of State of the United States that the information conveyed by the Governor's Office relative to the approaching executions was furnished by wire in response to the telegraphic request of the State Department, copy of which is handed you herewith.

These three telegrams, of course, are being transmitted together for the reason that each bears upon the same subject, namely the possible effect of the impending hanging on international relations involving the United States and Mexico, and the possibility of subjecting Americans residing in Northern Mexico to an unnecessary risk through the holding of an execution of the nature outlined above.

It will be observed, in reading the telegram attached hereto, that the Secretary of State of the United States, fully realizing the precarious position of Americans in Northern Mexico and the necessity of preserving harmonious relations with the people in the Southern Republic, suggests to the State Government of Arizona the advisability of granting commutations of sentence in the cases of the five condemned men, and urges that, in any event, the penalties imposed upon the prisoners above referred to be suspended for the purpose of enabling the State Department of the United States to deal properly and thoroughly with a subject fraught with such seriousness and unfortunate possibilities as is the summary putting to death of five men of Mexican birth, in whose welfare their fellow-countrymen have evinced the deepest interest.

As I recognize perfectly that the members of your Honorable Body will be quick to discern the great importance which attaches to the representations of the Honorable Secretary of State of the United States, and also the grave consequences that might accrue from the holding of the executions scheduled for tomorrow, I would be neglectful of my apparent duty were not to include in this message relative to a matter of such commanding importance, my earnest endorsement of the course of action suggested in the text of the attached dispatches.

Pursuant, therefore, to the telegraphic recommendations appended hereto, and in courteous deference to the Honorable Secretary of State of the United States, whose duties at the present time in connection with the Mexican situation are of a most delicate and imperative nature, it is my unqualified recommendation that the two Houses of the Second State Legislature of Arizona prepare and adopt a joint or concurrent resolution properly memorializing in the premises the Board of Pardons and Paroles of the State of Arizona, a meeting of which has been called by its Chairman today for the purpose, presumably, of considering the numerous recommendations filed with reference to the approaching executions.

George P. Hunt to House, Second Legislature of Arizona, May 27, 1915, George P. Hunt Collection, CM MSS-48, Arizona Collection, Arizona State University, Hayden Library.

The Draft Issue During World War I

In May of 1917, Congress promulgated the Selective Service Act. While Mexican citizens in the United States were not eligible for the draft unless they applied for their first naturalization papers, they were obliged to register with the local draft board, a requirement that Mexicans were loath to comply with for fear of being conscripted. In the following case, a member of the Mexican consulate in New York City was called up, thus creating an international stir.

The Mexican Ambassador, Ignacio Bonillas, has made formal representations to the State Department against the drafting of Mexicans into the national army, particularly in the border States. In some cases where it is shown that Mexicans have been taken through irregular practice of the exemption boards, the State Department has had the men released.

Other cases are complicated because of the difference in the Constitutions of the two countries. Mexico holds that a man born abroad of Mexican parents is a Mexican unless he voluntarily forfeits his citizenship. The United States holds that a person born here is an American citizen.

Juan T. Burns, Mexican Consul General in New York, who in a statement given out on Monday denounced the American selective draft law and compared the members of the 180 local exemption boards in New York to the "savage hordes of Villa," is still defiant, and Jesús Martínez, the Mexican Vice Consul, whose call for examination by Board 145 made Señor Burns angry, was still unexamined late yesterday afternoon. Burns, in a letter to the board, which has been forwarded to Secretary of State Lansing, informed the board that he had instructed Martínez to ignore the law, and added that if the board examined Martínez it "will have to come and get him."

Mr. Burns would not add to his statement made on Monday, and Vice Consul Martínez said he had been forbidden by Mr. Burns to say anything. Mr. Martínez did not appear angry about being called, and a friend of his said he was willing to comply with the law if the Consul General would permit him to do so.

Mr. Martínez will receive a notification from Board 145 today instructing him to appear for examination at the headquarters in City College at 9 o'clock tomorrow morning. The letter will inform him that under the law he must be examined and that as soon as he files the proper papers which prove him to be a citizen of Mexico, he will be exempted from liability. He will also be informed that if he fails to comply with the law, the matter will be turned over to the Department of Justice for such action as the case may demand.

New York Times, October 3, 1917.

Mistreatment and the Need for Mexican Labor

The Mexican government attempted to parley the need for Mexican labor in the United States during World War I into diplomatic advantage in order to insure better treatment of Mexican workers, especially in Texas. In 1918, after the massacre of fifteen Mexicans by Texas Rangers in Porvenir, Texas, in February, the Mexican government and Mexican American leaders began to pressure Texas officials to curb such violence. Andrés G. García, Inspector General of Consulates in El Paso, wrote to Tom Bell, Deputy Labor Commissioner in Texas, indicating that Mexico would diminish the flow of Mexican workers into Texas unless Texas Ranger abuse and the drafting of Mexican citizens into the military were curtailed. Bell apparently took this to heart and wrote to the governor's office asking that García's protests be given serious consideration.

Dear Sir:

I have the pleasure of informing you that I received your letter dated the 7th of the present month, to which I will respond.

As I expressed to you, Mr. Standish and Mr. Domínguez, during the conference we had on the 7th of the present month, many of my compatriots do not believe that their lives and interests are respected in this country, specifically in the State of Texas, where they have fallen victim to countless assaults, not only by civilians but more than anything by those people who represent authority as has been demonstrated by events that have taken place at "El Porvenir" ranch, where fifteen peaceful Mexicans were killed by Rangers.

Due to this common distrust, I regard what you are trying to perform as a difficult task, and I deem it essential that in order to facilitate it, Federal and State authorities, as well as civil and military, should take efficient measures to properly protect the lives and the interests of Mexicans, not only of those who are being brought into the country but also of those who are already here and who, as a result of this lack of guarantees, are rapidly migrating. With this, trust can be established, since it is a very important factor in initiating an immigration flow of workers that without great effort would be enough to fulfill the necessities of agriculture in the United States.

As I had verbally expressed to you, only under that condition will I be able to cooperate with you in the referenced project, and if you find it convenient, let it be known to the corresponding Authorities. I take the liberty of citing the following cases that in my point of view require this country's Authorities' attention, and that in great part, are responsible for Mexican workers leaving:

FIRST. Until now some Mexicans have been enrolled in the Army. Many of them, in spite of steps that we, Mexico's representatives in this country, have taken and despite irrefutable evidence presented that prove their nationality, remain in the Army.

Given that these Mexican citizens have been taken by force into the military, the same Government that claims they are citizens of this country should face the obligation of proving within a reasonable period their right over them, and not place that responsibility on people who lack education and the means necessary to demand justice.

I attach a list of those who are currently detained and who have been taken from this Consulate's jurisdiction in which you will see that what has been addressed on this matter is completely justified.

SECOND. The immigration laws of this country, in addition to the $8.00 dollar required fee that all foreigners must pay, make many difficult demands that are hard to understand and even harder to carry out. As a result of this, when laborers try to come into this country in search of work, they are faced with an infinite number of obstacles that are too difficult to overcome. Above all, it is harder for them to find employees in ports of entry who have enough patience to explain the regulations as well as to indicate how to execute them. Instead, they are humiliated by the rude employees who hate Mexicans. With regards to the conduct of some Customs and Immigration employees, much could be improved and, in turn, this would result in the acceptance of an immigration wave into the country and not a rejection of it.

THIRD. The attitude and conduct of many Rangers has been so hostile towards Mexicans that many of them consider Rangers to be the most serious threat to their lives and interests. Many of these Rangers boast and brag about their anti-Mexican attitudes and their open opposition to the present Government in Mexico.

To conclude I should tell you that even though the Mexican Consular Service's cooperation could help you a great deal in promoting immigration to this country, the support of the Central Government in Mexico would render more useful results and you should solicit it by addressing a letter to whom it may concern in Mexico City.

Andrés G. García, Inspector General de Consulados, to Tom Bell, Deputy Labor Commissioner, Texas, June 12, 1918, and Bell to T.C. Jennings, State Labor Commissioner, June 7, 1918, Archivo General de la Nación, Ramo Secretaría de Industria y Trabajo, 137-12-9.

Documenting Mistreatment

On March 24, 1920, the Mexican consul in El Paso alleged in a report to the Foreign Ministry that police and border guards had indiscriminately killed hundreds of Mexicans since 1910 in various parts of the United States. Below are some samples from this compilation.

Antonio Gómez. July 19, 1911

A fourteen-year-old man was imprisoned by authorities in Thorndale, Texas, for the homicide of an American citizen who had insulted him. A group of Thorndale citizens took matters into their own hands because they did not believe that Gómez was being tried by the appropriate authorities, and in a heartless manner lynched him. No investigation was conducted to find the persons responsible for the lynching.

José Castro. May 9, 1912

He was beat by his boss until his teeth were knocked out in Phoenix, Arizona. Justice of the Peace Parker declared that there was no crime to punish without summoning the offender to court.

José Puente. December 24, 1912

He was killed in a bar in Fort Worth, Texas, by an American bartender named C. B. García simply because Mr. Puente entered the bar without noticing that in the entrance there was a sign prohibiting Mexicans from entering that establishment. Mr. Puente was shot in the center of his forehead.

Desiderio Flores (father).
Desiderio Flores (son).
Antonio Flores. August 4, 1915

During an arrest, Sheriff Van Hutching, commander of the Texas National Guard and Mr. Fox, Ranger Commander, killed three individuals as a result of an accusation made against them by the Casa Armendáriz's foreman. No legal actions were taken.

Six unknown Mexicans. September, 1915

These individuals were killed early September, 1915, while looking for work, near Benito, Texas. They left a farm where they were unable to negotiate their salary with its American owner. As a result, the American sought out the nearest Texas Rangers and accused them of sedition, thus leading to their mass murder. No investigation was conducted.

Gregorio Rivera. February 25, 1916
El Paso, Texas

He was a sixty-two-year-old man killed by W. Ligget near Fort Hancock, Texas, due to a land dispute. When Rivera was thrown off his land, he told Ligget that the matter should be settled legally, to which Ligget replied, "This is the law," and killed him. Many neighbors went to the American authorities declaring that Ligget was a good person of honorable conduct.

Luis Rodríguez. December, 1919

Rodríguez was killed in Kale, Texas, by foreman Campbell who, after having had a minor argument with him, decided to pay off his salary without any problems. The following morning while Mr. Rodríguez and his wife were in the car that served as their bedroom and as they prepared to leave, Mr. Campbell entered and hit Mr. Rodríguez with his gun and, once he was on the ground, he proceeded to shoot him.

"Listas de algunos mexicanos que fueron muertos en los Estados Unidos de Norte América durante los años de 1911-1919, Compilados por el consul en El Paso, January 1920 ("Listas")," August 6, 1919, Archivos Históricos de la Secretaría de Relaciones Exteriores, 11/19/24.

The Comisiones Honoríficas Mexicanas and Las Brigadas de la Cruz Azul Mexicanas

Jesús Franco, an immigrant activist who was instrumental in the effort to organize Comisiones Honoríficas Mexicanas (Honorary Mexican Committees), left a lively account of the founding of the very first one in San Marcos, Texas, after a meeting of consuls in San Antonio on April 9, 1921, to discuss the inordinate problems facing Mexican immigrants during the recession; repatriation needs were the most pressing. In the same work, Franco also demonstrated the significance of the consul-sponsored Brigadas de la Cruz Azul Mexicanas (Mexican Blue Cross Brigades), a women's group dedicated to providing medical assistance and emergency relief to the immigrants.

The Consulate's workload intensified in order to tend to the numerous repatriation applications that were received. The flow and urgency of those demands was such that General Consul D. Eduardo Ruiz decided to hold a Convention of Consuls with the purpose of exchanging impressions, to study the problem, and to come up with uniform solutions and practices. This, in turn would develop the repatriation and protection program that the Government had sketched out. They had to make sure that both were reasonable and effective while keeping in mind abuses and injustices that many Mexicans had fallen victim to at the hands of their bosses, especially in the State of Texas, where they should be prevented and corrected.

The Convention was inaugurated on April 9, 1921, at the San Antonio Mexican Consulate in Texas.

* * *

I had attended the Convention as an attaché with the purpose of informing on specific cases regarding the necessities that I have observed in our compatriots, especially on a recent trip I made to the state of Oklahoma. In order to provide such reports, I was given a voice but not a vote.

The Convention has rendered fruitful results, since in only seven sessions held under the guidance and presidency of D. Eduardo Ruiz they have reached important agreements.

I do not deem it correct to publicize the discussions nor the procedures employed in reaching the final agreements of the Convention since they dealt with private matters, but I do believe it is necessary and free of all indiscretion to briefly include some of the agreements that were later made public in the regulations when recorded by the Honorific Commissions and the Blue Cross, printed and known by many Mexicans in the United States.

Honorific Commissions would be built to aid Consulates, to impart protection to compatriots in the United States, and to zealously care for the Mexican Nation with respect and dignity. They would represent our colony in their place of residence. They would be elected and removed annually by the people's vote.

146

Their purpose would be to listen and tend to all complaints on behalf of Mexicans, taking the proper steps under the law, and courteously proceeding before the authorities. They would carry out specific investigations and measures in each case, submitting a copy of the record to the corresponding Consulate so that it could make the necessary representations. They would resolve all possible issues that could be taken care of, immediately informing the corresponding Consulate.

They would obtain all possible testimonies to document accidents suffered by Mexicans at their place of employment, such as dismemberment, serious or fatal injuries, sending proofs to the Consul in their jurisdiction before submitting a claim and before signing any contract that might jeopardize our compatriots' rights in any way.

Delegations would be assigned among its members with the purpose of periodically visiting jails, schools, hospitals, and other institutions as well as factories and labor fields where Mexican citizens might be employed. These delegations would investigate extensively our compatriots' situation and would create a record of complaints regarding their bosses' behavior and the authorities' negligence.

They would celebrate national holidays and commemorate heroic dates, assigning in advance the work to the councils responsible for the respective celebration.

They would initiate and sponsor civic-instructive conferences among Mexicans, to remind them of their Nation and their obligations to the country in which they are currently residing. They would favor all publications, books, and pamphlets that praise Mexico.

They would register all Mexican citizens on their census, marking their names, age, occupation, and residency so as to transfer the information to the Consulate.

According to the Consul, they would name Honorific Sub-Commissions in places where a commission was not needed and maintain communication with the Consulates via the Commissions.

In serious cases or international matters, Commissions and Sub-Commissions would limit their action of gathering detailed and meticulous data to communicate it to the respective Consulate, since the Consulates are responsible for taking the adequate measures in a particular case.

Once the basics were discussed and the formation of the Honorific Commissions was metaphorically approved, they proceeded to formulate the Regulations for its functions, which were immediately recorded as complete, since they are the same that are currently in force.

* * *

The concept of the Honorific Commissions was an idea which crystallized in the bosom of the Convention. This idea conceived by Mr. Eduardo Ruiz and Mr. Luis Montes de Oca supported what I had deemed inseparable from it, the establishing of the Blue Cross. It would be composed of Mexican women of no particular social status, so that, taking advantage of its kindness and giving spirit, along with the protection that the Commissions would grant and the power that was semi-officially assigned, the Blue Cross would impart that other protection which can never be reached by the Government's efforts nor, let us confess, the endeavors of men of goodwill. I am alluding to that protection which is not only bread, but love and comfort as well as enthusiasm. What I am referring to is the Christian and caring charity of our beautiful female colleagues.

Regulations were drawn out for the Blue Cross as well, for which Mr. Eduardo Ruiz was made Supreme Commander and I, General Organizer.

Having accomplished my goal, I left the Convention in its study of other matters and headed for San Marcos in order to carry out any preparations needed to install the Honorific Commission and the Blue Cross Brigade, which were to be the first of their kind in the United States.

* * *

I was inspired with the best intention and filled with enthusiasm; I found that the opportunity was at hand, given that neighbors of that town had already asked that an Honorific Commission be established there through Mr. Gonzalo G. González.

I explained to them that these Mexican organizations had in great part education, understanding, and protection among their compatriots as their goals. I explained that this was one of the most clever steps that had been taken not only in remedying the current difficulties but in uniting our compatriots into a network that would remind them of the nation they represented, even though they resided in a foreign country. They are an honorable representation of our Nation, who as a loving mother never forgets her absent children; we in turn must always keep her in our hearts and in our minds in order to be useful to her. If they cannot keep her in their hearts or minds, then, at least in their bosoms. This is a friendly country which has received them, before it, they must be grateful, endowed with honesty, industriousness, good citizenship and fraternity, since not only does direct labor serve this country, but it efficiently honors its name and praises its merit through our actions.

Once the preparations were made, I came to an agreement with the Convention and on April 14 at 4:30 in the evening, all consuls arrived with the exception of three who had other engagements. We proceeded from the reception to the simple ceremony which constituted the first Mexican Honorific Commission in the United States.

I said a simple ceremony, but I must add that just because it was simple it does not mean it was not significant, since it was quite solemn due to the reunion of such an illustrious group of Consuls, foreign authorities, special guests, many American citizens, and a crowd of our own people. All were moved, all spirited, all carrying on their lips and in their hearts a cheer for the beloved Mexico who in dire moments has known to stretch out its loving hands and blessed arms.

That is how the first Mexican Honorific Commission was formally organized after the Convention.

Jesús Franco, *El alma de la raza: narraciones históricas* (El Paso, Texas: Compañía Editora "A la Patria," C. 1923), pp. 8-25.

Mexican Study of Immigrant Conditions

In 1928, the Secretaría de Relaciones Exteriores, Mexico's Foreign Ministry, issued a report outlining the treatment of Mexicans in the United States; it also made imposing claims for helping the immigrants. The fifty-two page-study detailed the travails facing immigrants, such as abuse by employers, segregation, physical attacks by prejudiced whites, police brutality, and inequities in the justice system. Shown here is the part of the report that points out the vulnerability of being undocumented.

The problem of emigration of Mexicans to the United States of America has been studied, however superficially; it is closely related to the protective work effected by our Consulates in the already mentioned country. Let us examine this work and what has resulted from it.

We have stated that many of our compatriots who arrive in this country arrive without fulfilling immigration requirements and, as a result, from the first day, they are liable to deportation by Immigration authorities. Therefore, they must hide their presence and, as a result, labor contractors make them sign abusive labor contracts through which the contractors gain a great number of advantages since they cannot be punished, because our compatriots, fearing deportation, will not complain. Of course, a large number of Mexicans are detained before entering American territory and are then deported, after being incarcerated anywhere between fifteen days to six months and subjected to truly distressing treatment, since they are placed in cells assigned to colored people and in some cases in cells for inmates accused of homicide and serious crimes.

* * *

Deportations of Mexicans carried out by the American Government are not only those motivated by illegal immigration, but also by those who have infringed on any police regulation or those pertaining to white slavery and the violation of the prohibition on alcoholic beverages, narcotics, and bearing arms.

It is well known in Mexico, too well known as a matter of fact, that our working-class compatriots do not take on civil marriages, that they contract ecclesiastical marriages only, and other times they carry on a married life of no legal value to any Mexican or American authority. When American Immigration authorities discover that our compatriots are in such conditions, and if the person involved appears to be physically strong, they disregard this detail pertaining to the lack of civil marriage proof and accept him as an immigrant who is accompanied by his wife and children. But they keep a careful record just in case that immigrant should cause any difficulty to any American citizen or corporation, since they can deport him for not being legally married. Whenever there is a labor shortage in any region of the United States of America and when it is not possible to send the unemployed to other regions, Immigration authorities carry out a general raid against our compatriots, deporting them in masses and not taking into consideration whether or not they are responsible for violating any laws or regulations.

The intervention of our Consuls could render positive results in avoiding injustices in these cases, but they hardly ever know of them. If they do find out, it is often too late and their negotiations are unsuccessful. In order to mend this irregularity wherever possible, our Washington Embassy has been instructed to appear before that Government so that Immigration Offices can continue notifying our Consuls on the deportation cases that are pending. As evidence of the trouble that this lack of notification brings about to our compatriots, we know of a specific case in which Abel Díaz, a fourteen-year-old boy, was lost for more than a month. This frightened his family terribly since neither they nor the Consulate were notified of his deportation.

In many cases, American authorities deport relatives of Mexicans, and this can seriously harm those who remain in that territory, especially when the one deported is the head of household. Very frequently, there are cases in which our compatriots are deported and they do not have time to collect their salaries from the companies that have employed them. They also do not have enough time to arrange and pick up their personal belongings, and our Consuls are brought in to take care of these interests. It is a good thing when the deportations are carried out by the American Government in places near the deportees' residences, but lately they have continued the deportation from the farthest places, and this has caused serious damage to the Mexican Government.

Secretaría de Relaciones Exteriores, *La migración de los mexicanos en el extranjero: labor de las relaciones exteriores en los Estados Unidos de América y Guatemala* (México: Imprenta de Archivos Históricos de la Secretaría de Relaciones Exteriores, 1928), pp. 21-22.

The Mexican Government and Segregation

The Mexican government was ever vigilant of the segregation of Mexican school children, as indicated by this 1930 report issued in May of 1931 by Manuel E. Otáñera, an official from the Mexican Foreign Ministry.

Recently, several Northern communities of Mexican residents in the United States have experienced great unrest as a result of certain measures that school authorities have taken in some American communities. These measures have been interpreted as an obvious tendency to exclude Mexican children from public schools intended for children of Anglo-Saxon descent.

The Department of Foreign Affairs has received constant reports from our General Consuls in San Francisco, Cal. and San Antonio, Tex., giving a detailed account of these matters which are described in the following manner:

Congressman Bliss presented a proposed law to the State of California's Assembly in which he authorized school officials of each district to establish separate schools designed to provide special education: first, to "Indian children" who are born either in or out of the United States and, second, to children of Japanese or Mongolian descent.

This project roused a general movement and uneasiness in all who are affected by such a decree, and although it has not been stated, whether or not they intend to include Mexican children under the denomination of "Indian children," our compatriots have deemed such a decree depressing and harmful to the education of our children, if it does include them. They united in protest with other foreigners affected, thus exerting moral pressure on legislative authorities in the American Federation. As a result of their respectful although eloquent attitude, they were able to convince Congressman Bliss to withdraw the proposed law and substitute it with a new one, which grants authority to school officials to establish separate schools for children in the already mentioned classes, only from kindergarten through the eighth grade, provided these schools be completely set up and equipped in the same manner as the other public schools of each place.

In Lemon Grove, Cal., a public school principal notified various Mexican citizens that their children could not continue to attend a certain school and that they should attend another under the name of the "School of Americanization," which had just been constructed and was exclusively designed for Mexican children. There, the children would be given a special English class. Parents of the segregated minors refused to send their children to the new school and organized a "Committee of Mexicans in Lemon Grove." They sought representation and filed a suit against Lemon Grove school authorities with the county's Supreme Court, for which they obtained a completely satisfactory response. The aforementioned court ruled on the case declaring that the suit was correct and ordered that Mexican children be admitted without any objections into Lemon Grove's public school.

In San Antonio, Tex., a wooden building that was to be named the "School of Americanization" was constructed, and since that building was destroyed in a fire, the project of segregation was suspended for a while. Subsequently, there was a complete change of school officials of the mentioned place, and it has been announced that the new school trustees, comprehending the injustices and inconveniences of the segregation project, have decided not to build any separate schools and will only enlarge the existing building to make room for all registered children without any racial discrimination.

A claim similar to that which was presented to judicial authorities in Lemon Grove was formulated by the parents of several Mexican children and taken before authorities in Del Rio, Valverde County, Tex.; a favorable judgment was also granted.

Finally, Morgan Junior High School in Mission, Texas, denied registration to four Mexican children. The parents went to the Board of Education of the school district in Mission, where school authorities gave them extensive explanations, trying to prove that it was not a matter of establishing racial differences, but of placing the children in South Junior High School where they still had room, since Morgan Junior High did not.

The last news that we received regarding incidents of this sort are quite satisfactory, since it is known that numerous school authorities of California, where the aforementioned decree is supposed to be expedited, have promised Mexican Consuls that even if it is passed into law, they will not employ their authority to create separate schools designed for children of other races, because they deem the judgment unnecessary and evidently antidemocratic.

The Mexican government, taking into consideration the sovereignty of each country to adopt and establish within its territory its principles of pedagogy that must regulate public education and identify the needs of students, according to their preparation and knowledge of the official language, has not deemed it necessary to formulate any complaint, as long as there are no measures which may indicate racial prejudices. The Mexican government has thus limited itself to closely observe the path of these events whose true end result should not be justified.

El Defensor, May 15, 1931.

Police as Criminals

Victimization by crooked law enforcement officials, while not as common as police brutality, nonetheless occurred all too often. In January, 1927, according to the Mexican Consul in El Paso, sheriff deputies in Stanton, Texas, persuaded three Mexicans to go inside a bank to inquire about a job. When the workers exited, the officials opened fire, killing two and wounding a third. The deputies alleged the Mexicans were trying to rob a bank and tried to claim a $5,000 reward. The document below tells the story of Gregorio and Piedad Herrera, who were robbed of $1008 by policemen in Bridgeport, Nebraska. Piedad was shot in the process.

On the 15th of November, 1920, four Mexicans, Gregorio Herrera, his father, and two brothers were at the railway station of Bridgeport, Nebraska, according to the complaint made in due course at the Consulate of Mexico in Kansas City, Missouri. They were waiting for a train to proceed to Denver, Colorado, when of a sudden, and without his giving any cause thereof, one of the brothers of Herrera was arrested by two special deputy sheriffs on duty and taken to the station. Gregorio went there to inquire why his brother had been arrested, and he was also arrested without any cause. From the statement of the Herrera brothers and the evidence since gathered, it appears that the two brothers were subjected to a personal search at the place where they were held, which was also unwarranted since they were not charged or even suspected of any offense or misdemeanor whatsoever; that, as a result of this search and unwarranted examination, the authorities of the United States who conducted it, satisfied themselves that Gregorio Piedad's brother, carried in cash $1008.00; and that when the said authorities became aware of that, they released both brothers, who immediately returned to their people at the railway station intending to proceed on their trip that had been so abruptly and inexcusably interrupted. But it happened that fifteen minutes later, one of the special deputy sheriffs above mentioned called again at the station and forcibly laid hold of Piedad Herrera, took him out of the station, took the money he carried from him ($1008.00), and firing his pistol on him, inflicted a wound in his leg which has kept him, and still keeps him, in a critical condition of health.

The Embassy of Mexico understands that upon the information lodged by the Herrera brothers, the authorities of Bridgeport instituted an investigation of the facts; but inasmuch as the case assumes characters of exceptional gravity, and seeing that the Herrera brothers have not only suffered from an abuse of powers, but also a genuine assault on the part of the lawful authorities of the United States (special deputy sheriffs), the Embassy of Mexico has the honor to apply to the Department of State and to bring the foregoing to its knowledge with the view that upon investigating the case, the persons responsible for this outrage be duly punished, the money taken from the victims be returned to them, and an indemnity paid to them as seems to be demanded by strict justice for the damage and injuries suffered by them.

Having no doubt that the Department of State, motivated by its high sense of equity, will be pleased to give this matter immediate attention, the Embassy of Mexico expresses its thanks in advance and renews to it the assurances of its most distinguished consideration.

Manuel Téllez, Mexican Ambassador, to Charles E. Hughes, Secretary of State, January 26, 1921, National Archives, Record Group 59, 311.1221, H43.

Mob Violence towards Mexicans

Civilian violence, like police brutality, was a source of constant grief. Lynchings were the most disconcerting, but less dramatic manifestations of mob violence toward unwanted Mexicans occurred more often. The document here is one of the many notes that the Mexican embassy delivered protesting these incidents.

Mr. Secretary:

I have the honor to inform Your Excellency that on the twenty-fourth of August of this year, a group of one hundred American citizens assaulted and ill-treated fourteen Mexican citizens, who were peaceful residents of the City of Kansas, simply because they attended a fair which was held in Shawnee Park in the said city.

The ill-treated Mexicans were able to escape from their assailants, thanks to the intervention of the police, and when they asked for the arrest of the offenders, the reply they received from the Kansas City Police Department was that they should have stayed at home if they did not want to have trouble with the Americans.

This is not the first time that Mexican citizens residing in the State of Kansas were subjected to insults of this kind, on account of their nationality. This is a circumstance that the Embassy should not allow to go without entering a strong protest with Your Excellency, as I now do, with the hope that the Government of Your Excellency will see fit to order such measures as it may deem necessary to avoid a repetition of attempts of that nature, and to the end that the citizens of my country may enjoy the guarantee that both the Constitution of the United States and that of the State of Kansas grant to all foreign residents.

I also kindly beg Your Excellency to bring your powerful influence to bear on the proper authorities so that the leaders, who are responsible for the outrage above referred to, be punished, and I avail myself of the opportunity to renew my assurances to you, etcetera.

Manuel Téllez, Mexican Ambassador, to Frank B. Kellogg, Secretary of State, September 11, 1925, National Archives, Record Group 59, 311.1213, Kansas City.

Lázaro Cárdenas and Mexican Immigration Policy

In the 1930s, Mexican officials, stunned by massive repatriation problems, entered into another phase of intense introspection regarding the problems of their compatriots in the United States. In November of 1938, President Lázaro Cárdenas uttered the following words in a speech that he gave during festivities commemorating the beginning of the Mexican Revolution.

Indeed, there is a large group of Mexicans who should be considered and are deserving of our attention. They have migrated from their nation searching in vain through foreign lands for a better way to attain their progress. After a persistent battle and arduous labor, they have convinced themselves that neither economy nor prosperity is possible on foreign grounds. No matter how benevolent and welcoming they may seem at moments of illusion, during a local crisis, those foreign lands become a hostile environment to those who, maintaining their citizenship and nationality, are put aside by those who, within their borders, have complete use of the land, their citizenship and nationality.

But this unfavorable circumstance, which carries with it onerous results to a frail nation which is undergoing a laborious process of internal reconstruction, does not do away with the obligation of solidarity and responsibility. We should not only declare our obligation with an effort to provide efficient aid to the demand for help, repatriation, and reintegration of our compatriots who are not only downcast by the circumstances, but find themselves away from their homeland. Therefore, it is necessary to unite in our approach by cooperating, by modifying the selfish notion that some of us experience, since this is a problem which the majority does not face, to allow the return of those who did not think about the consequences and chose to follow their instincts. Although the nation is presently preoccupied with the immediate resolution of our economic emancipation, they deserve all our consideration. In view of this, I take the opportunity of this well-deserved, joyous moment of personal concentration of farm workers, laborers, soldiers, and organized state employees, along with the people and working classes who participate in the commemoration of the Revolution, to ask for real cooperation in their repatriation, since officials are mindful of the need to become part of the efforts of the people I have already mentioned; the officials are eager to join them in the necessary and urgent effort of reintegrating our siblings into the nation. It is necessary to take into consideration that we are now expounding a reverse procedure to find the solution to a chronic problem in our governmental environment. We are convinced that the officials' efforts in and of themselves are unable to satisfy the essential reversal needed to reincorporate Mexican emigrants and, without the cooperation of other members of the nation, we would not find a friendly environment for the absent citizens, since in problems of national character, such as the one we analyze, the citizens should demonstrate all the social valor which is requested of them, as well as patriotism.

Ernesto Hidalgo, *La protección de mexicanos en los Estados Unidos: defensorías de oficios anexas a los consulados—un proyecto* (México: Talleres Gráficos de la Nación, 1940), pp. 5-6.

Chapter Six

Mexican American Mobilization

By the 1940s and 1950s, Mexican Americans attempted to resolve problems through receiving an education, electoral politics, litigation, and claiming their rights as citizens. The repatriation of Mexicans during the 1930s reduced the influence of immigrant leaders in the *colonias,* creating a void in which a Mexican American identity and leadership emerged. But Mexican Americanism did not appear magically after repatriation. The identity was advocated as early as World War I in areas such as Tucson and San Antonio, where immigration, primarily from the Mexican north, had come earlier. In Arizona the first two major Mexican organizations were called the Alianza Hispano Americana (Hispanic American Alliance) and the Liga Protectora Latina (Latin Protective League), names demonstrating a remoteness from Mexico. Luz Sáenz, a teacher and World War I veteran, joined with other veterans in organizing the Order of the Sons of America in 1921. Most of the members were U.S.-born and encouraged naturalization and participation in U.S. institutions for all Mexicans. Also in 1921, Ricardo Arenales founded the Pan American Round Table in San Antonio. It attracted Mexican American and Anglo businessmen and engaged in combating defamation.

Francisco A. Chapa, publisher of *El Imparcial de Texas* and a druggist, advocated Mexican Americanism as early as World War I. His newspaper promoted electoral participation and celebrated Mexican American exploits during World War I. It featured weekly listings of Mexicans killed or wounded in European armed actions. By the early 1930s, a more complete shift towards Mexican Americanization became apparent. Mexico, as a source of identity, did not survive the massive repatriations provoked by the Great Depression.

To be classified as white became an essential goal for many Mexican American activists. U.S. Mexicans realized, even in the immigrant era, that as colored people, they could be subjected to *de jure* segregation. For example, the strategy employed in the few successful school desegregation efforts discussed previously was based on the claim of whiteness. Many scholars have charged Mexican American leaders of being anti-immigrant. This was not necessarily true. While they often lamented the slowness with which immigrants Americanized and they pointed out that this invited unwanted repression, leaders like Alonso Perales and José T. Canales consistently defended Mexican immigrants against nativist attacks.

Mexican Americans enthusiastically supported the U.S. declaration of war against the Axis powers in 1941. In spite of continuing discrimination, patriotism among Mexican Americans, who felt more accepted than their parents in this optimistic era, ran high. In addition, unlike their parents, their ties to Mexico were weak or nonexistent. Some 300,000 Mexican Americans served in the armed forces. Those who did not serve in the military engaged in "Home Front" efforts, such as bond drives.

Mexican American G.I.s returned by the thousands when the war ended, to urban areas, to small towns, and to agricultural camps, where they married and had babies. The soldiers came back more confident, desirous of participating more fully in a society which they had fought to preserve. Many of the young, newly-married Mexican American couples found homes in the growing suburbs and were further acculturated to American life. Leaders of organizations that promoted Mexican Americanism, such as the League of United Latin American Citizens (LULAC), saw in Mexican American wartime involvement an embodiment of their hopes and aspirations.

But because Mexicans were still subjected to segregation or barred from public facilities in schools, theaters, swimming pools, restaurants, and housing tracts, war veterans always reminded Americans of their excellent war record and strove to eradicate their segregation. The American G.I. Forum became the most dynamic postwar Mexican American civil rights organization. It began in response to the refusal of a funeral director in Three Rivers, Texas, to bury Félix Longoria, a soldier killed in the Pacific theater. Dr. Héctor García, a former Army medical officer who saw action in Europe, and civil rights lawyer Gus García were key figures in organizing the Forum. Unlike LULAC, the American G.I. Forum openly advocated getting out the vote and endorsing candidates.

The young Mexicans who grew up in the 1930s and 1940s comprised a new generation who either had been born in the United States or who had been very young upon arriving from Mexico. In addition, more persons from their cohort group graduated from grammar and high school, a factor that provided this generation with greater expectations than those held by their parents. To them, the symbolism perpetuated in previous decades by immigrant leaders was not very relevant. Instead, they leaned more towards Americanization and were influenced by such leaders as Ignacio López, publisher of the bilingual newspaper in

California, *El Espectador,* who championed these ideals. In Houston, Félix Tijerina was another who embodied the kind of leadership that greatly influenced young Mexican Americans. Tijerina served as national president of LULAC in the 1950s, when the influential "Little School of 400," which sought to teach pre-school Mexican Americans four hundred English words, was established.

Through such New Deal agencies as the Civilian Conservation Corps (CCC) and the National Youth Administration (NYA), young Mexican Americans were also exposed to the greater Anglo society. Both were designed to enroll young people and keep them off the streets during this era of massive unemployment.

The Mexican American Movement (MAM), which emerged in southern California during the 1930s, under the auspices of the YMCA, became the quintessential Mexican youth organization. Made up of upwardly mobile youths, mostly college students, the group committed itself to improving the condition of Mexican people living in the United States through responsible citizenship and higher education. Their ideology minimized racism as the main detriment to success. Their newspaper, the *Mexican Voice*, in issue after issue, bombarded its readers with the ideal of progress through education and hard work. They paid lip service to a cultural pride that recognized *mestizaje*, a position that served as a link between the mestizo identity of their parents' era and the Chicano Movement position of the 1960s. Nonetheless, when confronted with a situation where they had to choose between Mexicanness and being American, they chose the latter. Moreover, the prevalent notion that Mexicans in the United States inherited traits that were shaped by Mexican history and were incompatible with modern society was accepted by the MAM organizers.

The gang activity of *pachucos* (zoot-suited street youth) provoked negative media coverage that inflamed widespread public and police backlash against Mexicans. The repression of Mexican American youth threatened the civil rights gains activists had previously obtained. California Mexican American activists came to their defense by forming the Citizen's Committee for Latin American Youth, with Los Angeles lawyer Manuel Ruiz as chairman. A committee was formed to provide legal support for the Sleepy Lagoon defendants, who were accused of killing another Mexican American teenager at a party in 1942. It included journalist-crusader Carey McWilliams, labor organizer Bert Corona, and Josefina Fierro de Bright from the Congress of Spanish-Speaking People. The group employed a carefully crafted strategy in order to avoid exacerbating an already intense xenophobia aimed at Mexicans during the war.

The Zoot-Suit Riots became the hallmark event that exposed the antipathy that existed towards Mexican American youth. In the spring of 1943, servicemen stationed in the Los Angeles area commandeered taxicabs and spilled out into the streets of East Los Angeles, beating up every Mexican teenager that crossed their path. They did this with the tacit support of the press and their superiors and the police.

In spite of these racist manifestations, Mexican Americans were becoming more integrated into mainstream society and they displayed stronger capabilities in breaking down obstacles to economic and social mobility. School segregation seemed to be the most formidable barrier blocking their progress. In a LULAC-sponsored initiative, for example, attorneys from the Lawyer's Guild succeeded, through the 1946 landmark *Méndez v. Westminster* case, in desegregating a number of southern California schools by arguing that segregation violated the constitutional rights of Mexican children guaranteed by the Fourteenth Amendment. At least five thousand Mexican American children were affected. As expected, the Westminster decision had a momentous effect on the future efforts to segregate Mexican children.

Segregation policies were most stringent in Texas and Arizona, and there, Mexican American leaders waged the most intense efforts to desegregate schools. In Texas, LULAC could point to successes even before the war. Schools in Del Rio, Goliad, and Beeville were integrated during the 1930s, but the bulk of the battle remained for later years. For example, LULAC commissioned the Westminster case lawyers in 1948 to successfully challenge segregation in Bastrop, Texas. In Arizona, the *Sheely v. González* decision in 1952 abolished segregation in Tolleson, a town near Phoenix. Often, however, officials did not act promptly in issuing desegregation orders and it took continuous prodding from the Mexican community to bring about true integration.

The Mexican government and Mexican intellectuals also joined the Mexican American civil rights campaign to further better treatment through its consular service. The Comité Contra el Racismo (Committee Against Racism) was organized by a number of Mexican intellectuals, including the poet and career diplomat Jaime Torres Bodet. Its original purpose was to promote cooperation between the two countries against the fascist threat in Europe, but it extended its work to combat racism against Mexicans in the United States.

After the war, Mexican American politicos also turned more intensely to the ballot box in order to achieve their objectives. Electoral participation had been expressed as early as the 1890s by Arizona's Alianza Hispano Americana and New Mexico's El Partido del Pueblo (The People's Party). The number of potential Mexican voters increased by World War I, especially in New Mexico, Texas, and Arizona. But in *colonias* made up mainly of recent immigrants, as was the case in Los Angeles and other large cities, electoral power for Mexican Americans would have to wait until the 1950s when the immigrants' children matured into adults.

The success-oriented Industrial Areas Foundation (IAF), a grassroots project founded in Chicago by the legendary organizer Saul Alinsky, had a solid history of empowering poor neighborhoods through political organizing; it created the Community Service Organization (CSO) to empower Mexican Americans in Los Angeles. The tactics of the IAF suited the aspirations of Los Angeles' Mexican Americans, who increasingly leaned towards confrontational tactics. After a major voter registration drive by the CSO that enrolled 15,000 Mexican Americans in Los Angeles, Edward Roybal won a seat on the city council in 1949. But efforts to enter state-level politics were disappointing. In 1954, Edward Roybal unsuccessfully sought the Democratic nomination for lieutenant governor. Four years later, he ran for a slot in the County Board of Supervisors and lost. That same year, 1958, Hank López, a Harvard-educated lawyer, won the Democratic Party nomination for California Secretary of State, but lost in the general election.

In East Chicago, Indiana, naturalized immigrants formed the First Mexican American Political Club with the goal of uniting the *colonia* as a voting bloc. East Chicago politicos would have to wait until the 1960s before they became a dominant force in the Democratic Party of Lake County, when a large generation of Mexican Americans reached voting age.

Because Mexican Americans comprised a very large portion of the population in New Mexico, it is there where they had the greatest amount of success. In 1919, for example, the Mexican-born Octaviano Larrazola served as governor. Dennis Chávez occupied a U.S. Senate seat from the 1930s until his death in 1962. His successor Joseph Montoya, elected in 1964, stayed in power until the 1970s. More importantly, Hispanics controlled numerous local positions as would be seen in Tierra Amarilla, where Chicano movement stalwart Reies López Tijerina was opposed by a Mexican American establishment.

Similarly, Mexican American politicians, always Democrat, enjoyed some success in South Texas. Since the nineteenth century, Mexican constituents had elected native *tejanos* to local positions in the machine-dominated Laredo area and throughout the Lower Rio Grande Valley. Anglos with seigniorial power dominated the machines, but Mexican Americans' local political systems managed to obtain major concessions for some of their people. José T. Canales, who managed to break away from the Jim Wells Machine in the early 1900s, was the most successful politician in the early part of the century. Elected repeatedly to the state legislature, he was successful in deterring Texas Ranger abuses during the period of the Mexican Revolution. Others, such as Eligio "Kika" de la Garza and Henry B. González, were elected beginning in the 1960s to the U.S. Congress. In 1957, the election of Raymond Telles as mayor in El Paso was the most encouraging electoral gain for Mexican Americans.

By the 1950s, Mexican Americans had begun to use the strategy used successfully by black civil rights activists of insisting that racism was responsible for many of their people's problems. The integration of the armed forces and the entry of black athletes into major league professional sports demonstrated that concessions could be wrested from the white establishment by pricking its conscience. Mexican Americans also abandoned the claim to white ethnic identity because the strategy was often used against them. If Mexican Americans demanded a jury of peers for trials where the defendant was Mexican, they were told that seating all Anglo juries did not exclude the Mexican race, since it was supposedly white.

By the late 1950s, Mexican Americans emulated even more the success of the black civil rights movement. In 1959, Edward Roybal, Bert Corona, and Eduardo Quevedo met in Fresno and formed the Mexican American Political Association (MAPA), an organization that began to inject the tactics of militancy into their activism. At an Equal Employment Opportunity Commission meeting in Albuquerque, New Mexico, during March of 1966, the watchdog group heard grievances from members of such organizations as Political Association of Spanish Speaking Organizations (PASSO), organized in Texas in the 1960s, and LULAC. They walked out after demanding that the Equal Employment Opportunity Commission put Mexican Americans on its board and punish large southwestern corporate employers that discriminated in hiring Mexican Americans.

At the end of the 1950s, Mexican Americans began to obtain political power at the national level. This was best manifested in the 1960 campaign to elect John F. Kennedy to the presidency. Kennedy's Catholic Irish background acted as a detriment among the general American electorate, but Mexican Americans identified with his Catholicism and to a degree with his ethnicity. Then at the 1960 convention, the Democratic Party selected as Kennedy's running mate, Lyndon Baines Johnson, a Texas politician who had worked with Mexican American voters for many years.

Members of such organizations as the G.I. Forum, MAPA, and the Alianza Hispano Americana responded to Johnson's call and formed the Viva Kennedy Clubs to deliver the Mexican American vote for the Kennedy-Johnson ticket.

In sum, middle-class reformers, who advocated integration, assimilation, and working within the system as the solution to problems facing Mexicans in the United States, dominated the Mexican Americanization process. This middle-class prescription began to change by the end of the 1950s, as Mexican Americans witnessed the successes Blacks were registering by using such tactics as demonstrations, pickets, and charging white America with racism. In addition, Mexican American politicians began to see themselves as major players in national politics by this era. The older leadership had acquired a new vitality when President Johnson, in his 1965 "Great Society" inaugural address, declared a "War on Poverty," which promised to eradicate Mexican American poverty. This augured both solutions and jobs. However, their optimism was dashed when Johnson's Great Society set its sights more directly on America's black population.

Traditional Mexican American leaders showed militancy when they walked out of the 1966 Equal Employment Opportunity Commission in Albuquerque, which reverberated among Mexican American organizations throughout the country. But most Mexican American conservatives saw their dignity disparaged by these militant tactics and their positions endangered.

In response to the protests, President Johnson named Vicente Ximenes to the Equal Employment Opportunity Commission, who in turn established the Inter-Agency Cabinet Committee on Mexican American Affairs. In October of 1967, Ximenes scheduled hearings in El Paso that coincided with the much-heralded ceremony in which the United States returned to Mexico the disputed Chamizal territory. President Johnson would be there along with Mexican president Gustavo Díaz Ordaz. The Mexican Americans invited were from the old guard, and most were unlikely to replicate the boldness shown in Albuquerque. After all, they seemed to have obtained the recognition they wanted from the Johnson administration.

Some of these Mexican American era leaders, however, such as Bert Corona of MAPA and Rodolfo "Corky" Gonzales, a former Democratic Party stalwart from Colorado, traveled to El Paso but boycotted the meeting. They decided to join young activists from the emerging Chicano Movement, led by Reies López Tijerina, a land rights activist from New Mexico, in protesting that the Mexican Americans invited to the conference did not represent the "grassroots" community, but were only interested in their own advancement. This event served to initiate a new era in Mexican American politics known as the Chicano Movement.

Early Mexican Americanism

Although born in Mexico, the San Antonio pharmacist, Francisco A. Chapa, was one of the earliest promoters of Mexican Americanism. Chapa belonged to many civic organizations and helped deliver San Antonio's Mexican American vote to Oscar Colquitt's efforts, in the late 1910s, to defeat the ban on the selling of alcohol in Texas. As publisher of *El Imparcial de Texas*, he wielded considerable influence among Texas Mexican Americans and devoted much of his energy to encouraging Mexicans in Texas to organize and vote. Chapa especially used the fact that many Mexican Americans supported war efforts and served in the military during World War I as a wedge for acceptance.

Before the European War, Texans of Mexican descent disregarded public matters that would have been of interest to them and, as a result of this pitiful abandonment, a void soon began to grow around them. Texans of other races would put them aside as a result of the lack of interest that people of our race had in their own issues.

Every time that any election would take place, they would abstain from participating in the political disputes and only by continuously asking them to vote, would they do it. In these same columns, we began a campaign whose goal was to elevate the political spirit of Mexican citizens who reside in Texas; although we did accomplish something, it was too small to consider a true success.

But Mexican citizens in Texas can still do a lot for themselves by taking advantage of the services that the American nation receives from their young people enlisted in the military, from those who have shed their generous blood in defense of the striped and starred banner.

Texas Mexicans were being eliminated in their own land, and they soon became outcasts due to their natural abandonment, due to the simple reason that they were considered incapable of performing useful tasks in things other than the difficult work in the fields and factories, and on railroad tracks. But now, Texas Mexicans are demonstrating great courage in the battlefields and they have not spared their services in order to win the war. That is why, like all other Americans, they have a right to partake of all the advantages of the triumph of this war that conquered freedom for the world.

Therefore, we urge Mexicans who reside in Texas to try to exercise their rights as citizens, to unite politically in order to get the recognition and respect they deserve.

El Imparcial de Texas, October 31, 1918.

League of United Latin American Citizens (LULAC)

Article II of the LULAC constitution, which was promulgated in Corpus Christi, Texas, in February of 1929 during its first meeting, established the principles that would guide this resilient organization for many years. The cornerstone of this document was the affirmation that civil rights could be achieved through the legal system.

The Aims and Purposes of This Organization Shall Be:

- To develop within the members of our race the best, purest, and most perfect type of a true and loyal citizen of the United States of America.
- To eradicate from our body politic all intents and tendencies to establish discriminations among our fellow citizens on account of race, religion, or social position as being contrary to the true spirit of Democracy, our Constitution, and Laws.
- To use all the legal means at our command to the end that all citizens in our country may enjoy equal rights, the equal protection of the laws, and the land opportunities and privileges.
- The acquisition of the English language, which is the official language of our country, being necessary for the enjoyment of our rights and privileges, we declare it to be the official language of this organization, and we pledge ourselves to learn and speak and teach the same to our children.
- To define with absolute and unmistakable clearness our unquestionable loyalty to the ideals, principles, and citizenship of the United States of America.
- To assume complete responsibility for the education of our children as to their rights and duties and the language and customs of this country—the latter, insofar as they may be good customs.
- We solemnly declare once and for all to maintain a sincere and respectful reverence for our racial origin of which we are proud.
- Secretly and openly, by all lawful means at our command, we shall assist in the education and guidance of Latin Americans, and we shall protect and defend their lives and interests whenever necessary.
- We shall destroy any attempt to create racial prejudices against our people, and any infamous stigma which may be cast upon them, and we shall demand for them the respect and prerogatives which the Constitution grants to us all.
- Each of us considers himself with equal responsibilities in our organization, to which we voluntarily swear subordination and obedience.
- We shall create a fund for our mutual protection, for the defense of those of us who may be unjustly persecuted, and for the education and culture of our people.
- This organization is not a political club, but as citizens we shall participate in all local, state, and national political contests. However, in doing so, we shall ever bear in mind the general welfare of our people, and we disregard and abjure once and for all any personal obligation which is not in harmony with these principles.
- With our vote and influence we shall endeavor to place in public office men who show by their deeds, respect and consideration for our people.

- We shall select as our leaders those among us who demonstrate, by their integrity and culture, that they are capable of guiding and directing us properly.
- We shall maintain publicity means for the diffusion of these principles and for the expansion and consolidation of this organization.
- We shall pay our poll tax as well as that of members of our families in order that we may enjoy our rights fully.
- We shall diffuse our ideals by means of the press, lectures, and pamphlets.
- We shall oppose any radical and violent demonstration which may tend to create conflicts and disturb the peace and tranquility of our country.
- We shall have mutual respect for our religious views, and we shall never refer to them in our institutions.
- We shall encourage the creation of educational institutions for Latin Americans and we shall lend our support to those already in existence.
- We shall endeavor to secure equal representation for our people on juries and in the administration of governmental affairs.
- We shall denounce every act of peonage and mistreatment as well as the employment of our minor children of scholastic age.
- We shall resist and attack energetically all machinations tending to prevent our social and political unification.
- We shall oppose any tendency to separate our children in the schools of this country.
- We shall maintain statistics which will guide our people with respect to working and living conditions and agricultural and commercial activities in the various parts of our country.

Ruth Lamb, *Mexican Americans of the Southwest* (Claremont, CA: Ocelot Press, 1970), p. 116.

Alonso S. Perales on the Ideals of Mexican Americans

In the following essay, written in October of 1924, Alonso S. Perales delineated the classical arguments that embodied Mexican Americanism. Responding to a series of civil rights abuses in the 1920s, such as lynchings, he urged that Mexican Americans demand their constitutional rights as U.S. citizens. To do this, Perales insisted, Mexicans in the United States did not have to reject their cultural background.

There is no doubt that there will be someone who, while reading my writing, will ask the following questions: What is the goal of Mexican Americans? Are they trying to Americanize themselves? Do they want to deny their race? Do they beg Anglo Saxons to allow them to mingle socially with them? The answers are as follows: We, conscious Mexican Americans, under all circumstances, consider ourselves as American as the most American person there is, and we challenge anyone to prove us otherwise. We are not trying to deny our race. On the contrary, we are proud to have Mexican blood running though our veins. And our purpose is not to ask, much less beg, Anglo Saxons to allow us to mingle socially with them. What we long for is the respect of our unalienable rights and privileges. We would like equality of opportunity in the various battlegrounds of life as well as before courts of justice. We would like for persons of Mexican descent in violation of the laws that govern the country to be tried before a competent Court of Justice and to not be lynched, as was the case of the unfortunate young man Elías Villarreal Zárate in Weslaco, Texas, on November, 1921. We would like to go to a theater, restaurant, dance hall, or any other establishment whose doors are wide open to the general public, whenever we feel like it. We do not want to be ousted, as is frequently done, with the mere excuse of our racial origin. In one word, we ask for justice and the opportunity to prosper. There you have our goal. There you have our objective.

Alonso S. Perales, *En defensa de mi raza,* Vol. I (San Antonio: Artes Gráficas, 1936), pp. 28-29.

A Pioneer in Mexican Americanism

LULAC leaders differed in their approach to the meaning of Americanism. The view shown below is expressed by Eduardo Idar in an editorial that appeared in *El Defensor*, a newspaper in Edingburg, Texas, which pioneered the Mexican American ideal that demanded full constitutional rights for Mexican Americans. Idar, a labor organizer and a founder of LULAC, recognizes that Mexican Americans need to learn English, and to fit into Anglo American society, but he emphasizes the rights that accrue to Mexican Americans simply because they are citizens. In addition, he calls for having pride in being of Mexican background.

The constant rise in Mexican immigration was a serious and unresolved problem. But this has diminished considerably with the new restrictive laws, and henceforth, the process of assimilation will be easier for those who remain as a result of a logical and natural consequence which will elevate living and working conditions for the parents of our children and, to be honest, ourselves. A careful analysis of the facts and the consequences we have not been able to avoid will only lead to this conclusion.

The concept of our Americanization is not what we think; it is precisely the fulfillment of all our biggest and most beautiful desires. Before anything, it implies the conscience of the Mexican American who must realize that he is a citizen with rights equal to those of others and that he is not an outcast, that he is not a stranger, nor a newcomer. It implies a new conscience, an ample and complete concept of his duties, of his rights; in other words, it is necessary to subject yourself to the traditional model under the condition that the model be identical to that which other racial groups have been subjected.

It is estimated that in Texas, for example, there are approximately 800,000 Mexicans and foreigners, and, of these, about half are citizens who in their hands hold the weapon of citizenship that, when wielded well, proves to be wonderful when accompanied by intensive education, which must be enforced as soon as possible. We should not ask for rights; we should take them as the most natural thing in the world. It is logical that whoever takes what belongs to them encounters no resistance, but if they should ask if they may take them, then someone is bound to say no.

Racial prejudice is not as notable for the white Mexican as it is for the dark. This prejudice has found a new way of expressing itself in the classification of dark Mexicans as Indian, as is to be seen in California through the 1930 census. We usually tend to see the negative side of our situations and, due to a lack of documentation, we do not take into account the positive aspect of things. At the present time, an intense and profound scientific campaign for which considerable sums of money are spent, is being carried out to vindicate the Indian. This campaign is beginning to produce beautiful results on profound archeological investigations. It has been proven that we are not Indians, according to the true meaning of the word; instead we are *mestizos* and, even with this, it is completely proven that our Indian was far from being equal to the redskin. Our ancestors had an advanced culture during their time; it was a civilization defined by laws with an established government, religious practices, scientific research, and literature, etc. Another favorable aspect is the tactful pan-Americanism that does not allow our exclusion, and it is something that has been of interest to the United States government since many years ago, and now even more, due to several circumstances.

It is true that there are certain regions that hold a negative attitude toward Mexican people, and this is due to several reasons. The most important are the difficulty in making ourselves understood and the poverty of our grassroots, to which the degree of neglect or hostility which we are shown is attributable. It is necessary to judge carefully if this diminishes or increases with time. First of all, we should make the necessary efforts to solve this problem in an intelligent manner; we must, I believe, behave in an honorable, respectful, and always dignified manner before the Anglo Saxon. We must study English, exhibit good social conduct, solidify our deep and undeniable racial bonds, and protect our compatriots everywhere. If we do not do this, we are not worthy of interacting with each other.

El Defensor, May 22, 1931.

Consoling Loyalty to the United States of America

M anuel González, a founder of LULAC and a lawyer in San Antonio, provides another view of what Americanism means to Mexican Americans. In a public letter to his friend M.G. Pérez, published in *El Defensor*, González evoked an emotional patriotism and loyalty to the United States. His main premise was that Mexican Americans needed to Americanize and become good citizens of the United States by acculturation and by pledging allegiance to American patriotic symbols.

To develop within the members of our race the best, purest and most perfect type of true and loyal citizens of the United States of America, we must first understand just what is meant by such type of American citizen.

As a practical proposition, he must be that kind of person and of such a nature that ordinary human beings by the exercise of social conduct, taking into consideration present-day living conditions, are within the realm of possibility for assimilation. Conditions must be such that the people of Latin extraction, with their peculiar characteristics, idiosyncrasies, natural instincts, temperament, social and intellectual background, as well as the environment, and the whole scheme of life of that particular race of people as distinguished from the above named features characteristic of Anglo-Saxon race can emulate our countrymen of other racial extractions.

It certainly cannot be expected of an organization whose high ideals are well-defined, and which is centered around the pivot of absolute American principles, to develop its work and carry into effect its teachings within the short period of two years in which it has been functioning. Rather, it is an arduous task that requires faith, patriotism, patience, courage, and a feeling of racial pride.

The methods, therefore, to be employed in putting into practice the apparent meaning of this article will necessarily vary in a given locality where the living conditions of the members differ from members in other places. For instance, the same rule could not be applicable in an agricultural area, where the membership is composed in its great majority of, for instance, cotton pickers, as against members in a large industrial city where, perhaps, the members are composed of professional men, like doctors, lawyers, engineers, etc.

However, our task is to develop as much as possible the best and purest type of a true and loyal American citizen, in which case the problem simplifies itself to the point that where a member is well-educated and intelligent, the work of the League as to him is rather minimal, whereas, in the instance of the common laborer, the work to be done is very great. We must seek to better his social position, his economic situation, strengthen his political rights, and endeavor to inculcate in him the principles of Americanism, civic duties, and his plain rights as an American citizen.

For the League to be successful in its work, it is necessary that we get our brains and hearts saturated with its teachings and to try to live up to them the best way each person understands it, taking these suggestions in mind.

However, I would say that if you want to be a one-hundred-percent American citizen, you must first learn the history of the United States, the meaning of the American flag, understand the Federal Constitution, and have sufficient background of English history to really appreciate the sacrifices of our forefathers who gave us this blessed land of freedom, as it stands today. To be an upright industrious citizen in the community in which you live, you must share your community burdens by participating in its civic affairs. If you show your fellow members deeds worthy of notice, that you are patriotic in your ideas, that you devote time for constructive work of a charitable nature, and do those things that build up character, until you get a well-deserved reputation as an honorable and industrious man in time of peace, always ready to volunteer to serve your country in time of war, those characteristics would appeal to me as the qualities necessary for our people to conform with the first basic principle of our organization.

El Defensor, June 6, 1931.

The Social Security Classification

When the U.S. Census Bureau identified Mexicans as colored in 1930, Mexican American activists decided to fight the classification tooth and nail. In 1935, after Congress passed the Social Security Act providing a federal retirement plan for the first time in history, the Social Security Board asked employers to enroll Mexicans as nonwhite. When LULAC and other Mexican American organizations discovered this, a major campaign ensued to reassign Mexicans to the white category. It was obvious to Mexican American leaders that being colored in America only invited second-class citizenship. The telegram shown below from Texas Congressman Joe Eagle is part of this intensive campaign.

Referring to item twelve of your form SS-5 Treasury Department Internal Revenue Service attached to application for account number STOP Item twelve seems to place Mexican citizens in some class other than white or Negro and requires description of color or race to which employee belongs and states typical examples of other color classifications are Mexican, Chinese, etc. STOP The more than sixty thousand citizens in Houston of Mexican descent unitedly protest that classification STOP They insist they belong to the white race having descended from Spanish STOP They urge, in agreement with hundreds of thousands in Texas belonging to the same racial group, that this discrimination is humiliating to their pride and unjust to their proper status, and they beg and urge that such classification as excludes from designation as white race be promptly amended STOP In this protest by them through me, I, as their Congressman and friend, join most earnestly.

Joe H. Eagle, M.C. Texas, to Frank Bane, Executive Director of the Social Security Board, November 25, 1936, typescript in J. Rodríguez Collection, Houston Metropolitan Research Center, Houston Public Library.

A Poignant Defense of the Whiteness of Mexicans

The Social Security issue was just an initial step in the effort to have whiteness conferred on Mexicans in the United States. The documents below reveal the intensity of this effort, which by 1940 resulted in Mexicans being officially classified as white in the United States census. This was clearly evident in the pronouncement in 1936 by the Mexican American district attorney of Laredo, John Valls. He made this statement during an interview for *La Prensa* in response to the classification of Mexicans as colored by the Registrar in El Paso in October of 1936.

I am delighted and inspired by the firm and vigorous attitude that the Latin community of El Paso has adopted in protesting against the behavior of several officials who have classified the Mexican people as a colored race.

The noble pride of the Mexican people, who were naturally and justly hurt by this insolent distinction inspired by ignorance and prejudice, immediately proceeded to vindicate the greatest qualities of their race and the purity of their blood.

Just remembering that cruel ignominy and the insult held in those declarations, my blood boils with indignation, and the patriotic feeling in my heart is exalted with resentment and grief.

The Mexican race is sensitive and noble. Mexicans have completely sacrificed their lives whenever their freedom and rights have been threatened; they have always been inspired by the highest sentiments: their devotion to honor and their scorn for immodesty.

People who recognize God, the dictates of conscience, and men's rights possess the spirit of true Americanism, regardless if it originates in the States of Maine or Texas and whether it is called Puritan or Mexican.

I do not wish to express myself in a vindicative or implacable manner, but for my compatriots, for the Mexican people, I invoke that spirit of justice that demands respect and the confidence that it carries.

Mexican people carry with them a sound legendary prestige of romance and chivalry. The stories retold in their history speak of epic heroism, and generous hearts are pleased in recalling them.

Such honorable and patriotic people rebel with indignation before the classification of their race as people of "color."

Through the people's veins runs a blood so rich and vigorous, the best that a man's beating heart can receive.

Holding in one hand the Constitution of our country and in the other the Bible of our God, without having to ask for forgiveness for anything in the past, satisfied with the present, and with the greatest faith in the future, we, those who have Latin blood running through our veins, stand strong before the entire world with as much pride and patriotism as the most distinguished person in this country.

We do not ask for special privileges. All that we ask for is equality in our rights, according to the law, and in that manner we will create our future with success and valor.

La Prensa, October 14, 1936.

Faith in Americanization

The bedrock faith that Mexican Americans had in Americanization is shown in an article by a lawyer in Phoenix, Arizona, who is half Mexican and who emphasizes the need for Mexicans to Americanize in order to deal with such issues as the justice system.

The Need for Americanization Among the Mexican People of Arizona

Member of the Latin American Club of Arizona

The question has been asked me whether or not there are an unusual number of Mexican subjects in the penitentiaries or other penal institutions of the State of Arizona as compared to other nationalities, and it has been suggested that I give my opinion as to the causes and reasons why such Mexican subjects find themselves in the toils of the law in any number at all.

First, we must take into account the fact that there are two distinct groups of Mexicans in the particular locality with which we have to deal. For instance, we have the native-born Mexicans, which compose a large part of our citizenry and who are in most part law abiding and interested in the community in which they reside; and then we have a group of transients, nomads who roam about from place to place in the southwest, keeping close to the border and following employment in the farming districts when the produces are in season, or laboring for railway companies. This latter group is usually of the ignorant or uneducated classes who have never had the opportunity to better their social condition, and who are the most gullible people in the world when they find themselves in a foreign and strange country faced with foreign and strange ways and looking to the guidance of what they consider representatives of law and order.

Of the first group, little may be said because there are not many of that group that find themselves confined in the penal institutions of our state because of infractions of the law. Of late years this group has associated together in various communities with the aim to uplift and assist one another and other groups of Mexicans who may need assistance of any kind or character; this group forms a portion of our desirable citizenry. They have been here years and expect to continue as residents of this, the only country they know, and just as much their country as it is that of any other person residing within its borders. They follow their various professions, vocations, and labors diligently; they are, as a rule, educated in at least two languages; they are industrious and ambitious, but they have that well-known failing that is so popular among all merchants, to wit, they spend every cent that they make as a rule, and for that reason there are not a great many outstanding financiers in their midst.

Of the second group there are a great many that are serving all sorts of terms in different penal institutions. The astounding fact that of the number arrested a larger percentage are convicted than any other group of nationals is no doubt attributive to some of their characteristics enumerated above.

I have in mind especially two men who are awaiting the outcome of their appeal from a conviction imposing the death penalty. I happened to be present at the time one of these men was interrogated by the County Attorney when he was arrested, and it was apparent to me that the prisoner was at a point where he would answer any questions made to him in just the manner that the questioner wanted them answered. It was apparent to me that he had been questioned along the same lines many times before and that he had been told that it would be better for him to answer the questions in the manner desired by those in authority. This particular instance could not be remedied at the time that I observed it for the reason that the subject was too much in the influence of the authorities, and in my estimation he was at that very time insane mentally.

The only purpose of mentioning the above incident is the illustration of what I am about to say of the group referred to. When arrested, these men and women are easily intimidated and often admit things that have never occurred, for the sake of being pleasant and agreeable to those in authority of the country in which they find themselves. Again and again I have noticed that men of this type often times take the blame for things they have not done rather than state the true facts and involve some other person who had not yet been connected with the offense. The records will show that there are more pleads of guilty among this group than any other group of nationals.

The conclusion that I come to upon analyzing this set of facts is that the Mexican nationals in this country find themselves in trouble through timidity and ignorance of the law and customs of this country and in their faith in their fellow man. It is clear to me that a great many, as I have above stated, would avoid the penalties which they are paying if they would exercise the constitutional rights of our citizenry in keeping their own counsel by saying nothing and by availing themselves of competent legal services just as other more enlightened groups do. An educational campaign among these classes along the proper lines would do much toward making better and more law-abiding citizens than any other thing, and, too, they should be encouraged in fitting themselves and applying for naturalization.

William J. Fellows, "The Need for Americanization Among the Mexican People of Arizona," *El Latino Americano,* Vol. 1 (April 1934), p. 6.

Bert Corona and Mexican Americanism

Bert Corona, a lifelong warrior for civil rights, a union organizer, and an exponent of radical politics, recalled in a recent interview how he worked with the youth-oriented Mexican American Movement as a young man and in the more radical Congress of Spanish Speaking People. In Corona's mind, both movements converge or are considered part of this generation's political activity. Both organizations sought the betterment of Mexican Americans at a time in which they had become more aware of their rights. The Mexican American Movement urged education and social mobility for young people, while the Congress was concerned with improving the conditions in which Mexican Americans lived, regardless of whether or not they transcended the economic position to which they were relegated. Corona supported both positions.

In 1936, I was involved in two movements. The longshoremen were on a one-hundred-day strike and had shut down all the ports between San Diego and Alaska to Hawaii, and this was being discussed in a political science course that I was taking at the University of Southern California. It was affecting the shipment of drugs. Brunswick Drugs was one of the biggest in the nation; they manufactured a line of pharmaceuticals and drugs at a big seven- or eight-story laboratory building that still exists at 2nd and Central. So they came to our warehouse and asked if we could give them support; we were not organized, and we were not unionized. They were asking for support from hardware industry warehouses, paper warehouses, general warehouses, commercial warehouses, etc. At the same time I was going to church in the east side. My folks were Congregationalists, but we visited Presbyterian and Baptist and sometimes Methodist churches in East Los Angeles. A movement was started up called the Mexican American Movement and people like Félix Gutiérrez, Sr., and Paul Coroniel, Steve Gutiérrez from Pasadena. . . Some of these people were in the universities and colleges and others were teachers or social workers, Alberto Valadez in Placencia and other people. . . So that was focusing on the needs of the Spanish-speaking youth, Mexican youth, to obtain a decent education, obtain decent opportunities, etc. A series of conferences were organized through the South West YMCA to form the organization. Out of the leadership of Félix Gutiérrez and Juan Acevedo came a monthly magazine, *Mexican Voice*. I got very much involved in that and with the Mexican American Movement and the Mexican Youth Conference. In my place of work, very soon after the 1936 strike, longshore organizers, volunteers, and some, I guess, on staff came and began a drive to organize the wholesale drug industry workers and, of course, they also moved in to organize the paper warehouses. . . Zellerbach and others; hardware wholesale industry like California Hardware, Union Hardware; the paper hardware; and the drug warehouses. Those were the ones. Incidently, as we moved along in organizing these industries, I was a volunteer organizer. I was elected recording secretary of the local 26 of the Longshoremen and Warehousemen Union while working at Brunswick Drugs. I was not a paid officer. I helped to organize with paid organizers, before work and after work. Then I also participated very actively with a great deal of interest in organizing the waste material, used glass, used bottles, used metal, and used rags industry.

Workers were unorganized in many industries. They were being organized then by the Congress of Industrial Organizations, CIO, the automobiles, the rubber, the steel, the furniture, and many other industries, as well as the longshoremen organizing distribution and warehousing and packaging and other industries. The commitment to that was the rising movement of the Mexican American young people that were going to college, all these people that I mentioned. They wanted to work and organize for a better life for the Mexican youth that were coming behind them. These were people that were already in college or had made it through college. Some of them were excellent teachers like Dora Ibáñez—her father was a minister in La Verne; her brother Richard Ibáñez was a very prominent judge and attorney here. So they were people who were ahead, socially and economically, of the mass of Mexican immigrants and people born here. The two movements were parallel in their efforts focusing on different aspects. By 1938, there developed a movement called the Congress of the Spanish Speaking People, whose head organizer was a union organizer by the name of Luisa Moreno, who is still alive although very sick. She lives in Guatemala. She was the international vice president of the CIO and of the United Cannery Agricultural and Packing Workers of America. She had taken a year off to organize the Spanish Speaking People's Congress. In 1937 or '38, they tried to have the first Congress in Albuquerque, but they were driven out of there by the House Committee on Un-American Activities. They came before Congress and were red-baited. . . Dr. George Sánchez and the other professor there at the University of New Mexico, I can't think of his name. So they had to cancel the convening of the Congress, and it was moved to Los Angeles.

Bert Corona, interviewed by Luis Torres, September 29, 1992, Transcript made by the National Latino Communications Center (NLCC).

World War II and Mexican Americans

In the World War II era, California was popularly known as the place to be if you were a Mexican—internal migration from New Mexico and Arizona was tremendous. In addition, many World War II veterans moved to the Golden State. They were returning with more confidence in themselves and would not settle for the role to which Mexicans had been relegated in the generation of their fathers. In responding to the question of what Mexican American soldiers could expect in California, MAM activists, such as Félix Gutiérrez, felt optimistic about the possibilities that California offered veterans. In the following piece, the Mexican American message of how ex-soldiers should and could integrate into the larger society was promoted.

Several servicemen have written to us and asked for the "lowdown" on things "Mexican" in Southern California. It's very flattering because WE DON'T know the "lowdown" and we doubt if anyone does.

For the benefit of the servicemen, we will write down our impressions of the things we have seen and experienced . . .

JOBS

Jobs are the first thing and foremost in the minds of most servicemen. Right now, the industries are not too choosey in whom they hire, providing a person is qualified for the job. Opportunities are now open to Mexican American fellows and girls that were never there before the war. Many of our employees are breaking down prejudices because of their efficiency and desire to please. At the same time, especially among our younger fellows, their work is not as satisfactory as it should be. This impression is gained from a conference we attended where employers aired their views on employees of Mexican descent. After the war . . . that is the catch, will industries continue to hire on qualifications? Or will they return to the prewar attitudes of America for Americans?

Somehow, we feel that we have a little of both because in this war Americans of Mexican descent have proven that they are individuals and that they can tackle jobs of high skill, can supervise and lead, and that the employer can no longer generalize on the ability of the whole group. In other words, the industrial inroads made have been too great to be forgotten when peace returns.

HAVE SLACKENED

Yes, discrimination and prejudice have slackened a little. Public opinion has switched a little to the side of those of Mexican descent.

Whether this is a normal growth . . . the Good Neighbor Policy . . . the war . . . education . . . we don't know. We do know that things are better than before the war.

For example, we see things that we never saw much of before. Young fellows of Mexican descent with commissions in the Air Corps, Infantry Signal Corps, Navy, walking down First Street or Broadway in Los Angeles. We see Mexican girls walking down the street arm in arm, or in groups with others not of Mexican descent. Ditto for the boys. We see *paisanos* dating blonds from the westside. And yet at the other extreme we still see our gang groups dating their own chicks in their own social neighborhood group. Another thing that we have noticed is that the above-average American of Mexican descent is moving away from his "*vecindad.*" The trend is to move into American neighborhoods. As one fellow told us, "I want my kids to have a better chance. I want to be American. To get work, get a better deal in a mixed school." We see intermarriage . . . As yet this is not a general practice, but it is happening among our "adjusted" youth and those who have lived in mixed neighborhoods. Even the newspapers who once capitalized on a few *pachuco* and servicemen incidents to make them large gang wars, are now cooperating by giving gang juvenile delinquency very little new space. This you can chalk up as one point for democracy.

"Nosotros," *Mexican Voice,* Vol. 6 (Summer 1944), p. 12.

A Veteran Returns to Mexico

Vito Zavala, a veteran of the war and a prisoner of war, was the object of discrimination in Texas after the war. He went to live in Mexico, where he was born, although his parents took him to the United States when he was only three. In February of 1945, Zavala wrote to *Fraternidad,* the publication put out by El Comité Contra el Racismo in Mexico City. The letter reprinted below is indicative of the feelings of many Mexican American veterans, who after fighting for their country and for freedom, were discriminated against upon returning to the United States.

I have just become aware of a magazine titled "Fraternidad" (Brotherhood), which is part of the same committee, and since its content was of interest to me, I take the liberty of sending you this letter to tell you a story which other young men like me have experienced. I feel that it supports the objectives you pursue.

My name is Vito Zavala. I am twenty years old. I was born in Mexico, but when I was three, my parents went to live in the United States, and for that reason I have spent most of my life in that country. When the war between the United States and Germany broke out, I volunteered to serve in the North American military. I was then seventeen. After a year of training, I was sent to Sicily in a battalion of five hundred and one paratroopers. I was held captive by the Germans and was sent to a concentration camp. Some time later, I was exchanged and returned to the United States.

Upon my return to North America, after having fought for the democratic principles that I so much admire, I thought that the United States, the country for which I fought, would treat me as one of them. I was wrong. One day, while I was at Minor Wells in the State of Texas, I went to a restaurant dressed in my Army uniform. I asked for service and it was denied to me. I asked the reason for this, and I was told that I was Mexican and that I could not be served. I insisted once again, telling them that I was also a soldier in the Army, but they did not pay attention to me, and I was told that that place did not serve Mexicans, even if they wore an Army uniform.

Disillusioned, deeply hurt in my dignity as man and as a Mexican, thinking that my sacrifice of fighting for Democracy had been useless, if such absurd racial prejudices still existed in the country for which I had gone to expose my body, I asked to be discharged from the Army, and I came to Mexico, my country.

Here, in my nation, I feel like a new man. I am working and no one looks at me as though I were strange. I can go in wherever I want and obtain whatever services I need. I am happy to have returned and to know that my compatriots here in my homeland are working to abolish shameful discrimination practices.

Yours truly, sincerely.

"Carta de un mexicano," *Fraternidad: Órgano del Comité contra el Racismo,* Vol. 2 (June 1, 1945), p. 13.

Protesting Lack of Recognition During World War II

A *LULAC News* editorial in 1945 called aggressively for equal treatment by reminding Americans of all that Mexican Americans had done during World War II for the United States, a country built on principles of equality. The piece is a good example of how civil rights activists used the fact that Mexican Americans had fought against totalitarianism as a wedge for demanding full integration into American life. The piece also expresses umbrage over being mislabeled as nonwhite.

"We do not serve Mexicans here." "You will have to get out as no Mexicans are allowed." "Your uniform and service ribbons mean nothing here. We still do not allow Mexicans."

These, and many other stronger-worded ones, are the embarrassing and humiliating retorts given our returning veterans of Latin American descent and their families. They may all be worded differently, and whereas some are toned with hate and loathness while others are toned with sympathy and remorse, still the implication remains that these so-called "Mexicans" are considered unworthy of equality, regardless of birthright or service. This situation is ironic indeed, in view of the fact that these same "Mexicans" have just finished helping this country to defeat countries to the east and west who would impose upon the world a superior people, a superior culture.

Why this hate, this prejudice, this tendency to discriminate against a people whose only fault seems to be that they are heirs of a culture older than any known "American Culture," to find themselves a part of a land and people they have helped to build and to defend, to find themselves a part of a minority group whose acquired passive nature keeps them from boldly demanding those rights and privileges which are rightfully theirs? Can it be the result of difference in race, nationality, language, loyalty, intelligence or ability?

There is no difference in race. Latin Americans, or so-called "Mexicans," are Caucasian or white. There are only three races: the Caucasian, the Negroid, and the Mongoloid. Racial characteristics place the Latin American among the white. Who dares contradict nature? There is no difference in nationality. These "Mexicans" were born and bred in this country and are just as American as Jones or Smith. In fact, the ancestors of these "Mexicans" were here before those of Jones or Smith decided to take up abode. Difference in language? No. These "Mexicans" speak English. Accented, perhaps, in some cases, but English all over the United States seems to be accented. That these "Mexicans" can speak Spanish is not a detriment; it is an asset. After all, there are not too many people in this country who can boast a knowledge of the most widely spoken languages in the world. Difference in loyalty? How can that be when all revere the same stars and stripes, when they don the same service uniforms for the same principles? Difference in intelligence and ability? Impossible. For every profession and category of work, from menial labor to the most scientific and technical matter, there is a qualified group of "Mexicans." All they need is the opportunity minus the discrimination and jealousy.

We could go on and on naming erroneously imagined differences to be used as a basis for this hate and find each one false. This condition is not a case of difference; it is a case of ignorance. Yes, ignorance. Odd indeed to find this banal state of mind in a country of such enlightenment and progress. But then, ignorance is like a disease that is contagious, but contagious only for those who wish to suffer from it. Ignorance, bigotry, prejudice, and intolerance all down through the centuries have tried to crush intelligence with cruelty, reason with brutality, and spirituality with madness. This quartet of banalities constitutes the curse of the world. Ignorance is the parent of the other three.

Yes, ignorance broods hate and all its resultant actions of jealousy, misunderstandings, erroneous opinions, and premeditated feelings of discord and confusion. In this particular case of unjustified failure to foment a fraternal feeling between two groups of Americans, it is an ignorance of facts that poisons the atmosphere. An ignorance of the cultural contributions of Americans of Latin American descent to the still young American Culture; an ignorance of the blood, sweat, and efforts given to this country for its betterment; an ignorance of the sufferings withstood and the lives given to preserve this country free and independent through its various periods of strife and conflict; and finally, an ignorance of a sense of appreciation for a long, profitable, and loyal association with a group of Americans whose voice cries out in desperate supplication:

"We have proved ourselves true and loyal Americans by every trial and test that has confronted us; now give us social, political, and economic equality and the opportunity to practice and enjoy that equality. We ask for it not as a favor, but as a delegated right guaranteed by our Constitution, and as a reward for faithful service."

"Editorial," *LULAC News*, Vol. 12 (October 1945), pp. 5-6.

The Optimism of Returning Soldiers

Raúl Morín, a World War II veteran and civil rights activist, captured the optimism felt by Mexican American G.I.s in his much heralded book, *Among the Valiant*, which chronicled the feats of Mexicans in World War II and the Korean War. This work made the much accepted claim that Mexican Americans were the most decorated ethnic group because of heroic action. Below he discusses the expectations felt by returning Mexican American veterans that they would no longer be second-class citizens in the United States.

It felt very good to have come back from the wars. Things were happening to us that had never happened before. This was a new America for us . . . we felt like shouting . . . *Hey! We did it! The Allies won the war, and the Americans played a prominent part in it. Americans! . . . that meant us!* As returning veterans, we were being welcomed enthusiastically everywhere. We were openly admired, loved, and respected. It was a wonderful feeling; we were overwhelmed.

Most returning American war veterans found very few changes in their hometowns. Overjoyed with excitement incident to being home again, they gave no thought nor noticed many changes in the American way of life. Furthermore, most of them did not want it to be any different from that of the day they had left. This was home . . . they preferred it this way—this was the way they remembered it in their dreams during the long days overseas.

For the returning Mexican-American veteran, things *were* different, and furthermore, he did not want to find things the way he had left them. Not that he had not dreamed of coming home to his loved ones, but there were a few things he did not care for when he got back.

For too long we had been like outsiders. It had never made very much difference to us, and we hardly noticed it until we got back from overseas. How could we have played such a prominent part as Americans over there and now have to go back living as outsiders as before? We began to ask ourselves, how come? How long had we been missing out on benefits derived as an American citizen? Old-timers had told us and we had read in books how the early settlers had invaded our towns and had shoved us into the "other side of the tracks." But we ourselves had never made much attempt to move out of there. The towns had grown up; population had increased; state, county, city, and community government had been set up, and we had been left out of it. We never had any voice. Here, now, was the opportunity to do something about it.

Soon now, we left the other side of the tracks and began to move into town. We moved to better neighborhoods, and thanks to the GI Bill, we continued our education. We were able to buy new homes. We began to go into business for ourselves, obtain better positions of employment, and some even managed to get chosen, appointed or elected to public office.

We acquired new ways in everyday doings. New thoughts and dreams entered our minds. We embarked on many unheard-of-for-us-projects and developed many ideas and new perspectives. In the old days, our lives were governed mostly by patterns set by our elders. We had accepted without question edicts, taboos, restrictions, traditions, and customs that our ancestors had brought over from the old country. Many such were long since outdated in Mexico proper. After having been to many other parts of the world, meeting other people from different parts of the country, we cast aside these old beliefs and we began anew in America.

Raúl Morín, *Among the Valiant* (Los Angeles: Borden Publishing Co., 1963), pp. 277-279.

El Club Chapultepec

The clarion call for the ambitious young was education and self-improvement. Conceivably, education could eradicate the discrimination and mistreatment Mexicans suffered. Youth clubs, such as Houston's El Club Chapultepec, made up of young Mexican American girls, followed this ethos. They strove for education and mobility. In June 1937, when a young Mexican had been killed in his Houston city jail cell by his jailers, the group protested in writing. Its letter condemned police misconduct, but a major cause of such injustices, the statement read, stemmed from Mexicans' difficulty with English. It was crucial for Mexicans to learn to speak and write good English, a goal the club established for itself.

The Chapultepec Club of the Houston Y.W.C.A. has the following to offer as findings from their study of minorities. Here in Texas they [the club members] happen to constitute a minority group themselves and are called Mexicans. Some of the group were born in Mexico and have not taken out citizenship papers. [The] reason [is as] follows: Many were born in Texas and are therefore American citizens but are still called Mexicans. The group is made up of an excellent cross section of the Mexican colony in Houston. There are several high school graduates in the group, and, of course, every year more Mexicans are staying in school until graduation.

These are the problems that these young Mexican girls and women face in Texas, and they wonder what the future will be for them and their children. From this study, they hope sincerely for recommendations from the National B. & P. Council on action they can take to better understanding, respect, and opportunity. They recognize that minority groups elsewhere in the United States face some, though not all, of the same problems.

1. Texas is next door to Mexico, and there are bordertown problems to be considered, historically as well as at present. Texas history is founded on troubles, oft created by Texans, to get land and cattle from the Mexican people. [N]ow the problem of stolen automobiles is causing the same problem, and also the water power of the Rio Grande River is causing hard feelings.

2. Texas cannot, due to Chamber of Commerce and patriotic society activities, forget that Texas lost a tragic battle at the [A]lamo in San Antonio and won a battle at San Jacinto. This causes teachers to preach a patriotism not kind to Mexican children. Mexicans have been known to stay out of school [in Houston] when that part of history was being taught because of abuses inflicted by pupils and even teachers.

3. Mexicans in [a] desire to get ahead have at times denied their nationality calling themselves French, Italian, and Spanish. This induces the Mexican colony's disfavor. Nationalistic spirit [is] being cultured at present [and] this of course can be as dangerous an attitude as the denial [of] one. If they should move back to Mexico, they are considered traitors for having lived in Texas.

4. They do not take out citizenship papers because those who have are still called Mexicans and treated as such.

5. The Mexican people find it impossible to rent or buy in any decent section of town and are forced to live in dirty, crowded conditions in houses out of which Americans have moved.

6. Playgrounds and parks show distinct distaste to their presence on them, and in some cases they are ordered off or forbidden on. This problem is caused by the youth and not the recreation leaders.

7. Falsely accused of many crimes in the city and because of some difficulty with the English language, they are taken advantage of frequently.

8. Mexican people are paid less in wages on all jobs, and a great many jobs and industries are closed to them.

9. Mexican lawyers receive no respect from other lawyers nor even from our judges. It is a well-known fact that a case is practically lost if a Mexican lawyer handles it. Justice is very one-sided, and they have had some rather serious cases recently.

10. They are called "brown people," "greasers," etcetera, and of course want to be called white.

This letter is also going to Beatrice Langley, and at the same time the group is also sending a letter to the American Youth Congress protesting certain movies which have been shown in Texas portraying the Mexicans in a very bad light.

Tom Kreneck, "The Letter From Chapultepec," *Houston Review*, Vol. 3 (Summer 1981), pp. 268-269.

The Citizen's Committee for Latin American Youth

Lawyer Manuel Ruiz, chairman of the Citizen's Committee for Latin American Youth in Los Angeles, wrote this piece in response to the anti-*Pachuco* hysteria that had hit Los Angeles during the war. In 1942, twenty-two teenagers were tried for the killing of another Mexican teenager at a party in Sleepy Lagoon. The group was convicted on very weak evidence and sentenced on charges ranging from assault to first-degree murder. In 1944, an appeal resulted in reversal of the charges because of the biases that permeated the first trial. But the event clearly demonstrated that exaggerated hostility existed towards Mexican American youth. In fact, Mexican American leaders quickly attempted to turn this dilemma of *Pachucos* to their advantage. Wartime rhetoric in the press turned public opinion against Mexican American youth, whose attire was considered odd or foreign by mainstream society. Here, Ruiz attempted to reverse the negative stereotypes by depicting Mexican American youth as poor, isolated, and ignored by mainstream society. He argued that this neglect only had a negative effect on building the unity necessary during the war.

It all started when the law enforcement authorities decided to crack down. There had been some hesitation to do so; in fact some of the leaders of the Latin American community in Los Angeles had indirectly been sounded out by the expedient of being let in on the "problem." Those in authority, too, realized that there were international aspects involved, which could easily result in delicate complications. It was too late to deal with the causes for delinquency in those areas where the Latin American preponderated. While preventive measures would solve the problem as to the next crop of youngsters coming up, something had to be done NOW, concerning those juveniles who were giving vent to their exuberance on the community at large.

The police question of how to crack down was not a simple one. The orthodox course of rounding up the leaders, and making summary examples of them, was out. Already too much time had been lost in looking for the leaders. Inspector Lester of the Los Angeles Police Department, Juvenile Detail, admitted that the department had been unable to find leaders. The only alternative left then, was simply to make mass arrests, and leave it up to the courts to separate the chaff from the wheat. Once this course was decided on, it was rapidly put into execution.

When groups of twenty and thirty arrestees began to appear on the police blotters, the element that makes for news and sensationalism was seized upon by the press. Instead of arresting two or three troublemakers for disturbing the peace at some dance, the authorities arrested, on one occasion, as high as seventy-two; the charge was unlawful assembly. Whenever a group of young boys, even on slight pretext, could be rounded up, they were arrested. If circumstances did not permit this direct action, the group, which might consist of anywhere from four to ten boys, was made to disperse.

Naturally, the wholesale arrest procedure gave a distorted picture. Although the rate of juvenile delinquency convictions did not rise over any other similar period of time among youngsters of Mexican extraction, this significant factor was lost, as the press continued to lay emphasis on group apprehensions. The part of the public that informs itself by news headlines received a picture of roving gangs of bloodthirsty, marihuana-crazed young men, committing arson, rape, and robbery.

Then something happened. The stage was set for international intrigue. Three prominent officials in Los Angeles County were directly misquoted to the effect that these boy gangs were inspired by Nazi and Fascist agents. The misquotations prompted by communistic sources laid the trouble at the feet of Mexican Sinarquists. Rome, Tokyo, and Berlin countered to the effect that the boys were not henchmen, but simply victims of Anglo-American persecution, while the United States extended the good neighbor smile and glad-hand to Latin America, its racial bigotry was patent in that thousands of boys of Latin American extraction were without cause being thrown into jail and persecuted, and that the nations to the South had better guard themselves in the future. From a distorted local problem, the matter had now become a distorted international problem.

Knowing that wherever there was smoke, there must of necessity be a fire, the United States Department of Information sent Mr. Allan Cranston, assistant to Mr. Elmer Davis, to look for its existence and, by applying the correct remedy, extinguish it. The Los Angeles County Grand Jury had already gathered facts indicating the dangerous flame had been nurtured many years by an apathetic community. Karl Holton, Los Angeles County chief probation officer, and Judge Robert Scott, presiding judge of the Juvenile Court in Los Angeles, had constantly called attention to it, but the facilities they had had to work with had been limited, and public support had altogether never been forthcoming.

But the flame had burned brightly. There it was! The community had blinded itself to the fact that there was in our midst a large group of children of immigrant parents. Somehow or another, the people had not considered this problem as one of recent immigration. Many had gotten sidetracked on arbitrary racial theories imported from the deep south, which had made matters worse. Our Atlantic seaboard cities, accustomed to handling recent arrivals and their children for more than a hundred years, recognized symptoms and causes and by experimentation learned curative techniques. Los Angeles had had only one brief experience some twenty years ago, and that with a Russian community of recent immigrants. By recognizing that problem as one of immigration, it had been attacked as such at the core and dissipated.

Because of our failure to diagnose the problem, owing to the general idea that immigrants solely come from Europe, certain erroneous conceptions resulted—thus, the statement of one high public school official, "Why these people are not recent arrivals, they were here before the Americans came, their capacity is limited, they slow up other school children, and therefore should be segregated." Another important person has said, "They are lazy, have no ambition, and won't take advantage of opportunities offered them."

Effective parental cooperation of these minors has not been organized chiefly because of the existence of a law in this State to the effect that no foreign language may be used in the public school system as a means to teach any curricular subject, whether it be Americanization, hygiene, or anything else. Spanish may be taught, but the Spanish language cannot be used to teach. For years, this language barrier has been criticized by those who know that parental education of newly arrived immigrants is important, but nothing has been done about it. Those in public office who are advocating the importation into the United States of Mexican workers, as a temporary help to economic manpower dislocation, would do well to advocate legislation to hasten processes of assimilation. At cross purposes with this law of superimposing English has been the reluctance upon the part of parent immigrants to give up their mother tongue, Spanish, by reason of their proximity to the Mexican border and a feeling that soon they would return to Mexico.

As for the children, first generation Americans, the approach to their parents in Spanish will not deter the latter in our program of Americanization. The apparent retention upon the part of many youngsters of a thick Spanish accent, interpreted by some as a lack of interest in American institutions, is simply the result of their residing in communities where all of the oldsters speak Spanish in the home. This situation exists almost 100 percent in some localities where we find the younger people actually learning English with a Spanish accent. This bilingual problem does not exist, however, where the youngster of Mexican extraction has gone to school in an Anglo-American neighborhood.

Coming from poor families from the old country, the youngsters have gone into manual and vocational occupations, to more quickly and directly help the family larder. Those who have managed to get along farther in skilled occupations, wherein they compete with Anglo-Americans, have been called uncomplimentary words and refused jobs. Economic discrimination has existed. Younger brothers, noting the said experience suffered by their older, more ambitious brothers, have naturally not wanted to repeat what to them has been a mistake and are listless to pep talks about the advantages of training, thus resulting in an opinion on the part of some people, that many of these people lack ambition and won't take advantage of opportunities in education offered them.

This brief article, however, cannot linger with causative details. To succinctly put the matter, the problem has by Federal impetus finally been placed in its true perspective. As a direct result of this impetus, a citizen's committee for Latin American youth has been organized in the City and County of Los Angeles. From a study of facts this committee has suggested a specific program by way of requesting and recommending definite steps to be taken. Thus, some of the measures advocated as sound, for the betterment of the total population, are couched in the following language:

(1) We request the Mayor of Los Angeles and the Los Angeles County Board of Supervisors to work together where possible and individually where necessary to achieve the following objectives:
a. Increased training school facilities for war work in Spanish-speaking neighborhoods.
b. Special transportation facilities for Spanish-speaking people to existing training schools until better located schools are established.
c. Additional Spanish-speaking personnel in present and future training schools.
d. Night use of indoor school facilities for recreational purposes in Spanish-speaking communities.

e. Use of these recreational facilities on weekends.

f. Additional athletic equipment, lockers, and other facilities for recreation centers.

g. Additional Spanish-speaking supervisors for recreation projects.

h. Spanish-speaking attorneys as public defenders in local courts.

i. Enforcement of antidiscrimination ordinances governing public places, and the erection of suitable signs indicating equal access without discrimination for all persons.

j. Establishment of more forestry camps for juveniles between the ages of 13 and 15 on probation.

k. Release of boys on probation to enrollment in vocational National Youth Administration and similar training programs.

l. Use of Spanish-speaking law enforcement officers on cases involving Spanish-speaking juveniles.

m. More Spanish-speaking law enforcement officers in Spanish-speaking communities.

n. Provision in the regular training curricula of law enforcement officers for education in minority group's problems as is already done in New York, Chicago, and other major American communities.

o. Execution of police powers of law enforcement agencies equally and without undue emphasis against persons of Mexican extraction.

p. A general agreement with the press to cut to a minimum the publication of names of juvenile delinquents.

q. Establishment of nurseries in Spanish-speaking neighborhoods for mothers employed in war work.

r. Establishment of special training classes to provide Spanish-speaking personnel for jobs mentioned above in cases where competent personnel is now available.

s. Establishment of a procedure whereby competent Spanish-speaking personnel can be certified for temporary civil service jobs for the duration of the war in cases where present civil service regulations make it impossible to employ competent Spanish-speaking personnel.

(2) We request the State Youth Correction Authority to use current funds for the establishment of additional recreation facilities.

(3) We request the President of the United States to issue executive orders relaxing restrictions on friendly and allied aliens who are now denied full participation in and enjoyment of:

a. Federal housing projects.

b. National Youth Administration.

c. Civil service.

d. Restricted war contracts.

e. Civilian defense.

f. Privilege of enlistment in armed forces.

(4) We request the War Manpower Commission and the President's Committee on Fair Employment Practice to increase their efforts to open war industry jobs to workers of Mexican extraction and to provide more Spanish-speaking personnel in local offices of the United States Employment Service and to open a branch of the United States Employment Service in Belvedere and other communities where need is indicated.

(5) We request the Office of War Information:

a. To intensify its Spanish-speaking language information work among Spanish-speaking peoples in this area in order to increase their understanding of and participation in the war effort.

b. To assist in an information campaign designed to inform the local English-speaking population of the part played by the local Spanish-speaking population in the war, and

c. To assist in an information campaign designed to publicize the progress of the local program for better understanding between Americans and between the Americas.

(6) We request the United States Treasury Department to conduct a vigorous war bond drive in the Spanish language in this area.

(7) We request the American Red Cross to establish training centers and blood donor centers in Spanish-speaking communities under the supervision of Spanish-speaking personnel.

(8) We request the United Service Organization to establish centers in Spanish-speaking communities under the supervision of Spanish-speaking personnel.

(9) We request the Coordinator of Inter-American Affairs:

a. To open a regional office in Los Angeles to coordinate our internal policy toward Latin Americans and our foreign policy toward Latin America, and

b. To publicize the progress of the local program for better understanding between Americans and between the Americas.

Manuel Ruiz, "Bomb or Bubble," typed manuscript of article that appeared in *Crime Prevention Digest,* Vol. 1 (December 1942), 10 pages, In Carey McWilliams Collection, Special Collections 1243, Box 29, University of California, Los Angeles.

The Spears Bill

In 1945, a Texas state legislator named J. Franklin Spears lent his name to a bill that would make it illegal to discriminate against and segregate Mexican Americans. Mexican American civil rights activists, heartened by this gesture, rallied to support the politician's efforts, which to their disappointment was not put to the vote. Reproduced here is the bill itself as written by Spears.

Be It Enacted by the Legislature of the State of Texas:

Section 1. Friendly relations between the people of this State and the people of our neighbor Mexico and of Central and South America is hereby declared to be a public policy of this State.

Section 2. It is found that a large proportion of Texas citizens and residents are of Mexican or Latin American origin; that there is a substantial amount of travel in this State by persons of Mexican or Latin American origin; that discrimination against such persons of Mexican or Latin American origin exists in this State by persons who own or operate public places which cater to the public for business or profit; that a continuation of such discrimination causes social unrest and domestic strife, which affects the public safety, welfare, and health of citizens of this State and generates feelings of ill will and malice which adversely affect intrastate commerce and business and is against the public welfare. It is hereby declared to be the public policy of this State to eliminate such discrimination.

Section 3. All hotels, lodging houses, restaurants, eating places, opera houses, theatres, moving picture houses, melodeons, museums, circuses, caravans, race courses, fairs, and other public enterprises which are owned or operated within the State of Texas for the purpose of catering to the public for business or profit are hereby declared to be dedicated to the public interest and vested with a public use and to be public utilities to the extent necessary for the effective carrying out of the provisions of this Act.

Section 4. The term "catering to the public for business or profit" as used in this act shall mean any business enterprise (other than a private club, lodge, or society with a limited membership which is selected according to a plan approved in advance by a majority of its members) which holds itself out for patronage by members of the public and sells goods, services, or entertainment to the public for the purpose of profit.

Section 5. The term "Mexican or Latin American origin" as used in this act shall mean any person who is a citizen of the Islands of the West Indies or who is related in the third degree by affinity or consanguinity to any person who is or was a citizen of any of these countries or places.

Section 6. No person, firm, association of persons, or corporation, or their servants or agents that own or operate any business enterprise or place of business engaged in catering to the public for business or profit shall deny to any person because of his or her Mexican or Latin-American origin equal facilities, privileges, accommodations, or services with any other person who is a member of the public in such business enterprise or place of business.

Section 7. Any person, firm, association of persons, or corporation and/or their servants or agents who shall knowingly violate the provisions of Section 6 hereof, shall be guilty of a misdemeanor and upon conviction thereof shall be fined in an amount of not more than five hundred ($500) dollars or imprisoned for a period of not more than thirty days or both.

Section 8. Any person, firm, association of persons, or corporation and/or their servants or agents who violate Section 6 hereof, shall be liable to the person or persons discriminated against for the actual damages suffered, plus the sum of one hundred ($100) dollars exemplary damages, all of which may be recoverable in a suit at law brought in a court of proper jurisdiction.

Section 9. All of the provisions of this act shall be liberally construed for the accomplishment of the purposes herein set out.

Section 10. All laws and parts of laws in conflict with the provisions of this act are hereby repealed.

Section 11. The fact that there are thousands of men and women in our armed services of Mexican or Latin American origin and millions of such persons in the armies of the United Nations who are giving their lives that others may enjoy freedom and liberty, and the fact that prejudice and the lack of understanding on the part of some of our citizens are denying to these fine soldiers in Texas the things that they are fighting for abroad, creates an emergency and an imperative public necessity that the constitutional rule requiring bills to be read on three several days in each house be suspended, and said rule is hereby suspended, and this act shall take effect and be in full force from and after its passage, and it is so enacted.

S.B. 1. A Bill by Spears, undated transcript, typescript in LULAC collection, Houston Metropolitan Research Center, Houston Public Library.

Méndez v. Westminster

Below, the landmark *Méndez v. Westminster* of 1946 is reproduced. This case was proba-bly the most sweeping victory for desegregation warriors from the Mexican American generation. Affecting thousands of children in California, it served as a precedent and learn-ing experience for Mexican American civil rights activists who continued to desegregate schools in other regions of California and the Southwest throughout the 1940s and 1950s.

MÉNDEZ et al. v. WESTMINISTER SCHOOL DIST. OF ORANGE COUNTY et al.
Civil Action No. 4292.

District Court, S. D. California, Central Division.

Feb. 18, 1946.

1. Courts -282(3)

   Education is a state matter but not absolutely or exclusively, and a violation by a state of a personal right or privilege protected by the Fourteenth Amendment in exercise of the state's duty to provide for education would justify the federal court in intervening.

2. Courts -282(3)

   A complaint, alleging an invasion by common school authorities of the equal oppor-tunity of pupils of Mexican ancestry or descent as result of their segregation to acquire knowledge, conferred jurisdiction on District Court if the actions com-plained of were deemed those of the state. Jud.Code § 24(14), 28 U.S.C.A. § 41(14); U.S.C.A. Const.Amend. 14.

3. Schools and school districts -11

   The public school system of California is a matter of state supervision, being of gen-eral concern, though the various local school districts enjoy a considerable degree of autonomy. Const.Cal. art. 9.

4. Courts -282(3)

   Common school authorities in California are representatives of the state to such an extent and in such a sense that district court has jurisdiction of action against them to restrain segregation of children of Mexican or Latin descent in alleged violation of the equal protection of Laws requirement of the Constitution. Const. Cal. art. 9; Education Code Cal. § 2204; Jud.Code § 24(14), 28 U.S.C.A. § 41(14); U.S.C.A.Const.Amend. 14.

5. Schools and school districts -20

The segregation of public grade school children of Mexican or Latin descent is contrary to general requirements of the school laws of California. Education Code Cal. §§ 16001 et seq., 16004, 16005, 8002-8004, 8501; Const.Cal. art. 9, § 1.

6. Constitutional law -220

The "equal protection of the laws" as applied to the public school system in California is not provided by furnishing in separate schools the same technical facilities, textbooks and courses of instruction to children of Mexican ancestry that are available to the other public school children regardless of their ancestry. U.S.C.A. Const.Amend. 14.

See Words and Phrases, Permanent Edition, for all other definitions of "Equal Protection of the Laws."

7. Schools and school districts -20

A paramount requisite in the American system of public education is social equality, wherein the system is open to all children by unified school association, regardless of lineage. Jud.Code § 24(14), 28 U.S.C.A. § 41(14).

8. Constitutional law -220

Special treatment of public elementary school children with foreign language handicaps in separate classrooms can lawfully be made only after credible examination by the appropriate school authority of each child whose capacity to learn is under consideration, and the determination of such segregation must be based wholly upon indiscriminate foreign language impediments in the individual child, regardless of his ethnic traits or ancestry. Jud.Code § 24(14), 28 U.S.C.A. § 41(14); U.S.C.A Const.Amend. 14.

9. Constitutional law -70(1), 72

The court could not exercise legislative or administrative functions to save from inoperativeness school board's discriminatory action against public school pupils of Mexican ancestry, denying them equal protection of the laws. Jud.Code § 24(14), 28 U.S.C.A. § 41(14); U.S.C.A.Const. Amend. 14.

10. Constitutional law -220

Segregating public grade school children of Mexican or Latin descent denied to them equal protection of the laws, notwithstanding English language deficiencies of some of the children. Jud.Code § 24(14), 28 U.S.C.A. § 41(14); U.S.C.A.Const. Amend. 14.

11. Injunction -94

Injunction against segregation of public grade school children of Mexican or Latin descent in violation of equal protection of law requirements would lie. Jud.Code § 24(14), 28 U.S.C.A. § 41(14); U.S.C.A.Const. Amend. 14.

Class suit by Gonzalo Méndez and others against the Westminister School District of Orange County and others to enjoin the application of alleged discriminatory rules, regulations, customs, and usages.

Judgment for plaintiffs.

David C. Marcus, of Los Angeles, Cal., for petitioner.

Joel E. Ogle, Co. Counsel, and George F. Holden, Deputy Co. Counsel, both of Santa Ana, Cal., for respondents.

A. L. Wirin and J. B. Tietz, both of Los Angeles, Cal., for American Civil Liberties Union, amicus curiae.

Chas. F. Christopher, Ben Margolis, and Loren Miller, all of Los Angeles, Cal., for National Lawyers Guild, amicus curiae.

McCORMICK, District Judge.

Gonzalo Méndez, William Guzmán, Frank Palomino, Thomas Estrada and Lorenzo Ramírez, as citizens of the United States, and on behalf of their minor children, and as they allege in the petition, on behalf of "some 5000" persons similarly affected, all of Mexican or Latin descent, have filed a class suit pursuant to Rule 23 of Federal Rules of Civil Procedure, 28 U.S.C.A. following section 723c, against the Westminister, Garden Grove and El Modeno School Districts, and the Santa Ana City Schools, all of Orange County, California, and the respective trustees and superintendents of said school districts.

The complaint, grounded upon the Fourteenth Amendment to the Constitution of the United States and Subdivision 14 of Section 24 of the Judicial Code, Title 28, Section 41, subdivision 14, U.S.C.A., alleges a concerted policy and design of class discrimination against "persons of Mexican or Latin descent or extraction" of elementary school age by the defendant school agencies in the conduct and operation of public schools of said districts, resulting in the denial of the equal protection of the laws to such class of persons among which are the petitioning school children.

Specifically, plaintiffs allege:

"That for several years last past respondents have and do now in furtherance and in execution of their common plan, design and purpose within their respective Systems and Districts, have by their regulation, custom and usage and in execution thereof adopted and declared: That all children or persons of Mexican or Latin descent or extraction, though Citizens of the United States of America, shall be, have been and are now excluded from attending, using, enjoying and receiving the benefits of the education, health and recreation facilities of certain schools within their respective Districts and Systems but that said children are now and have been segregated and required to and must attend and use certain schools in said Districts and Systems reserved for and attended solely and exclusively by children and persons of Mexican and Latin descent, while such other schools are maintained, attended and used exclusively by and for persons and children purportedly known as White or Anglo-Saxon children."

196

"That in execution of said rules and regulations, each, every and all the foregoing children are compelled and required to and must attend and use the schools in said respective Districts reserved for and attended solely and exclusively by children of Mexican and Latin descent and are forbidden, barred and excluded from attending any other school in said District or System solely for the reason that said children or child are of Mexican or Latin descent."

The petitioners demand that the alleged rules, regulations, customs and usages be adjudged void and unconstitutional and that an injunction issue, restraining further application by defendant school authorities of such rules, regulations, customs, and usages.

It is conceded by all parties that there is no question of race discrimination in this action. It is, however, admitted that segregation per se is practiced in the above-mentioned school districts as the Spanish-speaking children enter school life and as they advance through the grades in the respective school districts. It is also admitted by the defendants that the petitioning children are qualified to attend the public schools in the respective districts of their residences.

In the Westminister, Garden Grove and El Modeno school districts, the respective boards of trustees had taken official action, declaring that there be no segregation of pupils on a racial basis but that non-English-speaking children (which group, excepting as to a small number of pupils, was made up entirely of children of Mexican ancestry or descent), be required to attend schools designated by the boards separate and apart from English-speaking pupils, that such group should attend such schools until they had acquired some proficiency in the English language.

The petitioners contend that such official action evinces a covert attempt by the school authorities in such school districts to produce an arbitrary discrimination against school children of Mexican extraction or descent and that such illegal result has been established in such school districts respectively. The school authorities of the City of Santa Ana have not memorialized any such official action, but petitioners assert that the same custom and usage exists in the schools of City of Santa Ana under the authority of appropriate school agencies of such city.

The concrete acts complained of are those of the various school district officials in directing which schools the petitioning children and others of the same class or group must attend. The segregation exists in the elementary schools to and including the sixth grade in two of the defendant districts, and in the two other defendant districts through the eighth grade. The record before us shows without conflict that technical facilities and physical conveniences offered in the schools housing entirely the segregated pupils, the efficiency of the teachers therein and the curricula are identical and in some respects superior to those in the other schools in the respective districts.

The ultimate question for decision may be thus stated: Does such official action of defendant district school agencies and the usages and practices pursued by the respective school authorities as shown by the evidence operate to deny or deprive the so-called non-English-speaking school children of Mexican ancestry or descent within such school districts of the equal protection of the laws?

The defendants at the outset challenge the jurisdiction of this court under the record as it exists at this time. We have already denied the defendants' motion to dismiss the action upon the "face" of the complaint. No reason has been shown which warrants reconsideration of such decision.

[1,2] While education is a State matter, it is not so absolutely or exclusively. Cumming v. Board of Education of Richmond County, 175 U.S. 528, 20 S.Ct. 197, 201,44 L.Ed. 262. In the Cumming decision the Supreme Court said: "That education of the people in schools maintained by state taxation is a matter belonging to the respective states, and *any interference on the part of Federal authority with the management of such schools cannot be justified except in the case of a clear and unmistakable disregard of rights secured by the supreme law of the land.*" (Emphasis supplied.) See, also, Gong Lum v. Rice, 275 U.S. 78, 48 S.Ct. 91, 72 L.Ed. 172; Wong Him v. Callahan, C.C., 119 F. 381; Ward v. Flood, 48 Cal. 36, 17 Am.Rep. 405; Piper et al. v. Big Pine School District, 193 Cal. 664, 226 P. 926.

Obviously, then, a violation by a State of a personal right or privilege protected by the Fourteenth Amendment in the exercise of the State's duty to provide for the education of its citizens and inhabitants would justify the Federal Court to intervene. State of Missouri ex rel. Gaines v. Canada, 305 U.S. 337, 59 S.Ct. 232, 83 L.Ed. 208. The complaint before us in this action, having alleged an invasion by the common school authorities of the defendant districts of the equal opportunity of pupils to acquire knowledge, confers jurisdiction on this court if the actions complained of are deemed those of the State. Hamilton v. Regents of University of California, 293 U.S. 245, 55 S.Ct. 197, 79 L.Ed. 343; cf. Meyer v. Nebraska, 262 U.S. 390, 43 S.Ct. 625, 67 L.Ed. 1042, 29 A.L.R. 1446.

Are the actions of public school authorities of a rural or city school in the State of California, as alleged and established in this case, to be considered actions of the State within the meaning of the Fourteenth Amendment so as to confer jurisdiction on this court to hear and decide this case under the authority of Section 24, Subdivision 14 of the Judicial Code, supra? We think they are.

[3] In the public school system of the State of California the various local school districts enjoy a considerable degree of autonomy. Fundamentally, however, the people of the State have made the public school system a matter of State supervision. Such system is not committed to the exclusive control of local governments. Article IX, Constitution of California, Butterworth v. Boyd, 12 Cal.2d 140, 82 P.2d 434, 126 A.L.R. 838. It is a matter of general concern, and not a municipal affair. Esberg v. Badaracco, 202 Cal. 110, 259 P. 730; Becker v. Council of City of Albany, 47 Cal.App.2d 702, 118 P.2d 924.

[4] The Education Code of California provides for the requirements of teachers' qualifications, the admission and exclusion of pupils, the courses of study and the enforcement of them, the duties of superintendents of schools and of the school trustees of elementary schools in the State of California. The appropriate agencies of the State of California allocate to counties all the State school money exclusively for the payment of teachers' salaries in the public schools and such funds are apportioned to the respective school districts within the counties. While, as previously observed, local school boards and trustees are vested by State legislation with considerable latitude in the administration of their districts, nevertheless, despite the decentralization of the educa-

198

tional system in California, the rules of the local school district are required to follow the general pattern laid down by the legislature, and their practices must be consistent with law and with the rules prescribed by the State Board of Education. See Section 2204, Education Code of California.

When the basis and composition of the public school system is considered, there can be no doubt of the oneness of the system in the State of California, or of the restricted powers of the elementary school authorities in the political subdivisions of the State. See Kennedy v. Miller, 97 Cal. 429, 32 P. 558; Bruch v. Colombet, 104 Cal. 347, 38 P. 45; Ward v. San Diego School District, 203 Cal. 712, 265 P. 821.

In Hamilton v. Regents of University of California, supra, and West Virginia State Board of Education v. Barnette, 319 U.S. 624, 63 S.Ct. 1178, 1185, 87 L.Ed. 1628, 147 A.L.R. 674, the acts of university regents and of a board of education were held acts of the State. In the recent Barnette decision the court stated: "The Fourteenth Amendment, as now applied to the States, protects the citizen against the State itself and all of its creatures--Boards of Education not excepted." Although these cases dealt with State rather than local Boards, both are agencies and parts of the State educational system, as is indicated by the Supreme Court in the Barnette case, wherein it stated: "Such Boards are numerous and their territorial jurisdiction often small. But small and local authority may feel less sense of responsibility to the Constitution, and agencies of publicity may be less vigilant in calling it to account." Upon an appraisal of the factual situation before this court as illumined by the laws of the State of California relating to the public school system, it is clear that the respondents should be classified as representatives of the State to such an extent and in such a sense that the great restraints of the Constitution set limits to their action. Screws v. United States, 325 U.S. 91, 65 S.Ct. 1051; Smith v. Allwright, 321 U.S. 649, 64 S.Ct. 757, 88 L.Ed. 987, 151 A.L.R. 1110; Hague v. Committee for Industrial Organization, 307 U.S. 496, 59 S.Ct. 954, 83 L.Ed. 1423; Home Tel. & Tel. Co. v. Los Angeles, 227 U.S. 278, 33 S.Ct. 312, 57 L.Ed. 510.

[5] We therefore turn to consider whether under the record before us the school boards and administrative authorities in the respective defendant districts have by their segregation policies and practices transgressed applicable law and Constitutional safeguards and limitations and thus have invaded the personal right which every public school pupil has to the equal protection provision of the Fourteenth Amendment to obtain the means of education.

We think the pattern of public education promulgated in the Constitution of California and effectuated by provisions of the Education Code of the State prohibits segregation of the pupils of Mexican ancestry in the elementary schools from the rest of the school children.

Section 1 of Article IX of the Constitution of California directs the legislature to "encourage by all suitable means the promotion of intellectual, scientific, moral, and agricultural improvement" of the people. Pursuant to this basic directive by the people of the State many laws stem authorizing special instruction in the public schools for handicapped children. See Division 8 of the Education Code. Such legislation, however, is general in its aspects. It includes all those who fall within the described classification requiring the special consideration provided by the statutes regardless of their ancestry or extraction. The common segregation attitudes and practices of the school authorities in the defendant school districts in Orange County pertain solely to children of Mexican ancestry and parentage. They are singled out as a class for segregation. Not only is such method of public school administration contrary to the general requirements of the school laws of the State, but we think it indicates an official school policy that is antagonistic in principle to Sections 16004 and 16005 of the Education Code of the State.

Obviously, the children referred to in these laws are those of Mexican ancestry. And it is noteworthy that the educational advantages of their commingling with other pupils is regarded as being so important to the school system of the State that it is provided for even regardless of the citizenship of the parents. We perceive in the laws relating to the public educational system in the State of California a clear purpose to avoid and forbid distinctions among pupils based upon race or ancestry except in specific situations not pertinent to this action. Distinctions of that kind have recently been declared by the highest judicial authority of the United States "by their very nature odious to a free people whose institutions are founded upon the doctrine of equality." They are said to be "utterly inconsistent with American traditions and ideals." Kiyoshi Hirabayashi v. United States, 320 U.S. 81, 63 S.Ct. 1375, 1385, 87 L.Ed.1774.

Our conclusions in this action, however, do not rest solely upon what we conceive to be the utter irreconcilability of the segregation practices in the defendant school districts with the public educational system authorized and sanctioned by the laws of the State of California. We think such practices clearly and unmistakably disregard rights secured by the supreme law of the land. Cumming v. Board of Education of Richmond County, supra.

[6, 7] "The equal protection of the laws" pertaining to the public school system in California is not provided by furnishing in separate schools the same technical facilities, text books and courses of instruction to children of Mexican ancestry that are available to the other public school children regardless of their ancestry. A paramount requisite in the American system of public education is social equality. It must be open to all children by unified school association regardless of lineage.

[8] We think that under the record before us the only tenable ground upon which segregation practices in the defendant school districts can be defended lies in the English language deficiencies of some of the children of Mexican ancestry as they enter elementary public school life as beginners. But even such situations do not justify the general and continuous segregation in separate schools of the children of Mexican ancestry from the rest of the elementary school population as has been shown to be the practice in the defendant school districts—in all of them to the sixth grade, and in two of them through the eighth grade.

The evidence clearly shows that Spanish-speaking children are retarded in learning English by lack of exposure to its use because of segregation, and that commingling of the entire student body instills and develops a common cultural attitude among the school children which is imperative for the perpetuation of American institutions and ideals. It is also established by the record that the methods of segregation prevalent in the defendant school districts foster antagonisms in the children and suggest inferiority among them where none exists. One of the flagrant examples of the discriminatory results of segregation in two of the schools involved in this case is shown by the record. In the district under consideration there are two schools, the Lincoln and the Roosevelt, located approximately 120 yards apart on the same school grounds. Hours of opening and closing, as well as recess periods, are not uniform. No credible language test is given to the children of Mexican ancestry upon entering the first grade in Lincoln School. This school has an enrollment of 249 so-called Spanish-speaking pupils, and no so-called English-speaking pupils, while the Roosevelt (the other) school, has 83 so-called English-speaking pupils and 25 so-called Spanish-speaking pupils. Standardized tests as to mental ability are given to the respective classes in the two schools and the same curricula are pursued in both schools and, of course, in the English language as required by State law. Section 8251, Education Code. In the last school year the students in the seventh grade of the Lincoln were superior scholarly to the same grade in the Roosevelt School and to any group in the seventh grade in either of the schools in the past. It further appears that not only did the class as a group have such mental superiority but that certain pupils in the group were also outstanding in the class itself. Notwithstanding this showing, the pupils of such excellence were kept in the Lincoln School. It is true that there is no evidence in the record before us that shows that any of the members of this exemplary class requested transfer to the other so-called intermingled school, but the record does show without contradiction that another class had protested against the segregation policies and practices in the schools of this El Modeno district without avail.

While the pattern or ideal of segregating the school children of Mexican ancestry from the rest of the school attendance permeates and is practiced in all of the four defendant districts, there are procedural deviations among the school administrative agencies in effectuating the general plan.

In Garden Grove Elementary School District the segregation extends only through the fifth grade. Beyond, all pupils in such district, regardless of their ancestry or linguistic proficiency, are housed, instructed and associate in the same school facility.

This arrangement conclusively refutes the reasonableness or advisability of any segregation of children of Mexican ancestry beyond the fifth grade in any of the defendant school districts in view of the standardized and uniform curricular requirements in the elementary schools of Orange County.

But the admitted practice and long established custom in this school district whereby all elementary public school children of Mexican descent are required to attend one specified school (the Hoover) until they attain the sixth grade, while all other pupils of the same grade are permitted to and do attend two other elementary schools of this district, notwithstanding that some of such pupils live within the Hoover School division of the district, clearly establishes an unfair and arbitrary class distinction in the system of public education operative in the Garden Grove Elementary School District.

The long-standing discriminatory custom prevalent in this district is aggravated by the fact shown by the record that although there are approximately 25 children of Mexican descent living in the vicinity of the Lincoln School, none of them attend that school, but all are peremptorily assigned by the school authorities to the Hoover School, although the evidence shows that there are no school zones territorially established in the district.

The record before us shows a paradoxical situation concerning the segregation attitude of the school authorities in the Westminister School District. There are two elementary schools in this undivided area. Instruction is given pupils in each school from kindergarten to the eighth grade, inclusive. Westminister School has 642 pupils, of which 628 are so-called English-speaking children, and 14 so-called Spanish-speaking pupils. The Hoover School is attended solely by 152 children of Mexican descent. Segregation of these from the rest of the school population precipitated such vigorous protests by residents of the district that the school board in January, 1944, recognizing the discriminatory results of segregation, resolved to unite the two schools and thus abolish the objectionable practices which had been operative in the schools of the district for a considerable period. A bond issue was submitted to the electors to raise funds to defray the cost of contemplated expenditures in the school consolidation. The bonds were not voted and the record before us in this action reflects no execution or carrying out of the official action of the board of trustees taken on or about the 16th of January, 1944. It thus appears that there has been no abolishment of the traditional segregation practices in this district pertaining to pupils of Mexican ancestry through the gamut of elementary school life. We have adverted to the unfair consequences of such practices in the similarly situated El Modeno School District.

Before considering the specific factual situation in the Santa Ana City Schools it should be noted that the omnibus segregation of children of Mexican ancestry from the rest of the student body in the elementary grades in the schools involved in this case because of language handicaps is not warranted by the record before us. The tests applied to the beginners are shown to have been generally hasty, superficial and not reliable. In some instances separate classification was determined largely by the Latinized or Mexican name of the child. Such methods of evaluating language knowledge are illusory and are not conducive to the inculcation and enjoyment of civil rights which are of primary importance in the public school system of education in the United States.

It has been held that public school authorities may differentiate in the exercise of their reasonable discretion as to the pedagogical methods of instruction to be pursued with different pupils. And foreign language handicaps may be to such a degree in the pupils in elementary schools as to require special treatment in separate classrooms. Such separate allocations, however, can be lawfully made only after credible examination by the appropriate school authority of each child whose capacity to learn is under consideration and the determination of such segregation must be based wholly upon indiscriminate foreign language impediments in the individual child, regardless of his ethnic traits or ancestry.

[9-11] The defendant Santa Ana School District maintains fourteen elementary schools, which furnish instruction from kindergarten to the sixth grade, inclusive.

About the year 1920, the Board of Education, for the purpose of allocating pupils to the several schools of the district in proportion to the facilities available at such schools, divided the district into fourteen zones and assigned to the school established in each zone all pupils residing within such zone.

There is no evidence that any discriminatory or other objectionable motive or purpose actuated the School Board in locating or defining such zones.

Subsequently the influx of people of Mexican ancestry in large numbers and their voluntary settlement in certain of the fourteen zones resulted in three of the zones becoming occupied almost entirely by such group of people.

Two zones, that in which the Fremont School is located, and another contiguous area in which the Franklin School is situated, present the only flagrant discriminatory situation shown by the evidence in this case in the Santa Ana City Schools. The Fremont School has 325 so-called Spanish-speaking pupils and no so-called English-speaking pupils. The Franklin School has 237 pupils of which 161 are so-called English-speaking children, and 76 so-called Spanish-speaking children.

The evidence shows that approximately 26 pupils of Mexican descent who reside within the Fremont zone are permitted by the School Board to attend the Franklin School because their families had always gone there. It also appears that there are approximately 35 other pupils not of Mexican descent who live within the Fremont zone who are not required to attend the Fremont School but who are also permitted by the Board of Education to attend the Franklin School.

Sometime in the fall of the year 1944, there arose dissatisfaction by the parents of some of the so-called Spanish-speaking pupils in the Fremont School zone who were not granted the privilege that approximately 26 children also of Mexican descent, enjoyed in attending the Franklin School. Protest was made en masse by such dissatisfied group of parents, which resulted in the Board of Education directing its secretary to send a letter to the parents of all the so-called Spanish-speaking pupils living in the Fremont zone and attending the Franklin School that beginning September, 1945, the permit to attend Franklin School would be withdrawn and the children would be required to attend the school of the zone in which they were living, viz., the Fremont School.

There could have been no arbitrary discrimination claimed by plaintiffs by the action of the school authorities if the same official course had been applied to the 35 other so-called English-speaking pupils exactly situated as were the approximate 26 children of Mexican lineage, but the record is clear that the requirement of the Board of Education was intended for and directed exclusively to the specified pupils of Mexican ancestry and, if carried out, becomes operative solely against such group of children.

It should be stated in fairness to the Superintendent of the Santa Ana City Schools that he testified he would recommend to the Board of Education that the children of those who protested the action requiring transfer from the Franklin School be allowed to remain there because of long attendance and family tradition. However, there was no official recantation shown of the action of the Board of Education reflected by the letters of the Secretary and sent only to the parents of the children of Mexican ancestry.

The natural operation and effect of the Board's official action manifests a clear purpose to arbitrarily discriminate against the pupils of Mexican ancestry and to deny to them the equal protection of the laws.

The court may not exercise legislative or administrative functions in this case to save such discriminatory act from inoperativeness. Cf. Yu Cong Eng v. Trinidad, 271 U.S. 500, 46 S.Ct. 619, 70 L.Ed. 1059.

There are other discriminatory customs, shown by the evidence, existing in the defendant school districts as to pupils of Mexican descent and extraction, but we deem it unnecessary to discuss them in this memorandum.

We conclude by holding that the allegations of the complaint (petition) have been established sufficiently to justify injunctive relief against all defendants, restraining further discriminatory practices against the pupils of Mexican descent in the public schools of defendant school districts. See *Morris v. Williams,* 8 Cir., 149 F.2d 703.

Findings of fact, conclusions of law, and decree of injunction are accordingly ordered pursuant to Rule 52, F.R.C.P.

Attorney for plaintiffs will within ten days from date hereof prepare and present same under local Rule 7 of this court.

Méndez v. Westminster School District, 64 F. Supp. 544.

Judge Peña Remembers Desegregation Efforts

In San Antonio, Judge Albert Peña remembered when, as a newly graduated lawyer in 1950, the G.I. Forum asked him to investigate continuing school segregation in Hondo, a town about thirty miles from San Antonio. The story, as Judge Peña recounts it, demonstrates how Mexican Americans mustered unity in the face of seemingly insurmountable odds to try to end the segregation of their children in the schools.

I graduated from law school in 1950, and in the early fifties, I became very interested in LULAC and G.I. FORUM. G.I. Forum requested that I investigate claims of school segregation in Hondo, Texas, which is about twenty, thirty miles from here. There was no money involved. Just go over there and check and see what you can do about it. And I told them that I was very happy to. Just out of law school and I wanted to do something like that.

Prior to that there was only one school segregation case in Texas and it was a case that Gus García and Juan Carlos Cadena—I'll give you the full name after a while— tried in a Federal Court, and it was an aggrieved judgment where they stated that you could segregate children of Mexican descent in the first grade to teach them English. But what was happening was that not only were they segregated, they never reached the second grade, so there were third, fourth, and fifth grade students who were still learning how to speak English.

They didn't really change anything as far as school segregation was concerned. . . It was the only case. The only school segregation case at that time. I went down—Hondo was an ideal situation of proving school segregation. When I first got there, I was to talk to the Max Orta family, they were the plaintiffs, and I knocked on their door and they wanted to know who was there and I told them I was a lawyer from San Antonio. They said, "Another lawyer from San Antonio? We paid out too much money for lawyers and they've never been able to do anything." I said, "I'm not here to. . . I'm just here to investigate and I'm not going to charge you anything for it." So here I was talking to them through a screen window and they were talking back to me. When I explained to them that I was there to investigate and if I could do anything about it, I would really be happy to help them, and it wasn't going to cost them anything, and I wasn't going to be paid by anyone either.

Finally, they let me in and we started talking about it. So they, in effect, retained me on that basis: I wasn't going to charge them anything. They had two schools, my investigation showed: one was called the West Ward School, and all *mejicanos* went to the West Ward School up to the seventh grade, regardless of where they lived. Then they had what they called the Main Plant.

What I did was, I investigated that. I talked to people and they told me this is true: seventh grade, if you're a *mejicano,* that's where you go. And after the seventh grade, they don't go to school anymore. So I went and talked to the superintendent and I told him what I had found. And I told him this is unconstitutional and we were requesting, on behalf of our clients, that they cease and desist segregating children of Mexican descent. He said, "I can't do anything for you. That's the policy of the Board." I informed him that I would appeal that decision to the School Board and ask for a hearing before them.

The reason we were taking this administrative route: because we didn't have any money to go into a federal court. We didn't have the resources to go into a federal court, so we decided to go the administrative route.

We did get a hearing before the School Board. And I had my client there. And they had some high-toned lawyers from Houston or someplace that were representing the School Board. They expected me to present my witnesses and my complainants, but I told them, "I only have one witness and my witness is your superintendent." I forget his name. "I'll put him on the stand." And I asked him, "You remember when I was in your office? And you remember that I pointed out that you had two schools, one was segregated and one was not, up to the seventh grade?" He says, "That's true. We don't call it segregation, we call it an opportunity for the children to learn how to speak English." "But they were separated?" "That's true." And I said, "That's my case. I don't have any more witnesses." "Aren't you going to call your complainant?" "No, I'm not going to call my complainant."

Of course, their lawyers could have called them, but they didn't. "This is my case and this proves that this school district has been segregating these children for a long, long time, etc., etc." He said, "Well, we'll let you know what our decision is." And their lawyer made a long spiel about I don't know what, but it made no sense. They eventually told us that they were going to turn us down. So we advised them that we were going to appeal their decision to the State Agency on Education.

What happened was that the State Agency just sat on it and wouldn't do anything about it, wouldn't give us a decision. So a year went by, and everybody in Hondo was mad at me. So I decided to do something about it. I told them, "We're going to have a meeting just prior to the September registration." So we had this meeting at the Guadalupe Church. Every *mejicano* in Hondo was there. And I told them, "I'm a brand new lawyer and maybe I'm not that good at this yet. But I think what we ought to do, if we really mean what we're talking about, what we ought to do is, tomorrow we ought to take all our children to the Main Plant and insist that they enroll them there and just stay there, until they do, if it takes a day, two days, a week. And I'll be there right with you. All the way."

The next day, every family in Hondo was there, except for one, and that one probably didn't know about it or disagreed with what we were doing. And every student, every *mejicano* student and their family was there. And we would line them up and they would say, "Well, you have to go to the West Ward." And what they'd do is get back in the line, and we just kept a steady stream of the people and . . . there was no violence, but we were having a good time."

There was at least five hundred people, maybe more. Lots of people. So what happened was that the media got hold of it in the afternoon. They did carry the story someplace. I don't think they carried it in San Antonio, and this was one of the problems that we had with a lot of these things: the media wouldn't cover it or give it any significance. But it did get some coverage, and when it did get coverage, the State Agency called a parent meeting and advised the Hondo School District to integrate the schools.

Interview with Judge Albert Peña on January 28, 1992, by Jesús Treviño, NLCC.

Mexican Americans and Ambiguity about Claiming Whiteness

By the 1950s, Mexican Americans discovered that claiming white ethnic identity could backfire. For example, demands for a jury of peers, when the defendant was Mexican, could be met with retorts that all Anglo juries did not exclude the Mexican race, since it was supposedly white. This changed in 1953, when lawyer Juan Carlos Cadena, later a judge in San Antonio, with partner Gus García, successfully argued before the U.S. Supreme Court that Pete Hernández's rights to a jury of peers were violated because no Mexican Americans were on the panel that convicted him of murder. Later, Cadena admitted that taking this position was tantamount to accepting a nonwhite status. The rendering of the Supreme Court of the United States is reprinted below.

HERNÁNDEZ v. TEXAS
Syllabus.
HERNÁNDEZ v. TEXAS.
CERTIORARI TO THE COURT OF CRIMINAL APPEALS OF TEXAS.
No. 406. Argued January 11, 1954.—Decided May 3, 1954.

The systematic exclusion of persons of Mexican descent from service as jury commissioners, grand jurors, and petit jurors in the Texas county in which petitioner was indicted and tried for murder, although there were a substantial number of such persons in the county fully qualified to serve, deprived petitioner, a person of Mexican descent, of the equal protection of the laws guaranteed by the Fourteenth Amendment, and his conviction in a state court is reversed. Pp. 476-482.

(a) The constitutional guarantee of equal protection of the laws is not directed solely against discrimination between whites and Negroes. Pp. 477-478.

(b) When the existence of a distinct class is demonstrated, and it is shown that the laws, as written or as applied, single out that class for different treatment not based on some reasonable classification, the guarantees of the Constitution have been violated. P. 478.

(c) The exclusion of otherwise eligible persons from jury service solely because of their ancestry or national origin is discrimination prohibited by the Fourteenth Amendment. Pp. 478-479.

(d) The evidence in this case was sufficient to prove that, in the county in question, persons of Mexican descent constitute a separate class, distinct from "whites." Pp. 479-480.

(e) A prima facie case of denial of the equal protection of the laws was established in this case by evidence that there were in the county a substantial number of persons of Mexican descent with the qualifications required for jury service but that none of them had served on a jury commission, grand jury or petit jury for 25 years. Pp. 480-481.

(f) The testimony of five jury commissioners that they had not discriminated against persons of Mexican descent in selecting jurors, and that their only objective had been to select those whom they thought best qualified, was not enough to overcome petitioner's prima facie case of denial of the equal protection of the laws. Pp. 481-482.

(g) Petitioner had the constitutional right to be indicted and tried by juries from which all members of his class were not systematically excluded. P. 482.

—Tex. Cr. R.—251 S. W. 2d 531, reversed.

Opinion of the Court.   347 U.S.

Carlos C. Cadena and *Gus C. García* argued the cause for petitioner. With them on the brief were *Maury Maverick, Sr.* and *John J. Herrera.*

Horace Wimberly, Assistant Attorney General of Texas, argued the cause for respondent. With him on the brief were *John Ben Shepperd,* Attorney General, and *Rudy G. Rice, Milton Richardson* and *Wayne L. Hartman,* Assistant Attorneys General, for respondent.

MR. CHIEF JUSTICE WARREN delivered the opinion of the Court.

The petitioner, Pete Hernandez, was indicted for the murder of one Joe Espinosa by a grand jury in Jackson County, Texas. He was convicted and sentenced to life imprisonment. The Texas Court of Criminal Appeals affirmed the judgment of the trial court.—Tex. Cr. R.—, 251 S. W. 2d 531. Prior to the trial, the petitioner, by his counsel, offered timely motions to quash the indictment and the jury panel. He alleged that persons of Mexican descent were systematically excluded from service as jury commissioners, grand jurors, and petit jurors, although there were such persons fully qualified to serve residing in Jackson County. The petitioner asserted that exclusion of this class deprived him, as a member of the class, of the equal protection of the laws guaranteed by the Fourteenth Amendment of the Constitution. After a hearing, the trial court denied the motions. At the trial, the motions were renewed, further evidence taken, and the motions again denied. An allegation that the trial court erred in denying the motions was the sole basis of petitioner's appeal. In affirming the judgment of the trial court, the Texas Court of Criminal Appeals considered and passed upon the substantial federal question raised by the petitioner. We granted a writ of certiorari to review that decision. 346 U. S. 811.

In numerous decisions, this Court has held that it is a denial of the equal protection of the laws to try a defendant of a particular race or color under an indictment issued by a grand jury, or before a petit jury, from which all persons of his race or color have, solely because of that race or color, been excluded by the State, whether acting through its legislature, its courts, or its executive or administrative officers. Although the Court has had little occasion to rule on the question directly, it has been recognized since *Strauder v. West Virginia,* 100 U. S. 303, that the exclusion of a class of persons from jury service on grounds other than race or color may also deprive a defendant who is a member of that class of the constitutional guarantee of equal protection of the laws. The State of Texas would have us hold that there are only two classes—white and Negro—within the contemplation of the Fourteenth Amendment. The decisions of this Court do not support that view. And, except where the question presented involves the exclusion of persons of Mexican descent from juries, Texas courts have taken a broader view of the scope of the equal protection clause.

Throughout our history, differences in race and color have defined easily identifiable groups which have at times required the aid of the courts in securing equal treatment under the laws. But community prejudices are not static, and from time to time other differences from the community norm may define other groups which need the same protection. Whether such a group exists within a community is a question of fact. When the existence of a distinct class is demonstrated, and it is further shown that the laws, as written or as applied, single out that class for different treatment not based on some reasonable classification, the guarantees of the Constitution have been violated. The Fourteenth Amendment is not directed solely against discrimination due to a "two-class theory"—that is, based upon differences between "white" and Negro.

As the petitioner acknowledges, the Texas system of selecting grand and petit jurors by the use of jury commissions is fair on its face and capable of being utilized without discrimination. But as this Court has held, the system is susceptible to abuse and can be employed in a discriminatory manner. The exclusion of otherwise eligible persons from jury service solely because of their ancestry or national origin is discrimination prohibited by the Fourteenth Amendment. The Texas statute makes no such discrimination, but the petitioner alleges that those administering the law do.

The petitioner's initial burden in substantiating his charge of group discrimination was to prove that persons of Mexican descent constitute a separate class in Jackson County, distinct from "whites." One method by which this may be demonstrated is by showing the attitude of the community. Here the testimony of responsible officials and citizens contained the admission that residents of the community distinguished between "white" and "Mexican." The participation of persons of Mexican descent in business and community groups was shown to be slight. Until very recent times, children of Mexican descent were required to attend a segregated school for the first four grades. At least one restaurant in town prominently displayed a sign announcing "No Mexicans Served." On the courthouse grounds at the time of the hearing, there were two men's toilets, one unmarked, and the other marked "Colored Men" and "Hombres Aquí" ("Men Here"). No substantial evidence was offered to rebut the logical inference to be drawn from these facts, and it must be concluded that petitioner succeeded in his proof.

Having established the existence of a class, petitioner was then charged with the burden of proving discrimination. To do so, he relied on the pattern of proof established by *Norris v. Alabama,* 294 U. S. 587. In that case, proof that Negroes constituted a substantial segment of the population of the jurisdiction, that some Negroes were qualified to serve as jurors, and that none had been called for jury service over an extended period of time, was held to constitute prima facie proof of the systematic exclusion of Negroes from jury service. This holding, sometimes called the "rule of exclusion," has been applied in other cases, and it is available in supplying proof of discrimination against any delineated class.

The petitioner established that 14 percent of the population of Jackson County were persons with Mexican or Latin American surnames, and that 11 percent of the males over 21 bore such names. The County Tax Assessor testified that 6 or 7 percent of the freeholders on the tax rolls of the County were persons of Mexican descent. The State of Texas stipulated that "for the last twenty-five years there is no record of any person with a Mexican or Latin American name having served on a jury commission, grand jury or petit jury in Jackson County." The parties also stipulated that "there are some male persons of Mexican or Latin American descent in Jackson County who, by virtue of being citizens, householders, or freeholders, and having all other legal prerequisites to jury service, are eligible to serve as members of a jury commission, grand jury and/or petit jury."

The petitioner met the burden of proof imposed in *Norris v. Alabama, supra*. To rebut the strong prima facie case of the denial of the equal protection of the laws guaranteed by the Constitution thus established, the State offered the testimony of five jury commissioners that they had not discriminated against persons of Mexican or Latin-American descent in selecting jurors. They stated that their only objective had been to select those whom they thought were best qualified. This testimony is not enough to overcome the petitioner's case. As the Court said in *Norris v. Alabama:*

> "That showing as to the long-continued exclusion of Negroes from jury service, and as to the many Negroes qualified for that service, could not be met by mere generalities. If, in the presence of such testimony as defendant adduced, the mere general assertions by officials of their performance of duty were to be accepted as an adequate justification for the complete exclusion of Negroes from jury service, the constitutional provision . . . would be but a vain and illusory requirement."

The same reasoning is applicable to these facts.

Circumstances or chance may well dictate that no persons in a certain class will serve on a particular jury or during some particular period. But it taxes our credulity to say that mere chance resulted in there being no members of this class among the over six thousand jurors called in the past 25 years. The result bespeaks discrimination, whether or not it was a conscious decision on the part of any individual jury commissioner. The judgment of conviction must be reversed.

To say that this decision revives the rejected contention that the Fourteenth Amendment requires proportional representation of all the component ethnic groups of the community on every jury ignores the facts. The petitioner did not seek proportional representation, nor did he claim a right to have persons of Mexican descent sit on the particular juries which he faced. His only claim is the right to be indicted and tried by juries from which all members of his class are not systematically excluded—juries selected from among all qualified persons regardless of national origin or descent. To this much, he is entitled by the Constitution.

Reversed.

Hernández v. Texas, 347 U.S. 475 (1954).

Dolores Huerta on the Community Services Organization

Dolores Huerta, the farm worker organizer, who along with César Chávez helped organize the United Farm Workers Union in the 1960s, vividly remembers the citizenship drives when she worked for the Community Services Organization (CSO) in Los Angeles.

Q: What are some of the things that CSO accomplished in those early days? What were the successes?

A: A lot of stuff. After we started expanding, one of the goals of the organization, well first of all, here in Los Angeles, they accomplished a lot, like getting the streets paved, up in Maravilla, getting the health clinics, the streetlights—they didn't have any streetlights in those days. It was just a whole string of victories that they won. Then, when they started expanding, they started going for legislation. As the CSO expanded, it fought these fights against the cops, like in Salinas . . . . In San Jose they fought some discrimination cases up there. César joined in San Jose; that's where he found César at, and I think the San Jose chapter was the one after the L.A. chapter. César would know this stuff too, because he became the director of CSO after he organized the San Jose Chapter. Then they came down to Stockton and I didn't see César for a long time. I guess Fred Ross was the one that organized me. He was the one that got me involved.

Q: So you became part of the CSO organization in Stockton?

A: In Stockton, right. And in Stockton we did the same thing; we fought the cops on illegal searches and seizures; we were planning to get a Bracero program in. Then we started the statewide campaign to get this pension for the noncitizens. By the way, they did a massive citizenship program here. We helped literally thousands throughout California, but here in L.A. it was just incredible, the citizenship program. Because people couldn't get old age pensions unless they were citizens. So we got the law passed so that they could, an amendment to the law so they could take their citizenship test in Spanish and immediately began massive citizenship programs and set up classes—just hundreds and hundreds of people became citizens so they could get their old age pension. But then at the same time, we started working on a law to take away the citizenship requirement, so that all of the people that were immigrants could get their old age pension. So we won that law in 1961, and I was a lobbyist for that law. We took the citizenship requirements from all of the public assistance programs: aid for the blind, aid for the disabled . . .

Dolores Huerta interviewed by Luis Torres, April 20, 1992, NLCC.

Keeping in Touch with JFK

The wealth of experience acquired in the Kennedy campaign was subsequently parlayed into political action that was to help Mexican American candidates locally. In the fall of 1963, Mexican Americans in Texas planned to revive the Viva Kennedy! Clubs in order to campaign for Kennedy's reelection bid in 1964. Tragically, Kennedy was assassinated just one month after LULAC mailed the letter below, inviting the President to a function hosted by LULAC that was planned for Kennedy's fateful trip to Texas in November of 1963. The President did attend a reception held at the Rice Hotel in Houston; the next day he was assassinated in Dallas.

In connection with President Kennedy's visit to Houston for the Albert Thomas Testimonial Dinner, I wish to urge that you do everything possible to have President Kennedy visit the LULAC State Director's Ball at the Crystal Ballroom of the Rice Hotel on the same night.

We can win in Texas. However, to do it again the VIVA KENNEDY CLUBS must be reorganized. Most of the membership of the VIVA KENNEDY CLUBS came out of the LULAC membership rosters and all of them will be present at this LULAC affair honoring one of our best known members.

If we could be assured of the President's presence at this LULAC affair, I could make it my business and it would be a great honor to have all of the VIVA KENNEDY CLUBS' members from Houston, Corpus Christi, Dallas, San Antonio, Beaumont, Galveston, El Paso, the Rio Grande Valley, and West Texas to be in Houston, and meet with the President and any of his official party to begin welding together the VIVA KENNEDY CLUBS for the coming campaign. Frankly, we are in trouble in Texas, but with the repealing of the poll tax in Texas, more Latinos than ever will vote in the coming presidential election. It is toward the necessary end of solidifying this potentially strong voting factor that I urge your utmost to have President Kennedy include a visit to us on his itinerary. As soon as I get a commitment from you, I can pass it on to all of the VIVA KENNEDY CLUBS' members in Texas to be present.

The Republicans are making a concerted effort to get Texas back into the Republican column next year. The reuniting of the VIVA KENNEDY CLUBS' members of Texas at Houston, Texas, will recall (and reignite) the spontaneous effort of the Latin Americans of Texas toward the Democratic Party, and which constituted one of the greatest political upsets in the history of Texas politics.

Finally, and this is most significant, this affair will be at the Rice Hotel, and at the same spot where President Kennedy made his historic speech to the Greater Houston Ministerial Association, September 12, 1960, which is generally regarded as one of the turning points in that presidential campaign.

This will be a fine opportunity for President Kennedy to meet with the Latin Americans of Mexican descent of Texas, who have always held him in the highest esteem.

As soon as you give me the word, we will start working to make this a memorable and happy occasion for us all.

John J. Herrera to President John F. Kennedy, October 24, 1963, Civic Action Committee file, Political Association of Spanish Speaking Organization's Collection, LULAC Collection, Houston Metropolitan Research Center, Houston Public Library.

Mexican Americanism Becomes Militant

Mexican Americans began to use more aggressive confrontation tactics by the mid-1960s. Mexican leaders had expected President Kennedy to address many of the problems they faced after they had helped him come to office, but his assassination dashed those hopes. Although his successor, Lyndon Baines Johnson, in 1966, had promised Mexican Americans that he would deal with their historical marginalization, leaders of such organizations as LULAC and MAPA decided not enough was being done and walked out of the 1966 Equal Employment Opportunity Commission Conference. Mexican Americanism became more militant during the 1960s, a factor that helped initiate the Chicano Movement. The piece below, from the MAPA official newspaper, *The Voice*, discussed why this action was taken.

All 50 Mexican-American delegates—including a group from Southern Califor-
nia—walked out in protest at a Federal Equal Employment Opportunities Commission
Conference in Albuquerque, N. M., recently.

The delegates, acting less than an hour after the all-day session started, charged the commission is indifferent to Mexican American needs and is guilty of discrimination in its own hiring practices.

It was the second walkout within a month, of Mexican Americans participating in EEOC conclaves. The first such walkout came in San Francisco, early in March over what attorney Robert E. Gonzales, President of the San Francisco Chapter of MAPA, claimed was gross ignorance of the problems faced by the Spanish-speaking community. Both meetings were chaired by Herman Edelsberg, the Executive Director of the commission.

In August 1965, MAPA delegates Eduardo Quevedo, Bert Corona, and Phil Ortíz, together with other delegates from the G.I. Forum, LULACs, and CSO, attended a Washington D.C. conference, which was slated as a workshop. The Hispanic-Americans present called attention to the fact that the five Commissioners could be replaced under Section 702 (2) of the Equal Employment Opportunity Law, at the rate of one per year, commencing as of July 2, 1964, unless they succeeded themselves by reappointment by the President.

It was pointed out at the Washington, D.C. meeting that the five Commissioners established policy, none of which members possessed of firsthand knowledge of the characteristics engrained in the emotional and social bicultural background of the Hispanic citizen.

The Albuquerque conference called by the commission was to have explored employment opportunities for Mexican Americans in the six Southwest states of California, Arizona, Nevada, Colorado, New Mexico, and Texas.

Alfred J. Hernández of Houston, national president of the League of United Latin American Citizens, said that while Mexican Americans comprise the second largest minority group in the United States, they are not represented on the commission.

"Our employment problems are severe and complex, yet we have no one on the commission with any insight into them," he charged.

Dr. Miguel Montes of San Fernando, president of the Latin American Civic Assn., complained that the EEOC has only one Mexican American compliance officer on its Washington staff and that there should be at least 20.

Criticism Voiced

"I find it difficult to see how the commission can go out and enforce laws on fair employment when it practices discrimination itself against the Mexican American," Dr. Montes said.

Agustín Flores of Riverside, president of the American G.I. Forum, complained that the commission has made no effort to reach the Mexican American community and that the EEOC put a regional office in San Francisco when it should have been in Los Angeles.

Delegates also criticized the fact that only one commissioner attended the much-publicized conference. In the telegram to the President, they charged "he came without any background in Mexican American employment problems."

Southern California delegates included Alex García, field representative for Rep. Edward Roybal (D-Los Angeles); Ralph Guzmán, director of the Ford Foundation's Mexican American study project at UCLA; Louis García, director of the San Fernando Valley's Joint Ventures Project; and Armando Rodríguez, of the Assn. of Mexican American Educators.

The Equal Employment Opportunities Conference was to have been a mass exercise known as "group dynamics" in arriving at predetermined conclusions and then to be funneled out to the public as "the consensus."

The Voice, April 21, 1966, from the files of Edward Escobar.

Chapter Seven

Defense in the Workplace

Mexican workers contributed a significant portion of the labor that made possible the industrialization and modernization of the United States during the late nineteenth and early twentieth centuries. Finding a job was the Mexican immigrant's priority, but once working, he or she encountered arduous conditions, usually in labor sectors designated for Mexicans only. Because Mexicans were the most recent arrivals in the vast labor markets of the United States, they were usually laid off first, especially during severe economic slumps. As a consequence, Mexicans became extremely vulnerable to job insecurity. And because mainstream American unions usually established their recruitment drives in industrial regions, where few Mexicans worked, they often did not include many Mexican workers within their ranks. In addition, racism in the unions resulted in ignoring adverse conditions in labor sectors where Mexicans worked.

Mainstream labor unions felt Mexicans were too difficult to organize. Rank-and-file native American workers, both white and black, greeted Mexicans with hostility because they saw them as competitors and as the cause of low wages. Reaction against Mexican workers at times manifested itself in outright violence. For example, during 1921, armed, hooded night riders forced Mexicans to leave Ranger, Texas, when a recession provoked unemployment. Assaults also occurred in Cisco, Texas, where white workers threw rocks at Mexicans and threatened their lives if they did not vacate the town. At the end of the 1921 recession, anti-Mexican violence subsided, but during another downturn in 1926, outbreaks returned, especially in Texas.

To defend themselves against these abuses, Mexican workers organized unions, but they also defended their interests through other less formal endeavors. For example, farm workers traveled in groups and insisted on being hired as such. Made up of families, close friends or *compadres*, these independent work crews were less vulnerable to exploitation.

The Mexican consuls, who were supposed to maintain their distance when labor conflicts involved compatriots, also served as brokers for Mexicans with their employers, and monitored procedures to prevent legal violations. When Cochise County officials jailed four thousand Mexican participants in the 1917 Arizona copper mine strikes, the Mexican Consul Ives Levelier helped hundreds of strikers get released.

Unionization efforts by Mexican workers were extensive in the early twentieth century, but they did not emerge in proportion to the degree of exploitation. Mexicans mainly dealt with workplace abuse through informal methods, such as "wildcat" stoppages and walkouts or sabotage and personal violence. Informal efforts are hard to document, of course, because they do not leave a well-defined paper trail. Nonetheless, numerous examples of institutional union efforts involving Mexicans can be cited.

Because of the industrial nature of mining, some of the first major efforts to organize were in that sector. A number of strikes led by Mexicans rocked the mining regions of southeastern Arizona during 1903, for example. William "Wenceslao" Laustaunau, A. F. Salcido, both from Mexico, and the Italian Frank Colombo convinced workers in Morenci Copper to stay out of the mines for three days. Armed workers milled through Morenci making demands until Arizona Rangers, sent in by the governor, arrested the strike leaders. Salcido, Laustaunau, and Colombo were imprisoned for their role in the strike; Laustaunau died in prison in 1906. When the Western Federation of Miners labor union conducted extensive organizing campaigns among Mexican miners in 1915, they responded enthusiastically and joined. Of the five thousand workers who struck in Morenci, Clifton, and Metcalf, 70 percent were Mexicans whose main issue was double wage standards—one for Mexicans and the other for Anglos. Aware of the huge wartime profits being made by mine owners in Arizona during World War I, the International Workers of the World (IWW), also known as the Wobblies, initiated strikes with a large Mexican following in the Arizona mines. Lázaro Gutiérrez de Lara, a Mexican immigrant radical, was one of the leaders. The workers primarily sought better wages, but the mining companies fought any concessions tooth and nail. They defeated the Wobblie initiatives by accusing them of un-American activities and sabotaging the war effort. In another Wobblie-led stoppage during 1917, the mine owners, in collusion with Bisbee, Arizona, officials, ejected all strikers, most of them Mexicans, and left them stranded in railroad cars in the New Mexico desert.

California had fewer Mexicans than Arizona at the turn of the century, but their numbers increased dramatically within a few decades. There they worked primarily in agriculture, replacing an Asian workforce that declined because of a restrictive immigration policy. In April of 1903, the American Federation of

Labor (AFL) was one of the first unions to organize Mexican and Japanese farm workers in the beet fields of Oxnard. The objectives were better wages and the right to deal directly with farmers, not middlemen or contractors. The strike was relatively successful because the contractors were eliminated. On New Year's day in 1915 in Santa Paula, another documented Mexican farm worker strike took place at the Limonería Ranch, when lemon harvesters refused to work on this holiday. After grape pickers were inspired by a three-day celebration of Mexican Independence Day, in September of 1922, Mexicans launched another agricultural strike in Fresno. It was not until the end of the 1920s, however, that major agricultural union activity appeared in California.

Labor organizing activity had also been evident in Texas since the early part of the century. Nicasio Idar and his son, under the auspices of the Texas Socialist Party and the American Federation of Labor, effectively organized among the tens of thousands of Mexicans entering the state between 1900 and 1930.

In the late 1920s and throughout the 1930s, Mexicans made intensive organizing efforts in California agriculture. By then, Mexican farm workers acquired a greater willingness to struggle against workplace exploitation. In this same era, Mexican working women began organizing more than ever before. The Los Angeles garment industry, which before the 1930s had used a multiethnic workforce, increasingly turned towards Mexican women, who were migrating into the city from agricultural towns during the Depression. In a 1933 strike, members of the International Ladies Garment Workers Union (ILGWU), many of them Mexicans, brought garment production to a halt despite city officials constantly harassing the workers at the behest of the industry owners. Eventually, the union signed a contract with a number of shops, and its members received better wages.

Mexicans participated significantly in the "Little Steel Strike" of 1937, one of the most famous events in U.S. labor history. Large companies, such as U.S. Steel, negotiated with the new unions, but smaller steel companies, such as Republic, Youngstown, and Inland, resisted. The Steel Workers Organizing Committee then focused its efforts on these smaller companies. A bitter struggle ensued when scores of workers, including thousands of Mexicans, walked out of these plants throughout the Midwest. In Chicago, the police killed ten workers when they tried to break up a peaceful meeting designed to muster inspiration among the strikers on Memorial Day of 1937. Lupe Marshall, a social worker, and Max Guzmán, a union activist who helped organize the rally, were among the many Mexicans who were arrested and beaten that day.

In response to labor scarcity during World War II, Congress established the Bracero Program in 1941, which allowed for the recruiting of guest workers from Mexico, a process that kept wages down and hindered unionization efforts during and after World War II. One of the last strikes before the arrival of *braceros* began on January 31, 1941, in Ventura County. American Federation of Labor (AFL) organizers persuaded lemon pickers, packers, and cannery workers to strike across the whole county. The stoppage lasted six months, during which time the growers, led by Charles C. Teague, refused to bargain with the umbrella negotiating team established by the AFL. The growers knew that unions would destroy their ability to obtain cheap labor and to break the strike. The growers recruited hundreds of "Okies" (dust bowl refugees) and then evicted the strikers from company-provided camps.

In the mid-1940s, the writer and scholar Ernesto Galarza started the National Farm Workers Union (NFWU), an offshoot of the Southern Tenant Farmers Union. The most significant strike initiated by the NFWU occurred in October of 1947 against the powerful DiGiorgio Fruit Company in Arvin, California. Hundreds of Mexican, Filipino, and white workers walked out, demanding higher wages. The strike was broken by the usual methods. With local authorities on the side of the DiGiorgio company, strikers were evicted and undocumented workers brought in as strikebreakers.

In Texas and Arizona, limited unionization took place among Mexican farm workers during the 1930s and 1940s. Pedro de la Lama, one of the founders of La Liga Protectora Latina, tried to organize a pseudo-union, Los Agricultores Mexicanos (Mexican Agriculturalists), in the Phoenix area during 1930. The effort was based in Tolleson, a town that became a base for unionization as late as the 1960s and the 1970s. In Texas, La Asociación de Jornaleros (The Journeymen's Association) was formed in 1933, representing occupations which ranged from hatmakers to farm workers. The union tried to represent too many trades and found itself spread out too thinly. As a consequence, the organization was not resilient enough to survive after Texas Rangers arrested its leaders at an onion harvester strike in Laredo in 1934.

Urban area unionization occurred in Texas as well. About 10,000 Mexican workers, mainly women, toiled in San Antonio's pecan packing industry, shelling nuts by hand. The owners paid them five to six cents per pound, a paltry wage which amounted to as little as two dollars per week. To offset such conditions, some 4,000 workers joined El Nogal (The Pecan Tree). On February 1, 1938, union members walked out of 130 shops at the peak of the shelling season in response to the packinghouse owners cutting their wages by one cent per pound. The San Antonio police quickly embarked on a harassment campaign to break the strike at the behest of the influential pecan processors. The pecan shellers succeeded in obtaining higher wages through this strike, which lasted one month, although soon after that, the industry mechanized and thousands of workers had to find other means to make a living.

Mexicans found it difficult to organize enduring unions in the 1930s because they lacked the support given to other workers by the federal government. From the outset of his administration in 1933, Franklin D. Roosevelt showed that his Democratic administration could be sympathetic to organized labor but his major creation did not include farm workers. The National Labor Relations Act of 1935, which obliged employers to bargain in good faith, facilitated the formation of a Congress of Industrial Organizations (CIO), a powerful giant that eventually put dozens of unions under its umbrella. The act, however, did not include agricultural and packinghouse workers—sectors that contained almost half of the Mexican workforce in the United States.

But thousands of Mexicans did work in areas that the CIO rapidly organized under the auspices of the new law: in mining, steel, and automobile plants. Mexican workers joined CIO-sponsored unions when automobile manufacturing and urban building booms expanded to California. In the Chicago area, Mexicans who were either born in the United States or had no intention of returning to Mexico became some of the most militant members of the Steel Workers Organizing Committee (SWOC). In the Southwest, Mexican participation in unions representing workers employed by such companies as Phelps Dodge, Anaconda, American Smelting and Refining, and Nevada Consolidated was extensive.

Mexican miners saw their greatest success in the formation of the El Paso-based International Union of Mine, Mill and Smelter Workers (The Mine Mill), a union that sprang from the earlier Western Federation of Miners. In 1936, the organization became affiliated with the CIO, and although multiethnic, Mexican American workers soon filled its membership lists. Mexicans were attracted to the union because it promised to address dual wage systems and the labor segmentation that had been the bane of Mexican miners.

The organizing of Mexican workers in the first four decades of the twentieth century cut across many labor sectors, but it concentrated mainly in mining and agriculture. The breadth of its activity was extensive, but victories were few, primarily because employers had the support of officialdom—local police, judges, city councils, etc. A report done for the Works Progress Administration on California indicated:

> While some gains have been made by the Mexicans as the result of organization, both through their own racial unions and as members of others of mixed racial makeup, these have been won at the cost of considerable violence and economic loss due to time spent in carrying on their struggles, during which income stopped.

Bread-and-butter issues mainly interested most Mexican unionists in the 1930s, but some Mexicans strove for civil rights through unions, using the class struggle as an ideological foundation. The California-based El Congreso del Pueblo de Habla Española (Spanish Speaking People's Congress), started in 1938 by Luisa Moreno, a Guatemalan, and Josefina Fierro de Bright, a Los Angeles Mexican American, stands out the most in this respect. Organizing New York's Latino garment workers first radicalized Moreno, but she soon moved to California and became an organizer in the United Cannery, Agricultural, Packing and Allied Workers Association (UCAPAWA). Other Southwest organizing activities among Mexicans consumed her time, including the pecan shellers' in San Antonio.

The Asociación Nacional México-Americana (ANMA), an organization similar to the Congreso, emerged in 1949 with similar goals. The organization grew out of the Mine Mill union, which was ousted from the CIO in 1950 because of Communist affiliation. Predominantly Mexican American, the membership recognized that the problems of working Mexicans transcended workplace issues and attempted to deal with a plethora of problems related to Mexicans in the United States, such as undocumented entry, substandard housing, inferior education, lack of political representation, youth unemployment, and police brutality.

Mexican Americans also sought equal opportunity to work in sectors from which they had been banned in the past. They were keenly aware that better paying jobs that were not as backbreaking and which conferred more status were reserved for whites. Obtaining such a job was a mark of mobility. One area to which Mexicans looked to achieve this mobility was government employment. One of the first issues of Houston's Latin American Club (LAC) became convincing the city council to put Mexican American employees on permanent status rather than "temporary." Even though many Mexicans worked full-time for the city, they did not get fringe benefits.

The Works Progress Administration (WPA) in the 1930s integrated some Mexicans into occupations that had eluded them in the past. Mexican Americans, such as Isaac Aceves and Ramón Welch in California and Ernest Mendivil and José del Castillo in Arizona, obtained work with the Federal Writer's Project, a section within the WPA with the smallest number of minority workers. Nonetheless, Mexicans mainly worked in construction with the WPA. When noncitizens were taken off the WPA rolls in 1937, because of pressure from nativists and from employers who found that the WPA competed for laborers, Mexican American civil rights activists protested this as another example of job discrimination.

Mexican Americans did experience upward mobility during the World War II era. As soldiers, many rose high in the ranks and learned leadership skills that would serve them well as civilians. Spurred mainly by the defense industry, employment in the technological manufacturing sector expanded dramatically. A more sophisticated generation of Mexican Americans jockeyed for entry into this sector that was dominated by white workers. In 1941, Roosevelt's administration established the President's Committee on Fair Employment Practices (FEPC) in order to stem discrimination in projects financed by the federal government. Opposition from southern politicians and the reluctance of war industries to hire minorities in skilled positions stymied the FEPC's effectiveness. However, Mexican American politicians and civil rights activists tried to make the agency accountable. Unfortunately, the policy of excluding Mexicans from other than menial jobs in war industries continued during the war.

During the boom years of the war, in cities in the Midwest and Southwest that had wartime industries, hundreds of daughters of immigrants, who had first settled the *colonias* earlier in the century, obtained industrial jobs that were normally done by men. Despite the women being replaced by men in these jobs after the war terminated, Mexican American women learned skills that allowed them to aspire to jobs outside the service and agricultural sectors where they had toiled before.

Daniel Venegas and the Workplace

During economic downturns, Mexicans confronted long-term unemployment and destitution, a worse predicament than the most laborious of jobs. Consequently, they put up with a great deal of abuse. Generally, the most distasteful job experiences stemmed from having "patrones que eran muy perros" (bosses that were mean dogs). Anglos and even Mexican Americans who supervised Mexican workers sometimes leveraged power by resorting to demeaning force. At times, these bosses severely injured or killed their charges during altercations. The 1920s writer, Daniel Venegas, interrupts the narrative in his novel of immigration to recount an experience that he had personally undergone as an immigrant worker.

This kind of treatment for the poor guys who work in the camps and in the railroad sections is so common that one doesn't even take notice. Moreover, on these jobs, the foreman is the slave driver of the Mexican infidel who has to do his bidding. He cares very little about the suffering of those who are so grateful to the company which employs them.

The author of this novel, who, not too long ago, had to join up with the infamous *traque* like the majority of those who come from Mexico, took perfect account of the abuses which the foremen commit against the workers. On one occasion, the foreman, for no other reason than because he could, forced the author and two other Mexicans to replace a "sweech," or direction changer, one half-hour before a passenger train was to come through. Take into account that one had to cut the beams and lift up the rigging, or the main part of those "sweeches," from under the embankment. Those who are familiar with this kind of work know perfectly well that this is impossible to do in half an hour, even more so with only three men. In spite of all of this, that foreman worked us like dogs, only making us become desperate. The train arrived without our completing the task, and we had to fix it on the spot so that it could go through.

After this, the foreman began to yell at us in a manner so vile that, unable to take any more of his insults, I talked back to him. He socked me. And I returned his lick. I got canned, even losing the time I had already worked. Cases like this happen daily on the *traque*, and more than a few foremen have gone as far as killing Mexicans, such crimes going unpunished, just as there have been Mexicans who have sent foremen to meet their maker. Of course, when the workers on the *traque* decide to rub out a foreman, it's because he's already heaped their plate full of injustice.

Daniel Venegas, *Las aventuras de Don Chipote o cuando los pericos mamen* (Houston: Arte Público Press, 2000), pp. 70-71.

Boss Violence in Track Work

Repair crew foremen were pressured to finish a job quickly to accommodate train schedules, but railroad work attracted mainly newly arrived Mexicans unacquainted with routine tasks. Consequently, a foreman's perception of malingering or insubordination often sparked violent temper tantrums. These conditions are seen in the press account of the beating of two Mexican railroad workers by their boss near New Braunfels, Texas, in 1921. Such incidents often sparked civil rights protests.

Two Mexican Men

Yesterday two Mexican men who worked on the railroad track repair crew near Dittinger were abused while they worked. They were brutally hit by the son of the foreman, an American citizen who runs the railroad camp to which they were assigned.

According to the reports that have been provided to us via telephone by the New Braunfels Mexican Honorific Commission, which has been looking into this matter, Benjamín López, one of the Mexican men who was hit, found himself quite tired due to the hard labor and, suffering an overwhelming thirst as a result of the extreme heat of the sun, decided to drink water. He approached the camp foreman's son who refused to give him permission to take a drink saying that it was not convenient that he waste his time that way under any circumstances.

López insisted and the other refused; the exasperated Mexican said something harsh. The American asked for the shovel that the Mexican man carried and gave him a violent blow on the back and knocked him down. Once the Mexican man was down, he continued to hit him without compassion. Dionisio López, the victim's brother who also works in the same camp, seeing what was happening, rushed to his brother's aid. He encountered the American who was armed with the shovel. The American battered Dionisio hard; he knocked him to the ground and continued to hit him.

The foreman saw what had happened, and when his son was about to stop hitting the Mexican men, the foreman ordered him to continue doing it until they were almost dead.

As soon as the New Braunfels Honorific Commission found out about this occurrence, it went to the location where it took place and carried out its preliminary investigation, from which it deduced that the Mexican men did nothing to receive such treatment. That aggression was unjustified and even cruel.

It was also arranged for the injured to go to the referenced city, where they were placed with the Blue Cross Brigade which, of course, gave them the aid they required.

According to the information gathered and because the attack occurred during work, the Honorific Commission estimates that justice will be effected in this case, imposing the punishment that the guilty deserve and granting the indemnity that our compatriots claim from the railroad company where they are employed.

The Mexican Consulate has been notified of the event and today will take the proper steps; since yesterday was not a working day, nothing could have been done at that time, but we are told that they will proceed to address this case appropriately.

La Prensa, June 21, 1921.

Labor Competition and Violence

As unemployment rocked the Texas oil industry, citizens of Eastland, a town near Temple, attempted in February to expel Mexicans hired during World War I. In nearby Ranger, mounted masked men ravaged the frame shacks of Mexican workers and warned them not to compete with American labor. *La Prensa* newspaper in 1921 captured the frustration Mexicans faced during these attacks. Similar attacks occurred in other parts of the country, especially in Texas and Oklahoma.

Mexicans in this country are willing to obey the law and be good citizens. They also show great restraint when attacked by Americans. Nothing is better evidence of this than the latest provocation in Ranger, which occurred because American farmers prefer to give employment to our people. A mafia has been formed to force Mexicans out. Yesterday leaflets were distributed warning Mexicans to leave town in twenty-four hours or they should expect to be expelled. Because Mexicans did not leave, last night one of the most severe breaches of individual liberty took place.

Taking advantage of the almost timid character of the Mexican people and knowing that they would not encounter any armed resistance, since Mexicans are rarely armed, numerous hooded individuals invaded the Mexican section of town and, without consideration to women and children, they physically shoved them out of their homes, throwing out their belongings into the street. After doing this, the band of men dispersed and the authorities did nothing and none could be identified. The occurrences took place from 9 p.m. to 12 p.m., three hours during which the police did nothing. One woman is in shock. This is typical of what Mexicans experience in the small towns of Texas and many others in the United States. It is no wonder Mexicans prefer to abandon their homes to the bigger cities rather than remain in the small towns.

The mayor has assembled the competent authorities and the [Texas] Rangers to assure that the streets are patrolled to protect honest Mexican workers. Mexicans, on the other hand, have gone to the consul in Ft. Worth to seek repatriation or assistance to move elsewhere.

San Antonio representatives from the Hammon Railroad, the Mackenzie Co., the Eastland Rock Crusher, and Mosely Contractors, have gone to the mayor of Ranger, M.H. Hagama, asking that something be done about the assaults and provocations against Mexicans who are working for them. The camps that were invaded by the band of assailants are located on Tiffin Road, at the Hammon Railroad yards near Sinclair and south of Eastland.

The assailants, who after accomplishing their misdeeds seemed very satisfied, furiously hit the men repeatedly, shoved around women and children and destroyed their camps. Twenty-one Rangers are patrolling the streets of Ranger, as some of the assailants are still armed. Nevertheless, many Mexican families are abandoning the town.

Consul Roberto García in Dallas conveyed to Francisco Pérez, consul in this town [San Antonio], an extensive petition signed by 158 Mexican residents of Ranger in which they complain about the treatment they received. They ask the Mexican government for help in preventing further outbreaks or for help in leaving the community where for six weeks many individuals have been out of work. The communiqué also asserted that Anglo Americans insult and assault Mexicans with impunity on a daily basis and that when a group, under the leadership of Primitivo R. Castillo, went to the authorities to get help, they were told that the most prudent action would be to abandon the town.

Yesterday, four families came to complain from Ranger. Their leaders, Luis Barrientos, Jaral del Berrío from Guanajuato; Camilo Zamarripa from San Luis Potosí; and Gregorio and Antonio Navarro from Zacatecas came to San Antonio to recount their misfortune. The masked attackers, armed with pistols and black jacks, insulted the Mexicans vilely and manhandled them in the most inhumane manner possible. According to these refugees, there are at least five-hundred Mexicans who cannot leave. In view of this, the consul, Señor Pérez, has communicated with the ambassador in Washington and the Mexican Foreign Ministry, asking authorization to transport to the border from Ranger many of the victims so they can return to their lands. A telegram was sent to Governor Pat M. Neff asking protection for the lives and interests of our compatriots in Ranger.

La Prensa, February 18, 1921.

LULAC Defends White Worker Threats

Unemployment during the Great Depression, as had been the case in the 1921 depression, led to antagonism towards Mexicans. On January 12, 1931, one-hundred-fifty Anglo workers in Knickerbocker, Texas, signed a petition and presented it to E.E. Foster, the Tom Greene County Commissioner, demanding that Mexican workers be fired from highway construction jobs. Foster replied that only Americans would be hired from that point on. In May, disgruntled workers in Malakoff, an oil company town near Dallas, took a more concrete action. On the 19th, the "Mexican Hall," a gathering place for Mexicans who worked for the Malakoff Fuel Company, was dynamited. After the blast, placards attached to the wrecked hall read, "LEAVE TOWN, DAMN *PRONTO.*" In January, 1931, a committee of white workers demanded that Mexicans be dismissed from county jobs (first document). In mid-June, more threats against Mexicans appeared in San Angelo, Texas, but local officials dismissed them, as the second document below shows. A few days later this dismissal brought a vitriolic denunciation from LULAC president Manuel C. González in a letter printed in *El Defensor.*

San Angelo, January 12. Approximately one-hundred-fifty unemployed men signed a petition to force E.E. Foster of Knickerbocker, Commissioner of Precinct 5 in Tom Greene County, to replace Mexican workers employed in highway construction by "white men" who reside in that area, and if he does not, he must resign his Commissioner's post. Foster stated that he would not do it, explaining that the Mexican workers are residents, and the majority are natives of this Precinct.

The County Commissioners, with Foster's exception, stated that they would not employ people of Mexican descent, and the Court adopted a resolution stating that in all jobs, local residents would be hired first; second, Texas Mexicans and Negroes of local residence; and, third, nonresidents.

This agreement was accepted after a group of one-hundred-fifty men, who claimed to be unemployed, gathered at the Court's park and sent a delegation to the Commission.

Foster declares that this resolution does not mean he will fire any of his employees.

El Defensor, January 16, 1931.

Chief of Police Sam Haynes and *The Standard-Times* last night were in receipt of anonymous letters, one signed "Darts" and the other "The Unemployed," which among other things, threatened the Mexican population.

Chief Haynes was inclined to believe the letters were the work of a crank, or possibly were written as a crude joke, and said he paid little attention to his letter.

However, both the police department and the Sheriff's department will co-operate in putting down any demonstration that might possibly start from the secret "organization," if such exists.

The letter to the police head said:

"We are making raids on all Mexicans in and around San Angelo in the near future. This is the first warning. We are prepared for trouble so keep your nose out of it."

"The Unemployed." "South with Mexicans."

The letter to *The Standard-Times*, which was posted in San Angelo at 2 o'clock yesterday afternoon, read:

"We are forming a club known as the Darts; our aim is to clean up our city and make working conditions better for Americans. You will hear from us from time to time as our good work progresses. Each member will work separate, not knowing any other member. All Mexicans must leave.

Darts."

The letter was hand-printed in capital letters in a pale red ink.

San Angelo Morning News, June 16, 1931.

Our organization feels that the Hon. Chief of Police Sam Haynes will not overlook the matter of the two anonymous letters signed "Darts" and "Unemployed" as the work of a crank. If we are not mistaken, there appears to have been some demonstration around the San Angelo vicinity recently by some of our countrymen demanding the dismissal of all Mexicans from the county road work, etc. A broadminded, truly patriotic American citizen who was the foreman in charge, refused to accede to the demands, despite the apparent pressure brought to bear upon him, maintaining that Mexicans by racial extraction, born or naturalized in the United States are American citizens entitled to all the privileges and immunities enjoyed by Americans of other racial extractions.

Care should be taken to distinguish between the so-called Mexican of this country and the other who has chosen to retain his Mexican citizenship. As to the first, we stand ready to defend their rights, legally, to the limits of our resources, from the encroachments and underhanded methods of narrow-minded, selfish, and conceited persons who on account of their un-American conduct sink to a lower level than those they seek to oust from America as being undesirable, especially if those so-called "Mexicans" are bona fide citizens of our country.

El Defensor, June 19, 1931.

"Black Lung" Disease

While Mexican consuls did not support radicals, they often objected to dangerous and unhealthy working conditions. Miner's consumption, the dreaded "black lung," affected Mexican miners so disproportionately that Gustavo G. Hernández, the Mexican consul in Globe, Arizona, wrote on May 21, 1918, to the Arizona State Federation of Labor and to Governor George W.P. Hunt, asking for an end to the conditions that caused this disease. Supervisors at the mine refused to take any responsibility for this debilitating disease, despite Hernández providing a list of persons afflicted with the disease.

I am enclosing herewith a copy of correspondence exchanged between this Office and Mr. Croaff, President of the Arizona State of Federation of Labor, which is self-explanatory.

Please find attached a list of twelve Mexican laborers who have died of "miner's consumption" from December last up to date, leaving their families in a destitute condition. As far as I have been able to gather, as you will kindly see also in the attached list, there are twenty sick men, unable to work, and I understand there are more of them, residing only in the little town of Miami.

More than anything, these men complain that the plugger is responsible for them getting sick. They also state that while working in a sound condition, money is deducted from their wages for the support of the hospitals, and now when sick, unable to work, without any funds whatever and having to support their families besides, they do not receive even from these mining companies, some sort of medical attention to relieve their suffering.

It strikes me the number of Mexican workers who are sick, more than any other nationality, but they claim that is because a great number of them are placed to work with these pluggers, in the worst and most dangerous places, a greater number than any other race.

As a matter of fact, I may say, as everybody knows too, that the Mexican laborer as a whole always accepts any kind of conditions without protest, and I think this is where the whole trouble lies.

I am taking the liberty to address these lines to you only for your information and for whatever action you may see fit to take on behalf of the worker, as you will readily see that upon the death of these sick men, there will be that number more of families cast into destitution, and it will keep increasing every day. In the meantime, I am endeavoring to take the matter up with managers of mining companies here.

Gustavo G. Hernández, consul in Globe, Arizona, to George W.P. Hunt, governor of Arizona, May 21, 1919, Archivo General de la Nación, Secretaría de Industria y Trabajo, 137-20-23.

The Mammoth Tank Battle

One of the most violent reactions to Mexican efforts to organize and obtain higher wages took place during November, 1897, at a coaling and water depot near Yuma, Arizona, called Mammoth Tank. In the midst of a "wildcat strike" against the Southern Pacific, José Rodríguez killed strikebreaker Francisco Cuevas. San Diego County deputies and Arizona officers were called to the scene because, although Rodríguez had fled, the atmosphere remained explosive. A battle broke out in which an undetermined number of Mexicans were killed or wounded and one deputy was wounded, according to the following report.

A conflict of forces occurred at about three o'clock this afternoon, at the railroad track renewal camp, near Mammoth Tank, California, between three officers of Yuma County and a crew of three hundred Mexicans, laborers. It is believed some five or six Mexicans were killed and wounded, and one of the officers, George Wilder, was badly battered and bruised.

Several shots were fired by deputies, the Mexicans only being armed with stones and clubs. The laborers went on a strike this morning for causes unknown, as stated by railroad people, but which will probably develop to have been a grievance against the contractors who supply the company with men.

Meeting of the officers at Mammoth Tank is said to be merely a coincidence. As the sheriff was returning on the train from Los Angeles, he received a telegram to stop off and arrest the leaders of the strike, and that the other two were in search of a Mexican named Juan Jueraos who murdered a man at Fortuna a few years ago.

A posse left on a special train at 8 o'clock this evening for Mammoth Tank and further trouble is anticipated.

Arizona Gazette, October 26, 1897.

"¡Solidaridad! ¡Solidaridad!"

While most Mexican workers responded mainly to simple "bread and butter" concerns, many of the organizers attempted to expose them to more abstract ideologies, such as socialism or anarchism. During a mine worker strike in southeast Arizona in 1915, Tomás Martínez wrote the following tract, which urges solidarity among the striking Mexicans. Martínez, a follower of Lázaro Gutiérrez de Lara who was a member of the Partido Liberal Mexicano, the organization started by Ricardo Flores Magón, couched his appeal in strong socialist rhetoric against capitalism.

Solidarity!

This is what is needed for our comrades who have declared a strike on the mining camps of Clifton Morenci. Solidarity is what laborers of Arizona should contribute, helping with our humble intellect and in-kind, if possible, in support of the effort. Pay close attention, comrades in misery: the capitalist class is united and it solidifies even more when the salary earner rebels against the oppressive and miserable system, a system in which it is our duty to help in any way and at all costs.

The so-called managers believed in the beginning that there was a solution to what they called the "Street Riot," the labor movement of us workers, tired of undergoing the daily exploitation to which we fall victim. These "Misters" who represent companies, including every single boss they have at their service, whether he is called Foreman, Policeman, Dog, or whatever, the government's little managers and "mouthpieces" have thwarted themselves because even the protection offered by Hunt, the "headmaster of this state," was withdrawn. This protection was composed of little toy soldiers to scare off agitators and protect the lives or interests of the capitalists, just like any man in the service of capitalism is a tool. Comrades, solidarity is necessary; an offense to one is an offense to all. Go forward, and you, comrades in Morenci, do not be dismayed because the vampires are already calm. Agitate. It is better to die at your post for the labor cause than to continue living in this state of misery in which we are held by this damn trinity: the Government, Capital, and the Clergy. Do not allow politicians to go as redeemers. You yourselves, guard cleverly and knowingly your own interests. Direct action is our own salvation.

Tomás Martínez, "¡Solidaridad! ¡Solidaridad!" *Rebelde,* 1915, CHI h-54, Arizona Collection, Hayden Library, Arizona State University.

The Bisbee Deportations

Labor unions in the United States were not entirely abandoned by government officials, as the letter from the former governor of Arizona, George W. P. Hunt, to President Woodrow Wilson demonstrates. Here Hunt discusses the condition of strikers, more than half of them Mexican, were deported to Columbus, New Mexico, from Bisbee, Arizona, on July 12, 1917, by Dodge Copper Company goons and cooperating law officials. He condemns the act and claims that allegations that strikers were disloyal during World War I are not true.

My dear Mr. President:

On the 1st instant I telegraphed you as follows:

> "I have just returned from Columbus, New Mexico, where the men deported from Bisbee July 12 are camped. The impressions of that visit, resulting from careful inquiry designed to disclose the mental attitude of these men, their processes and course of reasoning, the quality of their loyalty to the government, and their hopes and aspirations for the future, coupled with my natural repugnance for an act so un-American, so autocratic, as that which forced them from their homes, constrain me to urge that you insist upon an early recognition of their constitutional rights and a resumption of American justice in this State. I am deeply mindful of the cares which so heavily weigh upon you at this time, and I will gladly relieve them in any way or degree within my power, but I am convinced that it is vital to the maintenance of this Union's proud boast of democracy, to which your utterances and acts so eloquently testify, and to the restoration of confidence in the efficacy of the federal constitution, that these men be returned to their homes under ample federal protection, there to answer in the constituted courts of justice any charges of unlawful conduct that may be regularly placed against them. I am writing you more fully and in my capacity as conciliator submitting a formal report to the Secretary of Labor."

In amplification of the above telegram I wish to explain that on the afternoon of the 19th ult., acting upon the suggestion and advice of Conciliator John McBride, of the Department of Labor, with whom I had been cooperating in an effort to bring about a settlement of the labor disputes in the Globe-Miami copper district, I left Globe for Columbus, New Mexico, where between 900 and 1,000 of the men deported from Bisbee on July 12 are still encamped. The visit to the Columbus refugees was not paid with any idea that it would or could result in a settlement or compromise of the difference between the particular men affected and the companies by whom they were formerly employed, for not only has the relationship of employer and employee ceased to exist, but the undesirable though not extraordinary status of operator and striker was terminated by means so abrupt and so violent that it was not reasonable to suppose there remained any basis of reconciliation as between the principal parties.

Nevertheless, in pursuance of your summons to me to do what I could to act as conciliator and mediator in this State, it had been my intention to go to Bisbee from Globe, but before the situation in the latter place justified my departure, every striker and practically every strike sympathizer in the Warren District was deported, through the medium of a large armed force of so-called deputies under the leadership of Sheriff Harry Wheeler of Cochise County, and there remained in the Warren District no one to whom I could appeal for a settlement of existing differences. The workingmen were gone, and it is not to be presumed that the operators, successful and defiant in their stupendous act of usurpation of the functions of the law, or of lawlessness, were in a frame of mind to listen to appeals to their fairness. There remained only the possibility that by contact with the deported men there might be gained, not an explanation or defense of the grievances which led them to strike—for in view of the act which occurred, the original differences are forgotten—but an insight into the mental processes and course of reasoning through which they justify their efforts, during the existing emergency, to secure economic reforms; into the depth of their realization of the responsibilities resting upon them as citizens of or as men claiming the protection of a nation at war in a great cause, and of their sense of loyalty to that nation; into the intimate phases—the psychology, as it were—of their attitude toward employers of labor in general; toward mankind in general; toward the vital problems of mankind which wait upon the outcome of the present struggle; toward the war itself. Such an insight—not profound, to be sure, but such a partial insight as I might gain, it seemed to me would likely shed a little light upon the causes of labor's unrest, and so far as this country is affected, or at least so far as the metal industry is affected, might possibly aid in the formulation of a plan for dispelling the discontent and suspicion prevailing, and for remedying a condition that constitutes so great a menace to many necessary industries.

Of particular interest was the chance of learning whether or not the sinister influences of the enemies of this country were at work among the deported men. Numerous suggestions—in fact, broad statements—that they were have emanated from those who defend the deportation.

I spent five days in camp, talking to the refugees, singly and in groups, receiving their confidences and learning their views, judiciously questioning them when necessary to ascertain their real frame of mind. From first to last, I talked to as many as a third of the camp's population. A considerable number of them, who have for many years resided in Bisbee, some with, some without families, I have been personally acquainted with. I feel that I acquired, with reasonable accuracy, the information I sought.

There was not to be found the slightest evidence of German influence or the work of German money, now or heretofore. That charge, emanating from the defenders of the deportation, I am satisfied was a hoax pure and simple.

There are a considerable number of I.W.W.'s—more than there were at the time the deportation occurred, which is a perfectly logical effect of such a method—probably constituting one-half of the men in the camp. About one-third are affiliated with labor unions in no wise connected with the I.W.W., while approximately one-third belong to no labor organization. I found no line of cleavage, so far as it related to their views on any subject other than the technical one of membership, between the union men and the unaffiliated men. The I. W. W.'s were frequently distinguishable for unfortunate utterances, but more among them are men without convictions than is true of those who carry no red card.

These men—speaking of them by and large—are not unpatriotic. Just now, to be sure, their spirits are not exuberant, and their expressions do not disclose any excesses of patriotism, but nothing appears to be further from their thoughts than feelings or sentiments of disloyalty. They are just ordinary human beings, struggling in their own ways and according to their own lights for a betterment of the conditions which they expect will be their lot through life—hardly so much evidence of an aspiration for better things, in order that all mankind might be the gainer, as one could wish for, but forward-looking men with a rather personal outlook upon affairs. There are few extreme radicals among them. I talked with no one who struck me as being unamenable to reason.

George W. P. Hunt, chairman, Arizona Council of Defense, Committee on Federal and Interstate Relations, to Woodrow Wilson, President of the United States, September 3, 1917, CHSM-330, Arizona Collection, Hayden Library, Arizona State University.

Workers' Demands in Clifton, Arizona—1918

During the Clifton, Arizona, strike of 1918, two thousand Mexicans walked out of their jobs, but became so destitute that Vice Consul C. Emilio attempted to repatriate them to northern Mexico. The consul obtained the following declaration that some of the strikers made against the mines, dated February 1918. The document below recounts how the strike began and that an accord with the companies was reached. The mine managers, however, did not live up to the promises of the contract, according to the writers.

The undersigned Mexican citizens, in full possession of our faculties, respectfully express before you:

1st - That from June 1st of 1917, we declared ourselves on a union strike; five thousand work mates asked the Copper Companies who own mining camps in Clifton, Morenci, and Metcalf, that they justly raise our salary, taking into consideration the increased costs that are apparent in all articles of daily use and consumption.

2nd - That because of the contradictory propositions of the different Companies, we jointly agree to exert pressure in order to obtain our objectives by way of declaring a strike.

3rd - That November 1st of last year, jobs were reopened because of an agreement reached between a Commission of the Department of Labor of the Federal Government and the Companies, making a pact with our labor union for no retaliation and that at the end of two weeks the union would have all strikers back in their jobs, BECAUSE WE ARE NEEDED.

4th - Since the Companies violated the agreed upon pact that is mentioned in the previous paragraph (and they continue to violate it), we have been supporting ourselves in whatever way we can; meanwhile we have been meeting and protesting to make sure that the Companies carry out their promises, while the Companies, under pointless pretexts, make allegations that do not remedy our precarious situation.

5th - In view of the Companies who, far from carrying out their promises have been trying to PUNISH US for the simple fact that we made them see that bread costs more and therefore we needed a higher wage, have introduced new workers, contrary to what was agreed to as is declared in the beginning of the previous paragraph, which was not agreed to in the covenant even though there are strikers waiting for these Companies to carry out their commitment to place us back in our jobs.

In view of all that is expressed and after having depleted whatever resources we had within our reach, either through our labor union, lawyers, etc., without JUSTICE BEING CARRIED OUT FOR US and as time goes by, our situation becomes more and more difficult.

Dear Vice-consul, we come to demand aid and protection, so that as soon as possible these be imparted to us, returning us to our beloved Homeland, where we can obtain sustenance for us and our families through honest work, because we are now suffering miserably in exile.

Oficial Mayor, Secretaría de Industria, Comercio y Trabajo to SRE, March 28, 1918, Archivo General de la Nación, Ramo Secretaría de Industria y Trabajo, 137-17-5.

Agricultural Workers in California

Before the era of large-scale agricultural organizing in California, the *Labor Clarion*, on February 23, 1934, cited a report issued by the National Labor Relations Board after it investigated attempts by Mexicans and Filipinos to organize into unions. It painted a dismal picture of the conditions under which California agricultural workers lived.

After nearly a month's investigation, the commission delegated by the National Labor Relations Board to investigate the almost unbelievable reports from the Imperial Valley of violence, peonage, denial of constitutional rights and persecution of workers in connection with labor difficulties, has submitted its report to Washington.

The commission reports some terrible facts, of "filth, squalor, the entire absence of sanitation; of habitation unfit for human beings, lack of pure water, of general discomfort which breeds a social sullenness dangerous to the community, and with many workers unable to earn sufficient to maintain so much as a primitive or savage standard of living."

But worse than all these, in the opinion of the commission, is the suppression of what we in the United States claim as our birthright—the freedom to express our lawful opinions and legally to organize to better our lot and that of our fellowmen.

Altogether, the report reveals a terrible blot on our civilization—a blot that it must be the endeavor of every citizen, and especially every official, to eradicate at once. Let us have an end to this slavery and starvation in a land of plenty, and a restoration of those rights to which even the humble Mexican and Filipino are entitled under our constitution and laws.

"Organization Efforts of Mexican Agricultural Workers," p. 4, Bancroft Library, Berkeley, CR-2 Carton 37, folder NF73.

An Early Labor Society

An early form of labor organization was a cross between the older mutual aid societies and unions. As can be seen below, the articles of incorporation for the Sociedad Agricultores Mexicanos de Arizona in 1930, while not a labor union in the strict sense of the word, contains language that encourages workers to band together and put forth a united front when dealing with their employers. A similar organization, the Latin American League, was started some eleven years earlier in Los Angeles, California.

The name of this Organization shall be "SOCIEDAD AGRICULTORES MEXICANOS DE ARIZONA," and its principal place of business shall be the town of Tolleson, County of Maricopa, State of Arizona.

The purposes for which this organization is formed are the following:

FIRST: For the purpose of uniting the people of the Mexican race who depend on agricultural work or farm labor as their livelihood, to the end that they will be afforded better working facilities, and to the end that they will not be cheated or defrauded of their earnings by any person inclined to take advantage of them because of their nationality or because they do not speak the English language.

SECOND: For the purpose of establishing a better understanding between the Mexican farm laborers and the farmers of this State, and to assist the Mexican farm laborer to adjust to any difference or disagreement that may result between the laborers and the farmers.

THIRD: For the purpose of maintaining an office where the farmers may call for Mexican farm laborers, and to assist Mexicans in obtaining employment with the better class of farmers.

FOURTH: For the purpose of having social and instructive gatherings where farmers and professional men may instruct them and advise them regarding the laws of the land.

FIFTH: For the purpose of acquiring and maintaining sufficient real estate and personal property to conduct the business and objects of this Society.

This Society shall be a nonprofit organization and whatever dues are collected shall be used to defray the expenses of social, instructive, and public gatherings, and to defray the expenses of assisting the members in obtaining justice, and to assist sick members of this organization as far as possible. However, the dues shall not exceed the sum of two dollars per month.

Article of Incorporation, Sociedad Agricultores Mexicanos de Arizona, Incorporation Commission Microfilms, Arizona Department of Library, Archives and Public Records.

Mainstream American Unions and Mexicans

The American Federation of Labor (AF of L) made efforts to reach out to the Mexican labor movement in order to resolve issues common to workers on both sides of the border. A meeting was held in Laredo in November of 1918. It was called by Samuel Gompers, president of the AF of L, to bring together Mexican labor union leaders, such as Luis Morones, head of Confederación Regional de Obreros Mexicanos (Regional Confederation of Mexican Workers) and American government officials, such as Secretary of Labor Wilson. Mexican workers in the United States figured as a major point of discussion, as the following excerpt from a prepared statement of the CROM indicates. It asks the AF of L to use its influence to reduce the mistreatment of Mexican workers.

The United States, with the exception of a few honorable instances, are almost completely unaware of the state and condition that Mexican workers face, and possibly due to that ignorance, Mexican workers who live in this country are the object of unjustified discrimination and in some cases they are harassed in such a way that their situation becomes very difficult. Despite the fact that the American Federation of Labor has made public repeated declarations, and it may be said that it is inspired by a noble spirit of brotherhood and justice, it is with true sorrow that we have not been able to correct the evils that have created a hostility that has no reason for being, even if those who exercise this hostility are known to us as members of a civilized and egalitarian society.

These practices, which probably would not have been approved by the Federation, were witnessed by those who on various occasions have visited this country, and today, due to the high activity seen in all industries and work centers in the United States, migration of Mexican citizens has increased greatly and with it have appeared many difficulties, new obstacles that threaten to delay the unification that the American Federation of Labor and we wish for, if the evil that we point out is not destroyed.

But there still is more: the working people of the border cities and the working class in general, without gender or age distinction, fall victim to indescribable abuses on behalf of some United States authorities who insist on not recognizing that the Mexican worker is an agent of progress and civilization; and these abuses manifest themselves in the disgusting manner in which they mistreat mothers, sisters, and daughters of workers, who need to provide themselves with the basic necessities on a daily basis in the towns north of the Rio Grande.

All these acts, completely proven and widely known by the labor organizations in this country, incite protests and produce growing wariness; and it is indisputable that, lacking trust, unification is not possible.

We are certain that labor organizations in the United States condemn these acts that are in open battle with the interpretation they give of democratic practice, but we recognize that the American Federation of Labor is in a position to take efficient and immediate action to prevent harm to the interests of laborers (of whatever place of origin).

It will not escape your good judgment that hundreds of thousands of Mexican producers are not, cannot, exactly know the true causes behind the wrongs we mentioned. And if it is true that a feeling of brotherhood moves the Mexican Regional Confederation of Labor and the American Federation of Labor, they share in the wish for crystallizing such a beautiful ideal, then reality, a sad reality based on countless acts, which to the present have been creating the greatest obstacle for the unification of labor movements in both countries.

We sincerely wish to remove any obstacles that may oppose labor unification, and believing that the American Federation of Labor will give necessary attention to what we have expressed, we formally invite you to effectively execute justice in your country in all fields for the laborers we seek to unify.

El Imparcial, November 21, 1918.

Mexican Unions Emerge in the United States

By the end of the 1920s, the unionization efforts of Mexican agricultural workers in California increased. In March 1928, the Confederación de Uniones Obreras (Federation of Labor Unions) was founded in Los Angeles. In quick fashion, twenty-one chapters extended throughout southern California. Its total membership as of May 1929, was between 2,000 to 3,000. But because its members were migrants who lacked a stable residential base, the union had major difficulties in staying afloat. Nonetheless, the union initiated a massive walkout of cantaloupe workers in the Imperial Valley of California. Louis Bloch, an investigator for the California Department of Industrial Relations, concluded the following after investigating the causes of the strike.

Strike of Mexicans in Imperial County

1. A request from Alejandro Lubbert, Consul General of Mexico in San Francisco, to Governor C. C. Young on May 14, 1928, to investigate the alleged unjust imprisonment of Mexicans in Imperial County was referred to the Department of Industrial Relations by the Governor. Subsequently, the Mexican Ambassador in Washington, D.C. appealed to Secretary of State Frank B. Kellogg in protest against the situation and the protest was transferred to California's Governor.
2. Dr. Louis Bloch of the Division of Labor Statistics and Law Enforcement was assigned to the study of the trouble. His report shows several important facts. He found that
   a. Approximately between 3500 to 4000 Mexicans are engaged in harvesting the cantaloupe crop each year in the Imperial Valley.
   b. For the first time the Mexicans organized to combat grievances they claim are unjust and burdensome.
   c. They appealed to the Chambers of Commerce in the Valley to act as intermediaries in adjusting their complaints, but were unsuccessful in their efforts.
   d. The three major issues involved, according to the Mexicans, are (1) better housing conditions, (2) safeguards against defaulting contractors, and (3) proper insurance under the Workmen's Compensation Act.
   e. The organization of the men was so sudden that steps were taken to counteract the movement, and there is evidence that some of the steps were hastily taken and cannot be considered as reaching down to fundamental causes.
   f. Perhaps the complaint most important from the Mexican point of view is the retention of from 20 to 25 percent of the wages by the grower, who then gives the money due to the contractor, this for the purpose of making sure that the Mexicans will stay until the end of the season. Sometimes these contractors fail to meet their obligations, and growers have been known to do likewise. This irritating state of affairs has caused growing resentment among the Mexicans. It is doubtful whether the withholding of a portion of the wages of the workers is legal.

g. A number of Mexicans were arrested. Some of these arrests were made without sufficient cause. In some instances, bail was fixed at $1000, with occasional reductions to $500, and even the latter sum is impossible for the average Mexican.

h. The desire of the Mexicans for a rate for picking of 15 cents a crate of cantaloupes, an increase from the prevailing rate of 13½ cents, is evidently not as important as some of the other factors involved, because the 15 cents is now paid by many of the growers.

3. The situation warrants mature consideration for the future to avoid possible disaster for all, or nearly all, the growers. There were statements made that if the Mexicans left their employment, other Mexicans would be brought in from adjoining States. This might only lead to a repetition of the trouble, and would not prove a satisfactory means of a settlement.

4. All the Mexicans arrested are now out on bail, or on their own recognizance. It is believed the charge against them of disturbing the peace will not be pressed. If this proves to be the case, it will prove a temporary settlement of the condition now prevailing.

Governor Council Meeting, Thursday, May 31, 1928, Department of Industrial Relations, National Archives, Record Group 59, 311.122R61.

Unionism in the Agricultural Fields

After the cantaloupe strike of 1928, there followed a series of labor disputes in which Mexicans were the main actors. During 1930, two major outbreaks took place in the Imperial Valley among lettuce packers and trimmers led by an all-Mexican union, the Asociación Mutual de Valle Imperial (The Imperial Valley Mutualist Association). Between 1931 and 1941, Mexican agricultural workers struck at least thirty-two times in California, all the way from Santa Clara in the North to the Imperial Valley in the South. The workers walked out of canneries, and from harvests of peas, berries, beets, cantaloupes, cotton, citrus fruits, beans, lettuce, and celery. The roll call of these commodities tells us how extensively California depended on Mexican workers and also the wide range of products coming out of the Golden State. The following compilation, done by a Federal Writer's Project writer in 1938, provides a partial list of the strikes.

1930

February 11 to February 18. Lettuce packers and trimmers at Brawley, Holtville, Calexico, and El Centro, Imperial County. Struck for higher wages. Association Mutual del Imperial Valle (Mexican Union) and Agricultural Workers Industrial League (including Mexicans in membership) involved.

March. Not a strike, but disorder marked attempts to unionize the Mexican and other cantaloupe pickers, undertaken by A.W.I.L., organized by the Trade Union Unity League, a Communist faction, in Imperial Valley. Total of 103 arrested including nine organizers, some of whom were sentenced under the Criminal Syndicalism Law to prison terms ranging from 3 to 42 years.

1931

August. Cannery workers' strike, Santa Clara County, called by the Cannery & Agricultural Workers Industrial Union, an outgrowth of the A.W.I.L., or, as a matter of fact, a change of name in the same organization, broadened to include cannery workers. Mexican workers included in membership of union involved.

1932

May. Pea pickers, San Mateo County. Strike promulgated by the C. & A.W.I.U., which included Mexicans in membership.

1933

April. Pea pickers, southern Alameda and Santa Clara Counties. C. & A.W.I.U. controlled strike, membership including Mexicans.

June. Berry pickers and craters, El Monte, San Gabriel Valley, and at Santa Monica. Ordered by Farm Workers Union, also A.W.I.U. including Mexicans in racial composition. Mexicans aided by CROM, powerful Mexican labor party, which ordered boycott of Japanese goods in Mexican stores as a result of strike, which was directed against Japanese growers.

August. Lettuce field workers, Salinas and Watsonville areas. Strike ordered by Filipino Labor Chamber, joined by A.W.I.U. which included Mexican workers. Filipino leaders endeavored to restrict strike to Filipinos, while A.W.I.U. fought this and insisted on including both Mexican and Japanese workers.

August. Beet workers in Oxnard district. Strike ordered by A.W.I.U. which included Mexicans, and by the Filipino Protective Union.

September. Grape pickers, Fresno, Tulare, and San Joaquin Counties. Called by C. & A.W.I.U. which included Mexicans. Marked by unusual amount of violence and numerous arrests, particularly at Lodi where strikers were driven from the district.

October. Cotton pickers, San Joaquin, King, Tulare, Kern, Madera, Merced, Fresno, Imperial, and Stanislaus Counties. Called by C. & A.W.I.U., 55 percent of the strikers being Mexicans. Strike lasted 22 days in battle for higher wages and abolition of labor contractor system. Three killed and scores injured in this strike, which was marked by extreme disorder. Gained increase of 15¢ per hundred pounds in rate for picking cotton.

November. Cantaloupe field workers. Called by Mexican Workers Union, in battle for higher wages to meet increased costs of living. Although Mexican union lacked proper direction and leadership, some slight gains in wages were secured as the result of actions carried on by the Mexican organized workers.

June. Orange pickers, El Cajon, San Diego County. Mexican Union of Laborers & Field Workers called strike for higher wages.

November. Orange pickers, Santa Ana, Orange County. Campesinos y Obreros, Mexican Workers Union.

1936

February. Agricultural workers, Chula Vista, San Diego County. Strike for higher wages and better hours called by Union of Mexican Workers, with other unions involved.

April. Celery pickers, Venice and Culver City, Los Angeles County. Called by Mexican Confederation of Unions for higher wages and better hours. Attended by considerable violence. Called off by meeting of the C.U.O.M. (Confederation of Mexican Unions).

May. Bean pickers, Los Angeles County. Mexican Confederation of Unions, also Agricultural Workers Union involved. Wage increases granted but Mexican factions held out for recognition of their union.

May-June. Strawberry crop workers, El Monte, Los Angeles County. Called by Mexican Confederation of Unions, also Federation of Agricultural Unions, for wage increases, union recognition, and other demands. Considerable violence.

July-August. Citrus pickers, Santa Ana, Orange County. Confederation of Unions and Mexican Orange Pickers Union involved with others. Much violence and terrorism recorded. Wage increases agreed to but no union recognition.

September-November. Lettuce workers, Monterey and Salinas Counties. Mexicans included among others, probably members of Fruit & Vegetable Workers Union (A.F. of L.). One of the longest and bloodiest strikes in the State's history.

1937

January. Celery workers, San Diego County. Union of Laborers & Field Workers (Mexican), also two other unions involved, for higher wages. No settlement made.

May. Orange pickers, Santa Paula. 100 Mexicans involved. No record of any union concerned.

November. Agricultural workers, Santa Maria. Called by Fruit & Vegetable Workers Union (A.F. of L.), which included Mexicans in membership.

1938

August. Field hands, Orange County. C.U.O.M. members voted to join United Cannery & Agricultural Workers (C.I.O.). Struck against proposed wage cut by Japanese growers. Outcome not clear.

August. Lemon pickers, San Fernando Heights, Los Angeles County. Mexicans included in U.C.A.P.A.W.A., which won small wage increase.

September. Pea pickers, Hollister. Mexicans involved as members of the U.C.A.P.A.W.A. Wage increase demand lost.

September. Cotton pickers, Kern County. Some Mexicans in U.C.A.P.A.W.A. Demand for wage increases lost. Much violence, several riots, and numerous arrests.

"Organization Efforts of Mexican Agricultural Workers," pp. 24-28, Bancroft Library, Berkeley, CR-2 Carton 37, folder NF73.

Radicals and Mexican Agricultural Workers in California

Radical revolutionary organizations made overtures to bring Mexican agricultural workers under their wing as illustrated by the following article from the *Daily Worker,* written by Pablo Barbis, an Argentine Communist leader in California, during May of 1929.

The hundreds of thousands of Mexican workers in California belonging to the most exploited section of the working class constitute very important material to be reached and organized into the Communist Party.

At the Trade Union Educational League Conference, there were Mexican delegates in Los Angeles from both sections of the State. In Los Angeles the C.U.O.M., an independent union of Mexican workers, elected delegates to the Trade Union Educational Conference, and they will be represented at the Cleveland Trade Union Unity Convention as well as in various committees.

Reaching the Mexican workers is one of the main tasks before the Party in California. Because of their exploitation in this country, they are responding to the call for organization, and because of the situation in the home country, they can be drawn into our anti-Imperialist work. It is certain that the Communist Party, if it concentrates on the Mexican worker, will accomplish very good results in the future.

Pablo Barbis

"Organization Efforts of Mexican Agricultural Workers," p. 20, Bancroft Library, Berkeley, CR-2 Carton 37, folder NF73.

Emma Tenayuca

In the 1930s, Texas produced one of the most well-known labor crusaders in Emma Tenayuca. A member of the American Communist Party, she brought to her work a fervor born out of her dedication to the class struggle and an interpretation that Mexican workers in the Southwest were part of this conflict. Tenayuca helped organize the well-known San Antonio Pecan Shellers Strike against the Southern Pecan Shelling Company in 1938. Tenayuca gave such fiery speeches to animate the striking workers that she earned the nickname *la pasionaria* (the Passionate One). During the strike itself, *Time* magazine featured her in an article that exhibited some elements of red-baiting.

Everyone in San Antonio knows about little Emma Tenayuca, a slim, vivacious labor organizer with black eyes and a Red philosophy. She first shone in her native city a year ago during a garment strike, and has been at the forefront of most of its civil commotions since. With San Antonio's police chief, she carries on a feud that has landed her in jail on countless occasions. Among the Spanish-speaking San Antonio proletariat, she is known as "La Pasionaria de Texas." Since her husband, Homer Brooks, former Communist nominee for Governor of Texas, lives in Houston, their marital life is confined to irregular weekends, but Emma Tenayuca declares pertly: "I love my husband and am a good cook."

Last week "La Pasionaria de Texas" was up to her small ears in a pecan pickers' strike. In a good year, San Antonio's 147 pecan shelleries shell 21,000,000 lbs. of pecans. No successful machine has ever been invented to pick pecan meat from pecan shells, and the "world's largest pecan shelling centre" depends upon the family labor of Mexicans and Tex-Mexes (U.S.-born Mexicans). Wages were recently cut from 7¢ per lb. to 6¢ for halves, from 6¢ to 5¢ for broken pieces, which means that a pecan picker can earn from 30¢ to $1.50 per day. Everyone, including the owners of the shelleries, agree that these are miserable wages, but the industry claims that it can pay no more, that pecan picking is a pin-money job.

The pecan pickers took their troubles to Juan López, a naturalized Mexican priest with strong C.I.O. sympathies. With Father López's approval the International Pecan Shellers Union (a San Antonio local of C.I.O. Cannery Workers) called a mass meeting to plan a strike. Into the meeting to steal the show completely marched Emma Tenayuca. "La Pasionaria's" Communism was too much for Father López, and he retired from active direction. Not more than 1,000 of 11,000 workers struck. Soon pickets were parading with signs reading, *El Padre López es un mal Católico. C.I.O.*

"La Pasionaria" then retired from active direction, leaving the field to President Donald Henderson of the C.I.O. Cannery Workers, who flew from Washington to take charge. By this time it was apparent that the piddling pecan strike would probably turn out to be a C.I.O. showdown in Texas, where John L. Lewis has yet to make much headway.

From her office at the local Workers Alliance, Emma Tenayuca continued to pull strings with the assistance of her "gang," some 300 devoted followers whom she deploys with a masterly hand in picket line or mass meeting. But by week's end, the strike had gone into the legal trenches with hearings, investigations, applications for injunctions, and loud demands to the Governor for Texas Rangers to enforce civil liberties in San Antonio.

"La Pasionaria de Texas," *Time,* February 28, 1938, p. 17.

The Memorial Day Massacre

Below are transcripts of testimony offered by steelworker Max Guzmán and social worker Lupe Marshall at congressional hearings that investigated the Memorial Day massacre of 1937, in which Chicago police fired into a crowd of peacefully striking steelworkers and their families. Their declaration obtained during questioning by Senator Robert La Follette, Jr. demonstrates the extent to which Mexicans were involved in this kind of union activity.

Testimony of Max Guzmán

(The witness was sworn by Senator La Follette.)

Senator La Follette. What is your full name?
Mr. Guzmán. Max Guzmán.
Senator La Follette. How do you spell your last name?
Mr. Guzmán. G-u-z-m-á-n.
Senator La Follette. Where do you live?
Mr. Guzmán. 8927 Commercial.
Senator La Follette. Chicago?
Mr. Guzmán. Chicago, Ill.
Senator La Follette. What is your occupation?
Mr. Guzmán. Steelworker.
Senator La Follette. Where have you been employed?
Mr. Guzmán. Republic Steel Corporation.
Senator La Follette. How long have you worked there?
Mr. Guzmán. I worked since 1927 in the same mill.
Senator La Follette. Are you a member of the Steel Worker's Organizing Committee?
Mr. Guzmán. Yes, sir.
Senator La Follette. Were you present at the mass meeting in the yard near Sam's Place on Sunday?
Mr. Guzmán. I was.
Senator La Follette. Were you in the parade?
Mr. Guzmán. Yes. I was carrying a flag, a flagbearer.
Senator La Follette. Look at the exhibit 1413 and tell me if you can identify yourself in that picture?
Mr. Guzmán. Yes. I am to my right, right here, where I am looking.
Senator La Follette. You are the one that is carrying the flag, to the right of the picture?
Mr. Guzmán. Yes, sir.
Senator La Follette. But on the left hand of the column as it marched toward the police?
Mr. Guzmán. Yes, that is right.
Senator La Follette. Did you see anybody in the crowd as you were marching down there, at any time, who had any clubs, gas pipes, branches of trees, stones, bricks, rocks, or other missiles or weapons?

Mr. Guzmán. No, I didn't.

Senator La Follette. Look at exhibit 1400. Can you tell from the position of those flags which one you were carrying?

Mr. Guzmán. Yes.

Senator La Follette. The one further away from the picture?

Mr. Guzmán. Yes, that is right.

Senator La Follette. But you see that some of the men in that picture had branches of trees and sticks, do you not?

Mr. Guzmán. Yes.

Senator La Follette. You say you did not see them?

Mr. Guzmán. I did not see any when we started marching.

Senator La Follette. Well, did you see any during the time you were marching down there?

Mr. Guzmán. No.

Senator La Follette. Did you have any conversation with any of the police in the line?

Mr. Guzmán. Yes, I did.

Senator La Follette. State the conversation that you had with them.

Mr. Guzmán. Just when we got to the line of the policemen, there was a plain-clothes man, and he talked in a low tone, slow. He say, "Lucky you are carrying that flag or you would have been shot." That is what he told me. Then I explained to him that we were just peaceable demonstrators in a parade, and that we wanted to go through, and if they will escort us by, to see that nothing would happen, and they can march alongside of us. That is all the conversation I had with the police.

Senator La Follette. And did you hear any other remarks before the trouble started?

Mr. Guzmán. Someone from the back say, when the police told me, he say, "You should have a permit to go by," and then somebody from the back, I don't know who, he said, "This is a strike, and we have a right to picket peacefully." That is all the remarks I heard.

Senator La Follette. Did you see any missiles, bricks, or anything thrown at the police?

Mr. Guzmán. No, sir.

Senator La Follette. Did you hear any profanity from the crowd toward the police?

Mr. Guzmán. No, not that I heard.

Senator La Follette. What happened next?

Mr. Guzmán. Well, as we were talking to the police there, meaning we were, some of us were talking to them, when we got to the line there, the crowd spread out, and the people all seemed well spread, and then the shooting started, and then I went down.

Senator La Follette. Why did you go down?

Mr. Guzmán. The policeman on the front clubbed me down as soon as the first shots fired, and I went down and I remained down. They all passed—the policemen passed where I was lying, and then, when I was just about to pick myself up, another policeman grabbed me by my jacket and took me in the patrol wagon.

Senator La Follette. Do you know whether you were struck more than once?

Mr. Guzmán. Yes, I was struck on the head on the first blow. Then when they picked me up they struck me twice on the shoulders—once on each shoulder.

Senator La Follette. How many people were in the patrol wagon?

Mr. Guzmán. When I entered the patrol wagon there was only one other.

Senator La Follette. How many were in it at the time it started away from the field?

Mr. Guzmán. There were about, say, about 10 or 11. I couldn't say.

Senator La Follette. Any seriously wounded with you?

Mr. Guzmán. Yes, there was about five of them that I remember that were pretty bad, and the other ones were, oh, Guiseppe, another, Mr. Fisk, he wasn't wounded bad, not at all. He was not bleeding, and the rest of them were, almost every one of them, bleeding.

Senator La Follette. Now, at any time during this event did you see any of the marchers resisting or striking or attacking or throwing anything at the police?

Mr. Guzmán. No, sir.

Senator La Follette. Where did they take you in the patrol wagon?

Mr. Guzmán. Well, they took a long way around. We were on Avenue O all the way to Hegewisch, and then back to the Irondale, and then to the East Side police stations. That is about . . . say about 5 miles out of the way, where the first police station is located.

Senator La Follette. How long would you say it took to get there?

Mr. Guzmán. Well, I say, at least, it took a half hour to the first station.

Senator La Follette. Had any of the people in the wagon with you, who were injured, received any medical attention up to that time?

Mr. Guzmán. No.

Senator La Follette. Any first-aid attention?

Mr. Guzmán. No. I myself gave a handkerchief to a fellow that was bleeding very bad.

Senator La Follette. Do you know whether or not any of these people who were more seriously injured received medical attention later?

Mr. Guzmán. Yes. We were put in cells, and then the police came around in about 20 minutes or half an hour after, and the ones that were very serious they took them to the hospital, and I didn't want to go right away, and another fellow didn't go right away. Then we asked to be taken to the hospital anyway.

Senator La Follette. How long were you held at the South Chicago police station?

Mr. Guzmán. From Sunday night till Wednesday morning, till about 9 o'clock.

Senator La Follette. Did you have any interviews with any of the police or any of the city or county officials?

Mr. Guzmán. Yes. I gave my statement to the police.

Senator La Follette. And state, to the best of your knowledge and recollection, the questions they asked you and your answers.

Mr. Guzmán. Well, they asked me where was I born, and what was I doing at the place of the meeting, and where was I employed. I told them, and if I was married; I told them also; and if I was a citizen of the United States. I told them. And they asked how long I was married. I told them, told them 9 years, and when I told them 9 years—I gave my age as 26 years old—they said "Well, did you have to lie to get your license?" I say, "Yes." "Why did you do that?" "Well, I wanted to get married. That is about all," I said. They said, "Did you ever have any run-in with your wife

251

before you got married, and going around with her—do anything?" "Well," I say, "I think that is a little out of the question." They told me, "Well, all we wanted to know, if you had run around in any way. We are not going to tell anybody about it." I said, "Well, anyway, that is a personal question I wouldn't like to answer."

And then they asked me if I had any weapons, guns, or knives, or what did I do with them? I told them I did not have any. Then they told me I was a Communist. I told them no, that I don't even know what the word Communist meant, and they said when they finished with my statement, they said "Where is the gun you were carrying? Did you have any fight with the police? Did you do any shooting?" I said, "No, I didn't. I didn't carry any gun, or you would have found it on me"— something like that. That is about all this thing.

Senator La Follette. Did they attempt to threaten you or intimidate you in any way?

Mr. Guzmán. Well, the only thing they did, when they asked me if I was a citizen of the United States, I told them that I was not, that I was raised in this country, but that I was not born here; so they told me as long as I was not a citizen of the United States they could send me back to Mexico any time they felt like it.

Senator La Follette. Did you ask to talk to any friends or relatives while you were confined in the police station?

Mr. Guzmán. Yes, I did—the same Sunday night. I asked to be allowed to talk to my wife, but I was not permitted to.

Senator La Follette. You were not permitted to?

Mr. Guzmán. No, sir.

Senator La Follette. Did any of the other prisoners ask for similar privileges, to your knowledge?

Mr. Guzmán. Yes, they did.

Senator La Follette. Was it granted to them?

Mr. Guzmán. No.

Senator La Follette. When were you brought into court?

Mr. Guzmán. Wednesday morning at 9 o'clock.

Senator La Follette. Do you know what bond was set in your case?

Mr. Guzmán. Yes, $500. Then finally my wife or a friend of mine arranged for $500 cash bond, so I went out.

Senator La Follette. And after the court hearing where did you go? Were you put back in jail again?

Mr. Guzmán. Yes, put back in the cell, waiting room.

Senator La Follette. And what happened then?

Mr. Guzmán. Well, they took us to the county, and they had our fingerprints taken again, and then they started calling me out around 6 o'clock in the evening, and I didn't know I was going out, and that is when they released me. The bond was already set.

Senator La Follette. Did you have to sign any kind of statement before you left?

Mr. Guzmán. Well, just a doctor, physical examination.

Senator La Follette. And what was the purpose of that statement, did you understand?

Mr. Guzmán. No, I didn't. The only thing, the doctor examined me and gave me an O.K., and he asked me to sign, so I did.

Senator La Follette. Let a copy of this witness' subpoena be inserted in the record.

Senator Thomas. How long have you been in America?

Mr. Guzmán. Seventeen years.

Senator Thomas. Seventeen years?

Mr. Guzmán. Yes, sir.

Senator Thomas. Is your wife a Mexican?

Mr. Guzmán. She is a Mexican. She was born in the United States.

Senator Thomas. She is an American citizen, then?

Mr. Guzmán. Yes, that is right.

Senator La Follette. Mrs. Marshall.

TESTIMONY OF MRS. LUPE MARSHALL

(The witness was sworn by Senator La Follette.)

Senator La Follette. What is your full name, please?

Mrs. Marshall. Lupe Marshall.

Senator La Follette. How do you spell your first name?

Mrs. Marshall. L-u-p-e.

Senator La Follette. And how do you spell your last name?

Mrs. Marshall. M-a-r-s-h-a-l-l.

Senator La Follette. What is your occupation?

Mrs. Marshall. At the present time, a housewife and volunteer social worker.

Senator La Follette. Could you speak a little louder, please?

Mrs. Marshall. At the present time, I am a housewife and volunteer social worker.

Senator La Follette. Where do you work as a volunteer social worker?

Mrs. Marshall. Throughout Chicago.

Senator La Follette. Have you any connection with Hull House?

Mrs. Marshall. Yes, of some sort.

Senator La Follette. Are you a member of any labor organization?

Mrs. Marshall. I am not.

Senator La Follette. Did you go to the strike meeting at Sam's Place on Sunday, May 30?

Mrs. Marshall. Yes, I did.

Senator La Follette. How did you happen to go there?

Mrs. Marshall. I am very much interested in studying and doing research work among the Mexican people, relative to their attitude within the organized labor movement.

Senator La Follette. Well, are there many Mexicans employed normally at the Republic Steel plant?

Mrs. Marshall. I do not know how many Mexicans are employed in the steel plant, at the Republic plant, but I do know that there are 5,000 Mexican families in South Chicago.

Senator La Follette. What time did you get to the meeting?

Mrs. Marshall. About 3:15.

Senator La Follette. Was speaking going on when you arrived there?

Mrs. Marshall. Yes, there was.

Senator La Follette. Did you join the marchers?

Mrs. Marshall. Yes, I did.

Senator La Follette. Where were you in the parade when it started?

Mrs. Marshall. At the side. I was speaking to a young writer that was with me, that had invited me to go to that meeting, and he was busy with his notes, and I didn't know just where I should be in order to get the best account of the thing, and I joined a group of women that seemed to be going toward the front.

Senator La Follette. And as the parade went on across the prairie, what position did you occupy in relation to the head of the column?

Mrs. Marshall. Right near the front.

Senator LaFollette. Near the front?

Mrs. Marshall. Right near the front.

Senator La Follette. And anytime during the time when you were standing there, or before the parade started, or during the time that they marched across the prairie, did you see any of the marchers armed with sticks, stones, pieces of gas pipe, or any other missiles or weapons?

Mrs. Marshall. No, I didn't. What I did see, though, was that as I walked back and forth, trying to find a place, to place myself, I heard a man behind me yell at another in an angry tone, "Drop that stone. We don't want that stuff here."

Senator La Follette. Now, when the crowd of marchers got down so that they contacted the police line, where were you?

Mrs. Marshall. I was right at the front. I was right next to one of the flags.

Senator La Follette. Will you look at exhibit 1358 and see if you can find yourself there?

Mrs. Marshall. Yes, I do. I find myself.

Senator La Follette. Where are you?

Mrs. Marshall. I am to the left of the marcher that is carrying the flag, to the right facing the picture.

Senator La Follette. Now, how many other women did you see in this march, would you say?

Mrs. Marshall. Oh, there were many women.

Senator La Follette. You say "many"—how many would you say you saw, yourself?

Mrs. Marshall. Oh, you mean right in the picture here?

Senator La Follette. No, not in the picture. I mean in the crowd of marchers—approximately.

Mrs. Marshall. Oh, I would say about 200 women.

Senator La Follette. Did you see any children?

Mrs. Marshall. Yes, I did.

Senator La Follette. How many?

Mrs. Marshall. I couldn't say how many, but while the meeting was going on, there were children running around buying ice cream and popsicles there in the . . .

Senator La Follette. Did you see any children in the march?

Mrs. Marshall. Yes, I did. Some of the women that were in the group that I joined had children with them.

Senator La Follette. What was the general character of the crowd, would you say?

Mrs. Marshall. Jubilant. As the march proceeded, that is what made me join the group of women. They were singing, and some of the fellows were kidding each other and patting themselves on the back as we went along.

Senator La Follette. Did you hear any remarks made which indicated that the objective of the parade was to storm the plant?

Mrs. Marshall. No, I didn't.

Senator La Follette. Or to work injury upon the workers who had not come out on strike?

Mrs. Marshall. No, I didn't.

Senator La Follette. Did you hear any remarks indicating hostility toward the Chicago police?

Mrs. Marshall. No. The only remark that can be construed as such would be one remark that came from the speakers, from one of the speakers, in which they referred to the police as being part of the city; the police were to protect the city, and it seemed as if in this case they were protecting the company instead of the workers that were on strike.

Senator La Follette. Now, you were near the front line. Did you have any conversation with any of the police prior to the difficulty?

Mrs. Marshall. Yes, I did.

Senator La Follette. Who did you talk to?

Mrs. Marshall. I talked to the officer that testified here on this chair, addressed by the Chair as "Higgins," Officer Higgins.

Senator La Follette. And what was the substance of your conversation with Officer Higgins?

Mrs. Marshall. I did not address him. He addressed me. From my recollections the marchers did not reach the police, but the police advanced toward us in a running step, when we were about 15 or 20 feet away from them, and the people in back of us kept marching, and the police came toward us, so that we were pressed together, the police and the marchers, and I could touch Officer Higgins with a paper which I was carrying under my arm, and as soon as we approached, he called me a vile name—the women around us—called us a vile name, told us to get back.

Senator La Follette. Had anything been said to Officer Higgins?

Mrs. Marshall. No, we had just come in contact when he addressed us.

Senator La Follette. Did you hear any other conversation?

Mrs. Marshall. Yes, I did.

Senator La Follette. Tell me all that you can remember.

Mrs. Marshall. I couldn't see the individual that was carrying the flag on the other side of me, but I heard some conversation in a serious tone, and I thought it was the leader of the marchers that was addressing some official on the other side. He said something about picketing and going in front of the plant. I heard, also from the back, snatches. Somebody hollered, "Mayor Kelly said it is all right to picket." Others said, "We have got our rights." But the confusion was such that it was really difficult to catch the whole phrase of what was going on. Some of the officers further to my left as I was facing them seemed to be addressing the men. I heard something about "Get back! Get back!" And as these things were being said, the officers kept going like this with their clubs [indicating an up-and-down motion]. They were swinging their clubs like this [indicating] in front of our faces.

Senator La Follette. I want to ask you one other question, before you go any further. In your hearing, did any of the people in the crowd of marchers use any vile or abusive language toward the police?

Mrs. Marshall. No, they did not.

Senator La Follette. Did you see any of them threaten or make any threatening gestures toward the police?

Mrs. Marshall. No, they did not, not those that I could see in my immediate vicinity.

Senator La Follette. Did you see any shower of missiles or rocks or bricks?

Mrs. Marshall. No, I didn't.

Senator La Follette. Now tell us what happened next?

Mrs. Marshall. As I was addressing one of the officers in front of me, Mr. Higgins had moved away somewhat. The police were closing in, closing their ranks and crowding us, pushing us back all this time, and I said to one of the officers in front of me, I said, "There are enough of you men to march alongside of these people, to see that order is kept." And he answered me, "Like hell! Like hell! Like hell! Like hell there are!" There is an officer that was directly in front of me that had his gun out, and I recognized him in the picture in another scene, that he laughed real sarcastically in my face, and said something about sending these [blanks] back. He said a vile word there. And this happened so suddenly that it seems that I was still talking to these officers in front of me, when I heard a dull thud toward the back of the . . . of my group, and as I turned around there was screaming and going on in back, and simultaneously a volley of shots. It sounded more like thunder. I heard that, and I couldn't . . . for a minute I couldn't imagine what was happening. I had seen this man with his revolver out, but I couldn't believe that they were shooting, so I turned around to see what was happening, and the people that were standing in back of me were all lying on the ground face down. I saw some splotches of blood on some of the fellows' shirts. I tried to run, but I couldn't; the road was closed by these people there, and I didn't want to step on them, so I sort of held back.

Senator La Follette. Give picture "Q" a number.

Senator LaFollette. Can you recognize yourself in that picture, Mrs. Marshall?

Mrs. Marshall. Yes, I can.

Senator LaFollette. Where are you?

Mrs. Marshall. I was walking or running, rather, around the people that had fallen in back of me.

Senator La Follette. Now, will you look at exhibit 1418. Do you see that picture?

Mrs. Marshall. Yes, I do.

Senator La Follette. Now, looking at those two pictures, exhibits 1424 and 1418, look at 1424, the one shown you first. Then look at 1418, and tell me whether you can tell which one of those pictures was taken first.

Mrs. Marshall. 1418 was taken first.

Senator La Follette. 1418 was taken first?

Mrs. Marshall. First.

Senator La Follette. And 1424? Now, in your opinion, 1418 was taken after 1424?

Mrs. Marshall. No, 1424 was taken after 1418.

Senator La Follette. Now, will you look at 1414, and tell me when do you think that picture was taken in relation to the others?

Mrs. Marshall. This picture was taken before I was aware of what had happened.

Senator La Follette. Then you think that 1418 was taken first? Is that correct?

Mrs. Marshall. Yes, and then 1424.

Senator La Follette. Is the officer you are talking about in 1414, the one you think you saw in the moving picture?

Mrs. Marshall. The officer that has the gun.

Senator La Follette. Then these people were shot down from around you, as shown in 1414, and piled up in this heap, before you even knew what had happened?

Mrs. Marshall. Yes, sir.

Senator La Follette. And by the time 1418 had been taken you had turned around to look at the people who had been with you?

Mrs. Marshall. I had been knocked down by a club. My head had been broken open, and I was raising myself up from the heap of these people—1418.

Senator La Follette. And in 1424 you had recovered sufficiently and are fleeing; is that correct?

Mrs. Marshall. Yes.

Senator La Follette. Now, did you see any policeman come near this group of people who had fallen in a heap, as is shown in all of these "stills" and as is shown in the moving picture, at any time before you left the scene?

Mrs. Marshall. Well, I was somewhat dazed, and all I was aware of was that I wanted to get away from these people and walked back to where the field seemed to be clear. There were not so many policemen over on that side.

Senator La Follette. Now, Officer Higgins testified that you dropped a bag of pepper out from under your arm. He testified at least that a woman did.

Mrs. Marshall. He said it looked like me, but he was not sure.

Senator La Follette. Officer Higgins, will you come forward, please.

U.S. Congress, Senate, Committee on Education and Labor, *Violations of Free Speech and Rights of Labor: Hearings Before a Subcommittee of the Committee on Education and Labor . . .* 75th Cong., 1st session, June 30-July 2, 1937, Part 14, "The Chicago Memorial Day Incident," pp. 4941-4949.

Luisa Moreno

The veneration that Mexican workers held for Luisa Moreno, one of the founders of the Spanish Speaking People's Congress, is seen in a union song called "La Escuela de Betabeleros," about beet workers in Colorado, that portrays her as a working-class hero.

Beware beet pickers
Pay attention
And keep in mind to
Learn about organization.

Alerta betabeleros
escuchen con atención
y tengan en la memoria
lo que es organización.

Students carry on
Proceed without stumbling
This group's education
Is the basis of progress.

Estudiantes adelante
adelante sin tropiezo
el estudio de este grupo
es la base del progreso.

With great sacrifice
And with the CIO's commitment
Our lady comrade Moreno
Organized this school.

Con muy grande sacrificio
y empeño del CIO
la compañera Moreno
esta escuela organizó.

Let's pay attention to the past
Let's comprehend the reason
For if we are divided there is no progress
It will only happen if we are United.

Fijémonos en lo pasado
comprendamos la razón
divididos no hay progreso
solamente con la Unión.

Onward fellow men,
let's fight like lions.
Don't make any excuses
and join the Union.

Adelante, compañeros
y luchemos como un león.
No se valgan de pretextos
ingresemos a la Unión.

Local women await us
With great anxiety;
We bring facts and figures
Of what reality is.

Las locales nos esperan
con una gran ansiedad;
llevamos cifras y datos
de lo que es la realidad.

With a warm salute
Of union and fraternity
To health and happiness
Your lady comrade Moreno.

Con un estrecho saludo
de unión y fraternidad
la compañera Moreno
salud y felicidad.

With this I bid farewell
My ballad has ended
Loudly acclaiming
Go forward CIO!

Ya con ésta me despido
mi corrido terminó
aclamando en alta voz,
¡Adelante el CIO!

Vicki L. Ruiz, *Cannery Women, Cannery Lives, Mexican Women, Unionization, and the California Food Processing Industry*, 1930-1950 (Albuquerque: University of New Mexico Press, 1987), p. 168.

The Empire Zinc Strike

The most well-known strike sponsored by the Mine Mill Union took place in Hanover, New Mexico, against the Empire Zinc Company. One hundred workers, most of them Mexican Americans, walked out in the fall of 1950 after the company refused to grant the same working conditions that prevailed elsewhere. A film, "Salt of the Earth," was made of this strike, which contained emotional drama involving not just the workers, but also their wives and children. The company tried to starve the workers into submission and then used violence by hired guns and local police. In January of 1952, after the workers were victorious, Rod Holmgren, an organizer, wrote a vivid account of this struggle, which had lasted fifteen months.

The historic 15-month strike of the metal miners of Hanover, New Mexico, against the Empire Zinc Company has ended in victory. But the miners are still deeply enmeshed in a struggle with the courts to save their union from backbreaking fines.

The strike made labor history in the Southwest, where the Mexican-American worker has traditionally been discriminated against in every way. Almost all of the 100 strikers were Mexican-Americans. So are a majority of the 1,400 miners, millmen, and smeltermen in the Bayard Amalgamated Union, Local 890, the local of the International Union of Mine, Mill & Smelter Workers to which they belong.

The valiant band of 100 strikers and their wives and children fought—and finally won out—against these overwhelming odds:

- Empire Zinc, the company against which they struck, wholly owned by the New Jersey Zinc Company, which enjoyed net profits of $10,000,000 in 1950—the year the strike began.
- Police terrorism and intimidation which included wholesale arrests, the use of tear gas and gunfire in repeated attempts to smash the picket lines.
- Two cold and hungry winters when the strikers relied entirely on food and clothing contributed by brother unionists and other progressives in Bayard and all over the United States and Canada.
- Vicious attacks by vigilantes in the local newspaper and denial of the right to fully state the union's position in either the newspaper or the local radio station.
- Opposition by many local businessmen who cut off credit for strikers, and some of whom deliberately tried to provoke violence in the streets.
- In the final weeks, red-baiting by the CIO Steelworkers' Union, which cooperated with both the company and local businessmen in trying to smash the miners' union.

It took more, much more, than ordinary determination, courage, and unity to win in the face of these obstacles. Something special and unusual was needed; and the Bayard strikers showed in a hundred ways that they had that special quality.

One progressive newspaperman reported, after the strike had ground through its ninth month, that:

"A new way of life is emerging in Grant County. About 99 percent of the Empire Zinc strikers are Mexican-Americans. They lead the struggle to end the status of second-class citizenship which the ruling clique and its politicos have reserved for

259

Mexican-American workers. Like their counterparts in the Deep South, the ruling cabal is rife with '100 percent, white, Anglo-Saxon' supremacy. The Empire Zinc strikers have challenged the 'status quo' in Grant County, and those who profit from the status quo are determined to punish the courage of men and women who seek progress."

The strike had been in peaceful progress for about eight months when the company decided last June (1951) to resort to violence in an attempt to smash it. The courts, the sheriff, the district attorney, and dozens of hired gunmen were all mobilized to join in the effort.

Company lawyers went to District Judge A.W. Marshall and obtained an injunction (restraining order), which forbade the union or its members from "blocking" what the company called a "public road"—actually a road that is clearly marked "Private Road" at both ends.

The union was determined to continue its strike peacefully, so its members obeyed the court order and withdrew from the picket line, thus abiding fully with the terms of Judge Marshall's injunction. But a new picket line promptly sprang up. Walking the line were the wives and children of the strikers. The women told their husbands: "If you are unable to run the strike, we will; the strike must not be lost."

The wives had already shown their eagerness to fight side by side with the miners. Despite the Southwestern tradition that calls for Mexican-Catholic women to remain in the background, these wives had been on radio programs, drawn up and distributed leaflets, written letters to the papers, given money-raising parties, cooked food for the strikers, and solicited funds. Now they took over the whole job of running the strike.

Shortly before women took over the picket lines, Grant County Sheriff Leslie Goforth swore in a gang of "deputies," who later were exposed as paid gunmen hired by the Empire Zinc Company. In the days that followed, the Sheriff and his gunmen engaged in the most brutal assaults on the women and children at the picket line.

Tear gas was used. The women were beaten with blackjacks, run down by automobiles, slapped, beaten, kicked, insulted. But the line held.

The Sheriff then decided to break the picket line by arresting all the women and children. Within a few hours, the jail was filled. Children in jail were separated from their mothers for many hours. One tiny baby was forced to go without milk for a whole day.

The Sheriff told the women that if they would promise not to picket again, they could go free. With one voice they replied: "We'll stay here together, or we'll go free together." The sensational story of more than a hundred women and children being locked up in a small county jail leaked out to the rest of the country, and the District Attorney ordered Goforth to release the prisoners.

Back to the picket line went the women.

The next six months were marked by frequent attacks on the picket line as the company persisted in its attempts to rush scabs through the line into the mine. These attacks were paralleled by a long series of court actions, taken against individual members of the union and their wives, the local union itself, and the International Union.

The number of injured mounted steadily, but the wives held solid and united. Around the country, word spread of the heroic stand of women and children who were determined that the strike begun by their husbands and fathers should not be lost, regardless of the odds.

As the months wore on, another kind of "revolution" was in progress—in the homes of the strikers. With the women spending long hours on the picket lines and performing a wide variety of strike activities, someone had to clean house, cook, wash dishes and clothes, and tend the children. Some miners were receptive to these household chores. And as they worked at home, they achieved a new kind of respect for their wives.

The Company tried desperately to import scabs from other areas of the Southwest, but no honest worker would enter their mines when he heard the story of the strike. The only scabs the Company could recruit were the gunmen—deputies—and they didn't know how to mine the metal.

Settlement of the strike came at the end of January (1952), when the Company finally realized that this was a strike they could never break. The announcement of the victorious agreements came almost simultaneously with these events: (1) The Company transferred the mine superintendent, who had been responsible for organizing most of the violence against the strikers, to a distant operation; (2) The CIO Steelworkers' Union, which had opened a raid against Local 890, left town; the National Labor Relations Board had dismissed the Steelworkers' petition as "not timely," (3) Several of the local stores that had displayed placards denouncing the strikers and their union went out of business.

The contract by which the strike was settled called for wage increases averaging 24 cents an hour. The Company also gave ground on the disputed collar-to-collar pay issue by increasing payments for lunch periods from 6 cents to 11½ cents an hour. On paid holidays, another controversial issue, it agreed to increase payments to 3½ cents an hour.

The pact also provided for 3 weeks' vacation after 25 years' service, for a pension with a minimum benefit of $100 monthly after 25 years at age 65, and for a company-paid $2,500 life insurance plan covering every worker. A sickness and accident program was also contained in the new pact, providing for weekly benefits of $26 for 26 weeks.

The final agreement provided that all striking workers would be returned to their jobs without discrimination and with full seniority and other accrued rights.

The strike was won, but the court cases, mainly the injunctions, which arose out of it are still being fought out. Following a climactic "trial" early in March (1952) Judge Marshall—Grant County's "injunction judge"—levied fines totaling $38,000 against the International Union, Local 890, and 20 members and their wives. The Judge ruled that the International and local union and individuals had committed contempt against his injunction, and ordered that the fines be paid, not to the state or county, but to the Empire Zinc Company!

The union promptly announced that it would appeal the fines to higher courts. Leaders of Local 890 pointed out that not they, but the company, had violated the law.

But while the final outcome of the court cases may cripple the union financially, it cannot subtract from the magnitude of the victory in the strike itself, a victory described by the *National Guardian* as "American labor's greatest since the war."

To the five million Mexican-Americans living in the great Southwest, many of whom contributed to the strike, the victory meant a big stride forward in the long struggle for economic, political, and social equality.

Rod Holmgren, "The Empire Zinc Strike Victory," manuscript, Arizona Collection, Hayden Library, Arizona State University, MSS137.

Striving for Equal Opportunity

Efforts to end discrimination in the workplace were evident very early in this century. The following newspaper report from *El Tucsonense* shows how La Liga Protectora Latina, led by Pedro de Lama, carefully countered with charges of discrimination every aspect of a proposed bill in the Arizona legislature that would forbid Spanish-speaking workers from gaining employment in Arizona mines. The effort paid off and the bill was never voted in by the legislature.

Protest

In a special meeting held on the 23rd of this month, in order to take quick action against the measures of Bill No. 23 introduced in the Senate of the Legislative Assembly by Senator Roberts from Cochise County, the following resolutions were adopted:

Be it decreed by the Supreme Central Committee of the Latin Protective League (Liga Protectora Latina), whose headquarters are located in Phoenix, Arizona: Whereas in the Legislative Assembly of the State of Arizona, Senator Roberts of Cochise County introduced a proposed Law No. 23, which in its text directly affects all Latino workers who are now in mining camps and in various industries where steam-powered or electric machinery is used, as well as those who work inside the mines.

Thus, this proposed law leaves unemployed 90 percent of the individuals of Mexican origin and Mexican immigrants who do not have the required prerequisites of Bill No. 23 for speaking perfect English.

Be it resolved by the Supreme Central Committee of the Latin Protective League, an organized association with the purpose of protecting the interests of Latinos in this nation, with headquarters in Phoenix, Arizona:

FIRST: That we condemn in all its parts the direct action of Senator Roberts of Cochise County, introducing Bill No. 23, guided with the aim of prohibiting employment in industries in the State of Arizona to all Latinos who do not speak English, thus constituting an attack on individual guarantees of the residents of the State and of all those who out of necessity migrate to this country to look for an honorable way to earn a living for themselves and their families.

SECOND: That a committee composed of associates, Supreme President Dr. Lorenzo Boido, Hon. Lorenzo Hubbell, Supreme Secretary Pedro G. de la Gama, Supreme Trustee J. A. Valenzuela, and Ex-Supreme President A. A. Celaya, will present themselves on Monday 29th of the current month before the State Senate commission, with the purpose of protesting and declaring arguments opposing the mentioned measure known as Bill No. 23, because if it is passed into law, it will cause the most damage on workers now involved in diverse businesses in the state.

THIRD: That all the Branches of our institution join the movement, protesting against this measure, by having public meetings, inviting Mexican workers who do not belong to our institution, by collecting signatures so that at the opportune time the Supreme Central Committee will present them to both legislative chambers.

FOURTH: That it be recommended to the named commission that by all means possible proposed law No. 23 be defeated by personally directing itself to all Senators so that with their vote they cooperate in the defeat of Bill No. 23.

FIFTH: That a copy of these resolutions be sent to each senator of the Third Legislative Assembly of the State of Arizona, to the newspapers *El Obrero Mexicano* of El Paso, Texas, *El Tucsonense* of Tucson, *Justicia* from Phoenix, and *El Clarín Disperso* from Jerome, so as to have it published and people in general can take note.

After these resolutions were read three consecutive times, they were approved unanimously.

Phoenix, Arizona, January 23, 1917.

El Tucsonense, January 27, 1917.

"On the Day They Were Defeated"

During May, 1938, the Latin American Club in Houston pressured the city to pay their Mexican workers for taking off on April 22, the commemoration of the Battle of San Jacinto (where General Antonio López de Santa Anna was defeated in 1836). In response, city councilman S.A. Starkey retorted that he did not understand why Mexicans should get a paid day off to celebrate their own defeat. Houston's Latin American Club led a campaign that resulted in Starkey backing off from his statement. Eventually, the Latin American Club won permanent status for Mexicans employed by the city. A letter to the *Houston Press* from John J. Herrera, one of the city employees who was denied the day off, captures the indignation felt by Mexican Americans during this incident. Herrera, who went on to become a lawyer and a city judge, defended in his letter the rights of Mexican Americans as citizens who had proven their patriotism during World War I.

Editor *The Press*:

I read an article in *The Press* of May 5 in which Commissioner Starkey recommended that a holiday which 37 Water Department employees took off not be paid to them because that was the anniversary of the day on which "they were beaten."

As one of those 37 men, I am fully qualified to know the facts in the case and I want the readers of *The Press* and Commissioner Starkey to know them.

In the first place, the City Council, of which Mr. Starkey is a member, voted some weeks back that the holidays in the city employees' working year would be reduced from 12 to 7. One of these designated holidays was San Jacinto Day. Being employees of the Water Department of the City of Houston, we took the day off as did all the rest of the city workers.

When the day was not paid to us, as it was to most of the other employees, we thought the reason was economical and let it go at that. But truth, very much like murder, "will out" and at the succeeding City Council meeting, on being petitioned for the payment of a holiday which had been promised us, Mr. Starkey made the statement which I consider unjust.

Mr. Starkey's statement was uncalled for, and as one of those 37 men, he will find a World War veteran wounded in action who still carries bits of shells that struck him during sieges 'Over There,' two men who can trace their ancestry 10 generations back on Texas soil, and one whose direct forefather signed the Texas Declaration of Independence. All are American citizens and possess poll taxes. Most of them are property holders and heads of families.

Mr. Starkey, as a man chosen to lead our citizens in the ways of better government, should realize that the people of Houston expect him to speak and act in a manner which reflects the best interests of the people. In making such a prejudicial statement, Mr. Starkey is being very unfair, intolerant, and un-American.

I, of the 37, have this to say: I am glad that the other commissioners do not exclude me from working for the city because I have a "Mexican name," as Mr. Starkey so bluntly puts it; and I am happy in the knowledge that in the event of another war, the officials of the United States of America won't notice the apparent origin of my name and deny me the privilege to fight for the country I love so well.—J.J. Herrera, 1516 Houston Avenue.

Houston Press, May 10, 1937.

"If We Are Given the Opportunity . . ."

That Mexican Americans were aware of their rights and were willing to take to task the new promises of equality in the workplace for all races is seen in the efforts of David Flores, an East Chicago, Indiana, steelworker who felt that Chicago-area defense industries discriminated against Mexicans. In 1941, right as the war broke out, even President Roosevelt had signed a decree prohibiting discrimination.

I was formerly employed by the Inland Steel Company, and while working there, I took a welder's course at an accredited college here in Chicago. After completing my course, I asked the management for the occupation which would enable me to put into practice what I had learned. Unfortunately, I was denied that position because of my being a Mexican alien . . .

On last October 2, I went to the Hammond office of the U.S. Employment Service. The first question asked me was whether or not I was a citizen. The clerk then told me that there were a few welding jobs open, but the applicant had to be a citizen. When I mentioned the "President's Executive Order" concerning discrimination in the employment of workers, the clerk told me that orders were orders . . .

Very determined to keep trying until I succeed, I went to several of the other defense industries; the same as the Employment Office, I was asked the same question of citizenship . . .

By this time I was very disgusted with the whole situation, but I made a last attempt at the General Transportation Company of East Chicago. There I was hired without question regarding racial or citizenship status. This proves that not all companies are prejudiced against aliens . . . due to lack of work, I was laid off.

On November 24, I went to the U.S. Employment Service here in East Chicago, where I went through identically the same procedure as in Hammond, with the exception I felt it useless to register . . .

Another fact I wish to mention is that there are quite a few Mexicans who are naturalized citizens, but they are still denied consideration and the rights of citizens . . .

So you see there is that general discrimination against the Mexicans. We are supposed to take whatever is handed to us and be content. I am sure there are a great many of us who can prove ourselves worthy of better occupations and also achieve the same goals as other men, if we are given the opportunity . . .

David Flores to Fair Employment Practices Council of Chicago, December 15, 1941, Private File of Author.

The Mine Mill

Unions like the Mine Mill were in the forefront of breaking down the barriers to ending discrimination in the workplace because of race prejudice. George Knott, an official for the union, gave radio talks in Arizona dealing with union issues. The script that Knott used for one particular broadcast in February of 1943 discussed discrimination, Mexicans, and the role the Fair Employment Practices Council should play in ending this treatment.

Fellow workers of Morenci and Clifton, friends of the radio audience, last Sunday I spent some time in explaining the CIO position on discrimination. This Sunday I'm going to talk on the relation of discrimination to production. Discrimination is not something that occurs only in Morenci; it occurs in various communities throughout the entire United States. The Spanish people are not the only recipients of its poisonous reaction. There is also the Negro, the Chinese, Indian, Jew, Catholic, Protestant. All of these people are in some sections of this republic looked down upon and discriminated against. The pattern of discrimination, however, always seems to follow the same course and is always most prevalent in those sections where big business finds it advantageous to have it promulgated. In the Southwest, of course, it's the Spanish and Mexican worker; practically anywhere in the United States, the Negro suffers discrimination. In those industrial sections of the country where discrimination is practiced and the Catholic is in the minority, he bears the brunt of the lash; and where the Protestant is in the same position he, too, suffers; the Jew, of course, stands next to the Negro as outcast. Today this country is engaged in a global conflict, testing whether democracy as a form of life shall be extended to all of the peoples of the world, or whether we Americans and our allies must go down the path of medieval barbarism as portrayed by fascism. Abraham Lincoln once said, "This Nation cannot exist half slave and half free." Today, with all the world at our doorstep, with the advent of the powerful plane, Lincoln's words must apply to the world.

As a result of actively fighting to make sure that democracy shall survive this holocaust, every man's hand must be turned towards achieving this end. As late as six months ago, the President's Committee on Fair Employee Practices said that there was in America some twelve million peoples, Negroes, Jews, Mexican, etc., hundreds of thousands of them unable to get training in defense industries, many more already trained unable to secure work in their profession or vocation. In this period of our country's history, during the greatest manpower shortage that our Nation has ever known, while humanity teeters on the brink of disaster, we find people in America who still feel that they have a right to enjoy their prejudices. An old Chinese philosopher once said, "To think is hard work, but prejudice is a pleasure." Hadn't we Americans better begin to think in the terms of the invaluable production we are losing during this period, production that may mean the difference between dying and living for someone you love on some far-flung battle front. The CIO as a whole says yes, some small sections of the AF of L say no, the predatory wolves who wax fat on human misery say never. Think it over, Brother and Sister, all of us are at the crossroads, all of us are going through Hamlet's soliloquy, "To be or not to be."

To my Spanish and Anglo friends, I offer this advice: occasionally we may run across those kinds of people who disagree with these thoughts; don't make it a point to argue or fight over these issues. Remember that two wrongs never made a right. Pursue your way in peace. Organize in the knowledge that you are following the path that has been blazed before you by such Americans as Payne, Jefferson, and Lincoln. Fight in the end will give us might and victory.

Some months ago in Silver City, New Mexico, I chanced to meet Ernest De Baca, organizer for the American Federation of Labor. He asked me whether I had any knowledge that the Fair Employment Practices were coming to town. I replied that they were expected the following week. He told me that he was glad of that because he had an armful of discrimination cases to dump in their lap on Morenci. A month later I met one of the men in El Paso who was on that Committee, and he asked me whether the CIO intended to do anything about discrimination in Morenci, because it appeared that the Committee wasn't getting anywhere with the AF of L, that they had turned only two cases into their office and that neither one of the cases was provable. This, of course, was one of the final straws that influenced the International Office in directing that Morenci be organized. Additional considerations were given, of course, to the fact that the Phelps Dodge Empire, in the Southwest, has always acted as a break on organizational advances and has always been in the forefront with a low wage policy. This, of course, reacted unfavorably on the wage policy throughout the entire mining industry in the Southwest. At the Phelps Dodge Refinery in Douglas, Arizona, where the CIO is the accredited bargaining agency, the Union was told that the War Labor Board could not give them a greater increase in pay than fifty cents a day, because the American Federation of Labor had already accepted that sum and if the Board gave the CIO more, which they indicated they were willing to do, they would be discriminating against the AF of L. In Silver City and other Southwest mining areas, wage policy is decided on the basis of what Phelps Dodge is doing. It appears self-evident then that the only way to protect the working conditions of the miners in the Southwest is to crack the fountainhead from which it stems, and this, of course, leads us to the keystone of the Phelps Dodge Empire, which is Morenci. The National War Labor Board has already recognized the fact that the miners are under-paid.

Radio Talk By George Knott, February 14, 1943, Arizona Collection, Hayden Library, Arizona State University, CHI-H59.

Chapter Eight

Catalysts of the Chicano Movement: Farm Worker Organizers and Land Grant Crusaders

The United Farm Workers (UFW) in California and the land struggle waged by Reies López Tijerina through the Alianza Federal de las Mercedes (Federal Alliance of Land Grants) in New Mexico served as inspirations for the tumultuous youth rebellion of the 1960s known as the Chicano Movement, a process that left a tremendous legacy for civil rights. César Chávez founded the UFW before a defined Chicano *movimiento* emerged, but young Chicano activists discovered that the farm worker struggle reflected their own commitments to helping the common folk or the underdog. Still, Chicano militants often mistook Chávez's short stature and quiet demeanor for passivity rather than forceful leadership. Ultimately, this image became his most important asset for working with mainstream American society and most Mexican Americans.

But Chicano activists had no greater symbol of defying the establishment than Reies López Tijerina. While César Chávez evoked a Ghandi-like image, the tactics used by the Alianza to regain land lost to Anglos or to the federal government were dramatic and audacious. Besides the Alianza's militancy and boldness, the goal of establishing a free, independent community appealed to the emerging Chicano nationalists and separatists.

Farm Workers in the Chicano Movement Era

In reality, the UFW simply continued Ernesto Galarza's efforts to unionize farm workers through the National Farm Workers Union (NFWU) of the 1940s and the Agricultural Workers Organizing Committee (AWOC) of the 1950s. In the late 1950s, the Community Services Organization (CSO, see chapter six) sent César Chávez to Oxnard, California, to help unionize packing shed workers, but the organization did not support the organizing of workers actually working in the fields. When Chávez became National Director of the CSO in

1960, the CSO board still would not authorize this emphasis, so he resigned to pursue his ambition on his own, and he took with him a fellow CSO worker, Dolores Huerta.

Employing techniques that he had learned in the CSO, Chávez and his organizers canvassed each town and camp, signing up small groups in each community. By 1965 the fledgling union, now called the National Farm Workers Association (NFWA), signed up a thousand members and won some small disputes. But in September it was drawn into an unexpected major confrontation with all the grape companies in the Delano area. That month, Filipino workers belonging to the Agricultural Workers Organizing Committee (AWOC) struck against one of the major grape growers in the area. In a show of solidarity, Chávez's fledgling union joined the AWOC walkout, but even this combined strike effort could not force the growers to capitulate. To put pressure on the farmers from another angle, Chávez associated the farm workers' struggle with social causes, which blacks in the American South had done so much to advance. In April 1966, the union organized a march from Delano to the state capital of Sacramento that emphasized the lack of social justice for farm workers. The effort, which proved highly successful in getting national attention, also served to inspire future Chicano Movement activists, who either joined or read about the trek.

But neither the march nor the strike brought the grape producers to the negotiating tables, so the NFWA resorted to a boycott. Instead of a general boycott of all grape producers, which required more resources than the union could muster, the union targeted Schenley Liquor Company, which owned extensive vineyards in the San Joaquin Valley. The ban succeeded and Schenley granted all of the union's requests.

In April 1966, the giant table grapes DiGiorgio Corporation, in order to sabotage NFWA gains, allowed workers to join either the Teamsters Union or the NFWA. The Teamsters won, but under such a cloud of fraud that political pressure forced the grower to allow another election on August 30, 1966. To expand its base, the NFWA merged with the AWOC to form the United Farm Workers Organizing Committee (UFWOC), which won almost two-thirds of the vote and obtained a contract from the DiGiorgio company.

The union then decided to strike against the biggest table grape producer in the country, the Guimarra Vineyards Corporation, and boycott its products. The corporation, however, used union labels from companies that had contracts with the UFWOC, thus hiding their grapes' nonunion status, so the union decided to boycott the entire table grape industry. Unfortunately, this required such a great effort that strike activity was neglected. Moreover, farmers recruited thousands of strikebreakers from Mexico. Some frustrated unionists engaged in sabotage against the growers, but Chávez, who was committed to nonviolence, decided in March 1968, to use a hunger strike to bring his people into line.

The fast also helped promote the boycott, and cancellation orders for grapes poured into California, forcing California grape growers to relent and sign contracts with the UFWOC. Then the union decided to target Salinas Valley lettuce farmers during the summer harvest season of 1970. The lettuce farmers countered by negotiating "sweetheart" contracts with the Teamsters. Thousands of workers honored a strike called by the UFWOC, but the crop was harvested anyway. Again, the UFWOC decided to use the boycott, but Americans did not respond to this plea as they did to the ban on grapes.

Heartened by the Teamster collusion with the lettuce industry, table grape growers decided to turn to the Teamsters when contracts expired with the UFW. California agriculturists then launched a state initiative to outlaw the secondary boycott, Chávez's most potent weapon. The union, now called the United Farm Workers (UFW), successfully campaigned to defeat the bill, but the effort drained the resources of the UFW.

Then in February, 1975, Chávez announced a national boycott against Julio Gallo Wineries, the biggest business to sign a Teamsters' contract, and led about 3,000 marchers from San Francisco to Gallo's headquarters in Modesto, California.

These labor battles damaged California's crucial agricultural industry. Consequently, Governor Jerry Brown urged legislators to pass a bill called the Agricultural Labor Relations Act to provide California farm workers protection from which they were excluded when the U.S. Congress passed the National Labor Relations Act in 1935. The bill was passed, but after Jerry Brown's term, Californians elected the conservative George Deukmajian as governor, and he appointed Agricultural Labor Relations board members who favored the growers' interests.

The farm worker movement never again had the widespread support and successes that it enjoyed during this period. To be sure, because of César Chávez's influence, efforts to organize farm workers spread to Arizona, Texas, Florida, and the Midwest; these met with only modest success. By the late seventies, internal dissent had weakened the California-based UFW, and the rank and file began to challenge the leadership in the decision-making process. A third grape boycott was issued in 1984, mainly to protest pesticide use as harmful to the workers. The boycott was a far cry from the dynamic effort made in the 1960s.

Recently, the union has continued to fall on hard times and has lost many contracts signed in the 1960s and 1970s. In the early 1990s, no more than 100 contracts covered about 10,000 farm workers. A bane for the union has been the ability of agricultural interests to use undocumented workers. One consequence was that Chávez and many of the UFW organizers leaned towards the position that the union should obtain benefits for U.S. citizens and permanent residents and supported restrictive immigration for immigrants. In the 1980s, the farm worker movement lost its symbolic appeal for Chicanos, and indeed, until César Chávez's tragic death in 1993 at age 65, the struggle was not as public as in previous years. A grape boycott was still in place at the time of his death, for example, but few people knew about it. The degree to which the farm worker movement succeeded is not the most important measurement of Chávez's place in history. His legacy transcends a lifework's commitment to organizing at a grassroots level, especially farm workers. Today, Mexican Americans evoke the name and memory of this soft-spoken labor organizer when they commemorate past civil rights struggles, when they advocate for contemporary social reform, or when they seek a heroic symbol with which they can identify. The reasons for this can be found in his persona and image, which he so carefully cultivated at the height of his career.

La Alianza Federal de las Mercedes—A Spark

Reies López Tijerina's fame, on the other hand, was confined more to the era in which he struggled for the restitution of Mexican and Spanish land grants. The 1848 Treaty of Guadalupe Hidalgo became the basis of this New Mexico-based movement, which began in the early 1960s. The agreement guaranteed Mexicans all the rights of citizens and a right to their property. Followers of Tijerina wanted to regain the lands lost since the end of the Mexican American War to developers, both wealthy Anglos and Hispanics, and the federal parks system. Moreover, those who had held on to their property into this century struggled with taxes and a constant battle to obtain favorable water and grazing rights.

Tijerina, who was born in Texas in 1926, spent the better part of his youth migrating with his farm worker family and, upon reaching adulthood, became a traveling Pentecostal preacher. After a failed attempt at establishing a religious commune in Arizona, he took his retinue to northern New Mexico, his wife Patsy's home area, and preached among the predominantly Catholic *Hispanos* in the mountain valleys of Rio Arriba County. In the early 1960s, as the U.S. Forest Service began restricting *Hispanos'* grazing and water rights on federal lands, Tijerina became attracted to the land grant cause and helped form the Corporation of Abiquiu.

As the Abiquiu movement grew, its headquarters was moved from Tierra Amarilla to Albuquerque in 1963. The membership changed its name from the Corporation of Abiquiu to La Alianza Federal de las Mercedes. Tijerina then attracted attention to the cause by hosting conferences that had the air of civil rights rallies. More importantly, Tijerina, his wife Patsy, his brothers, and a cadre of faithful organizers traveled across the breadth of village country recruiting disgruntled *paisanos*. The *aliancistas* became more hopeful when Tijerina announced that his research in Mexico City archives revealed that the U.S. had violated the terms of the Treaty of Guadalupe Hidalgo by not respecting the legality of land grants.

To persuade officials to investigate their claims, Alianza members marched from Albuquerque to the steps of the state capitol in Santa Fe in July, 1966. Frustrated because Governor Jack Campbell had rebuffed the group's request, in October of 1966 the *aliancistas* occupied Echo Amphitheater, a campground in the Kit Carson National Forest that had been an original *merced* (land grant). The group established the Republic of San Joaquín del Río Chama and evicted the forest rangers assigned to the area. Government officials arrested Tijerina and five other *aliancistas,* but eventually released them on bond.

By the spring of 1967, a more sympathetic governor, David Cargo, replaced Governor Campbell and gave the Alianza permission to convene a meeting in the town of Coyote in May 1967. When District Attorney Alfonso Sánchez of Rio Arriba County discovered that crusaders intended to formulate plans to again occupy the Echo Amphitheater campground, he tried to prevent the meeting by blocking the road to the village and making a number of arrests. Governor Cargo was out of the state and could not intervene. Consequently, Tijerina and other *aliancistas* attacked the jail in Rio Arriba on June 5 to free their comrades arrested in Coyote and wounded two officers in the process. They discovered, too late, that their comrades had already been freed on bail. Within hours, Acting Governor L.C. Francis mobilized the National Guard and embarked on one of the most massive manhunts in New Mexico history. The state police, without warrants, searched the homes of Alianza members and their sympathizers.

When Governor Cargo returned, he demobilized the National Guard, but Tijerina and the other fugitives were quickly arrested. After the courthouse incident, the raiders were charged with second degree kidnapping, assault to commit murder, unlawful assault on a jail, and a number of more minor infractions. Nonetheless, a state judge freed the *aliancistas* on bail and dropped many of the charges against them. In his trial, Tijerina fired his lawyer and defended himself brilliantly. The jury, made up of *Hispanos,* found all of the defendants not guilty.

The federal government then put Tijerina, and four others who were present at the Echo Amphitheater confrontation, on trial in southern New Mexico for an array of federal violations. The jury, made up primarily of Anglos, found Tijerina guilty on two counts of assault against forest rangers, and a federal judge sentenced him to two years in prison.

273

Tijerina's nationally publicized exploits earned him a heroic reputation among Chicano Movement participants. They exalted him as a national leader in the struggle against the establishment and against old-guard Mexican Americans, who were considered *vendidos* (sellouts). Tijerina did not disappoint them. He invited Chicano Movement activists to New Mexico to plan *movimiento* strategy and then took a lead in protesting against the conference held in El Paso in the fall of 1967, where President Lyndon Baines Johnson decided to appoint Vicente Ximénez as director of the Inter-Agency Committee on Mexican American Affairs. Ximénez and other Mexican American leaders who attended this meeting were considered too tame for Chicano militants. After the courthouse raid, however, extreme violence characterized all activities surrounding the land grant movement, both by and against the *aliancistas*, a situation that began to erode Tijerina's hold on leadership. Bombings of the Alianza headquarters and the murder of Eulogio Salazar, one of the deputies wounded at the courthouse raid who was scheduled to testify against the *aliancistas*, distracted Tijerina and his followers from day-to-day organizing activity.

Nonetheless, in February 1968, Tijerina, surrounded by a coterie of the faithful, joined the Poor People's March on Washington organized by the civil rights leader Dr. Martin Luther King. Although King was assassinated during this period, the *aliancistas* still marched and spent sixty days at the nation's capital, making friends among civil rights leaders from the Native-American and African-American communities.

While in Washington, Tijerina announced his intention to conduct a citizen's arrest of a number of federal and state officials back in New Mexico, an action that by now was a routine part of his political-theater tactics. A side effect of these wild antics, however, was that law enforcement agencies kept Tijerina and the group under constant surveillance. On June 6, 1969, *aliancistas* again converged on Coyote and set up a tent city on private land to camp out while they held their annual conference. Tijerina was now at the height of his fame and prestige among Chicano Movement activists who attended this conference from different parts of the United States.

At the end of the conference, the participants watched in awe as Patsy Tijerina set fire to a National Forest Park sign. When a Forest Service employee tried to stop her, Reies Tijerina came to her aid, was beaten, and almost shot. The police dispersed the crowd, but arrested both Patsy and Reies. Eventually, all of the accumulated federal charges against Tijerina earned him a five-year sentence. For her part in the sign burning, Patsy Tijerina received probation.

Tijerina was granted an early release from prison on July 26, 1971, contingent on his not associating with the militant stance of the Alianza. But New

Mexico authorities in June 1974, incarcerated Tijerina, this time for charges stemming from the courthouse raid. He had served only a few months when Governor Bruce King released him in response to constant pressure from New Mexico influentials.

Throughout the 1970s, Tijerina devoted only token attention to land grant activity. He emerged from federal prison with a new philosophy: to work towards brotherly love between all races and ethnic groups and to better relations between the police and minorities. He also became obsessed with achieving heroic recognition. He led a caravan of adherents to Mexico City in 1972 and ingratiated himself with Mexican government officials, including President Luis Echeverría, himself bent on projecting a populist image among his people.

By the mid-seventies, the much strained relationship with state officials had eased. The City of Albuquerque funded his Brotherhood Awareness Center, the new name for the Alianza. But Tijerina still had a few antics up his sleeve. During his trip to Mexico, he asked President Echverría to investigate the land question in New Mexico. The Mexican leader responded by establishing an agency charged with helping protect Mexican Americans in the United States and a commission to investigate land claims. This latest gambit again alienated Tijerina from the New Mexico establishment. After a press outcry, Albuquerque officials revoked funding for his project.

Significantly, until the courthouse raid, the Alianza movement used a quiet, legalistic tact to regain land grants. But the raid event changed the course of the Alianza movement, attracting attention to Tijerina personally and leading him to pursue national attention at the expense of local exigencies. Eventually, even Tijerina's most avid supporters abandoned his crusade as his activities seemed opportunistic and zany. The Alianza continued to function until the 1980s when the weakened organization finally collapsed.

In spite of the merits inherent in Tijerina's cause, his lifework has not yet coalesced into the legacy that accrued to César Chávez. His erratic behavior, his less than achievable goals, and the eventual neglect of his original objectives account for much of this. His behavior, however, is probably also related to his jail experiences. No other major Chicano Movement leader spent as much time incarcerated, and while many were harassed by the police, it was not to the same degree.

Although *aliancista* activity divided many New Mexicans, it also brought attention to the plight of the poor in one of the most impoverished areas of the United States. In addition, Alianza activity also energized other Hispanics in New Mexico and throughout the country into civil rights activities and educational reform.

Chávez's Organizing: the Early Years

By 1963, the organizers of the National Farm Workers Association had collected some 80,000 pledge cards from workers, and through dues, the union built up $25,000 in the credit union, which was run by Chávez's wife, Helen. In 1964, when the movement had one thousand members, Wendy Goepel interviewed Chávez for *Farm Labor*. Here he expounds on his often-repeated notion that an effective union could only be built slowly and quietly through methodical organization, not knowing that the NFWA would have to reveal itself sooner than expected, when it joined the Filipino workers' strike in 1965.

When you mention union in California, most people think of AWOC, the Teamsters, or perhaps the ILWU. Here, there are nationwide superstructures; and it is assumed that one of these will eventually "reach down" and pick up the farm worker.

Some say it will be the Teamsters because they control the necessary transportation link from field to cannery or retail store; others speculate that it will be AWOC because of its activity in the valley during the past five years.

But some other observers feel that a little-known organization called the Farm Workers Association (FWA) is building a union in the real sense. FWA, with headquarters in Delano (Kern County), was begun by César Chávez. Some people may be more familiar with his name than with the organization.

César Chávez was one of the first staff members of the Community Service Organization (CSO), a political and social action movement among Mexican Americans in various California communities. He became a skilled community organizer under the tutelage of Fred Ross of the Industrial Areas Foundation. He worked for CSO in San Jose, Oxnard, Stockton, and elsewhere.

As an organizer, he had to learn what unity and conflict meant, and how they came about. He was forced to figure out why people joined an organization or supported an organization.

It is difficult, he has found, to remain a leader of your own people, rather than to use your people as a vehicle for improving your personal position—for gaining a new social identity for yourself. Many minority group organizations have gained strength in their early days, have earned the awareness of majority groups, and have then sold out the original purpose of the organization for some immediate awareness and appeasement offered to them: either the group has been absorbed or its leaders have been lured off into positions within the "mainstream" of social life. Chávez himself has turned down positions with the Peace Corps and others, to continue what he believes he must try to do and might be able to do.

The Farm Workers Association is almost two years old now. Chávez says, "If you look back, we've come a long way; if you look ahead, we have a long way to go." He says that there is nothing unusual about what he is trying to do now: "I'm just trying to do what everyone else has, and making a few changes where I know we've made mistakes before." But the secret of his success—if there is to be success—will lie in certain unique techniques of worker organization upon which the Farm Workers Association is built.

César begins by saying, "Some farm workers are bums just like some growers are. It's a big mistake to begin by idealizing the workers because they're the 'down and outers.' Most farm workers are just human; they live, like all of us, from day to day; they want happiness and they want to avoid confusion and pain."

Then he continues by asking questions: "The spirit of our Revolution: what has happened to it? Why do people belong to anything or get excited about anything? What do they want? What keeps them going?"

"When I was 19," he recalls, "I was picking cotton in Corcoran. A car with loudspeakers came around. The speakers were saying: 'Stop working. You're not making a living. Come downtown to a rally instead.' My brother and I left, with many others. Seven thousand cotton pickers gathered in a little park in the center of Corcoran. There was a platform, and a union leader got up and started talking to all the workers about 'the cause.' I would have died right then if someone had told me how and why to die for our cause. But no one did. There was a crisis, and a mob, but there was no organization, and nothing came of it all. A week later everyone was back picking cotton in the same field at the same low wages. It was dramatic. People came together. Then it was over. That won't organize farm workers."

"A couple of years ago," he continues, "I was driving home from Los Angeles. I passed a Pentecostal church at night and it was full of people and I thought to myself, Why do all the people come there so much? It must be because they like to praise God—and to sing."

***

A union is a group of people who have feeling for one another and a devotion to a common cause. During the first year, 1962, Chávez spent months just talking with people in various towns—in their homes, in places where they gathered at night, in the fields as they left their places at the end of a day. In the beginning, he says, it is important to let people know exactly what you are trying to do and what role they have in it. It is fairly easy to get people interested, but it is important to find out which people are committed and are willing to work, and which are not really serious. Sometimes it is very hard to know this at first. In the beginning, he recalls, it was easy to get everybody excited. They were ready to join quickly, but they had unrealistic goals and ideas about what they would get. The biggest problem of all is to build a group spirit and to keep people involved and concerned—prepared to make demands, prepared to show their strength and their unity over a long period of time. You have to just begin this by finding the committed people in every little community; this takes time. You begin by talking to people; then you call back on people. You spend evenings having "house meetings"—talking to three or four people who want to spend an evening talking about problems and discussing what they see that has to be done. You build a core of people who keep coming back to talk. You find certain people who are respected as leaders in every community; and you find that some of these leaders are committed to the task ahead. A union, then, is not simply getting enough workers to stage a strike. A union is building a group with a spirit and an existence all its own.

277

A union must be built around the idea that people must do things by themselves, in order to help themselves. Too many people, César feels, have the idea that the farm worker is capable only of being helped by others. People want to give things to him. So, in time, some workers come to expect help from the outside. They change their idea of themselves. They become unaccustomed to the idea that they can do anything by themselves for themselves. They have accepted the idea that they are "too small" to do anything, too weak to make themselves heard, powerless to change their own destinies. The leader, of course, gives himself selflessly to the members, but he must expect and demand that they give themselves to the organization at the same time. He exists only to help make the people strong.

A union must have members who pay dues regularly. The only people whom the Farm Workers Association counts as members are those who pay their $3.50 a month, every month. Chávez says that farm workers who are committed can afford to pay $3.50 a month in dues, even though they have low incomes. He feels that the members commit themselves to the organization by paying dues regularly. He feels that because they pay so much, they feel they are the important part of the organization, that they have a right to be served. They don't hesitate to write, to call, to ask for things—and to reaffirm their position in the association. Members enjoy certain concrete benefits, and are offered assistance with social, economic, and legal problems that they might have. These benefits can be, and are, used continually by the members. To many, the breadth of services and programs available to association members is new and is most welcome. And the idea that the members are, alone, paying the salary of a man who is responsible to them is very important, both to members and to César Chávez. "Of course," he says, "it is very hard to limit assistance and service to members; many people come to your door because they know that you might be able to help them out with some problem. But helping everyone who came would take up all my time—and more. Then I would have none left to work with the other members. People must come to see assistance to one another as the purpose of the organization, as its very reason for being." César has also learned that you do not build a strong, ongoing organization by simply performing services for any person who has a crisis and needs help. People must come to realize that they join and are associated with a group that they will help, and that will help them, if they ever need it. The people together are not too small.

The people together must learn to show their strength. One way that César feels is very important is through concern with legislation. Part of the "training process" that the membership goes through is to learn how legislation is passed, and why certain kinds are often not passed. One of the requirements of membership is to pledge to work on legislation. This is done through letter writing campaigns, for example. Delegations to Sacramento are also part of the program; about forty of the members went to the governor's hearings on farm labor, and those who had never been to Sacramento before went on a tour of the capitol. "Legislation will not solve the problems," Chávez says, "but it can certainly make the road smoother."

In the Farm Workers Association, a single membership covers a whole family. Membership fluctuates some, with the fewest members during the time when there is the most work available. During this time, people are too busy to remember to pay dues, and they just aren't as concerned with their problems as they are during slack season. In spite of seasonal fluctuations, the organization has continued to grow every month since it began. Today, the Farm Workers Association is no longer César Chávez. There are local leaders, Farm Workers Association representatives, who work together with one another and with César. Local leaders are responsible for the members in their own town—for helping them with the problems they may encounter, for keeping the local group together, for encouraging people to understand and to use the services available to them as members, for collecting dues, and for recruiting new members in the community. At the present time, there are local leaders and local groups in sixty-seven different areas in eight valley counties. The greatest number of local groups is in Kings County, followed by Kern, San Joaquin, Tulare, and Fresno Counties.

In every community, there are certain types of farm workers who are not potential members of the association. That group of workers who has recently arrived from Mexico is, for example, very hard to organize. They tend to think they are better off here than they really are. For one thing, it is difficult to explain American-style unionism to the "emigrado." Mexicans tend to assume that the United States Constitution forbids workers to cross a picket line, and that it should therefore be fairly simple to organize a strike and a union. "The Mexican revolutionary constitution is," Chávez says, "kinder to the working man than our own."

The workers who are hired year-round on one farm have a loyalty to the grower and are not willing to lose their security for any improvements in their conditions; they feel they would jeopardize their jobs by joining the association. Another group that usually won't join consists of the "old hands" among the local, temporary workers. These are the workers who have been in one area about twenty years—long enough to know where all the seasonal jobs in a three-of-four county area are. These workers have a fairly regular circuit of jobs, in and out of agriculture. When there is no work available, during certain periods, these workers can draw unemployment insurance from the cannery and other "covered" jobs that they have had. But it is not uncommon for them to collect unemployment insurance and do temporary farm work at the same time to supplement their income. These workers have something to gain, then, by keeping the "system" as it is, and something to lose by joining an association that would change the system.

Thus, there are different kinds of farm workers in any small community, and there is a certain amount of friction, overt or covert, between groups of workers. It is the seasonal farm workers who have been in the United States for some time, but who have not been able to find a full year's employment, who are most likely to be interested in joining the association and in seeing an eventual union of farm workers. Chávez notes that there will probably be real conflict in many little communities before the problems are finally resolved, because of the vested interests that certain workers think they have in the status quo.

The agricultural workers who are FWA members may, then, be characterized as local families who depend on seasonal farm work. Most of them live year-round in the southern San Joaquin. Almost all are family men. They are a stable group to work with, and they are capable members of an ongoing organization.

The biggest problem is keeping the local groups, all the people, united and ready to engage in "direct action" when the time comes. There are not many general meetings of the Farm Workers Association. Chávez observes that people do not like to go to meetings endlessly. If nothing important happens when they do go, they may become discouraged about the organization and the movement on the basis of the meeting. Too many meetings also give the appearance that nothing important is happening, that there is no progress. When a group must be built to work for a goal which is several years away, it is the most difficult to build and keep a group together. If a group has not grown to the point where some direct action can be taken against some outside person or some problem, then there is a dangerous tendency for the group to weaken or splinter and for in-group factions or group disorganization to take place. So, it is very important during the growth period of a group to tackle small problems which individual members have and which the members can work out with the help of local leaders of the organization. The task of confronting some person or some problem which the group feels is important, and the success obtained when the people work together gives individual members a sense of control over their own lives. It teaches them more about the complexities of modern society, and it gives them an opportunity to work constructively in small, functional units. It gives the group a continual reason for being.

The few large meetings that are held to show and feel the size and the unity of the association are carefully planned. There is appeal to pageantry and a display of the "signs and symbols" that are part of the association. There is a Farm Workers Association song, written by Mrs. Rosa Gloria, a member from Madera, which is sung at meetings. There is a symbol, which Chávez admits is a bit "flashy:" a thunderbird on a red and black field. And there is a slogan: "Viva la Causa," which is the unity to which workers pledge themselves. These "artifacts" are used in the meetings, in greeting one another, and on the association's letterhead stationery. But these large meetings have a limited function. The hard work is done daily in the communities by the leaders and the members.

Of course, the biggest temptation is to "do something dramatic." This would be easier and quicker than working day to day on small problems and keeping people together. "I figure, though," says Chávez, "that even if we had a 50-50 chance of carrying off a successful strike, the gamble would still be too great. You stand always to lose more than you gain by drama when you are working with people. Thirty men may lose their jobs as a result of a strike. You lose thirty members, and you gain thirty 'disorganizers.' So we must work on immediate goals—helping the members get a little better living through using the facilities of the association, through getting what they are entitled to, through learning how to participate more fully in social life. And the hard work of gaining official recognition, including strikes if necessary, will come."

Chávez says that he is not concerned that his organization be the core of a union for farm workers. He says that his membership is ready to unite with any other union, if any other succeeds. He, personally, doesn't want to be the one at the bargaining table.

Chávez conceives his real job to be education of the people. "You cannot organize a strike or build a union until the members who must do the real work understand what all this means, what kind of activities are involved. They must, first, be able to articulate their own hopes and goals." He would like very much to hold some short-term schools where the leader-members could discuss and study union organization together. Whatever the outcome of the Farm Workers Association, it is certain that the individuals who have learned and have profited from being members will be a lasting asset to their communities and to the society at large.

César says, finally, "Even if our work succeeds, I don't want to hang on forever. What I would really like is to be alone somewhere—in Mexico or in the mountains—and have time to read all the classics that there are in English and Spanish."

Farm Labor, I-5, April, 1964.

César Chávez on How It Began

Prior to the march on Sacramento, the militant NFWA had decided to call a boycott of the Schenley Liquor Company, which owned extensive vineyards in the San Joaquin Valley. NFWA planners recognized that a nationwide campaign against table grapes required time they did not have and an infrastructure that did not yet exist. So the union decided to concentrate on boycotting the liquor products of one company by targeting its Los Angeles market. In an interview taken just before his tragic death, César Chávez related the story of how the union became involved with Filipinos and the first contract with Schenley Liquors.

Q: And, you had a pretty understanding family, I presume?

A: Oh, my wife. Without her I couldn't have ever done it. Oh, yeah. I had eight kids, no money. In fact, besides the union, I had unemployment compensation checks, which when I went to register, I called myself a house meeting specialist in community development, and that was back in 1962. They didn't know what the hell it was, so they couldn't send me to a job because I could refuse it. No, that's not my job, that isn't my specialty.

Q: Let's race forward through history: the first grape strike and then as a consequence of that, the beginnings of the boycott, you seeing that as a tactic. Let's talk about the beginnings of the strike first: the goal is to get contracts. What are the first steps that led to that initial strike?

A: Well, see, we were led into it; we weren't ready. We didn't have any money. That bridge I hadn't figured out how we were going to do it. See, I told my wife, I said, "I can organize a huge organization of workers, but I don't know if I can take them to a contract, and it is going to take ten years this early in the game." She says without thinking. If it is not four years, we'll have a contract, if it's not four years! It will be ten to twelve years before we get a contract, and my ambition was that I would get a grower and just stick with a grower. And, literally, economics destroyed what I had to do forcingly, one little grower at a time. I didn't decide on that, because I was groping for how we were going to get into this. The boycotts were already set in our minds because of Ghandi, because of Dr. King. I had done a lot of reading about boycotts, so we knew it was going to happen. We also knew we were going to break our strike. We knew that, I mean it was inescapable. So, how do you beat them after you break your strike with what we had to deal with? And so, on September 8, 1965, in the morning, a family who are members of our union came to their office early in the morning saying, "There's a strike, there's a strike." Esther says, "There's a strike, there's a strike the Filipinos are striking, but they're not asking us to go out and strike." I said, "Well, what do you want to do?" They said, "Well, we don't know. We don't feel good working." I said, "Well, we can't go out on strike; we have to talk to the members." So, immediately I called Dolores and we began to set up. I called the leadership we had developed in those conventions. We had a meeting that night, and we said, "What are we going to do? Well, we can't, we got to support them. No, we're not ready, but we got to support them. It would look bad if we didn't." So we worked all that week and called a meeting on September 16, at the church hall. We were astounded; we had like 6,000 workers. We were ready to strike and we took a vote and we struck. And we said, "God will provide," and we struck. That's how it started.

Q: When you say, "God will provide," you need to take care of essential economic needs of people on strike.

A: There was absolutely no way that I could. I had no money. I had no idea. All I knew was that they wanted to strike, but the demand was that we couldn't work while others were striking. That was more important to me than the money to come. So, food and clothing, we could get that, but pay rent and all that stuff, we knew we couldn't get.

Q: So, what happened?

A: What mattered was that many people left. After a while they went to other jobs; some went back to work. We kept, remember that group I told you about, those who were greatly committed stayed for fifty-eight and a half months. That's how we beat them. When they say boycotting, I mean striking and they never left—they were like preselective. These are the ones that we knew would stay, and then we added a few others. But, then in time we began to get money. We got a lot of food first, and then people later became more publicized, to who, they gave money. But our ranks began to deplete by December; they were shrinking. You see, I knew they were going to break the strike. Then you begin to shrink, and then people begin to fight among themselves—I knew all that. We had already prepositioned ourselves to take care of that, so in February we called the march to Sacramento in 1966. What happened was that there was a lot of repression against us—cops and all that stuff. But also lots of red-baiting and people are believing we're communist. So therefore, we're going like this, and so we had to break through that, and we did. We went from Delano to Sacramento, and by the time we were at Sacramento, we had thousands of people believing us as workers. See, we wanted them to see that first of all we had numbers, that we were organized. We were doing something Mexicans love to do anyway, marching, and we had the Virgin with us. And people, see, people said no, no they're not communists, once they saw the church around us. That was the way we broke the red-baiting.

Q: The media is responsible or guilty of it, but you were dealing with symbols, whether it's the American flag or the Virgin de Guadalupe?

A: Oh, we did a lot of symbolism, because that's how we talked to people.

Q: Did the red-baiting stop somewhat after that?

A: No, well, they kept doing it, but the people no longer believed them. The workers didn't, at least most of them. No, the red-baiting stopped when they came to Delano for the California Senate Sub-committee on Un-American Activities came to Delano in '67. They had a hearing, and we knocked the hell out of them; that's when it stopped. The leader or the chairman of the committee was a guy named Bill Coby, a senator from Madera in '52. When I was doing the CSO chapters, we had registered sixteen-thousand Chicanos for the first time, all democrats in those counties. When he ran, he won by about five-hundred votes. We got him elected and he came to see me and sent me letters calling me a great American, and I saved the letters. And when he came to the meeting, I showed the letters to the committee and to the public, and we knocked the hell out of them. We broke his back on that.

Q: Let's talk about the march which ended up in Sacramento. I mean, that focused national attention and, ultimately, international attention on your work and the work of your colleagues, and beyond that to seeing a metaphor for what was beginning to be called a Chicano Movement in general. Like it or not, you and your unit became representative of this whole social . . . ?

A: I'm not sure that that's the case, but on the march itself, there was also, see, the community organizing. I had noticed the people who talked and made motions, and those were the ones that were active. The ones who just sat and listened weren't that active. So, how do we get people to be active? Because our people won't really talk a lot. So we started singing. We would sing because people would get up and sing, and that's pretty participating. Then I noticed that we had a little march; one of our members died and we marched. I said let's have an all night *velorio* and let's march. They liked it. And man, everybody was talking; it was like wow. So the march was a *peregrinación*, a pilgrimage, and it had all the elements. The symbolism and other things we needed to give the workers, like hope. Plus, now I read back in history about the *teatros*, so I had . . . now out of sheer coincidence, Luis Valdez came to see me. I said we have room for a street theater. *El teatro* played a great role in those days, but we still sang the songs that he wrote for us. All the songs we sang are his songs that he wrote for us. I mean songs that dealt with it. So we have the *teatro*, the Virgin, we had the flags, but see people are marching and they're participating. They're committing themselves because their *compadre* goes in the car and sees them in the march; they can't deny it or the boss comes. Now, they're committed, now they have got to support it because if not, then . . .

Q: It's a way of sort of publicly coming out.

A: Yeah, it was publicly coming out, and Dr. King had been very successful with that. So, anyway, it was a great experience for us. Oh, it was very difficult to march for twenty-one days, but it was like God-sent, it was so fantastic. It helped us a lot.

César Chávez interviewed by Luis Torres, April 20, 1992, NLCC.

Getting a Contract

The boycott against Schenley succeeded. The Sacramento marchers were resting in Stockton when a call came from Schenley's lawyers, who wanted to negotiate a contract and indeed one was signed. Other wine producers—Gallo, Christian Brothers, Paul Masson, Almaden, Franzia Brothers, and Noviate—soon signed contracts.

AGREEMENT

IT IS HEREBY AGREED by and between SCHENLEY INDUSTRIES, INC., a corporation, herein called the Employer, and THE UNITED FARM WORKERS ORGANIZING COMMITTEE, AFL-CIO, an unincorporated association, herein called the Union, as follows:

SECTION I. *RECOGNITION*

The Employer recognizes the Union as the sole and exclusive representative for the purpose of collective bargaining with respect to rates of pay, wages, hours of employment, and other conditions of employment of all employees of the Employer employed on all agricultural fields leased, owned, or rented by the Employer in Kern and Tulare Counties.

The Employer further recognizes the rights and obligations of the Union to negotiate wages, hours, and conditions of employment, and to administer this agreement on behalf of all covered employees.

The Employer and its representatives will not undermine the Union or promote or finance any competing labor organization.

The Employer and its representatives will not interfere with the right of any employee to join and assist the Union, and will make known to all employees that they will secure no advantage, more favorable consideration, or any form of special privilege because of nonmembership in the Union.

The Employer and its representatives will make known to all employees, supervisors, and officers, its policies and commitments as set forth above with respect to recognition of the Union and that employees in the bargaining units should give the utmost consideration to supporting and participating in collective bargaining and contract administration functions.

Any claim by the Union that action on the job of any non-bargaining unit employee is disrupting harmonious working relations may be taken up as a grievance.

Any work which the employees in the bargaining unit can perform shall not be contracted out to be performed by outside contractors except upon Union agreement.

SECTION II. *UNION SECURITY*

Union membership shall be a condition of employment. Each employee shall be required to become and remain a member of the Union, in good standing, immediately following thirty (30) continual calendar days of employment.

The Union shall be the sole judge of the good standing of its members. Any employee who fails to become a member of the Union within the time limit set forth herein, or who fails to pay the required initiation fees, periodic dues, and regularly authorized assessments as prescribed by the Union, shall be immediately discharged upon written notice from the Union to the Employer.

The Employer agrees to furnish the Union, in writing, the names of employees, giving the names, addresses, ages, Social Security numbers, and type or job classifications.

The Employer agrees to deduct from each employee's pay all initiation fees, periodic dues, and assessments as required by the Union, upon presentation of individual authorizations, signed by the employees, directing the Employer to make such deductions. The Employer shall make such deductions from the employees' pay once in each month and remit same to the Union not later than the 15th day of the following month. Vacation pay is subject to a monthly dues deduction.

The Union will furnish the forms to be used for the authorization. The Employer will furnish the Union with a duplicate copy of all signed authorizations.

SECTION III. *SUCCESSOR CLAUSE*

This agreement shall be binding upon the parties hereto, their successors, administrators, executors, and assigns. In the event an operation is sold, leased, transferred, or taken over by sale, transfer, lease, assignment, receivership or bankruptcy, such operation shall continue to be subject to the terms and conditions of this agreement for the life thereof. It is understood by this section that the parties hereto shall not use any leasing device to a third party to evade this contract. The Employer shall give notice of the existence of this Agreement to any purchaser, transferee, leasee, assignee, etc., of the operation covered by this Agreement or any part thereof. Such notice shall be in writing, with a copy to the Union, at the time the seller, transferer, or lessor executes a contract or transaction as herein described.

SECTION IV. *MODERNIZATION AND MECHANIZATION*

No new job, job rate, classification, or new equipment (however, this will not apply to replacement equipment which will not affect the jobs, job content, or classifications of its operators) will be introduced without prior consultation with the Union. Nor shall any job in any way be modified without such prior consultation and agreement.

The company shall not change or modify any job so as to remove it from or keep it out of the bargaining unit.

SECTION V. *HIRING*

Whenever the Employer requires employees to perform any work covered by this agreement, it shall notify the Union, stating the number of employees needed, the type of work to be performed, the starting date of the work, and the approximate duration of the job or jobs.

Upon receipt of such notice, the Union shall use its best efforts to furnish the required number of employees. If the Union is unable to furnish the required number of employees within 72 hours, or on the date of the beginning of the work (whichever date is later), the Employer shall be free to procure employees from any other source. The Employer shall, in such event, notify the Union in writing, within 24 hours, of the names and addresses of all employees so hired.

SECTION VI. *DISCRIMINATION*

In accord with the policies of the Employer and of the Union, it is agreed that neither party will discriminate against any employee on the basis of race, creed, color, religion, or national origin.

SECTION VII. *SENIORITY*

Seniority will be based upon length of service and such seniority will be extended beginning with the first date of hire. Temporary layoffs of not more than three months shall not constitute a break in the continuity of service, for the purpose of seniority. Layoffs, transfers, promotions, and vacations for employees shall be determined on the basis of seniority. Company shall furnish an up-to-date seniority list of all employees on a quarterly basis.

SECTIION VIII. *WAGES*

Schedule of Wage Rates. Appendix A, which is attached hereto and made a part hereof, sets forth the Schedule of Wage Rates which shall apply to all jobs in the bargaining unit.
Each employee shall be assigned the job title of his regularly assigned job.
Any Employee who is assigned to a higher paid job shall receive the higher rate. If he is assigned to a lower paid job, he will receive the rate which he would normally be paid on his regular job.
Base Pay. Incentive workers shall have guaranteed earnings of not less than the rate of pay for hourly workers.

SECTION IX. *RIGHT OF ACCESS TO COMPANY PROPERTY*

Duly authorized representatives of the Union shall be permitted on the Employer's premises, agricultural fields and camps for the normal course of union business.

SECTION X. *BULLETIN BOARDS*

The Employer will provide bulletin boards placed at such central locations as the Union may designate, subject to approval of the Employer, upon which the Union may post its formal notices.

SECTION XI. *LEAVE OF ABSENCE FOR UNION BUSINESS*

Any employee elected or appointed to an office or position in the Union shall be granted a leave of absence for a period of continuous service with the Union. Fifteen (15) days' notice must be given the Employer before the employee takes leave to accept such office or position or chooses to return to work. Such leave of absence will be without pay. Seniority shall not be broken or suspended by reason of such leave.

A leave of absence shall also be granted for temporary leave to attend Union business provided ample notice is given.

SECTION XII. *MAINTENANCE OF STANDARDS*

The employer agrees that all conditions of employment relating to wages, hours of work, and general working conditions shall be maintained at no less than the highest standards in effect at the time of the signing of this agreement, and conditions of employment shall be improved wherever specific provisions for improvement are made elsewhere in this agreement.

SECTION XIII. *WORK OPPORTUNITY*

If less than the normal work opportunity is available, preference shall be given to employees of the regular full-time workforce.

Supervisors outside of the bargaining unit shall not do any work regularly performed by employees in the bargaining unit except in cases of emergency.

SECTION XIV. *REPORTING PAY*

An employee reporting for work at his regularly scheduled starting time shall be guaranteed a minimum of four (4) hours' work or four (4) hours' pay at his applicable rate, unless such employee has been notified not to report at least two (2) hours before his regularly scheduled starting time.

Stand-by time. Employee shall be paid for all time he is required to remain on the job at his hourly rate or average hourly piece rate earnings.

SECTION XV. *RECORDS AND PAY PERIOD*

Full and accurate records shall be kept, including total hours worked, piece rate or incentive records, total wages, and total deductions. Employees shall be furnished a copy of the itemized wages and itemized deductions each payday, which shall include the employee piece rate production record.

The Union shall have the right to examine time sheets, work production, or other records that pertain to employees' compensation. Reason shall govern no abuse of this request.

SECTION XVI. *CAMP HOUSING*

Rentals to employees of available camp housing on the Employer's premises shall be made to employees on a nondiscriminatory basis and without favoritism. The factors of race, color, creed, religion, or national origin shall not be considered in the distribution of available rentals.

Camps and meal service shall be operated on a nonprofit basis therein.

Where the company presently provides free sleeping accommodations in its camps, these camps shall be maintained on this basis (subject to final approval).

SECTION XVII. *SAFETY AND HEALTH*

Sanitary Facilities. There shall be adequate toilet facilities in the field readily accessible to employees, that will be maintained in a clean and sanitary manner. These may be portable facilities and shall be maintained at the rate of one for every thirty-five (35) employees.

Drinking Water. Each place where there is work being performed shall be provided with suitable cool, portable drinking water convenient to employees. Individual paper drinking cups shall be provided.

First Aid. Adequate first aid supplies shall be provided and kept clean and sanitary in a dustproof container.

Protective garments, tools, and equipment necessary to safeguard the health of or to prevent injury to an employee's person shall be provided, maintained, and paid for by the Employer.

It is understood that the Employer shall immediately furnish protective equipment for sprayers, umbrellas for tractor drivers, curtains for tractors in wintertime, hooks or jacob's ladders for pipemen when going into large pipes, and gloves for gondola workers. Other protective garments, tools, and equipment shall be furnished as the needs arise.

SECTION XVIIII. *SAFETY COMMITTEE*

A Joint Safety Committee consisting of equal numbers of employees' representatives selected by the bargaining unit and management and representatives selected by the employer, shall be established at each farm.

The Safety Committee shall consider existing practices and rules relating to safety, formulate suggested changes in existent practices and rules, and make recommendations to local management with respect to the adoption of new rules and practices.

SECTION XIX. *LEAVES OF ABSENCE*

A leave of absence shall be granted to a regular employee for a reasonable period for any of the following reasons, without loss of seniority:

For jury duty or witness duty.

Up to two (2) years for illness or injury of employee requiring absence from the job, such leave to be without pay.

Military Leave. In the event an employee of the Company serves in the armed forces pursuant to the Selective Service Act, he shall not lose any seniority job rights or other benefit. Upon their discharge from the military, they shall be granted a job equal to that they would have had with the Company had they remained in continual employment of the company.

SECTION XX. *DISCHARGE*

The Employer shall not discharge any employee without just cause. Reasons for such discharge shall be presented to the employee in writing. The Union steward and/or official(s) shall have the right to interview the employee in private, not on company time. Individual performance in relation to a piece rate or incentive plan shall not be used for the purpose of disciplining or discharging an employee. This shall not, however, constitute any limitation on any of the Employer's rights to discipline or discharge for unsatisfactory performance by any employee.

SECTION XXI. *PROCEDURE FOR DISPUTES*

The parties to this agreement agree that for all differences, misunderstandings, or disputes which arise between the Employer and the Union in regards to wages, working conditions, and for other conditions of employment which arise out of the interpretation of this agreement, discharge, or any other dispute, an earnest effort shall be made to settle any difference immediately as follows:

In the event of any disagreement or dispute between the Employer and any employee covered by the terms of this agreement, or the Union, the matter shall be first taken up with the supervisor by the Union steward within twenty-four (24) hours from the realization that a dispute existed.

In the event that they are unable to adjust the dispute within one work day, the matter shall be taken up by an officer of the Union with the Employer branch personnel manager.

If there be no settlement between the last parties within two (2) work days, the matter shall be reduced to writing and taken up by the Employer's district personnel manager and a district officer of the Union.

In the event that these parties cannot resolve the dispute within ten (10) working days, the matter shall be submitted to an arbitrator selected by the union and the company. If they cannot agree on an arbitrator, one will be chosen by the Federal Mediation and Conciliation Service, and his decision on the matter shall be final and binding on both parties.

A grievance committee of five (5) workers shall be established by the Union which may participate at any step of the grievance.

Any disputes arising between the Union and the Employers under Section I—*Recognition,* Section II—*Union Security,* or Section V—*Hiring,* shall be taken up directly by the district's personnel manager and the district Union officer and shall proceed immediately to arbitration, if said persons cannot resolve the dispute within five (5) days.

The arbitrator's fee and expenses, the cost of any hearing room, and the cost of shorthand reporter and original transcript if requested by arbitrator shall be borne equally by the Union and Company incurring them.

SECTION XXII. *HOLIDAYS*

Holidays shall be granted to the employees in accordance with Appendix B to this agreement.

SECTION XXIII. *VACATIONS*

Vacations shall be granted to employees that have 1600 hours employment for one year in accordance with the Employer's policy.

SECTION XXIV. *STRIKES AND LOCKOUTS*

While the provisions of this agreement are being observed and carried out, there shall be no strike or lockout for the life of this agreement.

SECTION XXV. *EMPLOYMENT SECURITY*

Picket Lines. The Employer agrees that any employee may refuse to pass through any picket line sanctioned by the United Farm Workers Organizing Committee.

Farm workers will not be required to work when in good faith they believe that to do so would immediately endanger their health and safety.

No farm worker under this agreement shall be required to perform work that normally would have been done by employees of another company that is engaged in a strike, or to work on goods that will be handled or are destined to be handled by other workers engaged in strikebreaking.

SECTION XXVI. *MODIFICATION*

No provision or term of this agreement may be amended, modified, changed, altered, or waived except by a written document executed by the parties hereto.

SECTION XXVII. *DURATION*

This agreement shall be effective as of the 21st day of June, 1966 and continue through the 20th day of June, 1967. Thereafter, the agreement shall continue in effect from year to year, unless either party gives the other written notice of its intention to terminate, which notice shall be given sixty (60) days prior to any anniversary date of the first effective date of this agreement.

IN WITNESS WHEREOF, the parties have executed this agreement, in duplicate originals, this *12*th day of *October*, 1966.

UNITED FARM WORKERS ORGANIZATION COMMITTEE, AFL-CIO

By */s/ Dolores C. Huerta*
By */s/ Gpe. G. Alvizo*
By */s/ William L. Kircher*
By */s/ W. J. Bassett*

SCHENLEY DISTILLERIES, INC.

By */s/ Sydney B. Korshak*

Opeiu-30
AFL-CIO

APPENDIX A

WAGE SCHEDULE

Crew Leader	$1.95/hr
Truck Driver	1.85/hr
Tractor Driver	1.85/hr
Tractor Driver—Gondola loader	1.95/hr
Shop Mechanic's Helper	2.00/hr
Equipment Serviceman—Field	1.95/hr

Camp Repairman	1.85/hr
Pipeline Repairman	1.85/hr
Irrigator	1.80/hr
General Labor	1.75/hr
Juice Grape Field Checker	1.75/hr

PIECE RATES

Pruners

Hand-Spur	$1.65 plus $1.00/row of 1/8 mi.		
Hand-Cane	1.65 "	1.50/row	"
Machine-Spur	1.65 "	1.00/row	"
Machine-Cane	1.65 "	1.50/row	"

Juice Grape Pickers for House Pack

$1.60 plus $ .05/box

Straight Piece Work
Juice Grape Swampers $ .0275/box

Gondola-Juice and Wine Grape Picking

Grape variety tonnage rates should be adjusted so that average workers will earn $3.10/hr. on a piece rate.

Gondola crews' work day is 6 hours per day, but this will not preclude them from working longer if they so desire. Each crew will be given a ticket indicating tonnage weight of gondola at time of weighing. Each crew shall have one person observe gondola weighing.

In case of rows not 1/8 mile in length, use direct proportion to 1/8 mile.

Walter P. Reuther Library, Detroit Library, Wayne State University.

MAPA Supports the Union

An early supporter of César Chávez's union, the Mexican American Political Association (MAPA), through its short-lived newspaper, *The Voice*, devoted much of its space to union activities. An editorial that appeared in March 1966, demonstrates that Mexican American civil rights activists, even before the advent of the Chicano Movement, saw in the struggle of the farm workers a mirror of their own aspirations to better the conditions of Mexicans in the United States.

Editorial by Richard Forquer
Long History of Abuse

At the beginning of the 20th century, as California became more populated, it developed small farming communities. The communities were formed mostly by immigrant farm workers who worked the fields throughout the state.

With the revolution of 1910 in Mexico, a great many Mexican families moved into the United States. Most of these people did not speak English but were experienced farm workers. The railroads and farms, the booming business in California, found these people a ready and uncomplaining source of labor.

There developed a system of moving large groups of entire families to various parts of the Southwest and beyond where labor was needed. Many of these families lived in camps throughout the state. Growers were thus provided with much needed unskilled, untrained labor, particularly for seasonal farm work. These communities, called "colonies" or "barrios," were augmented beginning in 1910 by refugees of the Mexican Revolution.

Until the Great Depression of 1932, these communities were centers of commercial and social activity among the Mexican population. They contributed tremendously to the expanding economy. The communities developed without planning, guidance, regulation, ignored by political and social agencies without help of the Health Department, Building and Safety Departments of the local communities, and ignored as much as possible by Police and Sheriff Departments.

Most of them survived the depression of the '30s, the problems of World War II, and again survived the intense competition of the importation of labor from Mexico that was just ended in 1965. They survived, although ignored by the social agencies, medical agencies, politicians, and by the growers' industry itself, and still now provide important functions as a source of labor.

As a direct result of neglect and the growers' push to bring cheap labor into California, these communities have become pockets of poverty, existing with substandard living conditions, no medical care, no job training, no sewers, plumbing, water, electricity. They have, in spite of the adverse conditions of the past thirty years, been able not only to survive, but retain their culture brought with them from their homeland Mexico, which enhanced and enriched the historical tradition of our state.

These then are the reasons that the communities decided to unite and form some kind of protective agency that would help them survive the pressure of the well-to-do growers. The daring leaders gathered as many workers as they could and formed the Agriculture Workers Organization Committee (AWOC) and the National Farm Workers Association (NFWA). When these organizations tried to explain to the multimillion-dollar organization of the growers that all they wanted was a little more money for the workers so that they could eat better and be able to send their children to school with shoes and decent clothes, they met with great opposition. Instead of trying to meet the basic needs of their workers, the growers became hostile. They tried with the best of their ability to disrupt and cause dissension from within the workers' groups.

For these reasons AWOC and the NFWA decided to unite in calling a strike.

How long must a man suffer and let his family suffer the indignities of human bondage before he arises and fights back? For the Mexican farm worker it has been more than fifty-five years. Never before, in the history of California, has any poverty-stricken group dared to unite against an organization as large as that of the growers and even think of success.

These brave people not only started, they have persevered for six months with no support but the charity of well-wishers who believe in respect for human dignity.

Our history tells us that when a cause is just and human rights are concerned, people respond with yells of justice—and that we expect from this, the greatest strike in our history.

¡VIVA LA HUELGA!

The Voice, March 12, 1966.

El Plan de Delano and the Chicano Student Movement

To give the farm worker movement direction and purpose, Luis Valdez, the founder of El Teatro Campesino, wrote the "Plan de Delano." The piece was written to proclaim a noble goal for the farm worker movement that would inspire farm workers to join the union and demonstrate to the public that the cause should be supported on the basis of equality and justice. In 1968, the United Mexican American Students (UMAS) newsletter at Los Angeles State College published the proclamation in its newspaper, a perfect example of how the confluence between the Chicano Movement and the farm worker cause inspired the young militants.

The Delano Proclamation

This is the beginning of a social movement in fact and not in pronouncements. We seek our basic, God-given rights as human beings. Because we have suffered—and are not afraid to suffer—in order to survive, we are ready to give up everything, even our lives, in our fight for social justice. We shall do it without violence because that is our destiny . . .

We shall unite. We have learned the meaning of UNITY. We know why these United States are just that—united. The strength of the poor is also in union. We know that the poverty of the Mexican or Filipino worker in California is the same as that of all farm workers across the country: the Negroes and poor whites, the Puerto Ricans, Japanese, and Arabians . . .

That is why we must get together and bargain collectively. We must use the only strength that we have, the force of our numbers. The ranchers are few; we are many. UNITED WE SHALL STAND . . .

We do not want the paternalism of the rancher; we do not want the contractor; we do not want charity at the price of our dignity. We want to be equal with all the working men in the nation; we want a just wage, better working conditions, a decent future for our children. To those who oppose us, be they ranchers, police, politicians, or speculators, we say that we are going to continue fighting until we die or we win. WE SHALL OVERCOME.

That is why we must get together and bargain collectively. We must use the only strength that we have, the force of our numbers. The ranchers are few; we are many. UNITED WE SHALL STAND . . .

Chicano Student Movement News, November, 1968.

Boycott Strategy

In recent interviews, Jessica Govea and Eliseo Medina, two UFWOC boycott coordinators, remember the reason for the boycotts and the pitch that they made to people in order to sell them on this idea.

Jessica Govea:

The whole point of the boycott was to put enough economic pressure on the growers to get them to sit down and talk. That's all we wanted was to get them to sit down and talk like reasonable people about what conditions and what wages people would work for.

What it did was give us a way to take our message out to the rest of the country, into Canada, into Europe, because we had in the beginning, we had people in Europe boycott, running the boycott . . . and to communicate to them the conditions under which farm workers worked and lived.

It also made it possible for them, people out there, to participate in a struggle that could be won.

"What we're asking you to do is to become involved in our struggle and to help us by not buying grapes. That's what we're asking you." Actually that was the smallest thing we were asking people to do, because, when we went out, we had to lose all shame and be willing to ask for everything.

And we were asking people to quit their jobs and drop out of school and come work with us full-time. We were asking people to give us money; we were asking people to let us live in their home, and sleep on their floor.

We were asking people to feed us. We were asking for paper for leaflets . . . anything you could think of, we were asking for, because we didn't have it, and we needed it in order to do the boycott.

Before the farm workers boycott began, there were so many people that hadn't stopped to think about where the things that they ate, the things that were on their plates, where that came from, and who was involved in getting it there, you know, who was involved in producing that, and getting that nice head of lettuce or that nice tomato or those nice table grapes or whatever product it was.

Getting the food on their table. Conditions: we get paid lousy wages, we get abused, our kids don't have a chance of going, any kind of hope of going to college, or being something different if they want to be something different. Because that was the other part of it, that we weren't saying that everyone should stop being farm workers, because it's embarrassing to be a farm worker, which it was at that time. We were saying that it has dignity; it's a very important job, and it has dignity, but it needs to be treated that way, with dignity. And, so we took the message, we said, "This is who we are, this is how we live, this is what we want. We want dignity, we want fairness, we want a fair wage, we want to be able to save a little bit. We want to be able to think about the future."

We've taken the first big step. We went on strike. We were willing to make the sacrifice about that. We've been on strike now for three years, but we can't stop the grapes there because of the strikebreakers, because of the injunctions, because of the violence, etcetera.

Eliseo Medina:

. . . The longest time was in Chicago. I went there in '67 and I stayed until 1970. That's how long it took for the boycott to end. Now, César didn't tell me that's how long it'd take. He told me, "Oh, well, you just got to stop the grapes, and then you can come home." I didn't know what that meant.

I mean, I was twenty-one years old, never been to any big city by myself, had no idea where Chicago was. And they gave me a bag of buttons, one name of a supporter in Illinois, and something like fifteen, twenty dollars.

'Cause, you know, if you remember, Delano's a very little town. I mean it's . . . right now it's twenty thousand; in those days it was like ten thousand, and all of a sudden, you go in a city of, oh, almost a million people, and we are asking people not to do something, you know.

My whole world had been a Spanish-speaking world, you know, a farm worker world, and all of a sudden I had to go out and meet church people and unions and white people and all kinds of people. It was a big experience.

Huelga Script, March 8, 1995, pp. 4-6, NLCC.

The Texas Farm Worker Movement

In Texas, the UFWOC pursued a California strategy that included a march to Austin in 1966 to present its grievances. Antonio Orendáin, the UFWOC national treasurer, became the de facto leader of the Texas effort. This prompted a sympathetic story in the bilingual newspaper *El Sol* of Houston. The march served to galvanize the civil rights movement of Mexican Americans in Texas and included Dr. Hector García, founder of the American G.I. Forum and other veterans from organizations such as LULAC. In addition, soon-to-be militants of the Chicano Movement in Texas were politicized by this incipient activity.

The Strikers and Their Problems

EL SOL NEWS SERVICES—Houston, Texas—July 15, 1966. Approximately three-hundred and fifty-six miles south of downtown Houston is a little town called Rio Grande City. Until several weeks ago, this little town was rarely spoken of and the everyday events were little known outside of its own township limits.

For many, many years, the people of this area have been working in the fields, they have worked hard, they have been treated mostly as tools for profit, and they have been paid very low wages. Many reporters have stated that the going pay scale is about 85¢ per hour. They are wrong. The big growers work the field hands for as little as possible, and 85¢ is what is known as top pay.

The days are long and very hot. There are hardly any rest periods for the field hands; but the American of Mexican descent does not have to work under these conditions because there are Mexican nationals who with the permission of the U.S. Government can come and work in the fields for whatever hourly scale the grower wants to pay. These people are called the "Green Card" holders and they have permission to live in "Old Mexico" and work in the U.S.

Thus, the Mexican-American who lives in Rio Grande City really has problems in the form of competition from cheap labor across the border. The big growers know that the "Green Card" holders can live much cheaper than the Mexican-Americans . . . so he gets away with paying them less. These growers send buses to Roma, Texas, to pick up the "Green Card" holders to put to work in his fields, and he could care less about the Mexican-American field hand.

For a number of years there has been discontent over the situation in the Rio Grande City area from the field hand, but no one seemed able to unite the people together to form a common front. Then two men named Sánchez and Pérez started to talk to the field workers about organizing a union. They met with some success, but they did not have the background to really get the farm workers organized.

Eugene Nelson, who had been involved in the unionizing of the grape pickers in California, happened to be in Houston about the time Sánchez and Pérez were trying to organize the Rio Grande people. Nelson, Sánchez, and Pérez met, and they went to work together on the problems of trying to organize and unionize the field hands. The people liked Eugene Nelson, and they felt that in him they had a leader that could help them accomplish their goal . . . form a Union, and then get a minimum wage of $1.25 from the growers. Sánchez and Pérez did not like the fact that Eugene Nelson was so well accepted, and they have since become disinterested in the cause of the strikers.

Eugene Nelson has completely won over the people, and there is little doubt that they would follow only Nelson if he asked them to make a move or decision in either direction. Nelson has signed up a large number of people to join the union, and these are the strikers that originally started making the first march from Rio Grande City to San Juan, Texas.

The march is being made by the strikers to protest the low wages paid by the big growers . . . one of the better known ones is "La Casita," a California-owned organization. The striking marchers are asking for a minimum wage of $1.25 per hour. The march, which is now under way, is being made from San Juan, Texas, to Austin, Texas, to show the Texas lawmakers and other state government officials that they should very strongly consider the passing of a minimum state wage law of no less than $1.25 per hour.

El Sol, July 15, 1966.

Texas Rangers Suppress Farm Worker Organizing

In 1967, Texas Rangers suppressed a farm worker strike organized by the UFWOC in which a young boy was killed. The U.S. Commission on Civil Rights held hearings in San Antonio on Texas Ranger behavior and subpoenaed Ranger Captain A.Y. Allee to account for charges of brutality. The result of this hearing was published in a report that the Commission presented to President Lyndon B. Johnson in 1970.

In southern Texas, the attitudes of Mexican Americans toward law enforcement officials were more intensely hostile and fearful than in any other area. These feelings were most acute with respect to the Texas Rangers, the 62-man state police organization.

José Martínez, a farm worker from Pharr, Texas, who testified at the Commission's San Antonio hearing, was asked to characterize the feeling of Mexican Americans toward the Rangers. He replied: "Many people hate them, many people are afraid . . . they will be hit or kicked . . ." A Mexican American doctor from McAllen, Texas, said that he is afraid to be alone on the highway if there is a Ranger around. Older people tended to be particularly fearful because they remembered stories of earlier harassment of Mexican Americans by Rangers. The extent of the fear is indicated by the fact that the mother of a State senator—Senator Joe Bernal of San Antonio—gave a party to celebrate her son's safe return from Starr County, where Senator Bernal had had an angry encounter with Captain A. Y. Allee of the Rangers. This was during a period from 1966 to 1967 when attempts by the United Farm Workers Organizing Committee (UFWOC) to organize Mexican American farm workers in Starr County led to harassment of the union organizers by the Texas Rangers.

After closed meetings held in Starr County, Texas, on May 25-26, 1967, the Commission's Texas State Advisory Committee found that the Texas Rangers and local law enforcement officials in 1966 and 1967 had harassed members of the UFWOC seeking to organize Mexican American farm workers in Starr County. Denials of strikers' legal rights, the Committee found, included physical and verbal abuse by Texas Rangers and local officials, and the holding of union organizers for many hours before releasing them on bond. The Committee found that the Texas Rangers had encouraged farm workers to cross picket lines, and stated that the harassment and intimidation by Rangers of UFWOC members, organizers, and sympathizers "gave the appearance of [the Rangers] being in sympathy with the growers and packers rather than the impartiality usually expected of law enforcement officers." The Committee observed that:

> The majority of the farm workers and members of the Farm Workers Organizing Committee are Mexican Americans. To many [Mexican Americans] the Texas Rangers are a symbol of oppression; their appearance in Starr County only served to aggravate an already tense situation. While the Committee supports fair and objective law enforcement and recognizes the possible need of Starr County law enforcement agencies to seek outside assistance in

this situation, it questions whether the Texas Rangers are the appropriate source for such assistance.

The Committee recommended further investigation of its charges by the Commission. On December 12, 1968, the Commission heard testimony of several witnesses confirming the findings of the Committee. According to the testimony, the Rangers conferred with and acted on behalf of the growers and joined with local law enforcement officers in attempting to break the strike and denying the strikers and strike sympathizers their legal rights.

More than a hundred arrests were made of farm workers and union sympathizers on such charges as trespass, unlawful assembly, secondary boycott, illegal picketing, abusive language, impersonating an officer, and interfering with the arrest of another. It was reported that these arrests usually occurred after some significant success was achieved by the union. One witness testified that Ranger Captain A. Y. Allee told the workers he would get them jobs if they would discontinue their participation in the strike and that the strike would only have a depressing effect on the Valley.

The director of the Texas Department of Public Safety, Wilson E. Speir, and Captain Allee denied the allegation that they consulted with the growers during the strike and took the position that they enforced the laws impartially.

United States Commission on Civil Rights, *Mexican Americans and the Administration of Justice in the Southwest* (Washington, D.C.: United States Government Printing Office, 1970), pp. 16-17.

The Farm Worker Union in Arizona

During 1968, Cesár Chávez's union drive in California inspired Gustavo Gutiérrez to organize farm workers in Tolleson, Arizona, an agricultural community located a few miles west of Phoenix. He resigned his position with the Arizona Migrant Opportunity Program (MOP) and recruited Mel Hewey and Carolina Rosales, two other MOP employees, to help him establish the Arizona Farm Workers Organizing Committee (AFWOC) using local funds. By 1969, the AFWOC struck local grape growers and obtained contracts. The following document, taken from the first issue of their newspaper, *El Paisano*, in the spring of 1968, explains their program.

What Are We Doing?

The United Farm Workers Organizing Committee was the dream of a group of farm workers who have been meeting in different parts of Arizona. The main office of the United Farm Workers has been set up in Tolleson. Right now, we are taking a survey of farm workers in Tolleson. We are going door-to-door to listen to and discuss the ideas of the working people in town. We hope to make this census in every part of Arizona.

The United Farm Workers will be a militant and democratic labor union, fighting to improve the condition of farm workers. Our goals are:

1) to organize and work with farm workers in the fields so we can begin to value union with our fellow workers;
2) to give services to farm workers, such as help with welfare, social security, or when a contractor refuses to pay you;
3) to work for contracts with the growers with wage guarantees for union members;
4) to print a monthly newspaper with news of interest to farm workers;
5) to start a credit union for farm workers;
6) to someday become a local of the United Farmworkers Organizing Committee, AFL-CIO, in Delano, California.

All these things can be done when the people work together. In Unity There is Strength.

All this time there are three people working for the United Farm Workers. One of us works part-time, the other two, full-time.

JOIN US
TOGETHER
WE SHALL OVERCOME

El Paisano, C. 1968.

The Farm Worker Union Opposes Immigrant Workers

From the very outset, the UFW opposed immigration from Mexico because it built up labor surpluses that lowered wages and made it difficult to organize. Chávez and his supporters also believed that union enticements were less appealing to immigrants than to more settled Mexican American farm workers. In 1968, an article appearing in *El Paisano*, the official organ of the UFW in Arizona, demonstrated how the hiring of "green carders" (Mexicans with work permits) who resided on the Mexican side of the border across from Yuma, rankled the union organizers.

Each morning 3000 farmworkers cross into the United States from San Luis, Sonora. At 5 a.m. on the border, 20 trucks and buses are taking on their human cargo and hundreds of cars are lined up to show their green cards. *El Paisano* recently visited the Yuma-Somerton area to find out what effect this daily flood is having on our American workers.

AMERICANS BEING PUSHED OUT

These workers from Mexico are allowed to work in the United States because there is supposed to be a labor shortage on our farms. The truth of the matter is that the Agri-Corporations are giving steady work with cheap wages to the Green Carders. American workers are used only when there are not enough Green Carders.

To prove these statements we need only compare the lemon and orange harvests in Yuma. This winter's lemon harvest required many workers; Green Carders and Americans worked and earned fair wages. At the end of February the lemons gave out and Agri-Business needed few workers for the oranges. American workers (Chicano, Anglo, Negro, and Indian) were laid off. Contractors' buses from San Luis stopped picking up workers in Somerton. Drive-ins were not hired. Some workers reported that fruit sacks were given out to Green Carders first, and if any sacks were left, Americans were hired. If not, these workers then had to walk many miles to get back to town.

El Paisano learned of one contractor at Yuma Citrus Co. who is still hiring Americans. His crew is only allowed to work 3 or 4 hours a day in the poorer groves. Green Card crews work 8 hours a day in the better groves.

THE RESULT

Refugees from the Yuma area could be seen on freight trains. One witness saw whole families hitchhiking out of the area. A bunkhouse in Somerton which had 50 workers in February has only 12 workers in March and may soon close. Here in the Phoenix area these refugees added to the surplus labor, which results in only half-days of work in the green onions and carrots.

Wages are depressed in the Yuma area. Growers pay $2.40 a bin (about 1500 lbs.) or 10¢ a sack for oranges. The same work in Phoenix pays $4 a bin or 20¢ a sack.

REVOLT

Mr. Richie Jones of Somerton took 30 angry workers to the Curtis, Woodward, and Roach Co. and said they were not going to leave until they got hired. Mr. Jones told the company that if the men were not hired he would buy a page in Phoenix and Washington newspapers to tell the country what's going on. At first the company managers said they were sorry but "we are only hiring Green Carders." Finally they gave in and hired the 30 workers. In less than two weeks, all 30 men were laid off, a few at a time.

Even the Green Carders are fed up with the low wages. At the beginning of March, Green Card crews at the same Curtis, Woodward, and Roach Co. walked out in a strike for higher wages. The Roach Company hired American workers to take their place. One worker explained that he went to work hoping to take the Green Carders' jobs and also avoid starvation. The next day the Green Carders saw what was happening and went back to work.

El Paisano, April, 1968.

Young Organizers Meet in New Mexico

The Alianza Federal de las Mercedes movement became a magnet for activists through-out the country. As a consequence, the Alianza served to link Movement people across the Southwest, injecting standardized styles of Chicano expression. At the behest of Reies López Tijerina, young Mexican American organizers from Chicago, Colorado, New Mexico, California, and Texas, many of them students, met in Albuquerque on October 21, 1967. At this meeting, the idea of holding a mass national meeting of Mexican American youths was discussed. This led to the historic National Chicano Liberation Youth Conference of March, 1969. And finally, the concept of a Chicano political party emerged at this meeting.

In Albuquerque, New Mexico, on October 21, a group of young Mexican-American organizers from throughout the U.S. met. The theme of the intense discussion was unity among all young people who are committed to organizing among the Spanish-speaking of the United States.

They have begun the establishment of a national communications network with the purpose of maintaining a constant flow of information concerning organizational experiences. The intent is to expand this network in a concerted effort to break down the isolation of those involved in organizing in all parts of the country. Four coordinators were chosen to direct efforts in the four geographical regions represented: San Antonio, Texas; Albuquerque, New Mexico; Chicago, Illinois; and Los Angeles, California. It was agreed that the Information Center would be at least temporarily located in Los Angeles.

The coordinators in accord with the group defined problems for immediate study and solution. 1) How inclusive is the term La Raza and how does La Raza relate to other oppressed groups? 2) What is the relationship between young Mexican-Americans, the new militants, with established Mexican-American organizations? 3) What kind of form, direction, slogans will be viable for a national organization of young militants?

It was unanimously agreed that all would continue working locally as they have been but they add the new perspective of discussion of a national movement of young Mexican-Americans. Progress reports on all organizing efforts will flow into the information center and throughout the network.

ACTION: The first action of the young militants will be to picket the Hearings at El Paso on October 28, 1967. They invite all young Mexican-Americans to join in informing President Johnson that the young militants have had enough; they are on the move. Meet at 8:00 a.m. on October 28, 1967, at Hotel Paso del Norte in El Paso, Texas.

The first national meeting of the young militants ended with the strong feeling that a new movement was being born: a movement whose birth, growth, and power is inevitable.

For further information, write El Barrio Communications Project, 2808 Altura, Los Angeles, Calif. 90031.

La Raza, October 29, 1967.

Poor People's March

Militant factions of the Chicano Movement, including a contingent of *aliancistas*, led by Reies López Tijerina, joined the Poor People's March that was organized by Martin Luther King's Southern Christian Coalition. The Chicanos, as seen below, formulated their own set of demands in this effort.

EDUCATION

We demand that our schools be built in the same communal fashion as our neighborhoods . . . that they be warm and inviting facilities and not jails. That the teachers and other personnel live in the neighborhoods of the schools they work in. We demand a completely free education from kindergarten to college with no fees, no lunch charges, no supplies charges, no tuition, no dues . . . this in compensation for decades of poor education given our raza.

. . . that from kindergarten through college, Spanish be the first language and English the second language and that the textbooks be rewritten to emphasize the heritage and contributions of the Mexican-American in the building of the Southwest. We also demand the teaching of the contributions and history of other minorities which have also helped build this country.

We also feel that each neighborhood school complex should have its own school board made up of members who live in the community the school serves.

HOUSING

. . . the necessary resources to plan our living accommodations so that it is possible for extended family homes to be situated in a communal style . . . around plazas or parks with plenty of space for the children. We want our living areas to fit the needs of the family and not the needs of the city pork barrel, the building corporations or architects.

AGRICULTURAL REFORMS

We demand that not only the land which is our ancestral right be given back to those pueblos, with restitution given for mineral, natural resources, grazing, and timber used.

We demand compensation for taxes, legal costs, etc., which pueblos and heirs spent trying to save their land.

We demand the suspension of taxation by the acre and institute instead the previous taxation system of our ancestors; that is, the products of the land are taxed, not the land itself.

JOB DEVELOPMENT

We demand training and placement programs which would develop the vast human resources available in the Southwest. For those of our people who want further choices in employment and professions, we wish training programs which would be implemented and administered by our own people.

In job placement, we demand that first of all, racist placement tests be dropped and in their place tests be used which relate only to the qualifications necessary for that job. Further, we demand nondiscrimination by all private and public agencies.

We demand seed money to organize the necessary trade, labor, welfare, housing, etc. unions to represent those groups. We further demand that existing labor, trade, and white collar unions nondiscriminatory membership practices be enforced by a national labor relations act.

LAW ENFORCEMENT

We demand an immediate investigation of the records of all prisoners to correct the legal errors, or detect the prejudice which operated in those court proceedings, causing their convictions or extra heavy sentencing. As these cases are found, we demand that the federal government reimburse those prisoners for loss of time and money.

We demand immediate suspension of officers suspected of police brutality until a full hearing is held in the neighborhood of the event.

We demand suspension of the city-wide juvenile court system and the creation of a neighborhood community court to deal with allegations of crime. In addition, instead of the prowl car, precinct system, we want to gradually install a neighborhood protection system, where residents are hired every few families to assist and safeguard in matters of community safety or possible crime.

ECONOMIC OPPORTUNITIES

We demand that the businesses serving our community be owned by that community. Seed money is required to start cooperative grocery stores, gas stations, furniture stores, etc. Instead of our people working in big factories across the city, we want training and low interest loans to set up small industries in our own communities. These industries would be co-ops with the profits staying in the community.

La Raza Yearbook, September, 1968.

Tijerina Speaks Out on Martin Luther King's Assassination

When Dr. Martin Luther King invited Reies López Tijerina to join the Poor People's March, his enemies had him arrested to prevent him from participating. But pressure from Mexican American and Native American civil rights leaders convinced state police chief, Captain Joe Black, to intervene with local authorities to release Tijerina. By the time *aliancistas* joined the Poor People's March as it came through Albuquerque, however, the Rev. King had been assassinated. Tijerina was in Berkeley, California, at the time of King's assassination, where he gave this remarkable radio interview to Elsa Knight Thompson, a commentator on African American issues with station KPFA, before proceeding to Albuquerque to join the March.

Interviewer: I'm in the studio with Reies López Tijerina, who is head of the organization called Federal Alliance of Free City States—now that is more commonly known, I believe, as the North New Mexico Six-County Land Grant Movement, which you have headed.

Reies: Right.

I: I would like to begin, where we began when you came into my office last night, yesterday evening. Early we had the news of Martin Luther King's assassination. This morning, just as you walked into my office, some kind of a disturbance involving police cars and both black and white, obviously high school students, was taking place, under the windows of KPFA's office. And I said, "God help us all." And I liked your reply.

R: I said that God could not help us any longer. He has run out of patience, and we have mocked him too many times. We have—we've got him fed up, and I think that we are running out of time, and the patience of God is also running out. I don't think that we have left him any alternative. And he chose to help us; he has been trying to help us for hundreds and thousands of years, and we have been mocking and mocking his true justice, his true democracy by destroying mankind and establishing our own kind of democracy. So that's why I feel that there's no way: this is a typical day, a typical act, the assassination, cold-blooded murder of the symbol of peace and the representation of the rights of the poor through a meek and wise man, Dr. King. The government, I feel, is responsible, by encouraging, by not developing ways for the poor, ways for the oppressed. Only ways and means for the bankers, for the powerful, for the whites. And that is why I feel that the federal government of the United States is pushing its own people to destruction, to the end of this empire.

I: You were dealing, I believe, with Dr. Martin Luther King about the proposed march on Washington, which was to take place on the 26th of this month. Could you tell us something about what those plans were?

R: On August the 26th or 28th, 1967, I approached Martin Luther King in the airport of Chicago when they had this new politics convention, and I suggested to him a coalition between the brown people and the black people. Also the Indians and poor whites. He said it was high time. And that was all. I didn't hear from him until this year. I think it was February when he invited me to come to Atlanta, Georgia. March the 14th, I arrived in Atlanta, Georgia, and some twenty-five leaders of other organizations of the brown people, also white people, Indian people, and black people. It was there that the coalition was formed. It was there that Dr. King talked to us. It was there that Dr. King reminded and pointed out to the people in the P_____ Hotel in Atlanta, Georgia, that I had suggested to him the idea and that he had embraced it, and it was high time. A steering committee was formed out of the various races and groups to steer and direct the coordination, the plans on the Washington march that is coming April the 22nd, and that will escalate up to June, probably June the 15th.

I: The committee will begin, will meet in Washington on the 22nd of March, and the march will be on the 26th? Is that it?

R: On the 22nd, right. Yes, the steering committee and about one hundred leaders will visit various offices of the government, departments and Congress. And then after that, 3,000 people will arrive to stay in the capital. And then after that, people will start to arrive according to the plans by thousands from all over the United States.

I: And this was to go on and build and build?

R: Escalate, yes.

I: Yes!

R: This is one of the greatest plans . . . I don't know how to put it in this second language of mine, but it was the greatest of plans that Martin Luther King had come out with. It was something fantastic, beautiful, and it will be, I have no doubts, unless the committee changes the whole plan. But I understand, I have contact. I was called from Atlanta, Georgia, just last night, and up to now they're going ahead with the march.

I: And Rev. Abernathy, I believe, is taking Dr. King's place as the head of the leadership conference?

R: Yes, yes, right.

I: Have you had a chance to speak with Dr. Abernathy?

R: No, not yet. However, I am invited personally by Rev. Abernathy to speak in his church in the very near future; a week or two and I will be speaking to him.

I: And you are expecting, then, that from all over the country the minority people will come to Washington over a period of time?

R: Yes, yes. The Mexican-Americans, Spanish-Americans are uniting and recruiting people, just like the Indians and the black people for this great march. Well, this was called by Martin Luther King, Campaign for the Poor, the march for the poor people.

I. I seem to recall that when he announced this march that he said something about the fact that this would be the last massive attempt to convince the government and the American people by nonviolent means. And that if he, if this was not successful, that he would not try again.

R: Right. Yes, his philosophy had changed. His last speech, a closed-door speech, was plain. He said this march would not represent civil rights, but human rights. For the first time the black people would ask for land. Would demand land, not just jobs, education, and housing, but land. Just like the people in New Mexico are demanding land.

I: Well, perhaps we can talk now about what you are doing in northern New Mexico. How it started. You yourself were born in Texas, I believe?

R: Yes, in Fall City, Texas, September the 21st, 1926.

I: In a field?

R: In a cotton field, yes, ma'am.

I: And you were your mother's fifth child?

R: I was my mother's fifth child, yes. It was around, between 4 and 5 o'clock in the afternoon when my mother and my father were picking cotton and the pains arrived, and it was there that I was born in a cotton sack, half-full.

I: See, I have a good memory. I heard you say this once before. And you grew up where?

R: I grew up around the San Antonio area up to fourteen. Then I left for the beet and tomato fields in Ohio, Indiana, and Michigan. At the age of seventeen I started in a theological seminary for three years. I graduated, then I was a minister for the following ten years. In Arizona, while we were . . .

I: A minister, what kind of minister?

R: Nondenominational, protestant minister.

I: But your family were agricultural workers. And you yourself worked in the fields as you grew up.

R: Yes, yes. That was my trade, yes. Field work.

I: When did you go to New Mexico?

R: I decided . . . I had been there before, but I had refused to join the land claimants, the people that had been fighting in the . . . with the federal government, and claiming certain rights under the Treaty of Guadalupe Hidalgo signed between United States and Mexico, February the 2nd, 1848. However, picking cotton in the fields of Arizona, the neighbors burned my house and sixteen other houses of my fellow brothers, who together had decided to build a little village called the Valley of Peace. In the period of two . . . three years they burned our houses, our church, our store, our school. Seventeen homes after . . .

I: Who burned them?

R: The neighbors, Anglo Americans, civilized Anglo Americans.

I: Why?

R: Because we refused to send our children to their school and because they thought we were Communists. And Don Pelton, the FBI agent, was called to investigate. He refused flatly. Laurence White, the sheriff of Pinal County, was invited, or rather, asked many times to come and investigate the burnings. He refused flatly. And it was there and then that we decided to move into New Mexico. And that burning, destruction of our property, changed part of my life and the course of my life; from Bible, religious teaching, to civil and international law and land, which is what is involved in this whole struggle.

I: Now, the current struggle which is going on, as I understand it, concerns six counties in northern New Mexico.

R: Well, really, it concerns the whole state. We sometimes mentioned the five counties because it's where we make up the 90 percent of the population. And because we are face to face with the federal government. And because the Department of Agriculture is there, holding most of the land that the President of the United States confiscated outright from the villages. However, the land grants, 350, are scattered throughout the whole state of New Mexico.

I: Yes, but the fight is concentrated, for the moment, around this particular area?

R: Yes, right. Right. But the members of the organization are scattered throughout the state and also Texas and California. But the "showdowns," what we would call them, and the real trouble is in the northern part, yes!

I: Well, how did it start? I believe I recall something about the fact that at some stage you decided to take over a village?

R: Well, to understand this and to inform the public, which has been deprived of the truth through CBS, I mean, UPI and the Associated Press, who have been distorting the truth, I would like to state that the people of New Mexico, like the Hopi nation, have never surrendered to the confiscation of the land; have never surrendered to the federal government and to their ideas; who are against . . . which are against the three-hundred-year-old system and way of livelihood in New Mexico. There is a group, there was and there is, called White Caps in the Northern part of New Mexico. As the government builds fences around this common land that belongs to the villages, during the day, the people cut the fences during the night, on and on for the last hundred years. The government has conspired in a thousand ways to destroy the lives, the culture, the language, the property of this people. It has not succeeded in pushing the people out of the northern part of New Mexico.

So it was 1957 that I decided, when my property was burned, that I decided to investigate the claims, the cries of the people. I discovered that even though there were many pueblos, many people, they were not united. Every pueblo was for itself, just like the Indian pueblos. My first step after discovering that they held a true claim and that the treaty did stipulate the protection of such land, and that they did have the title, and the villages had title to this land, I decided to organize and unite the people of the various land grants, which are called pueblos. It is these pueblos who hold the land, not the individuals, not the heirs. The heirs hold certain rights through the village, through the pueblo council, or city councils, more popularly called. And in 1963, after due and thorough investigation, I decided to organize the Alianza Federal de Mercedes, Federal Alliance of Land Grants, whose papers and documents were confiscated by the federal government in 1967. Then we decided to dissolve the organization and convert it into a political organization, which is now called Federal Alliance of Free City States. The fight has been going on for the last 120 years.

It is not true that we started the fight. In many local papers it has been proven and written on the front page that the problem or the trouble did not start with Tijerina. It was there. But the people had not succeeded in bringing their claim, their cry across the nation. See, the nation was ignorant of this organized conspiracy and criminal confiscation of the federal government against the people. It was there and it has been there all the time. But the public has been kept ignorant of this fact. Only the local bankers, politicians, and rich men and ranchers know the facts, but they, in collusion with the news media, kept it quiet until now. They could no longer do it because the Alianza broke through the silence barrier.

It was when we were to hold a meeting, a nationwide meeting, in Coyote, New Mexico. *Coyote* is the Spanish word for Coyote. So it was there we published it in the news media, radio, press, and TV for a month. But there is a man that is being used by the senator of New Mexico, Senator Montoya, who wants to make a name for himself, and the news media provoked and teased this man by calling that meeting at Coyote a "Showdown Day" meeting, between the people and the government. So making the state police believe that there was going to be a shootout, the district attorney, Alfonso Sánchez, decided to pool all his resources and call the chief of police, Joe Black, and call all his state militia, state police, block all the roads, and start arresting everybody on the grounds of unlawful assembly. Naturally the people were too strong, too brave to swallow such a stupid accusation and grounds for arrest. They were enraged, they were angry, and in this state of anger, the following day after the mass arrest, they decided to arrest, by themselves, the District Attorney. They were furnished with a warrant of arrest, an official document signed by the *alcalde*, the mayor of San Joaquin. The deputies and the volunteers went to Tierra Amarilla, the next town, to arrest Alfonso

Sánchez. It was a plain citizens' arrest. It was turned into a shootout because of the state police. That day a hearing was to be held for the Alianza leaders who were being tried. And, of course, the following was published throughout the nation and the world that there was a revolution going on in Tierra Amarilla.

The governor, David Cargo, whose wife is a member of the Alianza, was in Michigan with Governor Romney. Immediately he was called and took a special Army jet to fly back to New Mexico. In the meantime, Mr. Francis, the Lieutenant Governor, summoned the National Guard, the state police, 150 mounted police, and they brought in three battle tanks, and helicopters, airplanes, and so on. And the whole state was turned into a state of confusion, and at Kirtland Airforce and Lee Airforce, all the personnel were pulled out of the airbase into the city of Albuquerque because they had been threatened by telephone that there were going to be bombs. Even the state penitentiary triplicated their guards. And the whole state was in a state of confusion.

I: This all started because a conference, a meeting was going to be held?

R: Yes, in Coyote, New Mexico, right. Yes, they blocked, they sabotaged our meeting and naturally, the people, well educated, they refused to allow stupid men to tamper and fool around with our rights, our constitutional rights. See, in New Mexico the people have been educated through the radio. We have a daily radio program. We have been teaching our people the rights that have been frozen, sabotaged by the federal government. The rights that were practiced by these people three hundred years, and rights that have been barred out of school. See, the Spanish language, traditions, and culture, and certain perpetual rights that we hold, have been frozen completely and were not . . .

I: All of these rights, I want to get this clear, the original Treaty of Guadalupe did reserve to your people these pueblo lands and certain rights?

R: Yes, yessir, yes.

I: And these rights had gradually been removed, is that . . .

R: Yes, frozen, frozen. The government has never legally dissolved any right or any pueblo whatsoever.

I: What was included in those rights? The right to your own schools and language . . .

R: Well, the language, the culture . . .

I: The language . . .

R: The culture, the cultural rights, which includes the language; property rights, which includes the mode of, or the way of living, that is concerning the property. See, we held no property individually, but a little home and a little garden. We could not hold over 150 square yards for ourselves. It was the pueblo, the village, that held all the land in trust for the villagers. So naturally, the government comes and respects the Indian pueblos, but the Spanish pueblos, it froze them, confiscated the land, took it, converted it into public land or U.S. Forest land under the Department of Agriculture and the Department of the Interior. So, naturally, that was an outright theft. We therefore accuse the federal government . . .

I: Well, did this take place gradually or was it done sort of all at once?

R: Yes, gradually. Gradually. To start with, the public has not been told that after the treaty was signed, our government took full responsibility as our government to protect our lives and our property. Our properties, patents, original patents and titles, were in Guadalajara, Jalisco. That was the Royal Audencia which kept the original patents of the pueblos and property rights. Well, in the year 1858, ten years after the signing of the treaty, these documents were burned mysteriously in Guadalajara, Jalisco, before the United States had the courtesy, according to its obligations, to ask Mexico for a copy of those titles. Then, in the year 1870, William A. Pile, governor of the Territory of New Mexico, with the help of the territorial attorney general, who was Thomas B. Catron, the king leader and the king of New Mexico for fifty years, the criminal shrewd person who masterminded the whole plan, took William Pile and Thomas B. Catron, kicked out the archives of Santa Fe—the documents that had been kept there for three hundred years. They were kicked out in the street, according to historians Twitchell and Bancroft. According to newspaper film of that day, an editorial called William Pile a "Pig Head" for kicking the Spanish archives out into the streets.

I'd like to state that during these years, there was no judicial protection for the land grant titles, for the pueblos, for our property. There was no protection from 1848 to 1891; there was no judicial or tribunal hearings for the adjudication of these titles. It was in the year 1891 when Frank Springer, a friend of Thomas B. Catron and a member of the Santa Fe Ring, asked Congress to establish a political court to adjudicate the titles. It was from 1891 to 1904 that the titles were adjudicated by tribunals of five judges who were all veterans of the Civil War, and veterans of the Confederacy, of the South, who hated the Spanish Americans and the Mexicans. And, naturally there were no documents when this court was established. It was a conspiracy, a criminal conspiracy by the federal government against my people, and now . . .

I: And now, wait a minute, where, what did the court, this court . . . what decisions did they reach?

R: What decisions could we expect after they destroyed all the documents!

I: But they did go on record as confiscating these lands?

R: Yes, they did. No, they went on record as disapproving 33.5 million acres of the 35 million acres we were claiming in New Mexico. Therefore they just approved 1.5 million acres.

I: They left one and a half million acres in the control of the pueblos?

R: Of the pueblos, right. And now that we have the documents, they were discovered in 1960, Kenneth Sanders, a friend of the Santa Fe Ring, comes to New Mexico to sell the documents for 50,000 dollars. The sheriff of Santa Fe County confiscates the documents, arrests the person, and the whole matter goes into court for seven long years. It was this year, last year in December of 1967, that the U.S. District Court of St. Louis, Missouri, decided in favor of Mr. Kenneth Sanders. The defender, the attorney for Kenneth Sanders, the thief, was Thomas B. Catron III. You can see how the Catrons have been guarding very well their shame [?], their organized crime, with the help of the federal government.

And as you can see, on May 20, 1862, the Homestead Act came about. And if you read the Homestead Act, it reads, and I quote, "No homestead shall be issued within boundaries of land grants." For your information, thousands of homesteads were given to people within the boundaries of land grants. Now this was during the '60s and the '70s before the courts were adju . . . I mean, the land grants were adjudicated by the Court of Private Land Claims, which was later in 1891 to 1904. Why did the government violate its own act of Congress to throw the people into confusion, hatred, and fighting among themselves? Because some, naturally, wanted their piece of 160 acres all to themselves, with a title. Other heirs or members of the villages wanted their old way, to let the pueblo administer the common communal lands. So naturally there were two factions, two sides; they started fighting. In comes the federal government and adjudicates and takes over the land. So, naturally, the government thought that it had it made, see, but as the police of our days teaches the black and the brown—that crime does not pay, what our federal government, the greatest giant ever built by taxpayers, is discovering that crime does not pay; even his own crime against the Spanish American people does not pay. Now he's all surprised, he's . . . he doesn't know what to do. And now he has discovered the time and his own crimes are catching up with our federal government.

I: Now, you are now in the process of fighting this situation through legal channels as well as other channels, such as publicity?

R: Many channels, right, yes.

I: What legal steps are being taken now? Is it an effort to reconstruct this whole history of the situation that you've been telling us about and thereby go into federal court to have these laws and these confiscations that you accuse the government of, undone? What is it that you expect to achieve through the courts?

R: Well, one step is the courts because of our enemies who are slandering and saying that we want to use force and violence, even though that's what they use themselves! And that is what they are using throughout the whole world. But then when it comes to us, they want to behave like little angels, as the name Anglo means, from the Latin, "angels." Now they want us to go through the courts. We are going through the courts to a certain extent and on certain questions. However, we are also preparing a document for the United Nations. And bringing in the United Nations, if we succeed in getting Mexico or Spain to present our petition to the United

Nations, to investigate the Treaty of Guadalupe Hidalgo, which is a farce, which is not a treaty, it's a proposal. Naturally, the only title the United States holds for the Southwest is the treaty. And if we can prove that it is not a treaty, then the U.S. has no title for the Southwest. Not only for the pueblos, but for the whole Southwest.

Again, the signature of the Treaty by Nicholas P. Triest is invalid, as Congress has stated in Document 129 of the State Department. Because James Polk, the president of the United States at that time, revoked the credentials of Nicholas P. Triest, therefore making him a simple citizen, and his signature on the treaty invalid. Now that crime, that conspiracy and fraud has been covered from the public. That is why they don't teach the Treaty, the history of the Treaty in schools. Because the public will find out, and then our government will be in trouble. We are also using other channels, such as occupying the land. We have never abandoned our lands. The government cannot claim adverse possession by prescription because of us abandoning the land—no sir, never! We have never abandoned the land. We are living within the boundaries of the land grants, of these pueblos' boundaries. And we are not the only ones that are asking, demanding. The Indians of the Taos Pueblo in Taos, New Mexico, the Hopi Nation, the Apaches, the Navajos are all asking and demanding. So are the Seminole Indians. So this is not something rare; it is not a case of only the Mexican-Americans, but all the people that occupied the land prior to the coming of the bad whites. However, we have many good whites that have bought land in good faith; we consider them to be our neighbors, our friends, our brothers. And they are even helping us to regain, recuperate our rights.

I: How many people are involved in this, in that part of New Mexico?

R: The people that are affected directly are about five million people throughout the Southwest. However, some of them do not know, do not know, but by the thousands they are coming to know, and awakening very fast, especially since last June the 5th, 1967, when the Tierra Amarilla historical event happened, when the whole nation was aware of what was going on in New Mexico.

I: And in New Mexico itself, how many people?

R: There's one million inhabitants. Out of that one million inhabitants, we feel that there are half a million Spanish-Americans. Also, we are fighting and teaching our people the difference between Mexican-American and Spanish-American and Chicano, La Raza, Hispano, Latino, and . . . all those names. We feel that we are not Spaniards, not Indians, as the history will state and prove; we are a new breed that for the last three hundred years has been multiplying at a very fast rate. In fact, according to scientific statistics, the Latin American people are the fastest-growing people in the whole entire world. And I'm referring to the "new breed." See, the new breed, according to law and records, is Indio-Hispano, just like Indo-China, which is called Indo-China because it is made out of India and China. These people are Indio-Hispanos. But we suffered the nicknames of our neighbors, because we are at the young stage, just like when the Hebrews were in Egypt for four hundred years. They were called dogs and many nicknames.

The Anglo had many nicknames two thousand years ago. "Anglo" is one of the nicknames that Julius Caesar gave them when they found them in the caves of Britannia. He called them "ángeles" because they had blue eyes and blond hair. It was a nickname, and "ángeles" means angels, and Anglo means "ángeles." So really, the Anglos chose that nickname the best. It's too bad that they are behaving and want the whole world to treat them as angels, when in effect it was nothing but a joke, a nickname. However, we too are now suffering from the invasion of many nicknames.

I: What name, now, as I understand it, is "La Raza?" Is it the combined Indian and Spanish blood?

R: "La Raza," as you can translate it into English, means the race, the race which could be any race . . .

I: Yes, yes. Yes, but used in the sense that I have heard it used in this movement, the people you are talking about are people of mixed Indian and Spanish blood heritage. Is that correct?

R: Blood, right, right. Correct.

I: And what name do you prefer to be known by?

R: I think the question has to be subjected to records, law, to cultural proofs. Any name we can prove and trace it back to being a nickname and something out of exasperation, just like when a young child goes into school, and has no friends. Everybody picks on him. This young blood, this new breed is just like going into school. Surrounded by older races, such as the Anglo, the Italian, the French, even the Spaniard. However, I would like to make a difference between "Hispano" and "Spanish." See, we never say that we in New Mexico are "Spanish Americans"; we say "hispano," "hispano-americano." *Hispano* means sprinkled with something from Spain, whether Spaniard or *español,* which means pure-blooded Spaniard. We're not calling ourselves, when we say "Hispano-Americano," Spaniard Americans, for we are not. We are saying "Hispano," which means a race, a people that is sprinkled with Spanish blood. However, according to Law II, Title 1, Book 6 of the Laws of the Indias, which ruled this continent for three hundred years, and which was the law that legalized the marriage between the Indian and the Spaniards; according to the law, we are *indio-hispanos.* That covers the Indian part and the Hispanic part.

When the treaty was signed, only three thousand pure-blooded Spaniards were left in New Mexico. For they knew about the Black Legend that the Anglo had written for three hundred years against Spain. And they knew that they were going to be persecuted and punished, so they left the country. However, 100,000 "new breed" *hispanos* stayed in New Mexico. Why? Because they didn't know anything about the conflict between England and Spain as we know it now. So they stayed there. And to their surprise they were betrayed, and the land was taken over, their cultural rights, their language was deprived. And now we see we have discovered that the Anglo wants us to believe and the world and himself to believe that we are Spaniards so he can feel better when he inflicts, humiliates, and deprives us of our rights. As we can see, he doesn't hate the Indian because the Indian has nothing against the Anglo, and the Indian is not a threat. We are: we have the blood, the documents, the legal rights, the continental rights, divine right, every right in the book, up and down. So there is a great difference between our lives, our history, and the history of the Indians and the history of Spain, the Spaniards.

I: There was quite an admixture of black blood at one point in the development of the Middle Americas, I believe, also.

R: Right, that has been absorbed at a very fast rate. However, the Inca, the kingdom of the Incas, the Aztecs, Apaches, Tejas Indians, the tribes of Mexico all absorbed and were sprinkled with Spanish blood. By the year 2000, there will be 600 million Spanish-speaking people: the giant who has been overlooked by the Anglo neighbor. That's why the Southwest, this brown people, and New Mexico are in a key position. We will be playing a very important role in the future in the relationship of the Anglo and the Hispanic or Latin American countries. And I think that it's time for our government to realize and attend to the cry, the claim, the complaints, the demands of the people of the Southwest, the brown people. Because the time will come when the friendship of the U.S. and Latin America will be decided on the Southwest behavior. We, who speak the English and Spanish languages, we feel that way, we are no longer thinking in terms or from a Southwest standpoint, but from a global, universal point of view. And we see our future role as one of the most important for the survival of the white structure, white power. That is why we are trying to persuade the Anglo to be friends, to give up his crime, his sins, his imperialistic ambitions and come down to earth to live with us!

I: And that's also why you want to work with the black people?

R: Right, yes. I think the black people are here to stay and their cry is a holy cry. No matter if they are divided into hundreds of organizations, the time will come when only the color will count, and the black people will decide their destiny and their friends and their course on base of color. As much as we hate, I am against that, that theory or philosophy. However, times and events and the nature of organized powers throughout the world are pushing us to that state, where the differences of religion, religious barriers are falling down. And other barriers are going up in its place: barriers of color. However, we can speak about combining colors; we can speak about combining colors, bringing harmony between colors. And this is a good time to start. To select and invite from all the various colors and peoples. Just like Martin, Dr. King, was doing in his last moment, bringing all the colors together to fight together, to bring . . .

I: That's why he wanted to include the white people on the Washington March.

R: Right, yes, ma'am. And we had a very good representation of the white people.

318

I: Everyone wants to talk about, sooner or later these days, about whether or not violence is justified in this terrible historical moment. You have been dealing with leaders and all these communities. What is your own feeling, Mr. Tijerina, as to the various strands of thought on this subject?

R: Well, I'm afraid, to tell you the truth, of the future. The future is dark, cloudy, and the people are angry. All the people except those that feel guilt. And our government has developed into a machine, a power equal to an angry bull with whom you can no longer reason. With a beast you cannot reason. And that is why I'm afraid of the future. We can see the behavior of the United States in Vietnam, where we have no business, yet we demand from the North Vietnamese equal behavior in relation to the United States. As if we had the same right to be in Vietnam as they have. And that is what will make it difficult.

This country of ours was born in blood. This country was born by destroying sixty million buffaloes, which was the food of the Indian, a peaceful people. People, the Indians, were put in reservations. As bad as Spain was, Spain never did put the Indians in reservations. And it is rather difficult to say, for example, Dr. King . . . there is a great example. He took strictly the peaceful way. And that's how our government, and the friends of our government deal with peaceful leaders. I think and I feel that the assassinations of John F. Kennedy, Malcolm X, and Dr. King were committed by the same power, the same group, the same side, the extreme right side. So it is rather difficult. However, since we have no bullets, no money, even if we wanted to use violence, we could not. So, we will not think in terms of violence.

But as little and small as we might be, we see a lion crushing and jumping on top of a cricket. A cricket has no claws, no jaws, no way to destroy the lion, but he might decide to jump into the ear of the lion and scratch the inside of his ear. That is a place where the lion cannot hurt him. For the lion scratches himself to dig out the cricket, and he will bleed to death.

What I am trying to say is that there is more than one way to skin a cat! And I think God is in command, and if he is the one bringing this empire to its place, I think he will do it the right way. There is always a way to approach a lion; there is always a weak spot on a lion, on a beast. Even if he refuses to reason, there is a weak spot. And also there is a strong spot on the weak, on the oppressed, on the people. I think, more and more, mankind is taking over. The public, the peoples of the world, are fed up, tired, and discovering that we, paying our taxes so faithfully, are building up this giant, this machinery, this criminal, and before long, we might come to that moment when the people will stop paying taxes and will disregard their property. After all, you have to pay so many things for your house, to keep it there. Insurance, city regulations, taxes, and repairs, and the worries are so many, and the government pushing more and more. So who knows if all of a sudden the people will start thinking about quitting their electricity and turning to candles! Fed up. Or quit the gas, or quit the taxes. See, the people are strong. If they discover their power, and the way the government is pushing our people, pretty soon we will have no other choice. Peaceful means: the cricket in the ear of the lion is very peaceful, but yet the lion cannot resist it. And he will fight to get the cricket out of his ears. And, so I feel that our government is facing trouble. That's all I can say, he's facing trouble. And the way the oppressors are killing . . . are killing the good leaders, by sniper, like a sniper, sniping; they don't come in the open, like Dr. King would march in the open, in the streets. Well these murderers, these killers hide. And the people might just decide to do that themselves, start hiding. Imitating the enemy.

So, it's pitiful, the situation is dark. And we ourselves are preparing ourselves to make friends with good people, with honest people, and we're trying to quit the criminals, the troublemakers, and our government is no longer the power whom we can control. Our power, our government is meddling in the business of every country in the world, making trouble all over, and then they ask, we ask ourselves, "Why do they hate us?" They're greedy because we have much money. It is not true. I think they hate us because we meddle in their business!

I: Because you are after what you consider to be your rights, you are going to go ahead, of course, I assume, with whatever plans are made to continue with the Washington march and with the alliance between the black and brown peoples?

R: Yes, we're going straight, going ahead. We're going to strengthen our ties, our unity. We have no other choice.

I: Thank you very much.

"Reies López Tijerina Interviewed by Elsa Knight Thompson," Hayden Chicano Research Collection, MM CHSM-483, Arizona State University.

Tijerina Runs for Governor

The Alianza Federal de las Mercedes attempted to turn into a political party even before the rise of a national Raza Unida Party, which López Tijerina joined later on. In the fall of 1968, Reies López Tijerina ran for governor of New Mexico and issued a twelve-point platform.

1. I promise to donate my salary as governor to the poor and the ill.
2. I promise to defend poor laborers and to fight for their jobs so that they have a fair salary for their honest work.
3. I promise to fight against the discrimination that is carried out against all poor, black, and Hispanic people in the State of New Mexico.
4. I promise to carry out all constitutional rights originating from the Constitution of New Mexico and the Constitution of the United States in the field of education with respect to the cultural rights of Indians, Negroes, and Hispanics.
5. I promise to establish a Civilian Review Board in order to investigate police brutality against the poor in New Mexico.
6. I promise to investigate the records of all organizations and corporations that have speculated with the rights of the people, including New Mexico banks and the Middle Rio Grande Conservation District.
7. I promise to end discrimination in draft boards that is aimed at Negroes, Indians, and Hispanics.
8. I promise to fight for those who have State welfare, so that they receive checks—even if it is up to $500.00 per month.
9. I promise to use all my powers as governor to find and punish the criminals who assassinated Eulogio Salazar, at Tierra Amarilla, New Mexico.
10. I promise to pardon those prisoners, all of whom the laws will permit, and those who, due to the lack of money, did not have an adequate defense in court.
11. I promise to recognize and protect the rights of Hippies and of all those who want to maintain their own personal lifestyle.
12. I promise to protect the rights that exclude the payment of property taxes for war veterans, natives of New Mexico, as well as the right to vote for those who are eighteen years old.

El Grito del Norte, September 16, 1968.

A Government Agency Is Critical of Suppression

In 1970, the United States Commission on Civil Rights issued a report concluding that enforcement agencies illegally thwarted civil rights movements. In particular, the report accused County Attorney Alfonso Sánchez of Rio Arriba County of repressing meetings and illegally arresting members of the Alianza Federal de Mercedes.

Law enforcement officials reportedly sought to prevent political organization of Mexican Americans in northern New Mexico in a series of incidents culminating in the so-called "Tierra Amarilla" raid in June 1967.

The Alianza Federal de Mercedes, known as the "Alianza," is an organization of Mexican Americans in New Mexico under the leadership of Reies López Tijerina. Its stated goal is to improve the status of Mexican Americans in the Southwest.

On June 3, 1967, an Alianza meeting was to be held in the town of Coyote, in the northern New Mexico County of Rio Arriba. A number of Mexican Americans had charged that Alfonso Sánchez, then the district attorney for the First Judicial District of New Mexico (which includes Rio Arriba County), and other law enforcement officials used their powers to discourage and intimidate Alianza members who planned to attend the meeting. On June 2, 1967, Sánchez, in a radio broadcast, announced that since the participants were planning to take property by force, criminal charges of unlawful assembly would be filed against all persons attending the Alianza meeting and that the penalty for this offense was six months in jail. Sánchez also said that extortion charges carrying a penalty of five years of imprisonment would be filed against all who participated in "taking over private land" (presumably a reference to the Alianza's interest in asserting Mexican American claims to land owned by Spanish settlers and their descendants in the past). He urged listeners not to attend the Coyote meeting. Meanwhile, sheriffs' deputies and the police were stopping cars on the highways leading to Coyote and handing out a notice similar in substance to Sánchez's radio statement.

On June 2 and 3, Sánchez allegedly ordered the arrest of eleven officers of the Alianza. Old warrants were outstanding against some of these persons, but no warrants or grounds for arrest seem to have existed against others.

Some of the Alianza leaders who were arrested were taken to the courthouse in Tierra Amarilla for arraignment. News of the arrests spread, and a group of armed Mexican Americans attempted what they described as a "citizens' arrest" of District Attorney Sánchez on June 5 at the courthouse to prevent further arrests. Violence resulted, the precise origins of which are unclear. Two law enforcement officers were wounded, and the invaders fled, reportedly taking two other law enforcement officials with them as hostages.

Meanwhile, for several days Mexican Americans in large numbers had been traveling to the Coyote meeting from all parts of New Mexico. They gathered on picnic grounds in Canjilon and proceeded to camp and prepare for the meeting. On June 5, soon after the shooting in Tierra Amarilla, armed sheriffs' deputies, State policemen, and National Guardsmen surrounded the picnic grounds in Canjilon, where the Alianza meeting was to be conducted, and reportedly kept men, women, and children in the picnic grounds by force for more than 24 hours without adequate shelter or drinking water. According to reports, there was no indication that more than a few of these people might have been involved in the shooting at Tierra Amarilla or even have known about it.

In September 1967, Commission staff members obtained sworn affidavits from a number of persons who attended the picnic at Canjilon describing their experience with the law enforcement officials. A married couple gave the following account:

> On June 5, we were on our way to a barbecue, which was taking place in Canjilon. There was also to be a meeting with the barbecue. At the barbecue, approximately about 5 p.m. the State police came and asked us to come out into the open, and we were told to sit on the floor, which at the time was completely muddy, and we did so."

According to these participants, about eighty armed State policemen surrounded them until they were allowed to return to the picnic place at night, where they found that all their food, left unattended, had burned, and there was no food or water to be had. Their account continued:

> . . . By this time there were approximately 450 National Guard guarding us . . . we were searched and during this time we couldn't go to the restroom, and my wife was threatened by a State policeman that he would shoot her if she went to pick up a little child from the house near the camping site. We were not allowed to go to the outhouse if we were not accompanied by a guard. We were released at the end of the 24 hours.

Another man who attended the meeting at Canjilon stated:

> At approximately 5:30 p.m., about twelve State policemen arrived, or at least there were about six or seven State policemen and about five other civilian officers. They held us with rifles behind our back and made us sit down, while questioning us.

They were then taken back to the picnic grounds. At one point this man said, he and his son, who was extremely frightened, were kept in a paddy wagon for 45 minutes, then released back to the picnic area.

> They kept me and my 5-year-old son there until 5 p.m. the next day, and we didn't have any drinking water or for cooking, so we had to drink water from a dirty water hole cause they wouldn't let us move. On June 6th, they let us come home at about 6 p.m. When I returned home that day, my boss had seen my picture on TV or in the news. He called me a criminal and said we were criminals, and he fired me from my job. My son still is very scared, and he cries every time he sees a policeman.

Commission staff members interviewed representatives of the New Mexico State Police and the State attorney general's office in connection with these events. These men denied that any civil rights violations had taken place. District Attorney Sánchez said that the picnickers at Canjilon were placed in protective custody to prevent violence between the State police and the Alianza. This fear of violence at Canjilon seems to have been based on the view of these officials that the Alianza was planning to wage guerrilla warfare in northern New Mexico. They claimed that none of the Alianza leaders, except Félix Martínez, was a native of New Mexico and that outsiders had stirred up northern New Mexico. The representative of the State attorney general's office said that newspaper reports of the incidents involved were biased and that an article published in the John Birch Society magazine, which characterized the Alianza as a Communist front organization, was the best account of these events. Alfonso Sánchez stated that he believed Tijerina had Communist support, that the Alianza planned an armed takeover of northern New Mexico, and that, therefore, the actions taken were reasonable.

United States Commission on Civil Rights, *Mexican Americans and the Administration of Justice in the Southwest* (Washington, D.C.: GPO, 1970), pp. 14-16.

Protesting the El Paso Conference

Reies López Tijerina encouraged and then joined young Chicano militants to protest the El Paso Conference, which President Lyndon Baines Johnson called to incorporate Mexicans in the War on Poverty. The militants claimed that the mainstream Mexican American leaders did not represent the rank-and-file Chicano community. A pre-El Paso meeting held in early October and covered by the militant *La Raza* newspaper showed these anti-establishment strains, which Reies López Tijerina promoted.

If the temperament of the more than 200 Mexican-American activists who gathered for the "Pre-El Paso Hearings" meeting in Malibu this past weekend is indicative of the mood of Mexican-Americans throughout the Southwest, the political sky at El Paso might be ablaze with fireworks from Oct. 27-29. President Johnson may think he has scheduled hearings he can control, but it would appear he is in for some real surprises.

Bert Corona of Oakland, MAPA's national president, summarized the feelings of the Chicanos present when he said, "Although Mr. Ximénez (President's advisor on Mexican American Affairs) has picked some wonderful men, such as Ernesto Galarza of Los Altos and Eduardo Moreno of Camarillo, . . . we resent the fact that he didn't trust the organizations and our people to pick our own representatives, for we probably would have selected Dr. Galarza and Mr. Moreno. But we don't know who some of the others may be, nor do we know where they have been in La Causa of La Raza. Furthermore, at the MAPA Convention in Riverside, Mr. Ximénez said that the long contemplated White House Conference, which President Johnson back in 1965 promised to hold and permit to be structured by Mexican-Americans, would not be held. He is not holding the Conference, it is true, but instead he is holding hearings where our people will repeat the numerous complaints we have repeated for years and which no administration has ever attempted to work with us to solve."

It seems that the President, after he promised the White House Conference, had second thoughts and realized the power of grassroots civil rights activists to use such conferences to their advantage and to criticize the administration. Still the Democratic Party will need the Mexican-American vote, so the White House began "Operation Window Dressing." An Inter-Agency Committee on Mexican-American Affairs, akin to the Bureau of Indian Affairs, was created and directives were sent out to all departments and Agencies to hire themselves some Mexicans—just the thing that Ronald Reagan is doing in California. The President even created a "Cabinet level" position to be filled by a commissioner (Mr. Vicente Ximénez mentioned above), who would preside over the growing Mexican-American Club in Washington, D.C.

The "hearings," which are intended to substitute for the Conference, will be honored with the presence of the Secretaries of Labor (Wirtz), Agriculture (Freeman), Education (Gardner), Housing and Urban Development (Weaver), and the director of the War on Poverty (Shriver). Vicente Ximénez will serve as chairman for the hearings.

At the same time, it was announced, but *by accident,* the President himself would be in El Paso on October 28 for the official ceremony of "signing of the Chamizal Treaty with President Díaz Ordaz. A veteran of the Albuquerque "walk out," after hearing of this "accident," said: "Here we go again. That man LBJ believes in black magic. After having his underlings hear a few Mexicans tell them what they know so well, LBJ will go to the Chamizal and say, '¡Viva la Causa! There boys, I have given some of the land back to Mexico. What else do you Mexicans want?' and he will expect us to go back home quietly and remain quiet until after the 1968 elections."

For weeks following these twin announcements, the argument among activists was whether Chicanos should *go* or *not go* to El Paso. The *vendidos* were convinced they should go "because LBJ calls." Many others wanted to go, but were aware that those going were going to be "used" for window dressing. To them the choice was between boycotting the hearings altogether or going but making sure that they didn't just come back home quietly without having accomplished a damn thing for the people.

And that was the feeling at the Malibu conference, even after Congressman Roybal tried to soften the blow by saying, "Since the hearings are taking place anyhow, you might as well go to the conference and have a good time like everyone else."

The turning point of the Pre-Hearings meeting at Malibu was Saturday morning. Dr. Ernesto Galarza, at present a consultant with the Ford Foundation, discussed in detail the hearings and the shortcomings of different ways of approaching the issue. Herman Gallegos, also with the Ford Foundation, gave a report of a two-year study that Dr. Zamora from Texas, Dr. Galarza and himself had done, of the present problems of the Mexican-Americans in the Southwest.

While several workshops were held on issues having to do with housing, welfare, jobs and manpower, and police malpractice, another workshop dealt with "Unity and Action." This final workshop dealt with plans for El Paso and will be reported here. (Resumes of the other workshops will be printed as soon as they become available.)

The "Unity and Action" workshop was composed mostly of delegates from the major statewide organizations of Mexican-Americans. Discussing Dr. Galarza's criticisms of the hearings, the unity workshop came up with a plan to guarantee that whatever happens in El Paso will result for the benefit of all Mexican-Americans and not just for window dressing the White House.

La Raza, October 15, 1967.

Patsy Tijerina

López Tijerina's young wife, Patsy, demonstrated great courage when she burned the National Forest Service sign on June 6, 1969. But as the story below indicates, the reasons she gave must have resounded among the populist following of both Reies López Tijerina and the Chicano Movement.

Patsy Tijerina, tried and convicted for burning one of two Forest Service signs that went up in flames at Gallina and Coyote last June, was placed on five years' probation by U.S. Judge H. Vearle Payne on March 6.

Judge Payne, who had earlier sentenced Reies López Tijerina to nine years in prison on almost identical charges from the Coyote Incident, threatened Patsy with as much as 10 years in prison if she does anything "wrong" during the five years' probation.

Judge Payne indicated he would consider it "wrong" if Patsy was active in the Alianza or worked in any way to help the people to regain their lands.

Patsy was charged with burning two signs–one at Gallina, one at Coyote. She was found guilty on the Gallina charge. The jury was hung on the Coyote charge.

At the time of the burnings on June 8, Patsy had publicly announced she would set fire to the signs as a symbolic protest against the oppression of the people and the occupation of their lands by the U.S. Forest Service.

In suspending Patsy's sentence and placing her on probation, Judge Payne said he was "reluctant" to set her free because ". . . she still seems to believe that those signs belong to the people."

"Yes, I still believe the signs belong to the people," Patsy says now. "The signs belong to the people because the land belongs to the people. The signs are on the people's land. Why shouldn't I believe that? If they don't want me to believe that, why don't they prove it? Why don't they prove the land is theirs and not the people's? Let them prove that. Let them show the Forest Service has titles for the land. Let them prove the government has titles. Let them prove the land wasn't stolen. Then I will believe them. Why don't they do that?"

Payne was even more "reluctant" to set Reies Tijerina free from the phony charges of the Coyote Incident. Payne sentenced Reies to three years in prison for the burning of the sign at Gallina, three years for the burned sign at Coyote, and three more for "assault" on Ranger James Evans, the man who would be Kit Carson.

The smell of the Coyote Incident grows worse: Reies is now serving three years in prison for "aiding and abetting" Patsy in burning down the Coyote sign. But the jury didn't convict Patsy for the "crime" of burning down the Coyote sign. How can Reies be sentenced to prison for "aiding and abetting" in a crime that wasn't committed? How does that happen? Why did it happen?

La Raza, January 1, (c. 1970).

Chapter Nine

Chicanismo, Youth, and La Raza Unida Party

Even though by the end of the 1950s, education conditions and other social conditions had improved for Mexican Americans, young civil rights activists, dissatisfied with gains made by the previous Mexican American generation, joined the soon-to-be Chicano Movement in increasing numbers. By the 1960s, most whites had abandoned the inner Southwestern cities for the suburbs (white flight), leaving minorities, including Mexican Americans, behind in decaying communities with neglected school infrastructures, poor housing, and inadequate employment opportunities.

Moreover, in the 1960s Chicano intellectuals took note of the efforts by African Americans to bolster self-esteem and provide the stamina to sustain a civil rights struggle by initiating a "black pride" movement that promoted racial dignity and glamorized African history. As a consequence, the Chicano Movement pursued not only a strategy of militancy, which would result in significant social change, but also energy and time was devoted to defining a cultural and racial identity that included taking pride in being mestizo (part Indian, part Spanish).

But it took more dramatic developments to inspire future Chicano Movement activists and to link with each other across geographical chasms. The activities of César Chávez's United Farm Workers, especially the march to Sacramento in 1966, attracted large numbers of Mexican American college students from California and from elsewhere. Similarly, the land grant movement of the Alianza Federal de Mercedes lured budding Chicano activists to New Mexico from throughout the United States, especially after the courthouse shoot-out in Tierra Amarilla (see chapter 8).

The California Chicano Movement

Much of the coalescing that led to the Movement took place in the atmosphere of universities and colleges, which in the 1960s were undergoing tremendous intellectual ferment. In December of 1967, a pivotal student meeting sponsored by the University of Southern California's newly formed United Mexican American Students (UMAS) attracted two hundred participants from throughout California. Chicano nationalism permeated the gathering, which addressed familiar issues—voting, education, and poverty—but also pledged support to the land grant struggle of Reies López Tijerina and the grape boycott of the farm workers union. Many other meetings were taking place in other universities in California and the Southwest.

But more than any other single event, the highly publicized school walkouts in East Los Angeles in 1968 served to attract young Mexican Americans to the Chicano cause. These events can be traced to the summers of 1966 and 1967 when the Los Angeles County Human Relations Council invited Mexican American leaders to meet with about two hundred teenagers in order to tackle issues, such as gangs, school dropouts, and access to a college education. Led by David Sánchez, some of the teenagers formed the Young Citizens for Community Action (YCCA) and continued addressing youth problems in East Los Angeles.

But the social ferment of this era radicalized the YCCA, which changed its name to the Young Chicanos for Community Action. In late March of 1968, the YCCA, now better known as the Brown Berets because of their headgear, and UMAS members organized a walkout of East Los Angeles high school students to protest inadequate education conditions. Mexican American parents soon joined walkout leaders to form the Educational Issues Coordinating Committee (EICC). Throughout April, EICC members picketed or spoke out at school board meetings when they felt the panel was not responding to the issues raised by the student strike.

Then in early June, Los Angeles County officers arrested thirteen persons (The LA Thirteen), most of them EICC members, because they had helped organize the walkouts. Among those arrested was high school teacher Sal Castro. As a consequence, school administrators chose to fire him, but when EICC protesters occupied the school board chambers during a meeting, board members reinstated Castro. After much legal maneuvering the County dropped charges against the LA Thirteen.

By 1969, the Crusade for Justice (CFJ) in Denver began to serve as a nexus for the Movement. CFJ founder Rudolfo "Corky" Gonzales, a disenchanted, former official in Denver's War on Poverty, led dramatic protests against police brutality and against the city's neglect of Mexican Americans. Gonzales' activities gained him prominence outside of Colorado; thus, when he organized the National Chicano Liberation Youth Conference in March, 1969, more than one thousand young people attended. Out of the Youth Conference came El Plan Espiritual de Aztlán (The Spiritual Plan of Aztlán)—the call for cultural separatism and self-sufficiency, a pledge for Chicano protest activity against the Vietnam war, and one of the earliest attempts to deal with the role of women in Chicano society (women had held an impromptu workshop that condemned Chicano male chauvinism).

Inspired by El Plan Espiritual de Aztlán, California students met at the University of California, Santa Barbara, less than one month after the Denver meeting and issued a blueprint, El Plan de Santa Bárbara (The Santa Barbara Plan), for implementing Chicano studies programs throughout the California university system. The Plan eschewed assimilation, promoted collective rather than individual success, and decided to bring all California Chicano student groups under one standard, called El Movimiento Estudiantil de Aztlán (MECHA).

The Chicano Moratorium

The war in Vietnam, a source of discontent among the nation's youth, also provoked protest within the Chicano Movement. While most Mexican Americans reluctantly supported the war, many young Chicanos resented the disproportionate casualty rate of Hispanics. Steering the Chicano Movement in the direction of antiwar dissent was mainly the work of the Brown Berets and a former UCLA student body president, Rosalío Muñoz. In the summer of 1969, Muñoz announced that he would publicly turn in his draft card at the Los Angeles induction center on September 16, the anniversary of Mexico's declaration of independence.

In the meantime, Brown Berets had returned from the Chicano Liberation Youth Conference in Denver, started the Chicano Moratorium Committee (CMC), and sponsored two antiwar demonstrations that attracted national attention. Soon Muñoz's efforts and those of the Brown Berets melded into one, and the committee planned a national protest day for August 29.

Muñoz, under the auspices of the National Chicano Moratorium Committee (NCMC), traveled throughout the country obtaining support from both Chicano Movement groups and from traditional Mexican American organizations. On the 29th, thousands of protesters marched down Whittier Boulevard towards Laguna Park in the heart of East Los Angeles while hundreds of riot, gun-equipped county sheriff deputies and LAPD officers were conspicuous on every street corner. By 3 p.m., the park was teeming with as many as 30,000 demonstrators, most of them under twenty-five years of age.

When a disturbance broke out in a liquor store next to the park after marchers left without paying for their drinks, the police began to disperse the rally. But when some of the demonstrators resisted, the police reacted violently and three people were killed. One of the casualties was Rubén Salazar, a *Los*

Angeles Times columnist. He died when a deputy sheriff fired a tear gas projectile into the Silver Dollar Café, where Salazar had sought refuge from the violence. Chicanos felt that the police had targeted Salazar because of his coverage of police brutality and because of his sympathy for Chicano Movement goals. But the coroner's jury exonerated the deputy who fired into the cafe, a decision that outraged the Mexican and non-Mexican community alike. Non-Mexicans saw Salazar as a mediating force between angry militants and a recalcitrant establishment. Moreover, the antipolice reaction from even conservative Mexican Americans demonstrated that the community agreed with many reformist goals of the Chicano Movement.

Relations between activists and the police worsened after the tragic events of August 29, 1970. The LAPD and other law enforcement agencies used *agent provocateurs*, spies, rumors, and red-baiting to discredit the NCMC and its Brown Beret core. Eventually, a Chicano fringe element tried terrorist tactics of its own, such as bombings, which many activists believed invited unnecessary repression. Out of this maturation process came La Raza Unida Party, which had its origins in Texas among the Mexican American Youth Organization (see below) and in Colorado's Crusade for Justice. The idea of the party developed as early as 1967 in an Albuquerque meeting called by Reies López Tijerina that many *movimiento* pioneers attended.

The Youth Movement in Arizona and New Mexico

Although *chicanismo* spread throughout the United States, its character reflected the region where the process emerged. At the National Chicano Youth Liberation Conference in Denver, a *chicanismo* that experimented with abstract political and cultural options emerged and provided a strong ideological link between California and Colorado delegates who predominated at the meeting. In contrast, members of the Mexican American Youth Organization (MAYO) in Texas and Chicano organizations in Arizona emphasized more provincial and pragmatic initiatives.

Still, California and Colorado *chicanismo* stimulated *movimiento* activity wherever it emerged. Salomón "Sal" Baldenegro, a founder of the Mexican American Student Association (MASA) at the University of Arizona in Tucson in 1968, learned of the Chicano Movement in Los Angeles, where he lived during 1967. Before long, he and other students formed the Mexican American Liberation Committee (MALC) off campus and organized walkouts at predominantly Mexican American high schools to protest their deterioration. In the spring of 1970, the group demanded through daily confrontations that Tucson officials convert the Del Rio Golf Course, located in the Mexican west-side, into a people's park. Out of MALC was born the short-lived La Raza Unida Party, which unsuccessfully ran candidates for local political offices.

331

In the Phoenix area during the spring of 1968, Chicano students at Arizona State University adhered to the Movement after hearing San Francisco-area leader, Armando Valdez, speak on their campus. That summer, a core group of students devised a strategy to instill *chicanismo* among other Chicanos as soon as classes convened in the fall. After forming the Mexican American Student Organization (MASO), along with white radical students, Chicano students occupied the ASU president's office for two days to demand the severance of contract with a linen service that employed Mexicans only in menial positions.

Some of the MASO students then joined with nonstudent community activists in 1969 to start a community development organization, Chicanos Por La Causa (CPLC). The initial activity of this group dealt with educational issues and politics. In the summer of that year, the CPLC ran a Chicano slate for an inner-city school board election which, although unsuccessful, provided experience for activists who today form the core of Chicano political leadership in Maricopa County. The following year, the CPLC organized walkouts at Phoenix Union High School to protests deteriorating conditions in that inner-city school.

While the *movimiento* activity of the Alianza Federal de las Mercedes received the most attention in New Mexico, other important activity occurred. María Varela, a former Student Nonviolence Coordinating Committee (SNCC) volunteer in the American South and Chicago, came to New Mexico in 1968 to work with the Alianza. Afterwards, she independently founded the Ganados del Valle Cooperative and the Tierra Amarilla Free Clinic. Elizabeth "Betita" Martínez, another out-of-state activist, published the Movement newspaper *El Grito del Norte* (the northern call). In Albuquerque, the Black Berets, also known as the Chicano Youth Association, militantly protested urban poverty, educational neglect, and police brutality. Through a project called "La Resolana," Tomás Atencio and other activists in Santa Fe gathered knowledge from *Hispano* village elders, a wisdom that could hopefully shape public policy affecting Mexican Americans.

The Rise of the Mexican American Youth Organization

In San Antonio, Texas, the style of Chicano politics that contrasted the most to the California Movement emerged. During the spring of 1967, five young men—José Ángel Gutiérrez, Mario Compeán, Nacho Pérez, Willy Velásquez, and Juan Patlán—met regularly and eventually founded the Mexican American Youth Organization (MAYO), the forerunner of the Texas La Raza Unida Party (LRUP). After MAYO members met with black civil rights leaders in the South and Chicano Movement activists outside of Texas, their desire to deal locally with issues of police brutality, labor exploitation, and educational problems was reinforced.

MAYO constructed an ideology derived from cultural nationalism, but with less pondering of identity and symbolic separatism than did California Chicanos. It drew more from existing culture, family values, Tejano music, and the use of Spanish. But ending blatant economic and social subordination through the use of confrontational tactics became the foremost objective among MAYO members. During this time, they supported strikes called by César Chávez's UFWOC, who sent organizers to unionize farm workers in South Texas, and confronted the Texas Rangers, who openly harassed pro-union workers and sympathizers.

MAYO organizers became adept at tapping federally funded programs such as Volunteers in Service to America (VISTA), which deployed Chicano activists to South Texas's poverty-stricken areas. With federal and state funds, MAYO provided health care to farm workers throughout South Texas through the Texas Institute for Educational Development (TIED). With Ford Foundation funds, the group organized the Mexican American Unity Council (MAUC) to promote Chicano-owned small businesses and to provide job training.

MAYO members held to the belief that confrontational tactics could convince cowed Texas Mexicans that the *gringo* was vulnerable. For example, by engaging in public confrontations with the feared Texas Rangers, they demonstrated that at least some Mexicans were willing to stand up to these often despised law officials. But MAYO's highly publicized antics also provoked the ire of established Anglo liberals and Mexican American *políticos*. San Antonio's Congressman Henry B. González, for example, almost single-handedly eradicated most of the funding sources for the young militants.

After being stymied in their community development efforts, in 1968 the young activists turned to gaining electoral power. Naming their effort the Winter Garden Project (WGP), they chose to start in Crystal City, the hometown of José Ángel Gutiérrez and his wife Luz. Although the population of this agricultural town in South Texas was more than 80 percent Mexican, the power structure in both local government and private business was Anglo American.

In 1963, a slate of five Mexican Americans under the auspices of the Teamsters' Union and the Political Association of Spanish-Speaking Organizations (PASSO) took over the Crystal City Council. But Anglo community leaders intimidated the inexperienced Mexican American officials and sabotaged day-to-day city operations. In the next election, the Anglo old guard regained the council seats. Gutiérrez and his MAYO cohorts returned to Crystal City in 1968 precisely to recover the elusive gains of 1963. But unfolding local dissatisfaction with the school system prompted the organizers to put their electoral goals on hold temporarily.

Tackling educational problems was not new to MAYO members who previously had traveled throughout Texas persuading students to boycott their classes as a form of protest. In the Crystal City high school, Mexican students resented that they could not participate fully in school activities and that the curriculum was geared toward the Anglo minority. In the spring of 1969, for example, a cheerleading aspirant, Diana Palacios, led her friends in confronting school administrators on the cheerleader selection process.

When school resumed in the fall, a similar issue surfaced during homecoming queen elections. Chicano students, frustrated because of a grade ceiling on the students eligible to be candidates, decided to protest. The WGP, led by José Ángel Gutiérrez, joined high school students and their parents to form the Ciudadanos Unidos (CU). In December, when the school board acted equivocally to their demands, practically all of the Chicano students walked out of their classes. The strike ended on January 6, 1970, when the school board acceded to the reforms demanded by strikers. The next move for Gutiérrez and the group was to gain political power in Crystal City.

La Raza Unida Party: A Failed Dream

After the successful school boycotts, Gutiérrez and other MAYO members formed an LRUP chapter and won five positions on the city council and school board in the April election of 1970. That same year, voters put LRUP candidates in Hidalgo, Zavala, Dimmit, and La Salle county offices. By the spring of 1970, Chicano activists from outside Texas were greatly impressed with the achievements they saw in Texas, a factor catapulting the LRUP, MAYO, and Gutiérrez into national prominence.

The Texas LRUP then set their sights on the November elections to compete for offices where Mexicans constituted a majority in communities throughout the Winter Garden area. Massive organizing campaigns were launched, but the Anglo-run Democratic Party mired it down in red tape before it made any real progress. Of the fifteen seats that LRUP vied for in the four-county region, it won only one.

Many LRUP delegates at the San Antonio convention in October of 1971 aspired to run for state level races such as the governorship, in spite of November 1970 defeats. Gutiérrez, who wanted to organize region by region, opposed this escalation, but delegates led by Mario Compeán, who held this position, won out.

In 1972, through an informal procedure, the party selected as gubernatorial candidate Ramsey Muñíz, a Waco lawyer. Tall, muscled, good-looking, and a former college football player, he projected an attractive image. Because of pressure from the LRUP women's caucus, Alma Canales from Edinburg was asked to run for lieutenant governor. Many LRUP militants felt Muñíz was too mainstream, but after giving a number of nationalistic speeches during an intensive campaign effort, the Waco lawyer allayed their fears. In the primary elections, the LRUP drew away enough Mexican American voters from the Democrats that conservative Dolph Briscoe defeated Frances "Sissy" Farenthold, a liberal.

By now, the LRUP concept had spread to other areas in such states as Arizona, California, New Mexico, Illinois, Wisconsin, and Nebraska. But "Corky" Gonzales and the CFJ in Colorado showed the greatest amount of enthusiasm. His vision of the LRUP was to take it nationwide and not to cooperate with either the Democratic or Republican parties. The CFJ held a number of LRUP conventions in 1970 and ran candidates for state offices. But in spite of an ardent campaign, the party lost by huge margins. In 1971, the California LRUP fielded candidates for local elections but did not muster sufficient signatures to qualify to run for state offices. That year, in Los Angeles, publisher of *La Raza* Raúl Ruiz lost the race as a LRUP candidate for the California Assembly but forced the Mexican American Democrat, Richard Altorre, into a run-off election with the Republican candidate; Altorre lost. The following year, Ruiz ran again for a seat in the Assembly, a campaign he had to interrupt to attend the historic Congreso de Aztlán in El Paso.

As the Muñíz and Ruiz campaigns rolled on in 1972, Corky Gonzales finalized plans for El Congreso de Aztlán, an LRUP national convention to be held in El Paso in September. For two years Gonzales had held planning meetings for this event, which attracted activists from across the country. In Texas, José Ángel Gutiérrez considered the national strategy as premature, but by not attending, Tejano activists risked losing a leadership role within the Chicano Movement.

Of the four leaders, who by 1972 had emerged as Chicano Movement symbols, only three participated in the Congreso. Corky Gonzales appointed himself as temporary chairman, José Ángel Gutiérrez as vice-chairman, and Gonzales gave an honorary position to Reies López Tijerina. César Chávez, because of his close alliance with the Democratic Party, was excluded. The most important issue at the Congreso became whether the pragmatic Gutiérrez or the ideological Gonzales would be elected party chairman. Colorado LRUP leaders encouraged rumors that had Gutiérrez making deals with the Republicans in order to obtain funding for LRUP programs in Texas. Nonetheless, Gutiérrez won, provoking a bitter split that could not be bridged by any number of overtures for unity; the national Chicano party initiative was still-born. Neither Gonzales nor Gutiérrez attended a chaotic meeting that Reies López Tijerina hosted two months later in Albuquerque in an attempt to save the party. Slowly, the fragile infrastructure crumbled, and in 1979 the LRUP held its last national meeting.

In the meantime, local LRUP efforts in California and Texas attempted to give the party some life. Raúl Ruiz and his LRUP cohorts returned to Los Angeles from El Paso hoping to derail the election of another Mexican American Democrat, Alex García, to the state assembly. But García defeated him resoundingly in the predominantly Mexican American district. In 1974, an LRUP candidate tried to enter the gubernatorial race but failed to get enough signatures to qualify. That same year, the LRUP led a failed attempt to incorporate East Los Angeles as a separate city.

In Texas, the LRUP returned to the statewide campaign of Ramsey Muñiz for governor, hoping to attract a broad base of Texas Mexicans as well as white liberals who did not support the conservative Dolph Briscoe. Because of the Muñiz campaign, Republicans stood to remove thousands of Mexican American voters who normally voted for Democrats. Consequently, Republicans supported federal aid for Zavala County, which allowed the LRUP to shore up county and municipal campaigns.

In the general election, Muñiz received 6 percent of the vote, giving Briscoe's Republican opponent a victory. But the other LRUP candidates, including Alma Canales, did more poorly. It was now clear to the LRUP that at the state level, the party only functioned as a "spoiler" that benefited Republicans. LRUP activists then returned to organizing in South Texas and the Winter Garden area, where Mexicans constituted the majority populations. Indeed in 1973, the party won a record number of local election, in these areas.

But these triumphs only encouraged the LRUP to renew races for statewide offices in 1974, again choosing Ramsey Muñiz as the gubernatorial candidate. Muñiz decided to widen his appeal among liberal voters by toning down Chicano nationalistic rhetoric, a move that the nationalists, led by Mario Compeán, opposed unsuccessfully. Sissy Farenthold again lost to Briscoe in the Democratic primary, and liberals, who blamed the LRUP for drawing off Mexican American votes, withheld support from Muñiz. The former football star did not even duplicate the 1972 role of spoiler in the general election because Briscoe, running against a weak Republican candidate, won handily.

After Muñiz's defeat, the LRUP convened a state meeting to ponder again their future in statewide elections. Muñiz was removed from the picture when he was arrested in 1976 on charges of narcotics trafficking. Gutiérrez and other regional leaders tried to maintain power in local bases, but only Gutiérrez succeeded by remaining political boss in Zavala County. In 1978, Mario Compeán ran for governor and received less than 2 percent of the total votes cast. The Republican Bill Clements won against a Democratic liberal, John Hill. In the meantime, disaffected LRUP members in Zavala County formed a breakaway faction and voted José Ángel Gutiérrez out of power; in 1982, he left electoral politics for good.

In the rest of the country, the LRUP also died a slow, painful death. After violent clashes with the Denver police department, Crusade for Justice (CFJ) membership declined so precipitously that the organization almost folded. In California, former members turned to Marxist politics or returned to the traditional parties. After 1978, Juan José Peña from New Mexico attempted to keep the fires burning, at times almost alone.

In the late 1970s, Chicanos began to pay more attention to the plight of newly arrived immigrants from Mexico and other parts of Latin America. In 1977, José Ángel Gutiérrez organized the National Chicano/Latino Immigration Conference in San Antonio. Its aim was to oppose an effort initiated by President Jimmy Carter's administration to stem illegal immigration. Unlike typical Chicano Movement meetings, this one attracted every major Mexican American organization in the country. The immigrant worker issue continues today as a major legacy left for today's civil rights activists by the Chicano Movement.

The Crusade for Justice still exists in Denver, espousing a dogma that the real Aztlán of the Aztecs is the Southwest. If Corky Gonzales were to make a call for a national meeting, it would not have the impact of the 1969 youth conference—even if as many people attended. Almost every university in the Southwest has a Movimiento Estudiantil Chicano de Aztlán (MECHA) organization. While many chapters simply sponsor social events and cultural celebrations, others are more politically active. Even so, the attention-getting platform that existed for Chicano student organizations in the 1960s is no longer there.

Significantly, even in the heyday of the Chicano Movement, Mexican Americans approached political change by working through the system; these efforts created organizations that survive to this day. The most notable accomplishment of Mexican Americanism was the founding of the Mexican American Legal Defense Fund (MALDEF) and the Southwest Voter Registration Project (SVRP). Both were funded by the Southwest Council of La Raza (SWCLR), a product of the Ford Foundation's attempts to bring about social change. MALDEF, to the present day, has pursued numerous cases affecting Mexican Americans collectively, such as those dealing with educational neglect, bilingual education, affirmative action, and the rights of undocumented workers.

Prior to the movement, Mexican American leaders understood that mass registration of their people could pave the road to empowerment in electoral politics. During the *movimiento*, Chicanos through the LRUP continued to focus attention on such obstacles. Willie Velásquez, who bolted the MAYO group in Texas, pursued his dream and organized the Southwest Voter Education and Registration Project. He felt that Chicanos should work through the existing structure, in this case the Democratic Party.

Nonetheless, the Ford Foundation-funded SVRP, like MALDEF, tapped the Chicano consciousness, which the Chicano Movement activists instilled among Mexican Americans, to proceed with their agendas. The combined efforts made by MALDEF and SVRP are responsible for considerable gains Mexicans have made through the ballot box in recent years.

Perhaps the most visible legacy from the *movimiento* is related to the formation of economic and community empowerment organizations. In part, this effort exists because of the consciousness raised by militant Chicanos who pressured mainstream Mexican American leaders in the 1960s to reassess old prescriptions in solving long-standing social problems. Ultimately, the Chicano Movement accelerated the struggle to end discrimination in hiring, a movement pioneered by Mexican American advocates, such as George I. Sánchez in the 1940s and which was continued into the 1960s by such groups as PASSO, LULAC, and the G.I. Forum.

Another very visible vestige of the *movimiento* is to be found in academia. Today, every major Southwestern university houses a program whose major agenda is the study of Chicanos. None have the orientation expected in El Plan de Santa Bárbara, however, albeit the spirit of commitment to the Mexican American community continues as an integral part of their mission.

Rodolfo "Corky" Gonzales Speaks Out

In 1967, before he emerged as a national Chicano Movement leader, "Corky" Gonzales spoke before a group of white and Chicano students at the University of Colorado. In presenting his case for the Chicano revolution, he appealed to his youthful audience by reminding them of the contradictions and lies that beset the teaching of history in establishment institutions and accused older white Americans of hypocrisy and racism, a position that he claimed was being abandoned by younger radical whites.

Social Revolution in the Southwest

My subject for the night is "Social Revolution in the Southwest." And I think that, looking out among you, that I can see some familiar faces of those people who have considered themselves revolutionists in a spirit. And you might want to know in what fashion this revolution is taking place and why it's taking place. And if you really want to know why, I'll give you some reasons why it is taking place and why it's going to come to a more positive head.

First of all, we just have to look at the overall situation across the United States, and especially across the Southwest, for the Mexican American, Spanish American people, and realize that the Southwest is very much like one of the colonies that have been colonized by England, by some of the European countries and those places that are economically colonized or militarily taken over by the United States of America.

We have the same economic problems of those underdeveloped countries, and we suffer from the same type of exploitation and political strangulation. And because of this, you have a new cry for militancy and a new move. And in doing this we start to evaluate what this society is all about. And we start to point to the defects; we start to point to the real errors in a society that our leadership in the past, including many of us who have wandered through a maze looking for the right answers to tell the people, the right answers for ourselves. And we come to grips with ourselves and realize that the old methods are passé; the involvement in politics in two political bodies that are stagnant, that are status quo, have nothing to offer us.

A Democratic Party that offers a fine philosophy and then doesn't live up to it; a Democratic Party that produces George Wallaces and Connallys from Texas and produces the different bigots that operate in a political world under the guise of these great, tremendous philosophies left down by some of the real progressive legislators of our time.

So, we look at this and we realize that the only thing we can gain from the Democratic Party, in most cases, is to become involved with a status quo party that is willing to use us, willing to give us double-talk, willing to give us window dressing and appointments and patronage. But this does not change the social problems of the poor. It does not change the social problems of different ethnic and minority groups.

The Republican Party is sterile, has nothing to offer, and they have money to deal with. And they have the same kind of a patronizing offer of jobs for one or two and nothing of progressive changes for the rest of the people.

339

So we evaluated this and looked around and started to inform and started studying the economics of our Southwest and realized how we've been HAD. And how we've been USED. And we started to want to make some changes.

And how are we going to make these changes? We had to start from the very bottom. It's true that most revolutions are usually started from the middle class, and we think that the middle class of this society is also revolting against its own society. That's why you have young radicals who are rejecting the war that they didn't make, rejecting the draft that is, as far as they're concerned, unfavorable, illegal, and they're rejecting the very morals, or lack of morals, in a society that is supposed to present all these beautiful answers to decent living and to fair practice and to democracy and equality and all these fine words that you read from your Constitution, your Bill of Rights.

All this fine talk comes out of the double-talking mouths of politicians . . . And you hear these words and the whole society across this country does not believe a politician. You don't believe L.B.J. because you know he won't rat on Bobby Baker. You know that the industrialists in this country are making millions of dollars out of the Vietnam War. That even the whole economy of this nation is balanced on that war, when that money utilized for war could be utilized for progress, could be utilized for housing, could be utilized for medical care and education for all people without any concern of race, creed, color, or ethnic group. Instead it's utilized because there are people that are power-hungry and money-hungry and they're willing to make their dollar. It doesn't matter how much blood is stained on it or whose blood it is.

And I think that when we recognize the hypocrisy of our country's political nature, you're going to reject it because politicians are not elected by the majority of the people in this country or the electorate. They are elected by a minority that is mesmerized and hypnotized by a high-priced, Madison Avenue technique, TV, until most people are punch-drunk when they go into the voting booth. Not only that, the candidates elected either have to be rich to be independent or they are bought by private industry and big business. Therefore, the laws and legislation of our country are not made for the people, by the people. They are made by lobbyists who are hired by the industries, hired by business people. And those civil rights laws that do come out of our legislatures are so riddled with amendments that they're not worth the paper they're written on. Because those laws do not change the engrained racist attitudes that this educational system teaches to our young people, teaches to the Anglo, teaches to our people. And because of this attitude—and I can point to many examples and maybe you read your own books and look at them—you realize that for us, the people with the Spanish names who are considered foreigners (when there are too many of us around) by easterners who didn't know we existed here on this side of the Mississippi and who don't realize the history. And those westerners who are here already have the attitudes, the traditional attitudes that the southern whites have about the black man. And therefore we have this to battle with.

And where do all these attitudes come from? They come from the educational system, from your mass media, from the story structure from movies and TV that place the Mexican American in a second-class category or in a villainous category. The man with a mustache usually symbolizes the guy with a knife in his pocket or the guy hiding behind a tree or coming out with a big rifle in his hand. He's usually the bandit: in "Ship of Fools," he's the pimp or the prostitute. If it's in "The Dirty Dozen," he's now the cowardly Chicano that's gotta crawl up that rope like a speed demon because he's afraid he can't get up, he can't cut it.

And yet, the only time we're afforded any of the real contributions we give this nation and we gave this nation is when we die overseas for somebody else's battle. When we die, you know, in the movie scripts for the Anglo captain, then we're heroes. When we die for unjust and unholy wars that are created by the administration, by the business people and military complex, then we are heroes. We're afforded medals; we're given credit for being part of our great nation. And then we look back and realize what has happened to us.

And the revolution is going to start because young people are now starting to evaluate exactly how they've been oppressed, exactly how they've been exploited, exactly how they have been HAD. And how their people were too kind, too good, and too warmhearted to open their arms to the raging hordes of people that came across the Mississippi that had no knowledge of the mining industry, had no knowledge of the farming industry, had no knowledge of the ranching industry—and yet were taught, and all the techniques that were here, were already here, and were *given* to these Anglo oppressors and aggressors. And the young people are starting to realize that they are not a conquered people and nobody, NOBODY, really knows anything about the Treaty of Guadalupe Hidalgo.

I think Mr. Tijerina has taken on a tremendous battle, but he has it based on international law and he has it based on legality and facts. And it points to a very, very stark reality that none of our young people have learned who they are, can identify with anything but the Anglo success image, and therefore he'd have to reject what he is and commit ethnic suicide, and sometimes it's escapist to gain a degree to escape from the misfortunes and the tragedy of a defeated people. And therefore, he doesn't have to identify with defeat as seen in the eyes of this society. He can identify with success and the better things in life. But he also must, or is expected to, commit ethnic suicide to do it.

And I say that there's no right for any nation, for any people, or any society to destroy a culture, to destroy a people. We see that day in and day out. Economically, the majority Anglo controls the economics, controls the politics, controls the finances, controls the employment doors. And then wants to make all the decisions. When there is money that comes in to, say the War on Poverty, say Labor Department training programs, *they* make the decisions. They're the Big Brother that hands down the ideas. They come into our communities to try and organize us, and they create more problems than if they stayed out of our community, went back to their middle-class society, and taught themselves something about living, something about life.

And we have been sort of disturbed because our leadership is kind of confused. We've all been confused and looking for the direction and the way. And the direction does not lie through picketing and demonstrating anymore. We have tried the due processes of going through laws to gain redress for police brutality, and legal and legitimate legislation to try to put it across, to change the migrant labor laws, to change the different laws that affect us. And what has happened? We run up against brick walls.

It doesn't matter when a so-called "liberal" candidate sponsors raising the minimum income, or the minimum wage from a dollar and a quarter to a dollar thirty-five, and thinks he's giving us something. Because a man that's not working doesn't care if it's three dollars and sixty cents, if he can't get a job.

And this is what happens in the Southwest. I don't know of any Anglos that find it very hard to be hired in the Southwest. And yet the natural resources of our people, the people who are here and part of the earth, find it very difficult to find a job on the same level because they immediately point to technology, skills, and all these different qualifications even to go out and shovel sand for the state highway department. The different requirements or tests that have nothing to do with the job you're going to do, have nothing to do with the type of work that you can do, have nothing to do with your actual capability of doing work. This is nothing but a restriction and a barrier to one group from the other, a complete control by an Anglo society that has turned its back on the culture that exists here.

Now this is a nation of tourists. The people go all over. They go to Italy to look in on little Italian villages and to enjoy the culture and rub shoulders with tradition. They go to Mexico to look at little villages and look at the people and the architecture and the art. And when they come back, they're cultured because they can say "mañana" and "sí, sí" and a few things like this, you know. Then they come here, right in their own country and they destroy culture. They destroy a whole nation of people. You know, if you live in a country club area of Denver and you can speak Spanish, you're cultured. If you live down on Armour Street, you're Mexican. And this is the difference.

Now when you start evaluating what all the contradictions of our country are, what you're taught in the school that is right and what is wrong, and then you go out into real life and you find out exactly that it's a lie . . . because in your school system you've been taught that the only successful image is an Anglo image, because that's the only successful man. Whether it be Custer, who just got shot down again (he's off the TV) but they're going to make a hero out of him because he had yellow hair . . . And we all know that he was exposed as a psycho, as an egomaniac, and as a fraud. Now he comes back because he *is* this image, and they try to develop him as a hero image again.

Now this myth has to be destroyed. And we have to destroy it. And I think that the young people of this nation should start realizing that the people that they're really fighting are the Establishment, the Society, the System. And you have to look at it and realize that it is completely contradictory to itself.

They teach us that the only image of success is Anglo, so that our kids can become Anglos and become patriotically brainwashed to go die and show their machismo (which our people do by gaining more Congressional Medals of Honor than any other ethnic group, who die double the proportion of their numbers in the armed forces, so they do have guts). But we have to direct our guts into a revolution; here where the battle really is, not over there to kill other people that are protecting or revolting for their own self-determination. We have to start self-determination here at home. And how do we do it? We have to destroy a myth, a myth that is taught to us by the school system, by the biggest financial and brainwashing machine in the history of our nation and in the history of the world.

Now, one of the other things that is taught in this educational system is that if you have money, you're a success. And it doesn't make a difference whether you're a cheat or a liar or a hypocrite or a coward. As long as you have money in this society, you are recognized as a success. So that as the poor people go to school and try to identify with success, they're going to reject their homes; they're going to reject the places they live; they're going to reject the values that their forefathers or their fathers and mothers are giving them. They're going to reject their culture and their language because this is not success. And money is success. Love of human beings, love of each other is not important. The only thing is, "Make that fast buck."

And everybody gets wound up making this fast buck so much that he forgets what life is all about. He forgets what love is all about. Even a process of complete extermination of himself, driving himself toward social neurosis (sterilization of the soul, is what I call it) and, I think, only to gain a fat stomach, to make sure he has two cars in his garage, that he keeps his house bigger and better than his next door neighbor's and his grass is cut shorter. He doesn't give a damn about his next door neighbor or the man across the street or anybody else, as long as they don't confuse or rather disrupt the crease he's putting in the sofa from his behind watching the TV. And he doesn't want his TV program disrupted. Because he's going to sit there like a drone and a fat slob and forget about the rest of the world as long as he keeps his belly full, as long as he *thinks* he's educating his children who are going to go and learn something. (And I hope they're learning more than he did. I hope they're learning that *he* is responsible for the society that exists today.)

And I think as I talk at the universities and as I talk across the country, I find that the young people, the young radical is willing to move. He's rejecting; he's rejecting this society because he knows it's rotten. And he's not rejecting it because a young, or an old, or a middle-aged Mexican sits up here and tells you, "This society is rotten." Because I'm not part of your society. I don't want to be a part of your society. I want to eat steak and frijoles and chili verde at the same time. But I don't want to have to live the kind of life that's being lived by your society.

And what are your own experts telling you about this society? What are your young writers, your intellects telling you? When a man reaches the real pinnacle of intellectual achievement, he rejects this society. He doesn't accept it. He realizes what it is. And I think that this has to be engrained. Not only into the middle-class radicals who are coming away from their society, but we have to teach our young people who are the first ones to be brainwashed by this machine. We have to teach them what the economic strangulation is. How they're politically exploited. How they are mistreated.

And now the young Anglo who's taking part in the antidraft movement, the young Anglo who's taking part in the struggle against the phony institutions like the CIA . . . These people are starting to begin to realize what the police state is all about. What we've been suffering for centuries, you're just learning about right now when you go out on that picket line.

There must be a tremendous fear going through the hearts of the people who love to be policemen. They can't cut it any other way. But they can get identity, they can get a uniform, a badge, and get authority because they can't cut it on the outside field and get this kind of position. And the type of person that's drawn to a police force is usually not the "love thy neighbor" type. He's looking for a place where he can exert this force; he can exert this superiority that he feels he has, this authority.

I saw a picture in the Free Movement newspaper, and I saw a young, slender Anglo student being held by four massive policemen: one guy had a billy club against his throat, one guy had his arm bent backward this way, the other had his arm bent front-ward the other way, and the other guy had him by both shoulder blades. And I just wondered to myself, how much fear and cowardice, how much insecurity do those four big slobs have that one of them can't handle this one young kid? And have enough respect for him and make the kid respect him that they can have a meeting of the minds? If the boy is wrong, he's going to be arrested, right? If he's not wrong, he's got a right to speak his piece. But why? It takes four, you see. But you're just learning about it. Sometimes it takes ten or twelve cops to do up a Chicano down at Curtis Park or to do up a Chicano down on Armour Street, or to do up a Chicano down on Lincoln. You see, it takes ten or twelve, it takes the whole riot squad, and they all come down and get their licks in.

But you're just learning about it now. We've been bleeding. And we've been getting angry. And we've been, our people have been brainwashed by the media. They want to be conventional; they don't say that this is wrong. They don't want to be labeled "communists" or "radicals" or "un-American." They don't want to be labeled anything because they are very patriotic and proud of their country. So what happens? We have to teach them not to be blind in their loyalties, to find out, to evaluate.

And let me tell you that the young students across this nation, not so many in our western universities . . . it seems that the further east we get from the border line, the more conservative some of our graduates get, meaning those of my name, my name and other names that are Spanish. But we find some of the young students out of Cal State, out of San Jose University, out of UCLA, out of the University of New Mexico . . . Young kids are writing revolutionary songs. Young kids that are going to be the new intelligentsia of a real revolution are coming forth, just like they're doing in the black revolution. Young kids that are not subjected to inferiority complexes that their fathers knew. Nor the beatings of the police on street corners like we knew. Young kids who know what their rights are and are not going to accept a second-class status.

And these young people are going to have a new direction. And that new direction is going to be to destroy, to destroy a system that is rotten. When you say that, when you say "destroy," then you mean complete anarchism. I don't mean that. Why doesn't everybody live up to their Constitution? Why don't they glorify Thomas Paine instead of George Washington? 'Cause they don't have enough guts for the truth. You know there's a big difference. Why don't they tell you the real history in your history books? Why do they make Sam Houston a hero of the Alamo? They say he was an American. He was a Mexican. He was a traitor. He swore allegiance to Mexico, for a Mexican land-grant to develop the area. And Travis and Bowie were mercenaries. They weren't heroes.

You better start learning about who our people were. You better start learning about what is happening across the country. And we're going to go teach our people in the barrios, where they're mean enough to fight, not just be weak. And redirect their attitudes and their directions toward the real revolutionary thought instead of going outside and showing their machismo and blasting each other in some alley, on some street, because they're mad and mean, and they know there's revolution in them but they don't know where to go.

We're going to teach them where to go. We're going to teach them about this system, the economic problems. We're going to teach them about the legislation that is rotten and corrupt. We're going to teach them about the politicians that are using our people. We're going to teach them about the welfare system that perpetuates itself in order to keep people in bondage. We're going to teach them about the different government finance programs that take our best leadership and rob us of leadership. We're not going to teach them how to starve, but how to live. And this is a big difference.

We're going to teach them about the fact that a guaranteed income in the armed forces is not the most heroic thing to do. That if this school system can teach them how to be patriotic and how to die for this country—and it doesn't matter what the reason is—we're going to teach them how to die in the barrios for a real reason and a real cause.

And you're going to see the Mexican American will be fighting a revolution entirely different than you've ever seen in this country, because you have people that have guts and courage. You have people that show it overseas. And you have people that will be selective because they love their own people. And when they learn about the directions, they won't be blasting each other. They'll be picking the right spots. And they won't be burning their own houses down, nor their brothers' houses down. There's going to be a selectivity that you've never seen before.

And they're looking for methods, they're looking for strategies. And the strategies are coming about. And there are new young, militant people all across the Southwest. You don't read about them. Rap Brown might burp in Maryland and you get a headline. But they don't want to let a nationalism set in for the Mexican American, Spanish American. Because they know that if the words of Tijerina, if the words of radicals, if the statements that we say here tonight are spread across the news media and are identified with by young Mexican Americans, Spanish Americans in the barrios, if it's identified with and they feel it's information that they've been looking for, then they'd probably have the strongest force they've ever fought against.

Because we're the last. We've been here the longest of anybody. This is our land. This is our country. And let me tell you this: we are still not completely absorbed by this society, by this monstrous new creation. I don't call it a modern culture 'cause there's no culture in this society. It's just a society. The values are mixed up and corrupted because you contradict, or rather this society contradicts everything it does. It comes in here and it gives the money. It gives you OEO grants to help you become educated. The minute you try to become educated the way you want to become educated in the land of the free, then certain limitations are placed on you. And the CIA is part of your organizations. And if you don't allow the CIA to come in and brainwash you, then you're suspended from this school. Right? And this is what takes place in a society that contradicts itself from day to day.

You know, Anglo society doesn't have an exclusive right to be horses' asses. We have our horses' asses, too. And we have to point them out and wipe them out. We have to obliviate them. If it's politically, we're going to stop voting for them. If it's economically, we're going to stop buying from them. But we're going to teach them that what they gain from us, they bring back and help the people grow. Help our own people to educate themselves. Help our own people for their own self-determination.

We know and we have to point to this: there is a tremendous nationalism in our people, even though they say there is factionalism, they fight. Of course, when thirty Anglos go up for one job, it's "competition." When two Mexicans go up for one job, "they're fighting each other." You see, that's the difference. When *you* do it, it's all right, meaning the Anglo society. When *we* do it, you know, it's not competition; we're killing each other off. When we make a sort of top-level position, immediately we're considered leaders, you know. And they create our leaders for us. And this, again, is because they want to make the decisions in everything that's done.

And we will start making our own decisions. We will make our own mistakes. And if they're wrong, we'll suffer from them. We can't do any worse than we've done with your leadership, 'cause your leadership has corrupted us. Your leadership in a city where we face a society is where our young people become involved in crime. The *campesino*, the men, the *caballeros*, from the *ranchitos*, the migrant laborers, the villagers, the people from the mountain villages. What do they bring to the city and this society? They bring honesty. If nothing else, they bring purity that can never be matched. And what does this society and this city do to them? Why do we end up on the bottom of the ladder economically? Why do we end up on the top of the ladder in the juvenile courts and in the phony institutions? It's because we are the oppressed. And this is where society destroys us.

And I think that our young people better start evaluating this. And those who go to the life of crime are not following the footsteps of *our* culture. They are following the footsteps of this society that produces ghettos and crimes, discrimination and prejudice and phony legislation. And contradictions that nobody can stomach anymore. And, I think, when we start evaluating this and we start telling our young people, "This is it. This is the way it is." Because we want to set a nationalism into our young people that they can identify who we are. That they can identify with Tierra Amarilla as a battle cry symbolic of machismo and a right to self-determination. That we can identify the *huelga* in California as a new move for economic betterment. That we can identify the different statements and philosophies of a new breed of people that are willing to put their life on the line and their head on the line and call a spade a "spade."

And as I said before, it doesn't matter what color a man is. He can still be a sellout. Santa Ana was a Mexican and he sold Mexico out. Batista was a Cuban; he sold all of Cuba out. And Trujillo was a Dominican and he sold out the Dominican Republic. And Franco is a Spaniard and he strangled the freedom of all Spaniards. He's a dictator. This doesn't mean that if there is a Gonzales, a Trujillo, a Santa Ana that's a despot, that he's going to be accepted. This is the thing we have to start teaching our young people. Because even if this is top leadership in the Establishment, they are the enemies. And this is what we have to teach. This is what we have to say.

And there is a revolution brewing. It's not amazing and it's not impossible. Because as I said, the minimum wage has usually been the hand that kept the sleeping in line and keeps him sleeping. And then along comes the OEO to try and keep him sleeping more. And then along comes a fifteen-dollar, a five-dollar raise in Social Security to keep him sleeping more. But let me tell you that a minimum wage—I'll say it again—does not mean a damn thing to the guy that doesn't have a job. And there's no employment for him. What does he care about a minimum wage? He wants food in his belly; he wants his children fed and educated. And there *is* possibility of revolution.

If a hundred and twenty cities can go up in flames in one summer, what can the now conditioned, experienced people that took part in that be planning for next summer? What new plans and ideas do they have? What did they learn from it? They learned a lot. And as the black revolution starts, this is the one thing: the Mexicano could not identify very well with picketing. He didn't want to be conspicuous. He didn't want to be, you know, a bad show. So he didn't like that. So we found only a certain portion would do it. Then we start demonstrations. Only a certain portion. It was still negative to him. It was still something he rejected. But let me tell you that the young cats across the Southwest are really identifying with the violence in the black movement. They're really identifying with action. 'Cause this represents a machismo that can come out of the barrios.

And I talked with a group of young east L.A. boys. For some five hours they kept me, and we talked about strategies, we talked about avenues. And they want to use the legitimate, they want to use the pressures, they want to change different things, they want equality. But they're mean and bad enough to burn the whole town down if it doesn't come about. And that's the difference. He's not the Chicano at the back of the church with his hat in his hand, saying his name is "John Miller" instead of Jaramillo, to be accepted. He's now a young, proud Chicano that's going to start identifying with who he is, what he is, and what his purpose in life is.

And I think this is important. As some people say, what's in the bag for you? And the bag is creativeness. If you are creative, you'll join the revolution, 'cause you're going to change something. You're going to mold a whole new future. And it's worth twenty or three thousand times more than sitting making that crease in front of the sofa, in front of the TV. And I'd rather be out in the front line of the revolution than hiding in a closet. Thank you very much.

Robert Tice, "The Rhetoric of La Raza," Rodolfo Gonzales speech, in unpublished manuscript, at the Arizona State University, Hayden Library, pagination uneven.

United Mexican American Students (UMAS)

Student organizations were the backbone of the Chicano Movement. Even many of the community-based groups, such as the Brown Berets, had student members. One of the first Chicano-style student groups was United Mexican American Students (UMAS) at California State College, Los Angeles. Its constitution, called "Proposals of Necessity," demanded that the college defer to many of the specific needs of Chicano students. Article three, reproduced below, is a powerful testimony to the desire for not only Chicano power, but Chicano student power.

The commitment of having an aggressive recruitment program must be concurrent with the growth of the community's participation in the decision-making functions of the college. To do this we have expanded the concept of Chicano Studies to a wider and more comprehensive idea. It has become clear to the Chicano community that they must help determine and implement the educational programs coming out of this college. They must have a voice concerning proposals and decisions that generate from Cal State, L.A., for the benefit of the community.

To implement such a voice, we have constructed a Mesa Directiva [Board]. This Board will consist of each program director dealing with the recruitment and retention of the Chicano. This would include the director of the Community Relations Center, director of the Chicano segment of EOP, and the Department Chairman of the Mexican-American Studies Department. In addition, we are proposing the appointment of a Research Director. His main job will be to develop and relate research projects and materials to the Chicano community. His job will be essential to the existence of an expanded Chicano Studies concept.

These four members of the Mesa Directiva will be joined by members of the community. The community members will be elected by all the community organizations, representing the greater East Los Angeles area. Such a body as the Congress of Mexican-American Unity can serve as a vehicle for their election. Included in the Mesa Directiva will be eight Chicano students from Cal State, L.A. UMAS. These sixteen board members will appoint a Chicano director to act as the coordinator and chairman of the Mesa Directiva. He will also function as a liaison to all departments and administrative bodies of the college and fill the position of Special Assistant to the President's Office. He will be under the direction of the Mesa Directiva. The duties of the Mesa Directiva will be:

  a. To approve all educational programs dealing with the Chicano community from any department, school, or body using Cal State, L.A. as a funding agency or institution of control.
  b. To propose policies to the EOP Advisory Committee concerning the functions of the Chicano segment of EOP.
  c. To review all decisions and policies made by any academic entity and/or college committee dealing with the Chicano. The Mesa Directiva will have the power to approve or reject any decision and policy dealing with the Chicano.

d. To assume the administrative jurisdiction of the Cal State Community Relations Center. The Community Relations Director will be responsible for the *Mesa Directiva.*

e. To recommend and have accepted by the college the permanent Department Chairman of the Mexican-American Studies Department.

It is widely recognized that the GRE exams are discriminatory to culturally different minorities. The Chicano student faced with graduation cannot be evaluated by an exam that does not take into account the academic and cultural factors particular to him.

The college must address itself to the problems facing all Chicano students, including the Chicano graduate student.

This *derecho* [proposal] takes into consideration the kinds of financial and academic barriers that prohibit the continuance of the Chicano student into a graduate school. The lack of sufficient academic supportive services hampers the success of a Chicano graduate student. Financial support that guarantees the Chicano graduate student time for intensive study, needs to be implemented. A significant enrollment of Chicano graduates into an effective graduate program can be promoted by an aggressive attempt by the college to provide such a program.

Part of the Urban Focus program must be to provide symbolic references that relate and identify with the Chicano community. The naming of South Tower to a Chicano name will increase this identification. UMAS recognizes the need for the college to symbolically proclaim itself Chicano—Chicano, in the sense that it is part of the entire Chicano community.

The EOP program has long recognized the necessity to prepare students for their ordeal in college. The Chicano student, lacking sufficient preparation to meet the challenges of the college, needs an orientation program that will academically and psychologically ready him for the college environment. A Summer Institute can provide this. We are not saying it will replace twelve years of elementary and secondary education, but we know that it will provide the student confidence. Confidence in his ability to function on the college campus. The specifics of this proposal have been devised and are now ready to be presented to the college.

An effective program has to be implemented to secure a thorough transportation system for all Chicanos in need. The closeness of the Chicano community does not insure the availability of an effective transportation system. The bus lines are extremely complex and time-wasting. The implementation of a paid car-pool program or the leasing of a Los Angeles City Bus Line are strong possibilities to alleviate this dilemma.

There is a difference between agreeing in principle and economics. The college may agree, in principle, to all of these proposals, but at the same time, may not see where the money is going to come from. First, UMAS requests for the approval of all these *Derechos* in principle. Second, we declare the need for the entire college membership to diligently seek funds to implement all of these *Derechos.*

Marguerite V. Marín, *Social Protest In An Urban Barrio: A Study of the Chicano Movement, 1966-1974* (Lanham: University Press of America, 1991), pp. 257-261.

Marcha de la Reconquista

The Los Angeles-based Brown Berets attempted to spread their ideology and organization by engaging in dramatic, publicity-worthy events such as "La Marcha de Reconquista" (The March of Reconquest), a trek from southern California to Sacramento. The following is the text of their leaflet, which clearly outlined the central focus of the *movimiento* in California.

Marcha de la Reconquista

Hermanos:

This leaflet is to inform you of a march we of the National Chicano Moratorium Committee are now undertaking. The march is to protest the police brutality against our people, the indignities and brutalities which our people suffer at the hands of the Department of Immigration, Nixon's senseless and maniacal war in Southeast Asia, and the cutbacks of E.O.P. and other grants to Chicano students.

The march starts on El Cinco de Mayo (May 5th) from Calexico, California and will terminate in Sacramento, California. This march will cover approximately 750 to 800 miles; it will take about two or three months to complete and has been named, "LA MARCHA DE LA RECONQUISTA." We are reconquering our rights! The events of the last few months have clearly shown us that it is useless to place any trust in the present political system.

1. The police kill our people and all is forgiven by calling their actions "a tragic mistake." Then when the Federal Government intervenes, and sets up a congressional investigation, Police Chief Davis and Mayor Sam Yorty of Los Angeles scream police harassment from the federal level to the point where the investigation is withdrawn. This does nothing more than give the police a license to kill, because now the Los Angeles City Council has voted to pay for the legal defense of these killers with our tax dollars.
2. Daily our brothers are arrested, held prisoners, and deported without due process of law. Now, despite Nixon's words to the contrary, that this country finds itself in an economic squeeze—the same situation is now causing mass deportation of our people. This we cannot tolerate!
3. The war in Southeast Asia continues, and as you well know, our Chicano brothers are still being sought for use as cannon fodder. This we cannot allow to happen!
4. There is now a concerted effort to force MECHA and other Chicano organizations off the college campuses. One of the tactics being used in California is the cutbacks in the EOP (Educational Opportunities Program) funding. On the one hand Governor Reagan withdraws funding for students because of a lack of money and on the other he gives $13 million to three campuses. That money will

be administered by three police department heads. These police officials will receive $55,000 each apart from their regular salaries, and they will not have to answer to anyone. We believe that in reality they will attempt to buy out the Chicano students who will be using their grants!

5. Governor Reagan is now pushing a welfare "reform," which is nothing less than the enslavement of Chicanas and other poor women and provides their children with less than subsistence aid. He is following the same tactics that the slave traders and plantation bosses used to destroy the black families hundreds of years ago. It is obvious that racist reactionaries like Reagan, Yorty, and Chief Davis are using the Chicano as a whipping boy, trying to drum up support in the racist recess of a middle America's troubled soul. "We must now discredit and demoralize the type of men who perpetuate policies of Chicano Genocide!" We call on all of you to join and support our March as often as you can.

Marguerite V. Marín, *Social Protest In An Urban Barrio: A Study of the Chicano Movement, 1966-1974* (Lanham: University Press of America, 1991), pp. 263-274.

Police Brutality

Police brutality became a defining issue within the Chicano Movement. While every generation of civil rights activists had addressed this issue since the nineteenth century, *movimiento* militants voiced concerns about such misconduct with the greatest stridency. A study by the United States Commission on Civil Rights in the late 1960s supported the contention of activists regarding the arbitrary and violent treatment that police administered in barrios throughout the Southwest.

Some of the incidents reported to the Commission had resulted in death. These generally involved resistance to arrest or an attempt to escape from police custody. Mexican-Americans have asserted that the police officers would not have used deadly force against an Anglo under similar circumstances.

One such incident occurred in Stanton, California. According to one of the leaders of the local Mexican-American community, two young men en route home late one night were stopped, questioned, and searched by a police officer. The officer reportedly assigned no reason for his actions but said he was going to take them to jail because they lacked identification. At that point, it was reported, one of the young men, aged 18, started to run away from the officer, whereupon a cruising police car stopped and an officer who saw the youth running fired his revolver, killing the young man. The officer was prosecuted on a charge of involuntary manslaughter, but the case was dismissed after the prosecution presented its case.

A similar incident occurred in Alpine, Texas, in June, 1968. According to reports of local residents, a police officer was chasing Henry Ramos, a 16-year-old Mexican-American driving a car, in order to get information about his brother. The officer, it was reported, had a reputation for being rough and abusive and had been accused in the past of harassing Ramos, his brother, and other Mexican-Americans. The chase ended when the boy stopped his car and fled on foot, and the pursuing officer shot him once—fatally. A police investigation resulted in the filing of a charge of murder without malice against the officer and an indictment by the local grand jury.

United States Commission on Civil Rights, *Mexican Americans and the Administration of Justice in the Southwest* (Washington, D.C.: GPO, 1970), pp. 4-6.

Blowouts!

The walkouts at East Los Angeles high schools served as the most salient catalyst for ushering in the Chicano Movement. Below, the students explained their rationale for the walkouts in their manifesto, issued through the *Chicano Student Movement News*, the publication of UMAS.

Student Demands

BLOWOUTS were staged by us, Chicano students, in the East Los Angeles High Schools protesting the obvious lack of action on the part of the L.A. School Board in bringing E.L.A. schools up to par with those in other areas of the city. We, young Chicanos, not only protested but at the same time offered proposals for much needed reforms. Just what did we propose?

To begin with, we want assurance that any student or teacher who took part in the BLOWOUTS-WILL NOT be reprimanded or suspended in any manner. You know the right to protest and demonstrate against injustice is guaranteed to all by the Constitution.

We want immediate steps taken to implement bilingual and bicultural education for Chicanos. WE WANT TO BRING OUR CARNALES HOME. Teachers, administrators, and staff should be educated; they should know our language (Spanish), and understand the history, traditions, and contributions of the Mexican culture. HOW CAN THEY EXPECT TO TEACH US IF THEY DO NOT KNOW US? We also want the school books revised to reflect the contributions of Mexicans and Mexican-Americans to the U.S. society, and to make us aware of the injustices that we, Chicanos, as a people have suffered in a "gabacho"-dominated society. Furthermore, we want any member of the school system who displays prejudice or fails to recognize, understand, and appreciate us, our culture, or our heritage removed from E.L.A. schools.

Classes should be smaller in size, say about 20 students to 1 teacher, to insure more effectiveness. We want new teachers and administrators to live in the community their first year and that parents from the community be trained as teachers' aides. We want assurances that a teacher who may disagree politically or philosophically with administrators will not be dismissed or transferred because of it. The school belongs to the community and as such should be made available for community activities under supervision of Parents' Councils.

There should be a manager in charge of janitorial work and maintenance details, and the performance of such duties should be restricted to employees hired for that purpose. IN OTHER WORDS, NO MORE STUDENTS DOING JANITORIAL WORK.

And more than this, we want RIGHTS—RIGHTS—STUDENT RIGHTS—OUR RIGHTS. We want a free speech area plus the right to have speakers of our own choice at our club meetings. Being civic-minded citizens, we want to know what the happenings are in our community, so we demand the right to have access to all types of literature and to be able to bring it on campus.

The type of dress that we wear should not be dictated to us by "gabachos," but it should be a group of Chicano parents and students who establish dress and grooming standards for Chicano students in Chicano schools.

Getting down to facilities. WE WANT THE BUILDINGS OPEN TO ALL STUDENTS AT ALL TIMES, especially the HEADS. Yeah, we want access to the heads at all times . . . When you get right down to it, WE ONLY DEMAND WHAT OTHERS HAVE—things like lighting at all E.L.A. football fields, swimming pools. Sport events are an important part of school activity and we want FREE ADMISSION for all students. We, CHICANO STUDENTS, BLEW OUT in protest. Our proposals have been made. The big question is will the School Board take positive action. If so, WHEN?

Chicano Student Movement News, March 15, 1968.

The McKnight Letter

Joe McKnight, a teacher at Lincoln High School, wrote an article in the *Lincoln High School Faculty Forum* defending the students who were contemplating a walkout in the spring of 1968. Conceding that, indeed, the pedagogic approach to teaching Mexican Americans needed reform, he drew the ire of more conservative teachers. After the walkouts, another teacher, Richard Davis, wrote an angry reply to McKnight's essay in which he repeated a number of unfounded stereotypes about Mexicans. These insensitive remarks presented an opportunity for activists to expose the misconceptions that mainstream society, and worse, educators held about Mexicans. The two essays were reprinted in *Con Safos* magazine along with a rebuttal by Gilbert González and Rodolfo Salinas, regular contributors to the journal. *Con Safos* was short-lived, but it was the least polemical of the *movimiento* publications. Sections are excerpted below.

The Mexican-American child has been victimized by a society which insists that he "melt" at all costs. To start with, Mexican culture is not alien to the American Southwest. We are the alien culture which has been superimposed by military conquest on a prostrate, indigenous people. And like all conquering races, we are arrogantly insisting that the subject people turn themselves into carbon copies of ourselves. And we asked whether the sons and daughters of the immigrant, in order to be "melted," did not have to implicitly reject their fathers' culture, heritage, and values as inferior. We of the majority culture patted ourselves on the back and congratulated ourselves on our great democratic "melting pot" tradition. We set up the American school system to be the instrument of the "melting" process. But seldom—oh, too seldom—did we give a second thought to the destructive loss of identity, to the paralyzing self-alienation that was a by-product of the transition. Here in the Los Angeles Eastside, the problem of assimilation is compounded by skin coloration. And we teachers and administrators—whether we wish to face it or not—are the representatives of that conquering, Anglo power structure, representatives who have been sent into the Eastside "barrios" to "melt" the indigenous population whether they want to or not.

And how does the Mexican-American experience himself in the midst of all this? I am afraid he comes to see himself as the passive object of someone else's action. He experiences himself as a thing to which, or about which someone else does something. Those who are familiar with existentialist thought know that man does not experience himself as being alive until he becomes the subject of his own actions—indeed, he is a dead, and an inanimate object, as long as events merely happen to him. To be alive, to be one with himself, man must control his own destiny. He must have choices and take responsibility for these choices. Even in the most oppressive circumstances, man always has the choice of saying "Hell no!" I am afraid this is what many voices in the Mexican-American community are only beginning to sing out loud and clear to the Anglo power structure. If we are not deaf, we can hear them.

Psychoanalysts are familiar with a type of patient whom they often see in their practice. He is a man lacking a sense of identity, alienated from his society and from his own emotions. If asked how he feels at any moment, he cannot honestly answer. Indeed, he lacks the capacity to feel at all. In a world where it is dangerous to feel, this patient has destroyed all his emotions. He is not a productive man who actively relates to his world. He is not the controller, but the controlled. When such a patient begins to break through his alienation and re-establishes contact with his emotions, he begins to give vent to feelings of explosive rage. Acceptance of self and the long-repressed hunger for "aliveness" are often preceded by total emotional involvement in rage and conflict. This is like Meursault. In Albert Camus' *The Stranger*, he says, "I started yelling at the top of my voice; I hurled insults . . . It was as if that great rush of anger had washed me clean—I felt ready to start life all over again."

A valid comparison can be drawn between this type of alienated patient and the alienated minority community served by Lincoln High School. We must be prepared to accept the rage and anger, and we must be prepared to respond to it in a productive way. I feel that our principal has attempted to do just that. However, he lacks the power, the muscle, to effect many of the far-reaching reforms needed at Lincoln, and more generally in all schools on the Eastside. But we, as Eastside faculties, do possess the needed muscle. Combined and united, we could effectively represent the best interests of the community we serve. We could become an effective pressure on the Anglo power structure represented by the Los Angeles School Board. Why have we not done this already?

The most compelling question in terms of the above is directly related to that fact that we, as a faculty, are in much the same situation as the community. We lack an identity. We have become so accustomed to passively having decisions made for us by the administration, and spoon-fed to us like dependent children, that we do not as yet experience ourselves as "active bearers of our own powers," to use a phrase from Eric Fromm.

We must find our identity by the creation at Lincoln of a faculty senate, a representative body of teachers empowered to make decisions concerning school policy, and able to represent the best interest of our students vis-a-vis the downtown school board.

The first business of a Lincoln Faculty Senate should be a series of resolutions calling for reforms that would reorient our school around Mexican-American culture. I would propose the following:

1. Selection of textbooks and teaching materials on an area basis rather than a district-wide basis. In the Mexican-American area these books should reflect Mexican and Mexican-American culture.
2. Where materials and books reflecting Mexican and Mexican-American culture do not exist, a committee should be appointed to write them.
3. Where appropriate books do not exist in English but do in Spanish, these books should be translated and used.
4. Mexican and Mexican-American history should be a required course in all Eastside schools.
5. Funds should be made available to educate Eastside teachers in the history, traditions, and customs of Mexico.

Certainly the above list does not exhaust all needed reforms. But I am sure that if the "salad bowl" concept is ever generally accepted by the talented Lincoln faculty, they can bring their creativity to bear on reforms to a far greater extent than any individual.

* * *

I take issue with Mr. Joe McKnight's whole article in the *Lincoln Faculty Forum*, dated February 5, 1968, regarding the Mexican-American problem. His article was of the "divide and conquer" technique, divide America into small nationalistic minority groups, and see which ones can get the most from the city, state, and federal governments. If there is civil disobedience, picketing, etc. among the Mexican-Americans, it is only because they see what they think is progress in their Negro brothers who have obtained grants, money, and concern. They don't want to be left out.

Jews, Germans, Irish, Chinese, Japanese, Italians, and many others have "melted" in the "melting pot," and have contributed to American culture without asking for special privileges. They did not have to "reject their father's culture, heritage, and values as being inferior."

Most of the Mexican-Americans have never had it so good. Before the Spanish came, he was an Indian grubbing in the soil, and after the Spaniards came, he was a slave. It seems to me that America must be a very desirable place. Witness the number of "wetbacks" and migrants both legal and illegal from Mexico.

Yes, I agree that he sees himself as a "passive object." Therein lies the whole problem, as well as the answer. When it comes to going to the best schools in the world, FREE, he is passive. Absenteeism is his culture. His way of life always mañana. Maybe he will get an education—mañana. When it comes to repairing his home, controlling child birth, planning for tomorrow, he is passive. Those that have melted into the melting pot have broken away from this kind of culture and have become lawyers, teachers, and skilled employees. But first he is going to have to throw off his passiveness and WANT to get ahead—on his own.

I take issue with all five of Mr. McKnight's suggested reforms. Mexican history is taught, what there is of it, from the Indians and Spaniards to Pancho Villa and the rest. This is taught in our California history, which is a requirement for the Jew as well as the Japanese students, in our California schools. Should we teach Jewish history to the Jews, Chinese history to the Chinese, Irish history to the Irish? This is America. It seems to me that American history should suffice. If anyone is interested in these other histories, he will make an effort to learn them. Would the evening classes at Lincoln have more students if Mexican history was taught? And as for educating Eastside teachers to the history, traditions, and customs of Mexico, I wonder if it is wise to compete with our neighboring country?

I say disregard all these self-appointed "minority leaders." America is great because we are all, each and every one of us, from a minority group, all contributing to the common good. The only way that America will survive is to "heat the melting pot a little hotter" and all put together. Dividing groups, one against the other, is the totalitarian method of destruction.

I taught my children one thing. "You can have anything in this world that you want, if you want it bad enough." That holds true for any American citizen. It all starts with EDUCATION, and the most important thing of all is to GO to school EVERY day to obtain it. On the Eastside, the schools are there, the teachers are there, but the students are taking the day or week off.

A Reaction to Mr. Richard C. Davis' Article

We take issue with Mr. Richard C. Davis's article regarding the present-day Chicano movement and the developments that led to it. Mr. Davis's lack of awareness, his one-sided view of history (as it is with too many other teachers) reflects the deep distortions and failings of our education system.

Davis mentions "Divide and Conquer" with the implication that it is a useless, a hopeless, and a negative measure for Mexicans to group themselves into a power group. Davis overlooks labor, the Irish, the Jews, and other such groups who have grouped themselves in order to achieve certain objectives. Objectives can be varied. For instance, labor groups, during the late 19th and 20th century, fought for better working conditions, better pay, better fringe benefits, and so on. The Irish united for political and economic objectives. The Jews have grouped for cultural and religious reasons, wishing to preserve Jewish traditions. One could go on indefinitely, but one outstanding phenomenon threads its way through each group movement, which is "group consciousness." This sort of identity gives a deeper meaning to one's life. This is what the Chicano is seeking, and he is just starting to break down the barriers (such as Davis' attitude) that have for so long inhibited the Mexican community and prevented the Chicano from discovering his true identity.

The Chicanos, Negroes, and Puerto Ricans have started to make progress only after they applied great pressure in various forms. Mr. Davis goes on with the myth of the "melting pot" and says that the Jews, Germans, Irish, Chinese, and Japanese have so melted. As recently as twenty-seven years ago the Japanese-Americans had their "melting" process come to a sudden stop and were placed in concentration camps. What about the "Forgotten American," the Indian, who was systematically murdered, deprived of his lands, and herded onto reservations? Some "melting" process!

Members of these groups (Irish, Germans, Italians) only "melted" when they lost much of their cultural and religious identity. Negroes, Chicanos, and Indians can't lose their skin color, so that the general Anglo culture has not accepted them no matter how much 'surface melting' they have done.

Concerning Mr. Davis's remarks about Indians before and after the Spaniards came, we have the following to say: What does he mean by "an Indian grubbing in the soil"? Does he mean to imply they were dirty, primitive, and wild? If so, he is guilty of a profound historical error. The Indians, at the time of the arrival of the Spaniards, had achieved a high agricultural society, and they were far advanced in other areas, such as the arts, astronomy, architecture, and construction. If Mr. Davis feels the Indians were dirty, then again he is in error, for the Indians, as compared to the conquering Spaniards, were much more hygienic. For example, they took frequent steam baths; and the Aztec capital of Tenochtitlan had a garbage collection system that preceded any in Europe.

Mr. Davis's opinions about Chicanos being passive in regards to home repairs, birth control, the future, better education, etc., seems to leave out such factors (possibly unknown to Mr. Davis) as racial and cultural discrimination, the conservative role of the Catholic Church, and the ineffective and destructive role of the school system. This latter system has its roots in Anglo culture, and these do not meet the needs of the Chicano. We also question whether the education the Chicano is supposed to be passive about is the "best" in the world? Certainly it has not taught history with great accuracy, if we are to judge by Mr. Davis's remarks concerning the history of this continent.

To be able to say that, "you can have anything in this world that you want, if you want it bad enough," and to imply that that holds true for any American citizen, is perhaps a good indication of how far out of touch with reality many of our teachers and the school system might really be. The problem goes back to the myth we have created about ourselves as a nation, and that we in turn try to sell to the world. The gap between our ideals and reality is apparent to the whole world. Why can't Mr. Davis see that? Our educators have left out many chapters, lied, or given one-sided views on many others. Maybe this is why Mr. Davis can't pick up on the credibility gap that is so obvious to millions of Chicanos, Afro-Americans, Puerto Ricans, and American-Americans (the Indians), plus many others around the world.

The tragedy of Mr. Davis's thinking, and that of our society as a whole, is that it creates a body of myths that it pays homage to, but that have very little relation to reality. American society is hooked, addicted to this mental drug that limits and distorts its perceptions about itself and the world.

YA BASTA

"A Barrio Trilogy with Addendum: A Dialogue on Our System of Education," *Con Safos,* Vol. 1 (Summer 1968), pp. 8-20.

School Walkouts by the Crusade for Justice

The school walkout became a *movimiento* tactic throughout the Southwest. Using this method brought attention to the Crusade for Justice, which was led by Rodolfo "Corky" Gonzales in Denver, Colorado. The group issued "non negotiable demands" to the school board on November 26, 1968. The use of the term "nonnegotiable" was probably a dramatic tactic by which attention could be brought to the issues at hand. It is doubtful if any group seriously felt they could achieve these demands.

A. That the school board through its office of education enforce the inclusion in all schools of this city the history of our people, our culture, i.e., language, etc., and our contributions to this country.

B. That all federal, state, and city support funds be withheld from any school that does not comply with the above statement.

C. That payment for the psychological destruction of our people, i.e., inferiority complexes, Anglo superiority myth, rejection of our own identity and self-worth, will be settled by a free education for all Mexican-American youth . . . from Headstart through college. All books, dues, materials, lunch, tuition, expenses, etc., will be free. Recompensation for the ethnic educational genocide perpetuated by this educational system can never repay in total the damage already inflicted on our people.

D. That bilingual education from elementary school through college become a reality and that the protection of our cultural rights as cited in the Treaty of Guadalupe Hidalgo, 1848, be recognized and abided by.

E. That each neighborhood complex have its own school board with no at-large membership.

F. That teachers live in the community in which they teach and that they are bilingual and are well versed in the history, culture, and contributions of our people.

G. The preservation of our values, culture, and family life. Any attempt to subdue our people into this sick society is an attack on our integrity and our honesty.

H. That the school system, teachers, refrain from counseling our children to join the Armed Forces; and admittance that the educational system and this society can neither provide the education nor the employment for our youth.

Christine Marín, *A Spokesman of the Mexican American Movement: Rodolfo "Corky" Gonzales and the Fight for Chicano Liberation, 1966-1972* (San Francisco: R and E Research Associates, 1977), p. 10.

The National Chicano Liberation Youth Conference

Gonzales's ability to capture headlines increased his prominence outside his state. When he called the National Chicano Liberation Youth Conference for March 1969, in Denver, Chicanos throughout the country knew who he was. More than one thousand young people attended and engaged in the most intense celebration of Chicanismo to date—most were from California. Out of this meeting came the significant Plan Espiritual de Aztlán.

El Plan Espiritual de Aztlán

In the spirit of a new people that is conscious not only of its proud historical heritage but also of the brutal "gringo" invasion of our territories, we, the Chicano inhabitants and civilizers of the northern land of Aztlán from whence came our forefathers, reclaiming the land of their birth and consecrating the determination of our people of the sun, declare that the call of our blood is our power, our responsibility, and our inevitable destiny.

We are free and sovereign to determine those tasks which are justly called for by our house, our land, the sweat of our brows, and by our hearts. Aztlán belongs to those who plant the seeds, water the fields, and gather the crops and not to the foreign Europeans. We do not recognize capricious frontiers on the bronze continent.

Brotherhood unites us, and love for our brothers makes us a people whose time has come and who struggles against the foreigner "gabacho" who exploits our riches and destroys our culture. With our heart in our hands and our hands in the soil, we declare the independence of our mestizo nation. We are a bronze people with a bronze culture. Before the world, before all of North America, before all our brothers in the bronze continent, we are a nation, we are a union of free pueblos, we are Aztlán.

Program

El Plan Espiritual de Aztlán sets the theme that the Chicanos (La Raza de Bronce) must use their nationalism as the key or common denominator for mass mobilization and organization. Once we are committed to the idea and philosophy of El Plan de Aztlán, we can only conclude that social, economic, cultural, and political independence is the only road to total liberation from oppression, exploitation, and racism. Our struggle then must be for the control of our barrios, campos, pueblos, lands, our economy, our culture, and our political life. El Plan commits all levels of Chicano society—the barrio, the campo, the ranchero, the writer, the teacher, the worker, the professional—to La Causa.

Nationalism

Nationalism is the key to organization that transcends all religious, political, class, and economic actions or boundaries. Nationalism is the common denominator that all members of La Raza can agree upon.

Organizational Goals

1. UNITY in the thinking of our people concerning the barrios, the pueblo, the campo, the land, the poor, the middle class, the professional—all committed to the liberation of La Raza.

2. ECONOMY: economic control of our lives and our communities can only come about by driving the exploiter out of our communities, our pueblos, and our lands and by controlling and developing our own talents, sweat, and resources. Cultural background and values which ignore materialism and embrace humanism will contribute to the act of cooperative buying and the distribution of resources and production to sustain an economic base for healthy growth and development. Lands rightfully ours will be fought for and defended. Land and realty ownership will be acquired by the community for the people's welfare. Economic ties of responsibility must be secured by nationalism and the Chicano defense units.

3. EDUCATION must be relative to our people, i.e., history, culture, bilingual education, contributions, etc. Community control of our schools, our teachers, our administrators, our counselors, and our programs.

4. INSTITUTIONS shall serve our people by providing the service necessary for a full life and their welfare on the basis of restitution, not handouts or beggar's crumbs. Restitution for past economic slavery, political exploitation, ethnic and cultural psychological destruction, and denial of civil and human rights. Institutions in our community which do not serve the people have no place in the community. The institutions belong to the people.

5. SELF-DEFENSE of the community must rely on the combined strength of the people. The front-line defense will come from the barrios, the campos, the pueblos, and the ranchitos. Their involvement as protectors of their people will be given respect and dignity. They in turn offer their responsibility and their lives for their people. Those who place themselves in the front ranks for their people do so out of love and carnalismo. Those institutions which are fattened by our brothers to provide employment and political pork barrels for the gringo will do so only as acts of liberation and for La Causa. For the very young there will no longer be acts of juvenile delinquency, but revolutionary acts.

6. CULTURAL values of our people strengthen our identity and the moral backbone of the movement. Our culture unites and educates the family of La Raza towards liberation with one heart and one mind. We must insure that our writers, poets, musicians, and artists produce literature and art that is appealing to our people and relates to our revolutionary culture. Our cultural values of life, family, and home will serve as a powerful weapon to defeat the gringo dollar value system and encourage the process of love and brotherhood.

7. POLITICAL LIBERATION can only come through independent action on our part, since the two-party system is the same animal with two heads that feeds from the same trough. Where we are a majority, we will control; where we are a minority, we will represent a pressure group; nationally, we will represent one party: ¡La Familia de La Raza!

Action

1. Awareness and distribution of El Plan Espiritual de Aztlán. Presented at every meeting, demonstration, confrontation, courthouse, institution, administration, church, school, tree, building, car, and every place of human existence.
2. September 16, on the birthdate of Mexican Independence, a national walkout by all Chicanos of all colleges and schools to be sustained until the complete revision of the educational system: its policy makers, administration, its curriculum, and its personnel meet the needs of our community.
3. Self-defense against the occupying forces of the oppressors at every school, every available man, woman, and child.
4. Community nationalization and organization of all Chicanos: El Plan Espiritual de Aztlán.
5. Economic program to drive the exploiter out of our community and a welding together of our people's combined resources to control their own production through cooperative effort.
6. Creation of an independent local, regional, and national political party. A nation autonomous and free—culturally, socially, economically, and politically—will make its own decisions on the usage of our lands, the taxation of our goods, the utilization of our bodies for war, the determination of justice (reward and punishment), and the profit of our sweat.

El Plan de Aztlán is the plan of liberation!

El Plan de Santa Bárbara

El Plan de Santa Bárbara in 1970 reflected the emerging Chicano Movement interpretation of the role that higher education should play in the Chicano community, eschewed assimilation, and produced the most resounding rejection of Mexican American ideology to date. The document established a blueprint for future Chicano Studies programs, and although those that exist today do not follow El Plan to the letter, many aspects of this document have greatly influenced both the content and the scholarly orientation of present day, Chicano Studies.

Manifesto

For all peoples, as with individuals, the time comes when they must reckon with their history. For the Chicano the present is a time of renaissance, of renacimiento. Our people and our community, el barrio and la colonia, are expressing a new consciousness and a new resolve. Recognizing the historical tasks confronting our people and fully aware of the cost of human progress, we pledge our will to move. We will move forward toward our destiny as a people. We will move against those forces which have denied us freedom of expression and human dignity. Throughout history the quest for cultural expression and freedom has taken the form of a struggle. Our struggle, tempered by the lessons of the American past, is an historical reality.

For decades Mexican people in the United States struggled to realize the "American Dream." And some—a few—have. But the cost, the ultimate cost of assimilation, required turning away from el barrio and la colonia. In the meantime, due to the racist structure of this society, to our essentially different life-style, and to the socioeconomic functions assigned to our community by Anglo-American society—as suppliers of cheap labor and dumping ground for the small-time capitalist entrepreneur—the barrio and colonia remained exploited, impoverished, and marginal.

As a result, the self-determination of our community is now the only acceptable mandate for social and political action; it is the essence of Chicano commitment. Culturally, the word Chicano, in the past a pejorative and class-bound adjective, has now become the root idea of a new cultural identity for our people. It also reveals a growing solidarity and the development of a common social praxis. The widespread use of the term Chicano today signals a rebirth of pride and confidence. Chicanismo simply embodies an ancient truth: that a person is never closer to his/her true self as when he/she is close to his/her community.

Chicanismo draws its faith and strength from two main sources: from the struggle of our people and from an objective analysis of our community's strategic needs. We recognize that without a strategic use of education, an education that places value on what we value, we will not realize our destiny. Chicanos recognize the central importance of institutions of higher learning to modern progress, in this case, to the development of our community. But we go further: we believe that higher education must contribute to the information of a complete person who truly values life and freedom.

The destiny of our people will be fulfilled. To that end, we pledge our efforts and take as our credo what José Vasconcelos once said at time of crisis and hope: "At this moment we do not come to work for the university, but to demand that the university work for our people."

Political Action

For the Movement, political action essentially means influencing the decision-making process of those institutions which affect Chicanos, the university, community organizations, and non-community institutions. Political action emcompasses the elements which function in a progression: political consciousness, political mobilization, and tactics.

Commitment to the struggle for Chicano liberation is the operative definition of the ideology here. Chicanismo involves a crucial distinction in political consciousness between a Mexican-American (or Hispanic) and a Chicano mentality. The Mexican-American (or Hispanic) is a person who lacks self-respect and pride in ethnic and cultural background. Thus, the Chicano acts with confidence and with a range of alternatives in the political world. He is capable of developing an effective ideology through action.

Mexican-Americans (or Hispanics) must be viewed as potential Chicanos. Chicanismo is flexible enough to relate to the varying levels of consciousness within La Raza. Regional variations must always be kept in mind as well as the different levels of development, composition, maturity, achievement, and experience in political action. Cultural nationalism is a means of total Chicano liberation.

Campus Organizing: Notes on MEChA

MEChA is a first step to tying the student groups throughout the Southwest into a vibrant and responsive network of activists who will respond as a unit to oppression and racism and will work in harmony when initiating and carrying out campaigns of liberation for our people.

As of present, wherever one travels throughout the Southwest, one finds that there are different levels of awareness on different campuses. The student movement is, to a large degree, a political movement and, as such, must not elicit from our people the negative responses that we have experienced so often in the past in relation to politics, and often with good reason. To this end, then, we must redefine politics for our people to be a means of liberation. The political sophistication of our Raza must be raised so that they do not fall prey to apologists and vendidos whose whole interest is their personal career or fortune. In addition, the student movement is more than a political movement; it is cultural and social as well. The spirit of MEChA must be one of "hermandad" and cultural awareness. The ethic of profit and competition, of greed and intolerance, which the Anglo society offers, must be replaced by our ancestral communalism and love for beauty and justice. MEChA must bring to the mind of every young Chicano that the liberation of his people from prejudice and oppression is in his hands and this responsibility is greater than personal achievement and more meaningful than degrees, especially if they are earned at the expense of his identity and cultural integrity.

MEChA, then, is more than a name; it is a spirit of unity, of brotherhood, and a resolve to undertake a struggle for liberation in a society where justice is but a word. MEChA is a means to an end.

Function of MEChA—To the Student

To socialize and politicize Chicano students on their particular campus to the ideals of the movement. It is important that every Chicano student on campus be made to feel that he/she has a place on the campus and that he/she has a feeling of familia with his/her Chicano brothers and sisters. Therefore, the organization in its flurry of activities and projects must not forget or overlook the human factor of friendship, understanding, trust, etc. As well as stimulating hermandad, this approach can also be looked at in more pragmatic terms. If enough trust, friendship, and understanding are generated, then the loyalty and support can be relied upon when a crisis faces the group or community. This attitude must not merely provide a social club atmosphere, but the strengths, weaknesses, and talents of each member should be known so that they may be utilized to the greatest advantage. Know one another. Part of the reason that the student will come to the organization is in search of self-fulfillment.

Give that individual the opportunity to show what he/she can do. Although the Movement stresses collective behavior, it is important that the individual be recognized and given credit for his/her efforts. When people who work in close association know one another well, it is more conducive to self-criticism and reevaluation, and this, every MEChA person must be willing to submit to. Periodic self-criticism often eliminates static cycles of unproductive behavior. It is an opportunity for fresh approaches to old problems to be surfaced and aired; it gives new leadership a chance to emerge; and must be recognized as a vital part of MEChA. MEChA can be considered a training ground for leadership, and as such, no one member or group of members should dominate the leadership positions for long periods of time. This tends to take care of itself, considering the transitory nature of students.

Function of MEChA—Education

It is a fact that the Chicano has not often enough written his/her own history, his/her own anthropology, his/her own sociology, his/her own literature. He/she must do this if he/she is to survive as a cultural entity in this melting pot society, which seeks to dilute varied cultures into a gray-upon-gray pseudo-culture of technology and materialism. The Chicano student is doing most of the work in the establishment of study programs, centers, curriculum development, and entrance programs to get more Chicanos into college. This is good and must continue, but students must be careful not to be co-opted in their fervor for establishing relevance on the campus. Much of what is being offered by college systems and administrators is too little too late. MEChA must not compromise programs and curriculum that are essential for the total education of the Chicano for the sake of expediency. The students must not become so engrossed in programs and centers created along established academic guidelines that they forget the needs of the people whom these institutions are meant to serve. To this end, barrio input must always be given full and open hearing when designing these programs, when creating them, and in running them. The jobs created by these projects must be filled by competent Chicanos, not only the Chicano who has the traditional credentials required for the position, but one who has the credentials of the Raza. Too often in the past the dedicated pushed for a program only to have a vendido sharp-talker come in and take over and start working for his Anglo administrator. Therefore, students must demand a say in the recruitment and selection of all directors and assistant directors of student-initiated programs.

To further insure strong if not complete control and direction and running of programs, all advisory and steering committees should have both student and community components as well as sympathetic Chicano faculty as members, tying the campus to the barrio. The colleges and universities in the past have existed in an aura of omnipotence and infallability.

It is time that they be made responsible and responsive to the communities in which they are located or whose members they serve. As has already been mentioned, community members should serve on all programs related to Chicano interests. In addition to this, all attempts must be made to take the college and university to the barrio, whether it be in the form of classes giving college credit or community centers financed by the school for the use of community organizations and groups. Also, the barrio must be brought to the campus, whether it be for special programs or ongoing services that the school provides for the people of the barrio. The idea must be made clear to the people of the barrio that they own the schools and all their resources are at their disposal. The student group must utilize the resources open to the school for the benefit of the barrio at every opportunity. This can be done by hiring more Chicanos to work as academic and nonacademic personnel on the campus; this often requires exposure of racist hiring practices now in operation in many colleges and universities. When functions, social or otherwise, are held in the barrio under the sponsorship of the college and university, monies should be spent in the barrio. This applies to hiring Chicano contractors to build on campus, etc. Many colleges and universities have publishing operations which could be forced to accept barrio works for publication. Many other things could be considered in using the resources of the school to the barrio. There are possibilities for using the physical plant and facilities not mentioned here, but this is an area which has great potential.

MEChA in the Barrio

Most colleges in the Southwest are located near or in the same town as a barrio. Therefore, it is the responsibility of MEChA members to establish close working relationships with organizations in that barrio. The MEChA people must be able to take the pulse of the barrio and be able to respond to it. However, MEChA must be careful not to overstep its authority or duplicate the efforts of another organization already in the barrio. MEChA must be able to relate to all segments of the barrio, from the middle-class assimilationists to the vatos locos.

Obviously, every barrio has its particular needs, and MEChA people must determine with the help of those in the barrio where they can be most effective. There are, however, some general areas in which MEChA can involve itself. Some of these are:

(1) policing social and governmental agencies to make them more responsive in humane and dignified ways to the people of the barrio; (2) carrying out research on the economic and credit policies of merchants in the barrio and exposing fraudulent and exorbitant establishments; (3) speaking and communicating with junior high and other high school students, helping with projects,

teaching them organizational techniques, supporting their actions; (4) spreading the message of the movement by any media available—this means speaking, radio, television, local newspaper, underground papers, posters, art, theaters; in short, spreading propaganda of the Movement; (5) exposing discrimination in hiring and renting practices and many other areas, which the student, because of his/her mobility, his/her articulation, and his/her vigor, should take as his/her responsibility. It may mean at times having to work in conjuntion with other organizations. If this is the case and the project is one begun by the other organization, realize that MEChA is there as a supporter and should accept the direction of the group involved. Do not let loyalty to an organization cloud responsiblity to a greater force—La Causa.

Working in the barrio is an honor, but is also a right because we come from these people, and mutual respect between the barrio and the college group should be the rule. Understand at the same time, however, that there will initially be mistrust and often envy on the part of some in the barrio for the college student. This mistrust must be broken down by a demonstration of affection for the barrio and La Raza through hard work and dedication. If the approach is one of a dilettante or of a Peace Corps volunteer, the people will know it and act accordingly. If it is merely a cathartic experience to work among the unfortunate in the barrio—stay out.

Of the community, for the community.
Por la raza habla el espíritu.

Rhetorical liberalism is omnipresent in higher education perhaps more so than in other sectors of society. Unquestionably, the contradiction between rhetoric and reality that is characteristic of "America" is a feature of the campus also. The existing interests and traditional structures have no intention of sharing power, providing access, extending prestige, and permitting plural participation. Power must be taken, here, as elsewhere.

The institutionalization of Chicano programs is the realization of Chicano power on campus. The key to this power is found in the application of the principles of self-determination and self-liberation. These principles are defined and practiced in the areas of control, autonomy, flexibility, and participation. Often imaginary or symbolic authority is confused with the real. Many times token efforts in program institutionalization are substituted for enduring constructive programming. It is the responsibility of Chicanos on campus to insure dominant influence of these programs. The point is not to have a college with a program, but rather a Chicano program at a college.

If Chicanos do not exert dominant influence over the program, better no program at all. For without the requisite control, Chicano participation provides an ersatz legitimization for the continuance of the pattern of dominant-subordinate relations that characterizes Chicano colonial status within the larger society. The demand for self-determination in higher education is not a question of puerile power discussions, but, in this area as in others of community life, a matter of survival, progress, and dignity. The practice of self-determination serves best the interest of the Chicano community and the long-range interests as a whole.

But old patterns may persist, the Anglo may move to deny and limit Chicanos, and there will be "Mexican-Americans" to serve him. Chicano faculty and administrators, and even student groups, can function as "tío tacos," the same as politicians, store managers, radio announcers, police officers, ad nauseum. It is all too easy for programs to be co-opted, for them to function as buffers of denial and agencies of control. In that case, better no program at all. Yet the colleges and universities, through Chicano programs, may serve the community.

The premises for Chicano programs are:

1. The colleges/universities must be a major instrument in the liberation of the Chicano community.
2. Colleges/universities have a three-fold responsibility: education, research, and public service to the Chicano community.
3. Only by comprehensive programs instituted and implemented by Chicanos and for Chicanos that focus on the needs and goals of the community will the larger purposes of the academic institutions and the interests of the Chicano community be served.

These premises are in turn local particularizations of a wider system of values, beliefs, ideas, organizational modes, and commitments to which the Chicano is dedicated. One of these that has a direct bearing on Chicano-university relations is that the concept of "community" is all inclusive. The Chicanos on campus are an organic, integral part of the Chicano community. Among Chicanos on campus there can be no distinctions or separations because of personal occupational differentiations. Moreover, the Chicano community on campus is an extension of the larger community. The base of the Chicanos on campus is the Chicano community. Participation for the Chicano means total access to institutions by the total community.

The primary goals of the various programs must be to serve the interests of the Chicano people through the institutions of higher learning. In education, as in other matters, there is one loyalty—the community, one criterion—service, to La Raza. In higher education, the thrust is directed toward the creation of parallel institutions that are controlled by Chicanos serving the interests of the community. These interests are defined only by Chicanos. Education cannot be isolated from other factors determining the situation of the Chicano in this society.

The base, the strength, of any action on campus depends on the Chicano community at that campus—employees, students, faculty, and administrators. This base must be well organized, and the group must possess general agreement as to its orientation before moving to secure programs. Without a position of strength, it will not be able to exercise control over the programs, and without unity of goals, the programs would be constantly in jeopardy because of internal differences. It is no accident that programs that best fulfill expectations are to be found where the student groups are strong, more sophisticated, and most demanding. Before moving overtly, the Chicano must assess the situation; he must be organized and committed; otherwise, co-optation and tokenism will result. The Chicano cannot depend on the goodwill and false promises of others. He must recognize that he will secure his rights only to the extent that he is strong.

369

The Movimiento and the Catholic Church

Chicano Movement activists took the Catholic Church to task for not tending to the needs of Mexican Americans. The most strident of these groups, Católicos por La Raza (Catholics for the People), emerged in Los Angeles. As seen below, the stridency and militancy typical of the Movement is seen in the following CPR document.

Because we are Catholics . . . because we are Catholics who have in recent times repeatedly made private and public attempts for the attention of the Church, and because we are Catholics concerned about the social conditions of La Raza, we persist in our view that it is the responsibility of our Church to act upon the following demands:

Creation of a Commission on Mexican American Affairs within the hierarchy of the Church. This Commission will be composed of representatives from community organizations (elected from, among others, the general membership of the CONGRESS OF MEXICAN AMERICAN UNITY), priests, and nuns. The Commission will research the problems facing the Chicano community. The initial task of the Commission shall be to:

1. Education
   a. Obtain a periodic accounting of Church assets and other holdings in order to determine the sources for funding the proposed programs.
   b. Establish a Chicano Educational Fund to meet the financial needs of our youth in education at all levels.
2. Housing
   a. Establish an agency, controlled by the community, with funds to approve loans or grants for building homes or making repairs and improvements.
   b. Create a housing agency to build low cost housing for all persons presently residing in the housing projects.
3. Health
   a. Commission will administer and control those Church administered or controlled hospitals in the Mexican-American community, such as Santa Marta.
   b. Create a fund to provide free or low cost health insurance for lower-income Mexican Americans.
4. Democratically elected Chicanos serve, with full voting rights and obligations, with those whose duty it is to administer the temporal affairs of the Church.
5. Leadership and Orientation Classes
   a. Leadership training classes shall be conducted throughout all parishes in East Los Angeles. Classes will be conducted by priests and personnel selected from within the CONGRESS OF MEXICAN AMERICAN UNITY.
   b. Orientation sessions shall be held for seminary students planning to enter the priesthood and for priests currently assigned to our *barrios*. Sessions shall consist of Mexican culture and thought, history, contemporary problems, etc. Sessions will be conducted by personnel selected from within the Congress of Mexican American Unity.

6. Parish priests currently do not have the time to be actively involved in the Chicano Civil Rights Movement. Presently much of our spiritual leadership in such matters comes from Protestants who cannot truly grant our Church's voice of conscience. Priests and nuns will be assigned on a full-time basis, to work actively with community projects and organizations.
7. Freedom of Speech for all Priests and Nuns
Priests and nuns will be allowed freedom of speech without fear of retaliation from the Chancery. Specifically, no priest or nun will be removed from any position for advocating a position in the realm of secular affairs.
8. Use of Church Facilities
Many community organizations currently meet in either government-owned buildings or Protestant churches. This anomaly contributes to the lack of communication between the Church and her people. It will serve both the needs of the community as well as those of the Church when those involved in social issues can use their own Church's facilities.
9. Public Commitments and Statements in Support of Issues Affecting the Chicano
The Church shall serve as the voice of conscience for the communities of poor people in their struggle for freedom and justice throughout the entire world. Specifically, it can and must make public statements of policy in areas other than those traditionally religious. The total power of the Church must be used to implement the aims and policies of Chicanos involved in their struggle for liberation against forces of repression, as for example:
   a. the farmworkers
   b. the East Los Angeles walkouts
   c. unrepresentative Grand Juries and other federal, state, and local administrative and judicial bodies.
   d. inordinate (20 percent) number of Chicano war dead from the Southwest
   e. the Vietnam War in all its hideous aspects
   f. hunger
   g. pollution

In conclusion we submit, THE CHURCH WILL REFLECT THE SOCIAL CONDITION OF THE PEOPLE IT SERVES!

Católicos por La Raza, n.d.

Early Chicana Feminism

Many Chicana activists at the time saw a need for a separate critique of the Chicano Movement. Enriqueta Longauex y Vásquez, a pioneer activist who attended the Chicano Youth Conference in Denver, lamented the chauvinism that she encountered at that meeting from her fellow male delegates.

While attending a Raza conference in Colorado this year, I went to one of the workshops that were held to discuss the role of the Chicana woman. When the time came for the women to make their presentation to the full conference, the only thing that the workshop representative said was this: "It was the consensus of the group that the Chicana woman does not want to be liberated."

As a woman who has been faced with having to live as a member of the "Mexican-American" minority as a breadwinner and a mother raising children, living in housing projects and having much concern for other humans leading to much community involvement, this was quite a blow. I could have cried. Surely we could have at least come up with something to add to that statement. I sat back and thought, why? Why? I understood why the statement had been made, and I realized that going along with the feelings of the men at the convention was perhaps the best thing to do at the time.

Looking at our history, I can see why this would be true. The role of the Chicana woman has been a very strong one, although a silent one. When the woman has seen the suffering of her peoples, she has always responded bravely and as a totally committed and equal human. My mother told me of how, during the time of Pancho Villa and the revolution in Mexico, she saw the men march through the village continually for three days and then she saw the battalion of women marching for a whole day. The women carried food and supplies; also, they were fully armed and wearing loaded "carrilleras." In battle they fought alongside the men. Out of the Mexican Revolution came the revolutionary personage "Adelita," who wore her *rebozo* crossed at the bosom as a symbol of a revolutionary woman in Mexico.

Then we have our heroine Juana Gallo, a brave woman who led her men to battle against the government after having seen her father and other villagers hung for defending the land of the people. She and many more women fought bravely with other people. And if called upon again, they would be there alongside the men to fight to the bitter end.

And now, today, as we hear the call of the Raza and as the dormant, "docile" Mexican-American comes to life, we see the stirring of the people. With that call, the Chicana woman also stirs, and I am sure that she will leave her mark upon the Mexican-American movement in the Southwest.

How the Chicana woman reacts depends totally on how the "Macho" Chicano is treated when he goes out into the so-called "Mainstream of Society." If the husband is so-called successful, the woman seems to become very domineering and demands more and more in material goods. I ask myself at times, "Why are the women so demanding?" But then I realize: This is the place of owning a slave.

A woman who has no way of expressing herself and realizing herself as a full human has nothing else to turn to but the owning of material things. She builds her entire life around these and finds security in this way. All she has to live for is her house and family, and she becomes very possessive of both. This makes her a totally dependent human, dependent on her husband and family. Most of the Chicana women in this comfortable situation are not particularly involved in the movement. Many times it is because of the fear of censorship in general—censorship from the husband, the family, friends, and society in general. For these reasons she is completely inactive.

Then you will find the Chicana with a husband who was not able to fare so very well in the "Society" and perhaps has had to face defeat. She is the woman that really suffers. Quite often the man will not fight the real source of his problems, be it discrimination or whatever, but will instead come home and take it out on his family. As this continues, his Chicana becomes the victim of his machismo, and woeful are the trials and tribulations of that household.

Much of this is seen particularly in the city. The man, being head of the household and unable to fight the system he lives in, will very likely lose face, and for this reason there will often be a separation or divorce in the family. It is at this time that the Chicana faces the real test of having to confront society as one of its total victims.

La Raza, July 7, 1969.

Mexican Americans Protest the Vietnam War

Chicano Movement militants were not alone among Mexican Americans in opposing the war in Vietnam. The following declaration was issued by the Congress for Mexican American Unity, a group of moderate Mexican Americans in Los Angeles led by Esteban Torres.

The Congress of Mexican American Unity, an affiliation of more than 300 diverse organizations in Los Angeles, wishes to inform you of its opposition to escalation of the Vietnam War. The overwhelming majority of our people can no longer remain silent in the face of the Cambodian invasion.

This political and moral tragedy can only bring more sorrow to the Mexican American communities who already bear the heavy burden of the Vietnam War, by the disproportionate sacrifice of their youth.

Social progress in our barrios, Mr. President, depends largely on our people's faith in the honesty and goodwill of our elected leaders, such as you. Your action, which is contrary to your stated commitment to peace and social progress in the ghettos, has led us to question that faith . . .

We hope and pray that you will alter your course and give more consideration to national issues that are tearing our country apart; the hope and aspirations of our people are dependent on it.

. . .the National Chicano Moratorium will convene to show the world that the Chicano will no longer fight against their brothers in far off lands and that the Chicano recognizes that the fight is here at home against a government that oppresses and jails its poor people and as we know, even kills them . . .

The Chicano will take to the streets Saturday to protest U.S. aggression throughout the world: and (1) the war in Vietnam, (2) the high rate of Chicano casualties, (3) the attitude the U.S. has as the world's policeman, using our brothers to die for their interest, (4) the police aggression used in our own barrios, and (5) the United States' imperialistic position throughout the world.

We Chicanos have come to a realization that the Vietnam War is the ultimate weapon of genocide of nonwhite peoples . . . The random genocide in the barrio, *campo* [fields] and ghettos is escalated to a calculated cold-blooded policy to enslave the Vietnamese people and rape their land of its resources. It is a war of example to other third world colonies both outside and inside the borders of the United States that they dare not resist or they will be napalmed or gunned down . . .

Mexican American Sun, May 14, 1970.

Rosalío Muñoz's Assessment of LAPD-Mexican American Relations

The Los Angeles Police Department (LAPD) and other law enforcement agencies used *agent provocateurs*, spies, rumors, and red-baiting to disrupt the *movimiento* and to discredit it. Chief Edward Davis targeted mainly the National Chicano Moratorium Committee (NCMC). On at least two occasions, the LAPD raided the committee offices and intimidated its members, causing many to leave. The NCMC attempted to counter police intimidation with a series of protests, all of which ended in violence. The most lamentable occurred on January 31, 1971, when the LAPD fired at a crowd of rioting Chicanos, killing one and wounding thirty-five. Rosalío Muñoz wrote the following letter to the *Los Angeles Times* to explain the Mexican American side of this controversy even before this violent incident took place. The poignant letter outlines a distressing historical relationship between Mexicans and the police in California.

We, of the Chicano Moratorium Committee, are writing to you in response to your plea for some social facts to understand the strained situation between Chicanos and the police. The current conflict between Chicanos and the police is a political confrontation that historically has its roots in the mid-1800s when another police government body— the U.S. Army—forcibly took the land away from the Mexicans in this area. Subsequent brutal acts by border patrol and immigration law enforcement officers frequently leading to reciprocal violent defensive reactions by Mexicans made the situation more acute. The deportation of 312,000 persons of Spanish surname—many, American citizens— by immigration law enforcement officials during the Great Depression for political-economic reasons further strained and intensified the anger of people of Mexican descent toward the law and law enforcement.

Denying the Mexican American population in Los Angeles protection from rioting vigilante servicemen during the 1943 "Zoot Suit" riots, raised further doubts in Mexican Americans as to whom it actually was that the police were there to "protect and serve." Labeling the riots "Zoot Suit" only served to reveal the racist motivations of the press by applying an historically permanent label that implied "the Mexicans did it," thereby simultaneously protecting the servicemen from public ridicule. The Sheriff's department Captain Ayers' "biological basis" racist report to the county grand jury during this period, which stated that people of Mexican descent were biologically prone to criminal behavior, further intensified public racist attitudes towards Mexican Americans, which also had the effect of permitting more aggressive police behavior toward a "biologically crime-prone" population. The report was commended as an "intelligent statement" by LAPD Chief Horral. Subsequently, in 1960, Chief Parker revealed his racist attitudes toward Mexican Americans [absorbed by the LAPD] when he said that Mexican Americans were like "wild Indians from the mountains of Mexico" and that genes had to be considered when discussing the "Mexican problem." Today police have changed the label to "Communists" to discredit legitimate Chicano grievances and elicit public support for police, initiated violence.

It has been a Chicano experience that when he has attempted to protest peacefully against the educational institutions that produce an excessively high Chicano student drop-out rate; against the wealthy Catholic Church that has milked the Chicano of his meager financial resources with no reciprocal benefits; and against the U.S. involvement in the Vietnam war which has resulted in a severe overrepresentation of Chicano deaths [in effect depriving the Chicano community of its future youth resource], his efforts have always been met with police-initiated political violence. In this respect, the police have been given and have adopted a sentry role to protect and serve these institutions that are gradually, socially and psychologically, destroying a class of people along with their rich, proud heritage and tradition. Chicanos, by day and night, are reminded of their low status in society by a sentry helicopter that was not a "called for" service by the Chicano community. The Chicano lives in a totalitarian-like atmosphere within a broader Los Angeles community that is comfortably [with the exception of the black community] functioning as a democracy. Being a population group numbering close to a million in this area, we have no city or county-elected Mexican American political representative to assist us with our problems. Our behavior can only be seen as a normal response to an abnormal condition created by those in political power.

The police brutality that occurs ten to twenty times a month in East Los Angeles again communicates to us our worth to the broader society that does not seem to care. We have not received federal protection against this abuse since the law was initially enacted in 1872. We desperately wish to be part of this society, but your powerful sentry repeatedly sends us away bleeding. We are now directly protesting against the sentry. But it is not only the day-to-day police brutality that we have experienced for numerous decades that gravely concerns us, but rather a far more severe problem that our society is not even aware of, and that is that the police are increasingly becoming more a powerful political force in our increasingly less-free democratic society. The recent Skolnic Report to the National Commission on the Causes and Prevention of Violence warned that "the ranks of law enforcement have become an ultraconservative social force which shrilly protests positive change." The report also concluded that the increasing police militancy is hostile to the aspirations of dissident groups in society and that the police view protesters as a danger to our American political system. Although this is a national report, the situation is identical in Los Angeles as confirmed not only by our experience, but by the recent UCLA report of the May 5, 1970, student-police confrontation, which stated that "police attack was discriminatory, focusing on minority group members and long hairs."

Rather than calling off our protest, and returning to a life of fear under police totalitarian aggression, we have to continue to protest for purposes of survival. If Chicanos lose their right to protest in society because of police violence, you likewise are losing your freedom in America. In this respect, our insistence on the right to protest guarantees the right of all people in America to protest. If we allow police violence to intimidate us, it is really the broader society that is victimized.

(Note: The above letter written by Rosalío Muñoz, co-chair of the Chicano Moratorium Committee, was extensively edited by the *Los Angeles Times* before being published. This is the original letter.) Printed with permission of the Brown Berets.

Los Angeles Times, January 23, 1971.

Arizona State University Chicano Students Awaken

At Arizona State University, even before one word was spoken about issues of identity or ideology, Mexican American Student Organization (MASO) students, joined by white radical students, took militant action in the laundry sit-in. A former leader of MASO, now a university history professor, F. Arturo Rosales remembered this event some twenty-two years later.

When we called the first official meeting of MASO, the Mexican-American Student Organization, we had maybe 100 students. Considering that we only had about 300 Mexican-Americans on campus, that was a big chunk.

We weren't exactly sure what we were going to do. We still hadn't articulated the ideas of recruitment or having relevant courses on campus. We had just vague ideas.

Ted Caldes came to talk to us about an issue that he thought would be relevant and that we should know about. Ted, a special representative for the AF of L, told us the union was trying to organize laundry workers. There were laundries all around town that did big linen service. It wasn't very hard to find one where the workforce was all minority and the management was all white. In those days you took it for granted that you could get away with that sort of thing. That's basically why the Phoenix Linen and Towel Company was picked out to be organized.

Their major contract was with the university. The university had a contract with them to do the towels for physical education classes on campus.

Ted's appeal was, not only are we trying to organize these people, trying to get them a decent wage and so forth, but their laundry was blatantly discriminatory, which it was. He asked us if we wanted to take that on as an issue with the university and try to persuade the university to change the way the laundry was run. Ted knew that if the university would threaten to pull out, that the laundry management would change their policy with the workers.

We said, "Yeah. That's a great issue. We'll do it."

We decided that we weren't going to just follow the Ted Caldes version blindly. We were going to make our own reports to turn in to the university. So we sent Richard Martínez and María Martínez down to the laundry. They said, "We're just students. We'd like to inspect this place." And the boss let them in and gave them a tour. Then they came back and wrote this scathing report, a condemnation. Richard Martínez described some safety hazards there and the discrimination.

The report was about seven pages. We typed it on mimeograph stencils with the library's coin-operated typewriters. Then we mimeographed thirty copies and were going to present that to the university.

We decided to get a lot of student support, not just the Chicanos, so we publicized it. We were in the campus paper. We hadn't hit the city papers yet. We publicized through the *State Press* and leaflets that we were going to have a rally.

Ted was an old 1930s union man, really hard-nosed. He wasn't Marxist, I don't think, but he was really plain militant. He was always egging us on to go as hard as we could. We were students. We were afraid. We were timid. He said, "God damn it, if the

377

university doesn't do what you want, you can take over that office." So we were contemplating that the night before our rally. Just a few of us had a meeting over at Ted's office.

The university had not complied. They hadn't done anything, as far as we knew. They hadn't responded after we had given them the report.

The rally was supposed to be a monster rally, which it was of sorts, to show the university that we had student support.

I was elected, since I was one of the three MASO chairs, to be the master of ceremony and introduce the speakers of the rally.

At the end of the speeches, I told the students point blank the university was not paying attention to us, and the only thing they were going to understand was if we took more aggressive steps. I told them a group of us were going to go over and demand from President Durham that they drop the contract and "you're welcome to come."

I got off the podium and started marching toward the Administration Building. Some of the people I knew were going to be strong behind me. We hadn't even told our own MASO students that we had plans. They came along and then everybody else came along. The people in the Administration Building were caught by complete surprise. The secretaries, I even felt sorry for them. They were just scared shitless. They saw us coming in with signs and everything.

We sat down in the President's office. We sang songs and we just sat. Every space of that floor was full. We sang some union songs and some Mexican songs.

Gordon A. Sabine, *G. Homer: A Biography of the President of Arizona State University, 1960-69* (Tempe: Arizona State University Libraries, 1992), pp. 156-157.

Chicanos Por La Causa

In Phoenix, Arizona, the Mexican American Student Organization (MASO) from Arizona State University, along with community activists, started Chicanos Por La Causa (CPLC), funded by the Ford Foundation through the Southwest Council of La Raza in 1969. The initial activity of the group dealt with educational issues and politics. Father Frank Yoldi, a Spanish-speaking priest of Basque descent and also an activist, provided the young Chicanos with office space in a church building called Santa Rita Hall. Located in the middle of a low-income barrio, the building became the heart of the Phoenix Movement. A short history, written by an anonymous member of CPLC in 1971, captured the early philosophy of this organization.

Chicanos, La Raza, Mexican Americans, the Spanish-speaking—these are the people of Chicanos Por La Causa (CPLC). CPLC was formed because of them, exists for them, and belongs to them.

As a part of the Chicano Movement, CPLC is committed to bringing about constructive change which will benefit the Chicano community. It is particularly dedicated to supporting the Chicano community in its struggle to bring about systematic change in these institutions which continue to oppress Chicanos.

Chicanos Por La Causa was organized in 1968 when individuals involved in the Chicano Movement saw the need to develop a tool for obtaining resources (both technical and financial) to confront the educational, economic, youth, and housing problems of the Chicano community.

These individuals formed themselves into a board of directors, adopted the name of Chicanos Por La Causa, and applied for tax exemptions as a nonprofit organization from both the state and federal governments. In April, 1969, CPLC received its state tax exemption and the next year received its 501 (c) (3) federal tax exemption. This made Chicanos Por La Causa eligible to receive funds from foundations, churches, governments, labor unions, and businesses.

Since CPLC is a movement-oriented organization rather than a membership organization, anyone dedicated to helping the Chicano community help itself can be a part of CPLC and its activities. The board of directors consists of six Chicanos with this philosophy and sets the policy for Chicanos Por La Causa.

Philosophy

In the barrios of the Southwestern United States live the descendents of Spanish kings and Aztec gods. Born in a land stolen from their forefathers, this disenfranchised people have survived generations of oppression and neglect. Like the cactus in the desert, the Chicano has weathered the elements and endured. Through the years, beneath his rough but strong exterior, he has nurtured the tender fruit of his survival—the Chicano culture and the Chicano family. Young and old alike are now joining with

Chicanos Por La Causa declaring an end to their oppression and the beginning of a new spring for La Raza. The time has come for all Chicanos to join together to work, sacrifice, and make the necessary commitments to bring all Chicanos out of the desert of oppression and into the spring of justice for a new generation—the children—for they do not deserve the horrible sin.

"Chicanos Por La Causa," May, 1971, Hayden Library, Arizona Collection, Arizona State University, CHI.Q-43.

La Caravana de la Reconquista

In October, 1971, Brown Beret David Sánchez launched La Caravana de la Reconquista (The Reconquest Caravan) to spread the Brown Berets' philosophy beyond California. The caravan went through the semirural mining towns of Globe, Miami, and Superior, Arizona, where the reception, according to local newspapers, ranged from cool to hostile. The Brown Beret version, as seen below, saw this effort as a glowing success.

La Caravana de la Reconquista is traveling, and is a tour and caravan of the Southwest, to unify an understanding that "ALL CHICANOS throughout the Southwest are being discriminated against," and because of this, we are traveling to spread the word "CHICANOS UNITE."

During our last expedition, "La March de la Reconquista," we marched from Calexico to Sacramento, Calif., of which we were the first to set foot on almost all of California. "Now Chicano Power will travel."

Ahora, we are coming to your barrio; we have traveled many miles to prove our sacrifice for CHICANO SIGNIFICANCE "*POR LOS NIÑOS SE VALE.*" We have come to Hollywood, Jolie Vill, and San Pasqual.

When we first started, our motorcade was somewhat small but it was uniformed, and for us it was like the last surviving arrow that was fired. Traveling over the desert the vehicles roared with the wind, and off into the distance, we could hear the cries of Chicano Power.

As we approached the outskirts of Phoenix, it happened. Ten police cars pulled us over. The police told us to get out of the cars with our hands up, so we did, for our lives were at stake with police shotguns pointed at our heads. After search and intensive questioning, we were finally released.

We went on to organize Phoenix, Arizona, for the day of the rally. There at the Chicano power rally, many people had come from the Phoenix barrios of El Compito, El Golden Gate, El Marcos, and Las Milpas.

The next town we traveled to was the copper mining town of Superior, Arizona, where hundreds of Raza are working in the dangerous shafts, which are down to 48,000 feet. The sheriff in Superior blamed the Caravana for a high school walkout that took place at Superior High School, so the sheriff called in 120 state troopers to remove the Brown Berets. But when they came, they could not find us. Later in the week, we had a rally of 400 Raza from Superior.

During the next few days we visited the Raza from Tempe, Ajo, and Eloy, Arizona. And as we began to enter into Tucson, Arizona, at that time we were approached by police cars and a helicopter escort.

Tucson is a city that is filled with beautiful Raza who live and practice Carnalismo. We were very happy to visit and study the good characteristics of the Tucson barrios of Anita, Sovaco, Hollywood, Jolie Vill, and San Pasqual.

Because we had no place to stay, we went to a park that had no name and we took it over for eight days to name it "Joaquín Murrieta." Under one of the tents, we built a monument, which we unveiled, and there it stands today with the inscription "Parque Joaquín Murrieta."

We then left Tucson and headed for Douglas, a border town next to Mexico. During our stay there, we paraded down the street, right behind another group that was the U.S. Army recruiting band. After several days, we were able to gain the support of the people by engaging a Chicano march and rally.

Once again we were on the highway, headed for New Mexico. We crossed the state line, and in the small hick town of Lordsburg, we were hauted and raided by the sheriffs along with the U.S. border patrol. After a long investigation of all of us, they took one of our soldados in for not having papers, and they took him to a concentration camp the immigration inspectors call detention camp.

After losing our first casualty, we went on to Silver City, New Mexico, and now we are on our way to your barrio.

From personal files of Christine Marín.

Formation of the Mexican American Youth Movement (MAYO)

In a recent interview, José Ángel Gutiérrez explained with hindsight, and perhaps less passion than was his style in the early movement, how the MAYO founders came together and how they questioned the old guard.

The unity points were that we all had the same analysis. And we had the same similar kind of experiences, whether we were urban or rural. We were all young; we were all very bright, so we sought each other out to be in solidarity with one another. It made us feel good to be together. We were against the church, we were against the war, we were against [LULAC], and we were against the G.I. Forum. We were against so many things that we wouldn't know quite what we were for. And only in that group setting could we begin to define what we were for. But we were very careful, being students; we wanted to engage in a lot of reading. We wanted to find out about the Black Panthers, find out about the Southern Christian Leadership Conference, of Martin Luther King and Abernathy and all those. Wanted to find out about Tijerina—we had begun hearing about him. I wanted to find out about César Chávez; he had come down and made some linkages with the people in the valley. So we embarked on a very tough and demanding reading schedule and visiting schedule. We actually drove to Atlanta and to Delano and to—well, at that time it was Cochella, it was not Delano. And to Tierra Amarilla and then later to Denver to the Crusade for Justice. And we went up to Chicago, because there were some people up in Chicago making noises. So we sought out these folks. And by March of '68, we decided to form our own organization, the Mexican American Youth Organization. And the rest is pretty much history.

From the beginning we wanted to be a statewide organization. We thought we were going to be an organization of organizers. We did not want to be a mass membership group. We did not want to have any kind of dues structure or card-carrying kind of thing. We wanted to be the antithesis of LULAC and G.I. Forum, and we wanted to be like PASSO in terms of emphasis on electoral politics and street actions and collective action. But we didn't want to be tied in to the institutions that they were tied into, such as organized labor and business interests. We wanted to be independent. All of us had come from different schools. I had come via University of Houston, Texas A&I, and Southwest Texas Junior College. Ernie Cortez was at the University of Texas at Austin. Willie had been in the schools there in San Antonio and then St. Mary's University, Catholic School. Nacho Pérez had been down to the Valley, had been over at Pan American University at Edinburgh and then schools in San Antonio. Mario was all westside barrio, the schools there. We all already knew people, so when we decided to launch MAYO, we just went back to those groups that we had dealt with and recruited them to be organizers within the organization. Now our actions first took place in San Antonio. We started off with school issues. Education was our main concern. And since we were a youth organization, we did walkouts, blowouts as they are known in California and other places, school walkouts in the Edgewood, San Antonio school districts. And the media picked this up and made a big deal about it. So very, very soon, very rapidly, there were other actions across the state in Kingsville, Del Rio, Uvalde, Raymondville. And of course the farm worker thing got going really big. The L.A. blowouts occurred in Denver and Kalamazoo, Michigan. So those movements were saying the same things. When we read in the press what the demands were of the students in those other places, they were identical to ours. So we knew that this was the sign of the times, this was the mood. So we accelerated our learning process and our visiting schedule to make linkages and establish ties with people. There was a group of *Pintos* who adopted our name immediately and our program, because we probably were the more militant early on. We certainly were the more militant in Texas. We may have been the more militant across the country, but I have no way of knowing. I do know that we were always looked to when we traveled to other places. MEChA was not in existence. It was UMAS and some other names back then. But I recall that our rhetoric and our goals were very attractive to the young people.

José Ángel Gutiérrez, interviewed by Jesús Treviño, January 27, 1992, NLCC, pp. 10-11.

MAYO Membership Requirements

From the outset, MAYO members in Texas remained more practical in their outlook on organizing and in meeting their goals than Chicanos in California, but their tactical approach always encompassed militancy, and they expected sacrifice from their members.

1. A sincere desire to help La Raza as well as oneself.
   a. When one progresses, not to forget one's fellow Chicano.
2. A basic knowledge of what the movement is about.
   a. Romantic people and people out for kicks or publicity are not helping any. This movement is serious business—not a game.
3. No qualms of being labeled militant, radical, or other names for fear of losing job, prestige, etc.
4. A desire to put La Raza first and foremost. Can't belong to other political groups or owe allegiance to other philosophies—Young Democrats, Republicans, communists, etc.
5. Believe that all Chicanos have every right as human beings and that they are not inferior to any race or nationality.
6. Courage to follow orders as well as give them. When ordered to attack directly, must do so and he who gives the orders must be ready to lead.
7. Believe in the unity of the Chicano, La Raza Unida—not criticize other Chicanos in public—all internal problems to be solved at meetings.
8. Owe allegiance to no man but to the idea of justice for all the Raza—no idols, saviors, super Chicanos.
9. Support all fellow MAYOs in time of crisis. Wherever there is trouble, everyone goes. All go to Del Rio, Kingsville, etc.
10. Age should be no factor—but must have an ability to think young.
11. An alert and open mind together with a closed mouth.
12. Knowledge of what one is saying, a desire to study, learn, and articulate.

MAYO document, no date, José Ángel Gutiérrez files, Crystal City, Texas, 1973, In Armando Navarro, *Mexican American Youth Organization: Avant Garde of the Chicano Movement* (Austin: University of Texas Press, 1995), p. 250.

Walkout Fever Spreads

The school walkouts spread to some of the most unlikely places, as in the case of Sierra Blanca, a small West Texas town where Anglos were accustomed to having their own way and where they rarely heard dissenting cries from the Mexican community.

Families engaged in a student boycott of the school in the small West Texas community of Sierra Blanca Friday, received support from the Social Action Commission of the Catholic Diocese of El Paso.

Nearly 100 children—more than half of the combined grade and high school enrollment—have remained home since April 25 in a dispute centered around the beating of two Mexican American students and lack of Mexican American representatives in the school system.

In announcing the commission's support for the boycotting families, Father Robert Getz, Diocesan Social Action director, said, "There are obvious indications of injustices in the treatment of individual students and in providing Mexican American families a voice in the conduct of their children's education."

Parents of two children who received severe spankings from school authorities within the past two months have sought to press charges of assault, but have been rebuffed by the Hudspeth County attorney, according to the Social Action Commission. And three teachers who aided in the election of Mexican American PTA officers in April have been notified they will not be rehired when the fall school term begins. In their boycott, the parents of the town's Mexican American students are asking:

1. That the teacher responsible for severely spanking a 16-year-old girl be fired;
2. That the three teachers in question be rehired;
3. That a Spanish-speaking person be named to a current vacancy on the school board.

School board officials have announced that students participating in the boycott will not receive passing grades for the current year, and they will not discuss the matter until the next regular school board.

In a report on the controversy, the Diocesan Social Action Commission noted that three men have been fired from their jobs because their children are taking part in the boycott.

The 21-member commission has taken the stand that "the decision of the parents to withdraw children from the school until it exercises its delegated responsibility of educating the children more in keeping with the desires of the parents is justified."

Eastside, June 10, 1968.

Walkouts in Crystal City

The Crystal City, Texas, school walkouts organized by MAYO in 1969-1970 precipitated other Chicano Movement activity in the Winter Garden District, such as the rise of La Raza Unida Party. Below are the demands that MAYO organizers and their local supporters, known as the Ciudadanos Unidos, wanted school administrators to concede before they would call off the strike and return to classes. The detailed set of demands required that the school board allow greater input from the Chicano community in order to insure, among other things, that students would be less subject to discrimination and that course content would reflect the needs of the Mexican American majority in Crystal City.

Walkout Demands

Walkout demands were that all elections concerning the school be conducted by the student body. Concerning class representatives, the petition asked that the qualifications such as personality, leadership, and grades be abolished. These factors do not determine whether the student is capable of representing the student body. The students are capable of voting for their own representatives. The representatives are representing the students, not the faculty. All nominating must be done by the student body, and the election should be decided by a majority vote.

The present method of electing most handsome, beautiful, most popular, and most representative is elected [sic] by the faculty. The method of cumulative voting is unfair.

National Honor Society—the grades of the students eligible must be posted on the bulletin board well in advance of selection. The teachers should not have anything to do with electing the students.

An advisory board of Mexican American citizens should be a part of the school administration in order to advise on the needs and problems of the Mexican American.

No other favorites should be authorized by school administrators or board members unless submitted to the student body in a referendum.

Teachers, administrators, and staff should be educated; they should know our language—Spanish—and understand the history, traditions, and contributions of Mexican culture. How can they expect to teach us if they do not know us? We want more Mexican American teachers for the above reason.

We want immediate steps taken to implement bilingual and bicultural education for Mexican Americans. We also want the schoolbooks revised to reflect the contributions of Mexicans and Mexican Americans to the U.S. society, and to make us aware of the injustices that we, Mexican Americans, as a people have suffered in an "Anglo"-dominant society. We want a Mexican American course with the value of one credit.

We want any member of the school system who displays prejudice or fails to recognize, understand, and appreciate us, Mexican Americans, our culture, or our heritage removed from Crystal City's schools. Teachers shall not call students any names.

Our classes should be smaller in size, say about twenty students to one teacher, to insure more effectiveness. We want parents from the community to be trained as teachers' aides. We want assurances that a teacher who may disagree politically or philosophically with administrators will not be dismissed or transferred because of it. Teachers should encourage students to study and should make class more interesting, so that students will look forward to going to class.

There should be a manager in charge of janitorial work and maintenance details, and the performance of such duties should be restricted to employees hired for that purpose. In other words, no more students doing janitorial work.

We want a free speech area plus the right to have speakers of our own.

We would like September 16 as a holiday, but if it is not possible, we would like an assembly with speakers of our own. We feel it is a great day in the history of the world because it is when Mexico had been under the Spanish rule for about three hundred years. The Mexicans were liberated from the harsh rule of Spain. Our ancestors fought in this war, and we owe them tribute because we are Mexicans, too.

Being civic-minded citizens, we want to know what the happenings are in our community. So, we request the right to have access to all types of literature and to be able to bring it on campus. The newspaper in our school does not carry sufficient information. It carries things like the gossip column, which is unnecessary.

The dress code should be abolished. We are entitled to wear what we want.

We request the buildings open to students at all times.

We want Mr. Harbin to resign as principal of Fly Jr. High.

We want a Mexican American counselor fully qualified in college opportunities.

We need more showers in the boys' and girls' dressing rooms.

MAYO document, José Ángel Gutiérrez files, Crystal City, Texas, 1973.

La Raza Unida in Colorado

Through intense organizing and by holding a series of conventions in 1970, the Crusade for Justice in Colorado built up a formidable La Raza Unida Party infrastructure. In the first two meetings, the party nominated candidates for state-level races. The last parley was held in June of 1970 in Alamosa to hammer out the final platform; some 1,000 participants attended. For the most part Rodolfo "Corky" Gonzales' strategy at these meetings consisted of little more than vague promises of self-determination and nationalism, as the party platform reprinted below indicates.

Colorado Platform
La Raza Unida Party

HOUSING: To implement and/or utilize those resources now available and to strive for those resources necessary to accomplish adequate housing for La Raza.

We further resolve to utilize the necessary resources to plan our living accommodations so that it is possible to extend family homes to be situated in a communal style . . . around plazas or parks with plenty of space for the children. We want our living areas to fit the needs of the family and cultural protections, and not the needs of the city pork barrel, the building corporations, or architects.

EDUCATION: We resolve that schools be warm and inviting facilities and not similar to jails in any way. Also, that the Bill of Rights, i.e., the First Amendment be adhered to by the State Board of Education.

We also resolve a completely free education for kindergarten to college with no fees, no lunch charges, no supplies charges, no tuition, no dues.

We resolve that all teachers live within walking distance of the schools. We demand that from kindergarten through college, Spanish be the first language and English the second language and the textbooks be rewritten to emphasize the heritage and contributions of the Mexican-American or Indio-Hispano in the building of the Southwest. We also demand the teaching of the contributions and history of other minorities, which have also helped build this country. We also feel that each neighborhood school complex should have its own school board made up of members who live in the community the school serves.

ECONOMIC OPPORTUNITIES: We resolve that the businesses serving our community be owned by that community. Seed money is required to start cooperative grocery stores, gas stations, furniture stores, etc. Instead of our people working in big factories across the city, we want training and low interest loans to set up small industries in our communities. These industries would be co-ops with the profits staying in the community.

AGRICULTURAL REFORMS: We resolve that not only the land which is our ancestral right be given back to those pueblos but that restitution be given for mineral, natural resources, grazing, and timber used.

REDISTRIBUTION OF THE WEALTH: That all citizens of this country share in the wealth of this nation by institution of economic reforms that would provide for all people and that welfare in this form of subsidies in taxes and payoffs to corporate owners be reverted to the people who in reality are the foundation of the economy and the tax base for this society.

WAR IN VIETNAM: We resolve that:

(1) Draft boards be representative of the population.
(2) That members of the draft boards be thirty-five (35) years or younger and that these draft boards be appointed every four years concurrent with the election for Governor.
(3) That this war is unjust and only a form of genocide that has been used against La Raza to eliminate our natural resource—our youth! (9,000 deaths, 20 percent of the war deaths, 47,000 total killed.) The government's war machine has used the concepts of "Machismo" against La Raza and has succeeded in making La Raza one of the most decorated if not the most decorated minority in the country.
(4) We resolve and do condemn the war in Southeast Asia. This undeclared police action that has expanded into this present war situation is unjust and has been unjust in its conception.

June 20, 1970. Alamosa, Colorado.

Adopted at the third nominating convention of La Raza Unida Party.

Christine Marín, *A Spokesman of the Mexican American Movement: Rodolfo "Corky" Gonzales and the Fight for Chicano Liberation, 1966-1972* (San Francisco: R and E Research Associates, 1977), p. 38.

Chicanas and La Raza Unida Party

Martha Cotera, a La Raza Unida Party leader, remembered the many attempts to relegate women to a secondary position in the *movimiento*. Cotera organized Chicana feminist meetings in Houston during 1971 and 1972 that started an initiative that placed Chicanas in the forefront of today's international feminist movement. At these meetings a party platform for Chicanas was drafted and became part of Ramsey Muñiz's campaign for governor of Texas.

Crystal City is a good focus because there, like in other situations in the walkout, it took the support of the family, it took the support of the women, not only cooking, speaking, encouraging the children to come out and support the walkout and they in turn being supported, but supporting them before the school board. From the very beginning it was very natural that women were involved in the movement. Then they formed Ciudadanos Unidos in Crystal City. The people that took the role in Ciudadanos Unidos were men and women. The men were predominant because they had elected positions. . . but the women were there. I think what happens is that very often the women are very willing to do the work and they don't mind having a secondary role; they don't mind not having the elected and appointed positions. Bringing the women to greater awareness, in Crystal City itself was not something we had to do against the wishes of the men; it was something we had to do, in a way, against the wishes of the women. In other words, they didn't mind working, and they didn't mind being the ones to do a lot of the organizing and picketing and later being supportive. They didn't particularly want to run for office. So we had to do campaign workshops, political workshops that were consciousness-raising workshops. We organized a group of Mujeres Pro Raza Unida and a lot of people think that we developed a group because we were not getting recognition from the men. As a matter of fact, we developed a group to get more of the women to be aware that they needed to assume a political position. They were running out of men to run in Crystal City. There were some men that were left over, but they were working for Del Monte and places where they couldn't run. That's a little turnaround on what most people think . . . even men in Raza Unida are unaware that Mujeres Pro Raza Unida was to agitate the women and to raise their consciousness towards political participation and feminism. Not because they were not getting a chance at Raza Unida politics, but because there was so much to do and so much opportunity. Everybody had a chance that wanted to do something. These guys might sit around talking and think that we're running the whole show, but they weren't, when it comes right down to it; they were the least important people, dare I say that. The important people were the organizers, and the organizers were very often women. But they were not necessarily the ones running for office, and we needed them to run for office. We needed them because very often they had jobs that weren't threatened or they had no jobs. So they weren't threatened economically. They weren't vulnerable. Also we needed them because their sensitivity was real important to the organizing and development of the community. We needed them in the process; we needed their intellect and sensitivity; they were cornerstones of the family. We needed them not only physically involved, but also mentally engaged and involved and spiritually involved. Mujeres Pro Raza Unida worked for that purpose.

When it became a political issue was at the Houston Conference, not a party conference, but it was a Houston Raza Unida movement conference, I guess in 1970, maybe '71, when the party was already being organized. The party was getting organized before the actual convention. One thing that did annoy us in the movement conferences, as opposed to the party conferences, was that the movement conferences tended to be more sexist, tended to be more exclusive of women. We had a big Chicano conference in Houston; we had had one in Austin in 1970. We had a lot to do with the planning of it, and so it didn't turn out to be as bad. We had more women workshop leaders bringing their issues to the floor. And we weren't interested in the development of women just for leadership sake or legal struggle; we were interested in the input from women. And if we weren't there, they weren't getting that input—this was the Austin conference. The big thing there was that we did not have as many women participants as we wanted. So we spoke publicly about that: the need to include and involve more women in day-to-day activities of the total movement, whether it be farmworker or upholstery strike work or school organizing, that we needed that involvement. We put out a call to women to bring other friends and men to bring other women.

In Houston, we had a conference in the spring, and we had Doña María Hernández do one of the keynote addresses. We had a problem with the Houston conference because, for example, the arts conference didn't include Carmen Norma Garza as one of the presenters; she was definitely someone that we considered an up-and-coming artist, but they didn't include her. The housing . . . there was general exclusion of women, so we were very upset. We drew up a series of demands that we were presenting publicly. But before we did that, we had María Hernández come up to the podium as a speaker. She was an elderly lady; we loved her very much—the women adored her. She was a strong role model, a reformer from the '30s. Very politically involved, very radical. She came up to speak and some young punk screams, "Who wants to hear this lady? Anybody that wants to hear women, stand up or sit down". . . something like that. Made us really mad. So then we decided to take our petition to the podium. We had been drafting this petition along with other women. Everybody was very shy, and they pushed me onto the stage and this is the way a lot of leaders are made. When you get literally pushed out on the stage, you're not ready for it necessarily. That is when we started our demands. We felt that it was important for women to be involved in the movement overall for input and role modeling. Role modeling came in because of what they did to Doña María. She was our role model. She was important to us. I'm sorry that I cannot relate to José Ángel as a role model. I admire him a lot, but he didn't show me that women could do it and could stay committed and involved like Doña María.

What we felt in Houston is our awareness was there. It was not important for us to be on stage, but it was important for us to have our sensitivities and our needs for our family demonstrated, and evident, and taken care . . . that was what was important. And it was evident to us that as long as we had male workshop leaders, we were not going to get these needs met. We needed to start working on this awareness; not everybody felt the way we felt. We were just assuming that everybody knew that it was proper and right and critical for us to participate. We all assumed that everybody knew that it was important for the movement to include everybody's point of view and everybody's needs. But

392

this was not obvious from the feedback we were getting back from the audience, especially from the men, and even some of the women, not at that particular situation. But these guys were not aware of these two very important factors. And if they were not aware, then we, as a movement, needed to address those two issues.

The movement was for everybody, and everybody's input was important. To me that's what feminism is, no more and no less. That is when I decided that if people obviously did not know the history that I knew, that it was important to get that history out for men and for women to be aware that . . . oh, from the start, go home and do the dishes, and that is what you should be doing, and to do this is to be "*agringada.*" That came out right then and there. At the previous conference in Austin in 1970, there was a call for a Raza Unida conference, not a party conference. The same issue came out, that for women to participate to this level was to be *agringadas.* I felt that this was extremely dangerous, because I felt that we had a stronger history of participation than just about any women in the world. And certainly we had stronger women in the younger women. In our history as *mestizas.* I grew up with women's history. In Houston, I said, I've got to document. Obviously, not everybody has the same historical base or historical knowledge, so we have to document. That's when I started documenting.

Martha Cotera, *Profile on the Mexican American Woman* (Austin: National Laboratory Publishers, 1976), pp. 232-236.

The August 29th Movement

Socialist thinking also affected the Chicano Movement. The Socialist Workers Party and the Communist Labor Party had Chicano members who pursued Chicano issues. The Centro de Acción Social Autónoma-Hermandad General de Trabajadores (CASA-HGT Center for Autonomous Social Action-General Brotherhood of Workers) and the August 29th Movement (ATM), both founded in California and made up primarily of Chicanos, attempted to instill radical consciousness among Mexican Americans by launching an effort to push the Chicano Movement away from reformist goals. Reproduced below is an excerpt from an ATM pamphlet. The piece spells out how the group differed from the nationalist Chicano Movement organizations.

History of the August 29th Movement
(Marxist-Leninist)

The August 29th Movement (Marxist-Leninist), a multinational communist organization, had its roots in the movement of oppressed nationalities, especially the Chicano nationality, and in the working-class movement. The August 29th Movement (M-L) was named after the great anti-imperialist march and demonstration—the Chicano Moratorium Against the Vietnam War—which was held in Los Angeles, California, on August 29, 1970. For several years ATM issued a monthly political newspaper called *Revolutionary Cause*, which disseminated Marxism-Leninism to many people throughout the country. This newspaper was published in both English and Spanish. ATM has provided leadership to many different mass struggles throughout its history. ATM has carried out a continuing struggle against all forms of opportunism and has helped in the development of a correct Marxist-Leninist line for our movement.

ATM's history shows a steady development forward, although there have been many twists and turns. ATM was born in revolutionary struggle, and has made many contributions to that struggle.

ATM was originally the product of the merger of the August 29th Collective of Los Angeles, California; the East Bay Labor Collective of Oakland, California; La Raza Workers Collective of San Francisco; and a collective from Albuquerque, New Mexico. All of the collectives had their origins in the Chicano national movement or in the struggle of Latino people against their oppression.

A common thread which ran through the history of each group was their resolute struggle against the state and against the line of reformism and revisionism in the national movements. While none of these collectives began any systematic study of Marxism-Leninism until 1973 and their overall grasp of Marxism-Leninism was not very deep, they understood that the system of imperialism was at the root of the misery of the Chicano and Latino peoples and of all working and oppressed peoples. They knew that it had to be overthrown.

This placed them in direct opposition to the revisionists who preached "peaceful transition" and the reform of imperialism as a solution to national oppression. This also brought them up against the Trotskyites who opposed the national struggle and tried to split and wreck the growing unity of the national movement.

The collectives were very active in Chicano and Latino community work, in some workplace organizing, and in work among Chicano and Latino students. La Raza Workers Collective had developed mostly out of the struggle to free the seven Latino political prisoners from San Francisco's Mission District known as Los Siete de La Raza. This struggle attracted the support of many thousands of people and helped develop many revolutionary leaders for the movement.

La Raza Workers Collective

Los Siete organization was the predecessor of La Raza Workers Collective. It organized mass actions involving thousands, and developed *BASTA YA*, an anti-imperialist newspaper which grew to a circulation of several thousand per month. They struggled for a line of revolutionary struggle against the reformists and for internationalism in the face of the narrow nationalists and cultural nationalists. They developed a close working relationship with the Black Panther Party in its revolutionary period, with the Young Lords Party, with the Brown Berets, with the Red Guards, and with revolutionary whites as well. When the most advanced elements from among Los Siete organization formed La Raza Workers Collective, they took up active organizing efforts in the workplace. They helped to provide sound political leadership to struggles in the Laborer's Union and to a strike of Latino garbage workers, as well as to other struggles. This collective also participated in the antiwar movement and opposed the stand and role of the Trotskyites and revisionists. The Collective supported the 7 Point Peace Plan of the Vietnamese and opposed the Trotskyites, revisionists, and opportunists who refused to support the plan. The Collective was active in building support for the historic Farah strike of mainly Chicana women garment workers and in struggling against the national chauvinist line of the Revolutionary Union within that struggle.

August 29th Collective

The August 29th Collective traces its roots partly to the Brown Berets. The Berets, formed along the lines of the Black Panther Party, involved many hundreds of working-class Chicano youth from throughout California, the Southwest, and other parts of the country. The Berets stood for building revolutionary struggle against national oppression. It fought the reformists who tried to misdirect the movement into the lap of the Democratic Party, and it rejected the line of peaceful transition to socialism pushed by the revisionist CPUSA.

The Berets initially developed in East Los Angeles, in response to the national oppression faced by Chicano youth in the schools, and against the police brutality directed against the masses of Chicanos. It developed numerous "serve the people programs" and gave consistent support to the organizing struggle of the United Farm Workers of America. It helped to organize school walkouts, and built a mass movement to help free Ricardo Chávez Ortíz and other Chicano political prisoners.

The Brown Berets did not have a clear anti-imperialist line and were also plagued by a tendency toward militarism and adventurism. The most revolutionary elements in the Brown Berets waged a struggle against the narrow nationalists who rejected all alliances with other nationalities and who saw all white people as the enemy. Eventually the narrow nationalists launched an open attack against the revolutionary elements, and against Marxism-Leninism, which they condemned as a "white thing." This was aimed at isolating the class-conscious elements in the Berets. The revolutionary elements had helped to lead the Berets in its most revolutionary period, in great mass struggles and in mass confrontations with the state. They eventually left the Berets to form or join other revolutionary organizations, and this was to lead to the eventual decline of the Berets as a revolutionary organization.

Some of them helped to form the Labor Committee of La Raza Unida Party, which was to eventually become the August 29th Collective. In 1973, the collective helped to organize a walkout by the workers of ten furniture manufacturing plants in Los Angeles in opposition to the Nixon Wage Board and against the war in Vietnam. This walkout was organized in opposition to the most reactionary trade union bureaucrats of the Furniture Workers Union, local 500, and helped to expose them as social props to many of the workers. This walkout of mostly Chicano workers set a militant example for the Chicano national movement and was also a high point in the workers' struggle in Los Angeles. It provided inspiration to many Marxist-Leninists carrying out factory organizing, who by and large lacked any such experience in their labor work.

The ATM Collective also developed a Congreso Obrero in Los Angeles in 1973— a mass organization of Mexicano and Chicano workers set up for the purpose of helping to train them to organize on the job, to fight national oppression, and to study Marxism-Leninism. During this same period, the Collective also developed a Congreso Estudiantil which had the same purpose—to help train Chicano students to be organizers and to teach them Marxism-Leninism.

East Bay Labor Collective

The East Bay Labor Collective was formed in 1973 and developed mainly out of La Raza Unida Party. It did active work in building support for the Farah strike, helped build support for antiwar efforts, and did workplace organizing. In La Raza Unida Party, it consistently opposed the reformists who tried to turn the local chapters into election machines or into harmless social clubs which relied on legal struggle to fight national oppression. The revolutionary elements who later helped form the East Bay Labor Collective opposed these incorrect views, and fought to turn La Raza Unida Party into an organization of mass struggle.

Perhaps the most significant workplace struggle involving the East Bay Labor Collective was the Dasco strike of 1974. In the course of this strike, the East Bay Labor Collective had to wage a sharp struggle against the economist trade union line of the Revolutionary Union, which opposed bringing revolutionary politics to the workers, and instead preached militant reformism. The East Bay Labor Collective also opposed the chauvinism of the RU in this struggle, which denied the vicious national oppression faced by predominantly Latino and Asian Dasco workers. The strike involved hundreds of workers, and began in response to the firing of a member of the East Bay Labor Collective who was a shop steward at Dasco.

From the beginning, the East Bay Labor Collective struggled to expose the social props in leadership of the union, who opposed the strike, tried to sabotage it, and tried to work out a "deal" with the company. The East Bay Labor Collective promoted the equality of languages by making sure that all meetings, leaflets, etc. were translated into Spanish, and, with the help of the IWK, into Chinese as well.

The strike was very militant and lasted several weeks, in opposition to a united front of the bosses, the trade union bureaucrats, and the state, which quickly issued an injunction against the strikers. The strikers defended their picket line against scabs and against a team of hired thugs brought in by the company.

The East Bay Labor Collective also did work in the International Longshoreman and Warehouseman's Union, where they also had to struggle against the CPUSA and the RU, and in the Molders Union, where they once again had to take on the CPUSA. The East Bay Labor Collective also did work within the United Farm Workers in California. The East Bay Labor Collective helped to organize in the fields, and helped build support among the farmworkers for the struggle of the Vietnamese people against U.S. imperialism. It promoted support for the People's Republic of China and organized anti-imperialist educational programs among the farmworkers. It also distributed Marxist-Leninist literature to the advanced farmworkers.

Once more, it had to oppose the economist and chauvinist line of the RU. This struggle led the East Bay Labor Collective to pull out of work on a local RU "workers" paper because the RU refused to allow the paper to carry consistent articles on struggles going on within the Chicano national movement. The RU opposed this with their so-called "workers" line, which pitted the interests of the working-class movement against those of the national movements. Through their work, the East Bay Labor Collective was able to expose the opportunism of the RU to a significant section of the farmworkers in Salinas, California. The East Bay Labor Collective also waged a bitter struggle against the reformism of César Chávez, and opposed his class collaborationist line with a line of revolutionary class struggle.

Albuquerque Collective

The Albuquerque Collective was the youngest and most inexperienced of the four groups which came to make up the ATM. This collective formed mainly for the purpose of studying Marxism-Leninism. However, they were also active in helping to build support for the Farah strike, in La Raza Unida Party, and among Chicano students at the University of New Mexico. They had also done a small amount of labor work. Some of their members were active in support of a struggle involving custodial and service workers at the University, and mobilized support on their behalf. Due mostly to their inexperience, the collective made a number of sectarian errors in this struggle, in trying to combat certain reformist ideas among the workers.

The Struggle in La Raza Unida Party

The work of the Collectives in La Raza Unida Party (LRUP), particularly that of the ATM Collective, the East Bay Labor Collective, and, to a lesser extent, La Raza Workers Collective, was very significant. The LRUP was an organization which at one time had thousands of people in its ranks and many thousands of sympathizers in California, the Southwest, and in other parts of the U.S. To many Chicanos and Mexicanos, it offered the only alternative to the capitalists' political parties and to the revisionist CPUSA. The LRUP was mainly formed by elements from the Chicano petty bourgeoisie and intelligentsia, but had many working people in its ranks. It was formed to help combat the national oppression faced by Chicanos on the job, in the communities, in the schools, and other places, and it was meant to provide a militant voice of protest against that oppression.

In its early days LRUP had many reformists, narrow nationalists, and Trotskyites in positions of leadership, particularly in California and Texas. But from the beginning, the revolutionary elements in the Partido waged a consistent struggle against the efforts of the opportunist forces to make the LRUP an appendage of the Democratic or Republican parties, with a focus only on electoral politics or on the most narrow forms of legal protest. The advanced elements of LRUP, many of whom were to become Marxist-Leninists, fought to make the Partido an organization of militant mass struggle, to adopt an internationalist perspective, and to oppose imperialism resolutely.

The struggle eventually crystallized at the historic national conventions of the LRUP held in 1972 and 1973 in El Paso, Texas, and in Albuquerque, New Mexico. Over 2000 people attended the El Paso conference, during which the revolutionary forces were able to unite the vast majority of people from all parts of the country who had come to the conference, to oppose the program of José Ángel Gutiérrez of Texas. Gutiérrez wanted to make the LRUP a voting "pressure" block to wring concessions from the Democrats or Republicans. His basic message was this: work within the system, use the ballot to achieve liberation, and gradually Chicanos will gain full equality if they can provide votes for the capitalist parties.

Opposed to this was the line of the revolutionaries, which said that the enemy of the Chicano people was U.S. imperialism, that Chicanos must wage revolutionary struggle against it, and that they could never expect equality under this system. They said that the Chicano people could never gain liberation through the vote, but that LRUP needed to mobilize and organize the people to wage a militant struggle against imperialism. While the revolutionaries recognized that elections could be used tactically, they warned against reliance on this tactic to try to achieve an end to national oppression. These questions were hotly debated by the masses at the conference for several days.

Finally the program of the reformists was soundly defeated. The LRUP had taken a step onto the path of anti-imperialist revolutionary struggle. This was confirmed at the Albuquerque Conference, when LRUP delegates from throughout the Southwest and California adopted an anti-imperialist program which called for self-determination for Chicano and all oppressed peoples, support for the struggle of the Vietnamese people against U.S. imperialism, return of the lands stolen from Chicanos in the Southwest. The program made clear that national and class oppression would continue until the "existing economic and political system" was overthrown.

The Marxist-Leninists who helped develop this program and led the struggle for it were mostly from the collectives which later formed ATM. They represented the most advanced elements from among the Chicano people, and they helped to imbue LRUP with a revolutionary and internationalist spirit. They also helped various chapters to orient more of their work toward working-class Chicanos and Mexicanos. This took the form of workplace organizing and strike support work, as well as other forms.

Statement on the Founding of the League of Revolutionary Struggle (Getting Together Publications, 1978), pp. 77-87.

Bilingual Education and MALDEF

In the 1970s, bilingual education efforts suffered setbacks when a federal judge in Denver decided in *Keyes v. School District Number One,* a case being litigated by MALDEF, that putting children in bilingual classes violated antisegregation laws. In 1974, in the *Lau v. Nichols* case, the Supreme Court ordered federally funded school districts to "take affirmative steps to rectify the language deficiency [of minority students who did not know English] in order to open its instructional program to these students." While the ruling was made as a result of an Asian American initiative in San Francisco, this decision provided MALDEF with a rationale for pursuing bilingual education efforts after the defeat in Denver. The Lau decision is reprinted below.

LAU v. NICHOLS
LAU ET AL. v. NICHOLS ET AL.
CERTIORARI TO THE UNITED STATES COURT OF APPEALS FOR THE NINTH CIRCUIT

No. 72-6520. Argued December 10, 1973—Decided January 21, 1974

The failure of the San Francisco school system to provide English language instruction to approximately 1,800 students of Chinese ancestry who do not speak English, or to provide them with other adequate instructional procedures, denies them a meaningful opportunity to participate in the public educational program and thus violates § 601 of the Civil Rights Act of 1964, which bans discrimination based "on the ground of race, color, or national origin," in "any program or activity receiving Federal financial assistance," and the implementing regulations of the Department of Health, Education, and Welfare. Pp. 565-569. 483 F. 2d 791, reversed and remanded.

DOUGLAS, J., delivered the opinion of the Court, in which BRENNAN, MARSHALL, POWELL, and REHNQUIST, JJ., joined. STEWART, J., filed an opinion concurring in the result, in which BURGER, C. J., and BLACKMUN, J., joined, *post*, p. 569. WHITE, J., concurred in the result. BLACKMUN, J., filed an opinion concurring in the result, in which BURGER, C. J., joined, *post*, p. 571.

Edward H. Steinman argued the cause for petitioners. With him on the briefs were *Kenneth Hecht* and *David C. Moon.*

Thomas M. O'Connor argued the cause for respondents. With him on the brief were *George E. Krueger* and *Burk E. Delventhal.*

Assistant Attorney General Pottinger argued the cause for the United States as *amicus curiae* urging reversal. With him on the brief were *Solicitor General Bork, Deputy Solicitor General Wallace, Mark L. Evans*, and *Brian K. Landsberg.*

MR. JUSTICE DOUGLAS delivered the opinion of the Court.

The San Francisco, California, school system was integrated in 1971 as a result of a federal court decree, 339 F. Supp. 1315. See *Lee v. Johnson*, 404 U. S. 1215. The District Court found that there are 2,856 students of Chinese ancestry in the school system who do not speak English. Of those who have that language deficiency, about 1,000 are given supplemental courses in the English language. About 1,800, however, do not receive that instruction.

This class suit brought by non-English-speaking Chinese students against officials responsible for the operation of the San Francisco Unified School District seeks relief against the unequal educational opportunities, which are alleged to violate, *inter alia*, the Fourteenth Amendment. No specific remedy is urged upon us. Teaching English to the students of Chinese ancestry who do not speak the language is one choice. Giving instructions to this group in Chinese is another. There may be others. Petitioners ask only that the Board of Education be directed to apply its expertise to the problem and rectify the situation.

The District Court denied relief. The Court of Appeals affirmed, holding that there was no violation of the Equal Protection Clause of the Fourteenth Amendment or of § 601 of the Civil Rights Act of 1964. 78 Stat. 252, 42 U. S. C. § 2000d, which exclude from participation in federal financial assistance, recipients of aid which discriminate against racial groups. 483 F. 2d 791. One judge dissented. A hearing en banc was denied, two judges dissenting. *Id.,* at 805.

We granted the petition for certiorari because of the public importance of the question presented, 412 U. S. 938.

The Court of Appeals reasoned that "[e]very student brings to the starting line of his educational career different advantages and disadvantages caused in part by social, economic and cultural background, created and continued completely apart from any contribution by the school system," 483 F. 2d, at 797. Yet in our view the case may not be so easily decided. This is a public school system of California and § 71 of the California Education Code states that "English shall be the basic language of instruction in all schools." That section permits a school district to determine "when and under what circumstances instruction may be given bilingually." That section also states as "the policy of the state" to insure "the mastery of English by all pupils in the schools." And bilingual instruction is authorized "to the extent that it does not interfere with the systematic, sequential, and regular instruction of all pupils in the English language."

Moreover, § 8573 of the Education Code provides that no pupil shall receive a diploma of graduation from grade 12 who has not met the standards of proficiency in "English," as well as other prescribed subjects. Moreover, by § 12101 of the Education Code (Supp. 1973) children between the ages of six and 16 years are (with exceptions not material here) "subject to compulsory full-time education."

Under these state-imposed standards there is no equality of treatment merely by providing students with the same facilities, textbooks, teachers, and curriculum, for students who do not understand English are effectively foreclosed from any meaningful education.

Basic English skills are at the very core of what these public schools teach. Imposition of a requirement that, before a child can effectively participate in the educational program, he must already have acquired those basic skills is to make a mockery of public education. We know that those who do not understand English are certain to find their classroom experiences wholly incomprehensible and in no way meaningful.

We do not reach the Equal Protection Clause argument which has been advanced but rely solely on § 601 of the Civil Rights Act of 1964, 42 U. S. C. § 2000d, to reverse the Court of Appeals.

That section bans discrimination based "on the ground of race, color, or national origin," in "any program or activity receiving Federal financial assistance." The school district involved in this litigation receives large amounts of federal financial assistance. The Department of Health, Education, and Welfare (HEW), which has authority to promulgate regulations prohibiting discrimination in federally assisted school systems, 42 U. S. C. § 2000d-1, in 1968 issued one guideline that "[s]chool systems are responsible for assuring that students of a particular race, color, or national origin are not denied the opportunity to obtain the education generally obtained by other students in the system." 33 Fed. Reg. 4956. In 1970 HEW made the guidelines more specific, requiring school districts that were federally funded "to rectify the language deficiency in order to open" the instruction to students who had "linguistic deficiencies." 35 Fed. Reg. 11595.

By § 602 of the Act, HEW is authorized to issue rules, regulations, and orders to make sure that recipients of federal aid under its jurisdiction conduct any federally financed projects consistently with § 601. HEW's regulations, 45 CFR § 80.3 (b) (1), specify that the recipients may not

"(ii) Provide any service, financial aid, or other benefit to an individual which is different, or is provided in a different manner, from that provided to others under the program;

"(iv) Restrict an individual in any way in the enjoyment of any advantage or privilege enjoyed by others receiving any service, financial aid, or other benefit under the program."

Discrimination among students on account of race or national origin that is prohibited includes "discrimination. . .in the availability or use of any academic. . .or other facilities of the grantee or other recipient." *Id.,* § 80.5 (b).

Discrimination is barred which has that *effect* even though no purposeful design is present: a recipient "may not. . .utilize criteria or methods of administration which have the effect of subjecting individuals to discrimination" or have "the effect of defeating or substantially impairing accomplishment of the objectives of the program as respect individuals of a particular race, color, or national origin." *Id.,* § 80.3 (b) (2).

It seems obvious that the Chinese-speaking minority receive fewer benefits than the English-speaking majority from respondents' school system which denies them a meaningful opportunity to participate in the educational program—all earmarks of the discrimination banned by the regulations. In 1970 HEW issued clarifying guidelines, 35 Fed. Reg. 11595, which include the following:

"Where inability to speak and understand the English language excludes national origin-minority group children from effective participation in the educational program offered by a school district, the district must take affirmative steps to rectify the language deficiency in order to open its instructional program to these students."

"Any ability grouping or tracking system employed by the school system to deal with the special language skill needs of national origin-minority group children must be designed to meet such language skill needs as soon as possible and must not operate as an educational deadend or permanent track."

Respondent school district contractually agreed to "comply with title VI of the Civil Rights Act of 1964 . . . and all requirements imposed by or pursuant to the Regulation" of HEW (45 CFR pt. 80) which are "issued pursuant to that title . . ." and also immediately to "take any measures necessary to effectuate this agreement." The Federal Government has power to fix the terms on which its money allotments to the States shall be disbursed. *Oklahoma* v. *CSC*, 330 U. S. 127, 142-143. Whatever may be the limits of that power, *Steward Machine Co.* v. *Davis*, 301 U. S. 548, 590 *et seq.*, they have not been reached here. Senator Humphrey, during the floor debates on the Civil Rights Act of 1964, said:

"Simple justice requires that public funds, to which all taxpayers of all races contribute, not be spent in any fashion which encourages, entrenches, subsidizes, or results in racial discrimination."

We accordingly reverse the judgment of the Court of Appeals and remand the case for the fashioning of appropriate relief.

Reversed and remanded.

Lau v. Nichols, 414 U.S. 563 (1974).

LULAC Veers to the Left

By the 1980s, the strident line of political action and protest that came out of the Chicano Movement became internalized in LULAC—truly a dialectical synthesis between Mexican Americanism and *Chicanismo*. In the article below, LULAC officials take on the issues of social justice and make a plaintive plea for understanding the plight of Mexican undocumented workers at a time when "illegal" immigration began to attract negative attention among the general public. The first document was issued on July 1, 1982, by Tony Bonilla, LULAC president during that year, and the second was issued on May 18, 1983, by Arnold Torres, who succeeded Bonilla as president.

"The initial fears we had regarding the election of President Ronald Reagan have been fully realized during his 1½-year reign. It is clear that America has been enticed and entered the *AGE OF SELF-INDULGENCE*. The *AGE OF SELF-INDULGENCE*, which has come to mean that individual selfish interests prevail over the general welfare of society so emphasized by the U.S. Constitution"—so stated Tony Bonilla, National President of the League of United Latin American Citizens (LULAC) in opening the 53rd National LULAC Convention in San Antonio. "This self-indulgence is best manifested by the continued priority given to insuring 'welfare for the rich' and 'competition for the poor.'" The rich American need not share any burdens but rather is provided additional federal government perks which encourage an indulgence in extravagance. The poor on the other hand are fiercely pitted against one another for basic and ever dwindling necessities, to simply make life a tolerable existence," added Bonilla and offered, "This President makes no apologies to the 10.4 million Americans unemployed while further increasing their disenfranchisement."

The theme of the 53rd LULAC National Convention, *Economic and Political Power: Road to Freedom*, has been designed to orient the Hispanic community to the major challenges confronting us, while emphasizing that economic independence and political involvement are the major ingredients to realizing our rights as American citizens. Bonilla emphasized, "No longer must we only refer to our phenomenal growth as potential political power but we must insure that we fully maximize this growth in the marketplace and at the ballot box. The sheer growth cannot and will not bring about the change and integration needed by our community. We must organize and plan such growth to fully recognize and exert its strength." Therefore, LULAC proposes:

- Development of citizenship/bilingual education programs at local levels;
- Formalized network of voter registration programs;
- Creation of Political Action Committee (PAC);
- Private sector initiatives to establish long-needed linkage;
- Development of consumer assessment programs; and
- Ongoing analysis and advocacy of U.S. economic policy.

With regard to President Reagan's press conference of yesterday, he stated, "It would be unlikely to think that I would walk away from an unfinished job." Bonilla responded, "With all due respect to the highest office of this country at this time based on Mr. Reagan's tenure, I am hopeful he has no intentions of finishing the disastrous and ever-worsening economic program he has embarked upon." Bonilla further stated that the President continues to present falsehoods to the American public when discussing his economic program and its success. In today's *Wall Street Journal* it appears that America's corporate structure will not be the entity which will lead us out of recession, but rather they contend it must be the consumer. Bonilla stated, "Despite the beginning of today's 10 percent tax cut program, it seriously appears that consumers and the economy are not willing to take any further chances with the economic ideas of President Reagan. Despite the continued statements by this Administration that the end of this recession is near, they appear to be reading foreign newspapers of a foreign tongue, which only they appear to understand, for there is very little, if any, evidence that this economic program will ever bear any fruits except for the very rich."

LULAC is especially concerned with the plight of the Hispanic economic picture in view of the fact that the average Hispanic family size is 3.94 persons and their median family income is $14,700.00. The poverty level income is $9,300.00 and 28.4 percent Hispanics survive at or below the poverty level as opposed to the national level of 11.6 percent. 2.9 million Hispanics live in poverty in all its aspects. The government states that an urban family of four needs an income of at least $20,500.00 to provide for costs of living. So the average Hispanic family is $5,400.00 above poverty level and $5,800.00 below the level needed for costs of living.

* * *

OFFICE OF: Arnold Torres   DATE: May 18, 1983

Anticipating passage of S. 529—Immigration Reform and Control Act of 1983 by the Senate today, May 18, 1983, Arnold Torres, National Executive Director of the League of United Latin American Citizens (LULAC), this country's oldest and largest Hispanic organization, stated, "The Senate has chosen to support poor and clearly discriminatory legislation, and has failed to comprehend the complex reasons for population movements. It has made a conscious decision to apply quick-fix approaches to problems which have developed over decades, and to which this country has contributed." Torres was referring to the long-established practice of the United States to encourage and stimulate flows of undocumented workers to provide cheap labor to the U.S. economy since the 1900s, and to the consequences of a foreign policy in the Western hemisphere which has been instrumental in creating many of the push factors which now result in major flows of people to the United States.

Torres believes that the legislation in its final form will do very little to seriously decrease the flow of undocumented persons to the U.S. while presenting major government-sanctioned discrimination and exploitation. He stated, "The Senate failed once again to provide any protections or redress for employment discrimination. We recognize that this bill is to discriminate against undocumented workers, but the Senate has chosen to discriminate against all persons with certain physical and linguistic characteristics." Torres was extremely concerned with the inclusion of a transitional temporary worker's program, which contradicts the interest of stymieing the flow of undocumented workers. Torres said, "This country continues to want cheap labor at any cost, and if they are Hispanic, there is no need to protect their rights as human beings and workers. The Senate has contradicted itself by satisfying the insatiable appetite of the agricultural industry for cheap Mexican labor. They have shown that exceptions can be made."

In closing, Torres emphasized that LULAC and the Hispanic community has not, and will not, advocate that nothing be done to address the immigration issue. However, it cannot be part of a legislative effort, which is shortsighted and discriminatory. "S. 529 is not immigration reform, is not a compromise, nor is it honest. It is a desperate attempt to address a major issue, which requires more patience, honesty, intelligence, and pragmatism. It is difficult to anticipate that this bill can in any way quell the uneasiness that pushes people to the shores of this country. We had hoped that Congress would not settle for 'something better than nothing,' for there are more realistic approaches which would have had a more long-range effect and would have provided fair treatment to all."

"LULAC Press Release," Office of Tony Bonilla, LULAC President, July 1, 1982; "LULAC Press Release, Office of Arnold Torres, LULAC President May 18, 1983," Both documents donated to author by Pamela Manson.

Bibliography

Acuña, Rudolfo. *Occupied America: A History of Chicanos.* 3rd ed. New York: Harper and Row, 1988.

Álvarez, Jr. Roberto R. *La Familia: Migration and Adaptation in Baja and Alta California, 1800-1975.* Berkeley: University of California Press, 1987.

Aguilar, John L. "Expressive Ethnicity and Ethnic Identity in Mexico and Mexican America." In *Mexican American Identity.* Ed. Marta E. Bernal and Phylis I. Martinelli. Encino: Floricanto Press, 1993. 55-67.

Balderrama, Francisco E. *In Defense of La Raza: The Los Angeles Mexican Consulate and the Mexican Community, 1929-1936.* Tucson: University of Arizona Press, 1982.

—— and Raymond Rodríguez. *Decade of Betrayal: Mexican Repatriation in the 1930s.* Albuquerque: University of New Mexico Press, 1995.

Betten, Neil and Raymond Mohl. "From Discrimination to Repatriation: Mexican Life in Gary, Indiana, During the Great Depression." *Pacific Historical Review* 42 (1973): 270-388.

Broyles-González, Yolanda. *El Teatro Campesino: Theater in the Chicano Movement.* Austin: University of Texas Press, 1994.

Camarillo, Albert. *Chicanos in a Changing Society: From Mexican Pueblos to American Barrios in Santa Barbara and Southern California, 1848-1930.* Cambridge: Harvard University Press, 1979.

Campa, Arthur. *Hispanic Culture in the Southwest.* Norman: University of Oklahoma Press, 1979.

Cardoso, Lawrence. *Mexican Emigration to the United States, 1897-1931.* Tucson: University of Arizona Press, 1980.

Chávez, John. *The Lost Land: The Chicano Image of the Southwest.* Albuquerque: University of New Mexico Press, 1984.

Coerver, Don M. A and Linda B. Hall. *Texas and the Mexican Revolution: Study in State and National Border Policy, 1910-1920.* San Antonio: Trinity University Press, 1984.

Christian, Carole. "Joining the American Mainstream: Texas's Mexican Americans During World War I." *Southwestern Historical Quarterly* 92 (1989): 559-595.

De León, Arnoldo. *Not Room Enough: Mexicans, Anglos and Socioeconomic Change in Texas, 1850-1900*. Albuquerque: University of New Mexico Press, 1993.

——. *Ethnicity in the Sunbelt: A History of Mexican Americans in Houston*. Houston: Mexican American Studies Monograph Series No. 7, 1989.

——. *The Tejano Community, 1836-1900*. Albuquerque: University of New Mexico Press, 1982.

——. *They Called Them Greasers: Anglo Attitudes Toward Mexicans in Texas, 1821-1900*. Austin: University of Texas Press, 1983.

Escobar, Edward J. "The Dialectics of Repression: The Los Angeles Police Department and the Chicano Movement, 1968-1971." *The Journal of American History* 79 (1993): 1483-1514.

Heyman, Josiah McC. *Life and Labor on the Border: Working People of Northern Mexico, 1886-1986*. Tucson: University of Arizona Press, 1991.

Isuaro, Durán and H. Russell Bernard, eds. *Introduction to Chicano Studies*. New York: MacMillan Publishing Co., 1982.

Gamio, Manuel. *The Life Story of the Mexican Immigrant: Autobiographical Documents Collected by Manuel Gamio*. New York: Dover Publications, 1970.

——. *Mexican Immigration to the United States: A Study of Human Immigration and Adjustment*. New York: Dover Publications, Inc., 1971.

García, Ignacio M. *Chicanismo: The Forging of a Militant Ethos Among Mexican Americans*. Tucson: University of Arizona Press, 1997.

——. *United We Win: The Rise and Fall of La Raza Unida Party*. Tucson: MASRC, 1989.

T. García, Mario. *Desert Immigrants: The Mexicans of El Paso, 1880-1920*. New Haven: Yale University Press, 1981.

——. *Mexican Americans: Leadership Ideology and Identity, 1930-1960*. New Haven: Yale University Press, 1990.

García, Richard A. "The Chicano Movement and the Mexican-American Community, 1972-1978: An Interpretive Essay." *Socialist Review* 40-41 (1978): 117-136.

Gledhill, John. *Casi Nada; A Study of Agrarian Reform in the Homeland of Cardenismo*. Albany: Institute for Mesoamerican Society, University at Albany, 1989.

González, José Amaro. *Mutual Aid for Survival: The Case of the Mexican American*. Malabar: Robert E. Krieger Publishing Company, 1983.

González, Luis. *San José de Gracia: A Mexican Town in Transition*. Austin: University of Texas Press, 1972.

Gonzales, Manuel G. *Mexicanos: A History of Mexicans in the United States*. Bloomington: Indiana University Press, 1999.

Griswold del Castillo, Richard. *The Treaty of Guadalupe Hidalgo: A Legacy of Conflict*. Norman: University of Oklahoma Press, 1990.

——. *The Los Angeles Barrios, 1850-1890: A Social History*. Berkeley: University of California Press, 1979.

Gutiérrez, David G. *Walls and Mirrors: Mexican Americans, Mexican Immigrants and the Politics of Ethnicity*. Berkeley: University of California Press, 1995.

Hart, John M. *Revolutionary Mexico: The Coming and Process of Mexican Revolution*. Berkeley: University of California Press, 1987.

Justice, Glenn. *Revolution on the Rio Grande: Mexican Raids and Army Pursuits, 1916-1919.* El Paso: Texas Western Press, 1992.

Kanellos, Nicolás. *A History of Hispanic Theatre in the United States: Origins to 1940.* Austin: University of Texas Press, 1990.

Knight, Alan. *The Mexican Revolution.* Vol.1. London: Cambridge University Press, 1986.

Luckingham, Bradford. *Phoenix: The History of a Southwestern Metropolis.* Tucson: University of Arizona Press. 1989.

Marín, Christine. *A Spokesman of the Mexican American Movement: Rodolfo "Corky" Gonzales and the Fight for Chicano Liberation, 1966-1972.* San Francisco: R and E Research Associates, 1977.

——. "Go Home, Chicanos: A Study of the Brown Berets in California and Arizona." In *An Awakened Minority: The Mexican Americans.* Ed. Manuel Servín. Beverly Hills: Glencoe Press, 1974. 226-247.

Marín, Marguerite V. *Social Protest In An Urban Barrio: A Study of the Chicano Movement, 1966-1974.* Lanham: University Press of America, 1991.

Márquez, Benjamín. *LULAC: The Evolution of a Mexican American Political Organization.* Austin: University of Texas Press, 1993.

Martínez, John. *Mexican Emigration to the United States, 1910-1930.* San Francisco: Arno Press, 1971.

Mellinger, Philip J. *Race and Labor in Western Copper: The Fight for Equality, 1896-1918.* Tucson: University of Arizona Press, 1995.

Mirandé, Alfredo. *Gringo Justice.* Notre Dame: University of Notre Dame, 1987.

Martínez, Oscar J. *Troublesome Border.* Tucson: University of Arizona Press, 1988.

——. *Fragments of the Mexican Revolution: Personal Accounts From the Border.* Albuquerque: University of New Mexico Press, 1983.

Montejano, David. *Anglos and Mexicans in the Making of Texas, 1836-1896.* Austin: University of Texas Press, 1987.

Muñoz, Carlos. *Youth Identity and Power: The Chicano Movement.* London: Verso, 1989.

Nabokov, Peter. *Tijerina and the Courthouse Raid.* Albuquerque: University of New Mexico, 1969.

Navarro, Armando. *Mexican American Youth Organization: Avant-Garde of the Chicano Movement in Texas.* Austin: University of Texas, 1995.

Officer, James. *Hispanic Arizona; 1836-1856.* Tucson: University of Arizona Press, 1989.

Ortego, Phillip D. "The Chicano Renaissance." In *Introduction to Chicano Studies.* Eds. Livie Isuaro Durán and H. Russell Bernard. New York: Macmillan Publishing Co., Inc., 1982. 568-584.

Pitt, Leonard. *The Decline of Los Californios: A Social History of Spanish Speaking Californians, 1846-1890.* Berkeley: University of California Press, 1971.

Quiñones, Juan Gómez. *Chicano Politics: Reality and Promise, 1940-1990.* Albuquerque: University of New Mexico Press, 1990.

——. *Mexican Students Por La Raza: The Chicano Student Movement in Southern California, 1967-1977.* Santa Barbara: Editorial La Causa, 1978.

Raat, W. Dirk. *Revoltosos: Mexico's Rebels in the United States.* College Station: Texas A & M University Press, 1981.

Richmond, Douglas W. *Venustiano Carranza's Nationalist Struggle, 1893-1920.* Lincoln: University of Nebraska, 1983.

Reisler, Mark. *By the Sweat of Their Brow: Mexican Immigrant Labor in the United States: 1900-1940.* Westport: Greenwood Press, 1976.

Romo, Ricardo. *East Los Angeles: History of a Barrio.* Austin: University of Texas Press, 1983.

Rosales, F. Arturo. *Chicano! History of the Mexican American Civil Rights Movement.* Houston: Arte Público Press, 1997.

——. *¡Pobre raza!* Austin: University of Texas Press, 1999.

Rosenbaum, Robert J. *Mexicano Resistance in the Southwest: "The Sacred Right of Self-Preservation."* Austin: University of Texas Press, 1981.

Ruiz, Vicki L. *Cannery Women, Cannery Lives: Unionization and the California Food Processing Industry, 1930-1950.* Albuquerque: University of New Mexico Press, 1987.

——. *From Out of the Shadows: Mexican Women in Twentieth-Century America.* New York: Oxford University Press, 1998.

Sánchez, George J. *Becoming Mexican American: Culture and Identity in Chicano Los Angeles, 1900-1945.* New York: Oxford University Press, 1993.

Sandos, James A. *Rebellion in the Borderlands: Anarchism and the Plan of San Diego, 1904-1923.* Norman: University of Oklahoma Press, 1992.

San Miguel, Guadalupe. *"Let All of Them Take Heed": Mexican Americans and the Campaign for Educational Equality in Texas, 1910-1981.* Austin: University of Texas Press, 1987.

Santibáñez, Enrique. *Ensayo acerca de la inmigración mexicana en los Estados Unidos.* San Antonio: The Clegg Co., 1930.

Sheridan, Thomas E. *Los Tucsonenses: The Mexican Community in Tucson, 1854-1941.* Tucson: University of Arizona Press, 1986.

Shockley, John Staples. *Chicano Revolt in a Texas Town.* Indiana: University of Notre Dame, 1974.

Skerry, Peter. *Mexican Americans: The Ambivalent Minority.* New York: The Free Press, 1993.

Taylor, Paul S. *An American Mexican Frontier: Nueces County, Texas.* Chapel Hill: University of North Carolina, 1934

——. *Mexican Labor in the United States: Chicago and the Calumet Region.* Berkeley: University of California Press, 1931.

Treviño, Roberto. "Prensa y Patria: The Spanish Language Press and the Biculturalization of the Tejano Middle Class, 1920-1940." *The Western Historical Quarterly* 22 (1991):451-472.

Turner, Frederick C. *The Dynamic of Mexican Nationalism.* Chapel Hill: University of North Carolina Press, 1968.

Valdés, Dennis Nodín. *Al Norte: Agricultural Workers in the Great Lakes Region, 1917-1970.* Austin: University of Texas Press, 1991.

Venegas, Daniel. *Las aventuras de Don Chipote o cuando los pericos mamen.* Houston: Arte Público Press, 2000.

Vargas, Zaragoza. *Proletarians of the North: A History of Mexican Industrial Workers in Detroit and the Midwest, 1917-1933.* Berkeley: University of California Press, 1993.

Weber, David J. *Foreigners in Their Native Land. Historical Roots of the Mexican Americans.* Albuquerque: University of New Mexico Press, 1973.

Zamora, Emilio. *The World of the Mexican Worker in Texas.* College Station: Texas A & M University Press, 1993.

Index

A

Aceves, Isaac, 221
Adams, Jeff D., 54
affirmative action, 337-338
African Americans, iv, 3, 46, 64, 72, 116, 139, 162, 163, 181, 209, 216, 267, 274, 295, 306, 308, 318, 325, 328, 332, 376
Agricultores Mexicanos, Los (Mexican Agriculturalists), 219, 238
Agricultural Labor Relations Act, 220
Agricultural Labor Relations Board, 220
Agricultural Workers Organizing Committee (AWOC), 269, 270, 276, 294
agriculture labor, iii, 43, 45, 77, 78, 82, 86-87, 88, 116, 158, 174, 216-220, 222, 237, 238, 241-246, 258, 269-272, 276-303; in Arizona, 88, 174, 238; in California, 86-87, 217-219, 237, 241-246, 269-272; in Texas, 185, 218
Alamía, P. C., 66-67
Álvarez, Robert Jr., 128
Álvarez, Roberto, 128-129
alchohol prohibition, 46
Alianza Federal de Las Mercedes; *movimiento* inspiration, 269, 305, 328, 332; attraction to Hispano villagers, 272-273; courthouse raid, 273; decline of, 275; headquarters, 272; ideology of, 308-321; in context of Chicano Movement, 269, 274, 275, 305, 325; its members arrested, 273, 322-324, 322-324; march to Santa Fe, 273; mil-

itancy, 269, 273-274; occupation of public lands, 273-274, 312-314; opposition to in New Mexico, 161, 273, 311-313; origins of, 272-273; political clout, 275; success of, 275
Alianza Hispano Americana (Hispanic American Alliance), 104, 160
Alinsky, Saul, 161
Allee, Captain A.Y., 302
Alfaro, V., 57-58
Altorre, Richard, 335
American Federation of Labor (AFL), 217-219, 239-240
American G.I. Forum, 158, 162, 205, 338
American Legion, East Chicago, 101
Americanization, 114, 170-171, 174-175, 178-179, 183-184, 340, 342-344, 404
Anglo-American Settlers in Southwest, 1-3, 6, 22-25
Anglo-Mexican relations, 1, 3, 6-7, 39-41, 43-44 63-64, 66-67, 68-70, 111-113, 120-121, 168, 216, 226, 333-334, 386, 392
anti-war movement, iv, 330-331
Arenales, Ricardo, 157
Arizona Farm Workers Organizing Committee (AFWOC), 302
Arizona Federation of Labor, 230
Arizona Migrant Opportunity Program (MOP), 302
Arizona Republican, 55
Arizona State University, 377-378
Arte Público Press, i
Asamblea Mexicana, La (Mexican Assembly), 104

Asian workers, 45, 79
assimilation, 65, 330, 364-369
Asociación de Jornaleros, La (The
    Journeymen's Association), 219
Asociación Nacional México-Americana
    (ANMA), 220
Association for the Rights of Americans, 44
Atencio, Tomás, 332
Atristain, Miguel, 15
August 29th Movement (ATM), 394-399
Austin, Stephen F., 1
Ávila Camacho, Manuel, 138
Aztecs, iv, 337, 358
Aztlán, concept of, iv, 330, 335

B

Badillo, S.L., 58
Baldenegro, Salomón, 331
Barbis, Pablo, 246
Bell, Tom, 142
bilingualism, 27, 159, 168, 185, 189, 337,
    360, 362, 387, 389, 400-403, 404
Black, Joe, 308
Black Berets, 332
black lung disease, 228
Black Pride Movement, iv, 328
Bliss, Bill, 151
Bloch, Louis, 241
Bodet, Jaime Torres, 160
Bonilla, Tony, 404-405
Bonillas, Ignacio, 141
Box, John C., 73, 79
boycotts and, Gallo products, 271; grapes,
    270-272, 282, 296-297, 328; lettuce,
    271; pesticide use, 271; Schenley
    Liquor Company, 270, 282, 285
Bracero Program, 138, 218-219
Briscoe, Dolph, 335
Brown, Jerry, 271
Brown Berets, 329-330, 348, 350-351,
    381-382
Brown Scare, 4, 42, 52-53

C

Cadena, Juan Carlos, 205, 207
California Land Act (1851), 5, 23

California State College, Los Angeles, 348
California legislature, 4, 271
Calles, Plutarco Elías, 45, 79, 137
Campbell, Jack, 273
Camus, Albert, quoted, 356
Canales, Alma, 334, 336
Canales, José T., 67, 71-72, 158
Capital punishment, 103, 104, 105,
    110-116, 120-121, 122-125, 127,
    140, 176
Cárdenas, Lázaro, 138, 156
Cárdenas Martínez, León, Jr., 111-113,
    120-121
Cárdenas Martínez, León, Sr., 111-113
Cargo, David, 273, 313
Carranza, Venustiano, 43-45, 73, 135-136
Carter, Jimmy, 337
Caravana de la Reconquista, La (The
    Reconquest Caravan), 381-382; (see
    also Brown Berets)
Casa de Acción Social Autónoma—
    Hermandad General de Trabajadores
    (CASA-HGT), 394
Castro, Sal, 329
Catholicism, 1, 137, 162, 272, 370-371
Católicos Por La Raza (CPLR—Catholics
    for the People), 370-371
Centro Radical Mexicano, El (Radical
    Center), 104
Chapa, Francisco, 157, 164
Chávez, César, 269-272; as Movimiento
    leader, 269, 328, 333, 335; and boy-
    cotts, 270-271, 282; early organizing,
    269-270, 276-284; early victories,
    269-270, 285; employment in
    Community Services Organization,
    269-270, 276; death of, 272; fast, 269;
    non-violent image, 4, 196, 214, 226;
    and immigration, 271-272, 303;
    philosophy, 270, 277-284; religious
    orientation, 283; Teamsters and,
    270-271
Chávez, Dennis, 161
Chávez, N.B., 139
Chávez, Helen, 276
Chicana organizing, 391-393

Chicanismo, iv, 328, 330, 331, 333, 339-351, 353-354, 361-369, 384, 385
Chicano literature, 362, 366
Chicano Movement, 328-399; Arizona, 331-332, 377-382; California, 295, 328-331, 335, 348-351, 350-359, 364-376, 394-399; Chicago, 305; Colorado, 163, 329-331, 335, 337, 339-347, 360-363, 389-390; cultural nationalism, 329, 333, 345-346, 367-368, 379-380; legacy of, 338; in New Mexico, 272-275, 305, 309-322, 332, 337; terrorism, 331; in Texas, 332-338, 383-388, 391-393
Chicano political party, 305, 331, 334
Chicano Studies Program, 348, 359-360, 366-367
Chicano theater, 368
Chicano Youth Liberation Conference, 329, 330, 331, 337, 361, 372
Chicanos Por La Causa (CPLC), 332, 379-380
citizenship, 2-4, 12, 18, 35, 92, 118, 136, 141, 157, 159, 165, 167, 168, 170, 171, 175, 185, 211, 272, 375
Citizen's Committee for Latin American Youth, 159, 187-191
civil rights and African Americans, iv, 162, 274, 306, 318, 329, 332; and US Mexicans, 103-106, 114-115, 118, 158-160, 162, 181, 221, 261, 269, 272-273, 274, 275
Civilian Conservation Corps (CCC), 159
Clamor Público, El, Los Angeles, 26-27
Clements, Bill, 336
Clements, George P., 86
Club Chapultepec, El, 185-186
college students, Mexican Americans, 159, 295, 328-329, 330, 331, 332, 339, 343, 348, 353; white, 332, 339, 343
Colombo, Frank, 216
Colonias, 80, 104, 134, 138, 157, 160
Colquitt, Oscar, 164
Comisiones Honoríficas Mexicanas, 137, 146-150

Comité contra el Racismo, El, 164, 184
Communist Party, U.S.A., 220, 246
Community Services Organization (CSO), 161, 211, 269-270, 276
communty development organizations, 332, 333
Compeán, Mario, 332, 334, 336
Confederación Regional de Obreros Mexicanos, La (Regional Confederation of Mexican Workers), 236
Confederación de Sociedades Mexicanas, La, 105
Confederación de Uniones Obreras, La (Federation of Labor Unions), 238
Congreso de Aztlán, El, 335
Congreso de Habla Española, El (Spanish Speaking People's Congress), 159, 218, 258
Congress for Mexican American Unity, 374
Congress of Industrial Organizations (CIO), 218, 219
conquest of Mexicans in Southwest, iv, 2-7, 8-9, 20-21, 22-25, 31-32, 37-38, 272, 314-316, 361, 375, 379
consular service, Mexican, (see Mexican Foreign Ministry)
Córdoba, T., 58
Corona, Bert, 159, 162, 163, 177
Coronel, Paul, 176
Cortina, Juan Nepomuceno, 7, 28
Cota, Leonardo, 20
Cotera, Marta, 391
Couto, Bernardo, 15
Cristero Revolt, 79
Crónica, La, Laredo, 103, 120
Crusade for Justice, 329, 331, 337, 360, 361
Cruz Azul Mexicana (Blue Cross Brigades), 137, 146, 224
Cuevas, Luis, 15

D

Davis, Edward, 375
Davis, Richard C., 357-358
de García, José, 40

Defensor, El, Edingburg, Texas, 168-171, 228-229
de la Colina, Rafael, 138
de la Fuente, Rafael, 84-85
de la Garza, Eligio "Kika", 161
de la Lama, Pedro, 262
de la Rosa, Luis, 63
del Castillo, José, 221
Democratic Party, 284, 334, 336-337, 339
Department of Repatriation, Mexico, 136
deportation, 233-235
desegregation, 126-127
Deukmajian, George, 271
Di Giorgio Corporation, 218, 270
Díaz, Abel, 153
Díaz, Porfirio, 42, 47
Diez de Bonilla, Manuel, 19
Doak, William, 79-80, 96-97, 101-102
Douglas, F.W., 132

E

Eagle, Joe, 172
Educational Issues Coordinating Committee (EICC), 329
educational system, as Chicano Movement concern, 328, 329, 332, 333, 337-338; Corky Gonzales's views on, 340-342; and MALDEF, 337, 400; and Mexican American Generation, 157, 159, 160, 176, 179, 185-186
Espectador, El, California, 159
El Nogal union, 218
El Partido del Pueblo (People's Party), New Mexico, 160
electoral politics, 160-161
Empire Zinc Strike, 259-261
enganchistas (labor contractors), 77
English language, discrimination towards non-speakers, 6, 104, 262; need to learn, 91, 168, 165, 185, 189; used in teaching, 2, 105, 400-403
Equal Employment Opportunity Commission walkouts, 1966, 162-163, 214
Establishment, concept of, 331, 339-347
Escalante, M., 23

escuelitas, 137
exiles, political, 25, 105, 139, 155

F

fascism, 160, 188
Farenthold, Frances "Sissy", 335-336
farm workers, 298-299
Federal Writer's Project, 221
Fellows, William, 174
feminism, 370, 372-373, 391-393
Ferguson Forum, 116-117
Ferguson, James E., 72, 116
Fierro de Bright, Josefina, 159, 221
fiestas patrias, 147, 218, 330, 350, 363
Filipino workers, 270, 282
Flores, David, 266
Flores Magón, Enrique, 48
Flores Magón, Ricardo, 47-50, 59
Flores Magón Brothers, 47
Ford Foundation, 333, 337, 338
Foreign Miners Tax, 1850, 4
Forquer, Richard, 293
Fox, M., 70
Francis, L. C., 273
Franco, Jesús, 146
Fremont, John C., 2

G

Gadsden, James, 19
Gadsden Purchase, 1853, 3, 5, 16-19
Galarza, Ernesto, 218, 219, 226
Gallego, Rodolfo, 53
Gallo Wine Company, 226, 271
gangs, 159-160, 329
García, Andrés, 142
García, Gus, 158, 205, 207
García, Héctor, 158, 298
García, Teodoro, 74-75
Garfias, Enrique, 36
Garis, Roy, 93-95
Garner, John N., 86
Garza, Catarino, 39-41
genocide, 313, 340, 342, 351, 360, 361
Germans and Mexicans during World War I, 44
Ghandi, Mohandas, 269, 282

Gibler, Frank, 104
Goepel, Wendy, 276
Gold Rush, 4, 6, 31, 134, 139
Gompers, Samuel, 237
Gonzales Rodolfo "Corky", 329-330, 335, 337, 339, 341, 342, 343, 346, 347
González, Henry B., 161, 333
González, Manuel, 170-171
González v. Sheely, 160
Gorras Blancas, 6, 29-30
Govea, Jessica, 296-297
grape boycott, (see boycotts)
grape harvest strike, 270, 271, 282-283
grazing rights, 272
Great Depression, 79, 96-97, 105-106, 132, 293
Great Society, 162
Grito del Norte, El, New Mexico, 332
Guimarra Vineyards Corporation, 270
Gutiérrez de Lara, Lázaro, 217, 232
Gutiérrez, Félix Sr., 176, 177
Gutiérrez, Gustavo, 302
Gutiérrez, José Ángel, 332-336, 383-385; and Mexican American Youth Organization (MAYO), 332-333, 385; and Winter Garden Project, 333-334
Gutiérrez, Luz, 333
Guzmán, Max, 218, 249-257
Guzmán, Ralph, 215

H

Hayden, Carl, 34, 88-89
Hernández, Alfred J., 214
Hernández, Gustavo G., 228
Hernández, Pete, 207-210
Herrera, Gregorio and Piedad, 153-154
Herrera, John J., 264-265
Herrera, Juan José, 29
Hill, John, 336
Holmgren, Rod, 259-261
Homestead Act of 1862, 5, 315
Hoover, Herbert, 79
Huerta, Dolores, 211, 270
Huerta, Victoriano, 42
Huey, Mel, 302
Hunt, George W. P., 139, 228, 230

I

Ibáñez, Dora, 177
Ibarra, Vda. de Pompa, Esther, 122, (also see Pompa, Aurelio)
Idar, Eduardo, 168-169
Idar, Nicasio, 103, 218
ideology, Mexican American, 106, 157, 159, 160, 162-171, 174, 185-186, 216-217; México Lindo, 103, 107-110; Chicano, iv, 328-329, 331, 333, 335, 344-347, 361-363, 364-365, 394-399
Immigration Act of 1917, 77, 88
Immigration Act of 1929, 79, 98
immigration from Mexico, defense, 104, 113-114, 120, 134-135, 160, 262; Mexican Revolution, 42, 43, 45, 47, 69; poverty, 76, 78, 105-106, 134, 136, 223, 236; push-pull immigration factors, 42, 76, 77, 78, 79, 88, 98, 104, 137, 138, 142-143, 156, 219, 303; immigrant mobilization, 103-104, 106-107, 114-115, 120-121; undocumented, 45, 74, 77, 79, 80, 98, 100, 219, 221, 272, 337, 404-406; and unions, 270-271, 303
Immigration and Naturalization Quota Act, 1924, 46, 78
Immigration and Naturalization Service, 138
immigration policy, United States, 77-81, 86-100, 217, 272, 303, 337
Imparcial de Texas, El, San Antonio, 118, 240
indigenismo, 107, 109, 337, 359
Industrial Areas Foundation (IAF), 161, 276
industrialism, 78, 79, 104, 178-179, 216, 217, 218, 220
integration, 3, 4, 6, 160, 161
International Workers of the World (IWW), 59, 217, 236
International Union of Mine Mill and Smelter Workers (Mine Mill), 220, 267-268

Inter-Agency Cabinet Committee on Mexican American Affairs, 163, 274, 305

J

Johnson, Albert, 88
Johnson, Lyndon Baines, 162-163, 274, 340
Juárez, Benito, 107, 109
judicial system and Mexicans, 6, 7, 43, 45-46, 55-60, 79, 103-105, 111-113, 114, 120-125, 136, 137, 139, 142-145, 153-155, 160-161, 165, 185, 187-191, 207-210, 218, 219, 220, 221, 249-257, 273-275, 300-301, 307, 312-313, 322, 323-324, 327, 328, 330-331, 332, 337, 343-344, 350, 352, 372, 375-376; juries, 6, 162, 207-210
juntas patrióticas, 134

K

Kanellos, Nicolás, i
Kearney, Stephen Watts, 2
Kellog, Frank, 79
Kelly, Paul, 100-101
Kennedy, John F., 162, 212-213, 214
Keyes v. School District Number One, 400
King, Bruce, 276
King, Martin Luther, 282, 308
Knott, George, 265
Korean War, 183

L

Labor Clarion, 237
Land grants and land usurpation, iii, 5-6, 12, 22-25, 29-30, 31-32, 269, 272-279, 312-317; (also see *Alianza Federal de Mercedes*)
Larrazola, Octaviano, 161
Las adventuras de Don Chipote, o cuando los pericos mamen, 223
Latin American Club, Arizona, 174
Latin American Club, Houston, 264
Latin American Round Table, 157
Laustaunau, William "Wenceslao," 216
Lau v. Nichols, 400-403
Lawyers Guild, 160
League of United Latin American Citizens (LULAC), 158, 160, 162, 164, 167-172, 181-182, 205, 212, 214, 228, 298, 338, 404-406
Lettuce strike, 1970s, 271
Levelier, Ives, 217
Liga Protectora Latina, La (Latin Protective League), 104, 114-115, 262-263
Liga Protectora Mexicana, La (Mexican Protective League), 105
Lincoln High School Faculty Forum, 355-357
Lincoln High School, 355-359
Little School of, 159, 393
Little Steel Strike, 218, 249-257
Lone Star Republic, 2
Longauex y Vásquez, Enriqueta, 372
Longoria, Félix, 158
López, Hank, 161
López, Ignacio I., 158
López de Santa Anna, Antonio, 1-3, 346
López Tijerina, Reies, alliance with Native Americans, 316-317; as movimiento leader, 269, 274, 275; citizen's arrest tactic, 274, 312; court house raid, 273, 312-313, 322; ideology, 308-320; imprisonment, 274; legacy, 275; LRUP national convention, 335; March to Santa Fe, 273; militancy, 269, 274; occupation of public lands, 273, 312; Poor People's March, 269, 308; surveillance by police, 273
Los Angeles County Coroner's Jury, 331
Los Angeles County Human Relations Council, 329
Los Angeles County School Board, 329
Los Angeles County Sheriff Department, 370, 381
Los Angeles Police Department (LAPD), 375-376, 352
Los Angeles Thirteen, 359
Los Angeles Times, 331, 375-376
Lost Land identity, i-ii, 3-7, 20, 26, 28-32, 37-38
Lubbert, Alejandro, 241
lynching, 5, 6, 34, 52, 102, 111, 136, 137, 155, 166

M

Madero, Francisco I., 42-43, 135
Manifest Destiny, 1, 8-9
Marshall, Lupe, 218, 249-257
Martínez, Elizabeth "Betita," 332
Martínez, José, 300
Martínez, Tomás, 232
Martínez Preciat, Emilio, 236
Marxism, 337, 394-399; labor organizing, 221, 246-248
McCue, William, 122
McKee, Tom, 66
McWilliams, Carey, 159
Medina, Eliseo, 296
Memorial Day Massacre, 218, 249-257
Méndez v. Westminster, 194-204
Mendivil, Ernest, 33, 221
mestizaje (mestizo identity), iv, 90, 93-95, 299, 361
Mexican American Liberation Committee (MALC), 331
Mexican American Legal Defense and Education Fund, 337, 400
Mexican American Movement (MAM), 159, 178
Mexican American Political Association (MAPA), 162-163, 214-215, 293-294
Mexican American Poltical Club, 161
Mexican American Student Organization (MASO), 332, 377
Mexican American Unity Council (MAUC), 333
Mexican American Youth Organization (MAYO), 332-333, 385
Mexican Americanism, iii, 43, 106, 118, 157, 159, 160, 162, 164-171, 174-175, 176-177, 176-179, 185-186, 205, 207, 214-215, 221
Mexican Claims Commission, 74
Mexican Constitution of 1917, 136
Mexican Foreign Ministry, 135, 151; consuls, 23, 77, 98, 103, 105, 129, 135-147, 151, 226, 227, 230
Mexican Revolution, 1910, 42-46, 52-60, 76, 77, 103, 105, 139
Mexican Voice, Los Angeles, 159, 178-179

Mexican War, 2, 4-5
Mexico, antipathy against in United States, 43, 45, 51-54, 73; border issues, 42, 44, 45; immigration from (see immigration from Mexico); independence from Spain, 1; repatriation to (see repatriation to Mexico); Texas Rebellion, 1-2; War with the United States, 2, 3, 4-5; United States relations with, 42-46
México de Afuera (Mexico Abroad), 133
México Lindo ideology, ii, 103, 105, 107-110, 108-109
Meyer, F.W., 51
militancy, 162, 214-215, 269, 273-274, 282, 295, 305, 328, 331, 332, 333, 334, 338, 346-347, 352, 370, 374, 377, 383-384, 385
mine labor, 77, 78, 104, 132, 217, 230, 236, 381-382
Monteverde, J. Mariano, 19
Montoya, Joseph, 161
Morenci, Arizona strike, 217
Moreno, Luisa, 221
Morín, Raúl, 183
Morones, Luis, 239
Moroyoque, Juan, 53
Movimiento Estudiantil Chicano de Aztlán (MECHA), 330, 337, 366-368
Muñíz, Ramsey, 334-336
Muñoz, Rosalío Jr., 331, 375-376
mutual aid societies, 103, 104, 105, 107, 114

N

National Chicano Liberation Youth Conference, 329, 361
National Chicano Moratorium, 330-331
National Chicano/Latino Immigration Conference, 337
National Farm Workers Association (NFWA), 270, 276
National Farm Workers Union (NFWU), 219, 269
National La Raza Unida Convention, 335
National Labor Relations Act (NLRA), 218

National Youth Administration, 159
nationalism, (see Chicano cultural nationalism); immigrant, (see *México Lindo idealogy*)
Nelson , Eugene, 298
New Deal, 159
New Mexico National Guard, 273
New York Times, 61, 82
Newlands Reclamation Act of 1903, 76

O

Obregón, Álvaro, 45
Operation Wetback, 138
Order of the Sons of America, 157
Orendáin, Antonio, 298
Orta, Max, 205
Ortega Pérez, Anita, 36
Ortíz, Mike, 55
Otáñera, Manuel E., 151-152

P

pachucos, 159-160
Paisano, El, 302-304
Palacios, Diana, 337
Pan American Round Table, 157
Parker, Gilbert, 61
Partido Liberal Mexicano, (PLM, Mexican Liberal Party), 47-50
Peace Corps, 276
Pearson, M.E., 130-131
Peña, Albert, 205-206
Peña, Juan José, 337
Perales, Alonso S., 91-92, 100, 118-119, 158, 167
Peralta, Miguel, 139
Pérez, Eduardo, 139
Pérez, M.G., 170
Pérez, Nacho, 383
Pérez, Pedro, 33-36
Pershing, General John, 43
Pierce, Frank, 67
Pizaña, Aniceto, 63
Plan de Delano, El, 294
Plan Espiritual de Aztlán, El, (The Spiritual Plan of Aztlán), iv, 329-330, 361-363
Plan de San Diego, El, 43, 44, 63-64, 66-67

Plan de San Luis Potosí, El, 42
Plan de Santa Bárbara, El, iv, 330, 338, 364-369
Police, brutality and abuse, 43, 103-105, 136, 142-145, 153-155, 185, 219, 221, 249-257, 273, 300-301, 322-324, 329, 330-331, 332, 343-344, 350, 352; infiltration, 338; other relations with Mexicans, 352, 375-376
Political Association of Spanish-speaking Organizations, (PASSO), 162
political participation, 158, 164, 336
Polk, James K., 2
Pompa, Aurelio, 122-124
Poor People's March, 274, 306-307, 308
Population, Mexicans in U.S., 4, 6, 79, 104, 106, 138, 161, 333, 336, 376
Porvenir massacre, 68-70
prejudice towards Mexicans, 8-9, 51, 73, 82, 90, 93-95, 116-117; defense against prejudice, 91-92, 118-119, 160, 180
Prensa, La, San Antonio, 98, 120, 121, 226-227
President's Committee on Fair Employment Practices, (PCFEP), 222
Primer Congreso Mexicanista, El (The First Mexican Congress), 103
Protestantism and Mexican Americans, 137, 272, 311
Protestantism and Mexicans, 105, 110, 133, 275, 281

Q

Quevedo, Eduardo, 162, 214

R

race, 157-158, 162, 172-174, 181, 187, (also see prejudice)
racism, (see prejudice)
railroads, 45, 77, 78, 84-85, 225-225
Ramírez, Francisco, 26
Raza, La, Los Angeles, 335
raza cósmica, La, iv
Raza Unida Party, La (LRUP), 334-337; California, 335; Colorado, 335,

389-388; feminist critique of,
391-393; immigration conference,
1977, 337; national convention, 335;
New Mexico, 337, South Texas
elections, 334; Texas state-wide
elections, 334-336; Tucson, 331
refugees from Mexico, (see exiles)
Regeneración, 48
repatriation to Mexico, 4, 80, 96-97,
136, 138
resistance to Anglo-American hegemony,
2, 20-21, 28-30, 43, 44
Rivas, Cenobio, 66
Rivas, George, 66
Rivas, Martina, 66
Rivera, Librado, 48
Rodríguez, Antonio, 51
Rodríguez, Francisco, 139
Romo desegegation case, 126-127
Romo, Adolpho, 126-127
Romo, Ricardo, 42
Roosevelt, Franklin D., 220, 222
Rosales de Hernández, Carolina, 302
Rosales, F. Arturo, 302
Ross, Fred, 276
Roybal, Edward, 162, 215
Ruiz, D. Eduardo, 146
Ruiz, Manuel, 159, 187-191
Ruiz, Raúl, 335, 336

S

Saenz, Luz, 157
Saenz, Pablo, 107
Saenz, Moisés, 79
Salas, Fernando, 104
Salazar, Eulogio, 321
Salazar Ylarregui, José, 19
Salazar, Rubén, 330-331
Salcido, A. F., 216
Salt of the Earth, movie, 259
Sánchez, Alfonso, 273, 321
Sánchez, David, 329, 381-382
Sánchez, George I., 338
Santa Fe Ring, 6
Santa Ysabel massacre, 43-44

Santibáñez, Enrique, 98-99
Sarabia Juan, 48
Schenley Liquor Company, 270, 282, 285
Scott, Winfield, 2
Selective Service Act, 1917, 77
segregation of Mexicans, 103, 126-127,
128-129, 151, 160, 192-193, 205-206
Seguín, Juan, 3
separatism, 329-330, 361-363
Shaler, William, 8
Sheely v. González decision, 160
Sheffield, James, 79
Sleepy Lagoon incident, 159
Slidell, John, 2
smuggling from Mexico, 45-46, 74, 105
social class, i-iv, 3, 161, 162
Social Security Act, 1935, 172
Sociedad Mutualista Benito Juárez, 107
Sol, El, 297
Southern Pacific Railroad Co., 36
Southern Pecan Shelling Company, 184
Southwest Council of La Raza, 337, 379
Southwest Voter Registration Project,
337-338
Spanish language, 6, 26-27, 135, 159, 262,
281, 307, 313, 337
Spanish language newspapers, 26-27, 102,
120, 121, 159, 168-171, 228-229,
240, 262
Spears, Bill, 192-193
Spears, J. Franklin, 192
Starkey, S. A., 264
Steel Workers Organizing Committee
(SWOC), 220
strikes, 216, 217, 249-257, 259-261, 270,
271, 282-283

T

Taft, William, 51
Taylor, Zachary, 1
Teague, Charles, 86-87, 219
Teamster's union, 270-221, 276
Teatro Campesino, 284
Tejano identity, 337
Telles, Raymond, 161

Tenayuca, Emma, 247-248
Texas Constitution of 1836, 3
Texas Institute for Educational
   Development (TIED), 337
Texas Rangers, 43, 44, 61-64, 66-67,
   68-72, 302
Texas Rebellion, 1836, 1-2
Tierra Amarilla Free Clinic, 332
Tijerina, Félix, 159
Tijerina, Patsy, 272, 327
Tijerina, Reies López, (see López Tijerina,
   Reies)
Torres, Arnold, 405, 409
Torres, Esteban, 374
Treaty of Guadalupe Hidalgo, 1-3; basis for
   Tijerina movement, 272-273, 316;
   enacted, 2-3; supplanted by the
   Gadsden Purchase, 16-19
Trist, Nicholas P., 15
Tucsonense, El, 262

U

Unions, 216, 218, 220, 233, 231, 233-235,
   236, 238, 239, 243-257, 265-266,
   269-270, 276, 276-284, 294, 302;
   and women, 221, 270
United Cannery Agricultural, Packing
   and Allied Workers Association,
   (UCAPAWA), 221
United Farm Workers Organizing
   Committee (UFWOC), 270-271
United Farm Workers (UFW), 271
United Mexican American Students
   (UMAS), 330, 348-349
United States Commission on Civil Rights,
   299, 352
United States Congress, 1-2, 4, 5, 46, 77,
   134, 161
United States Forest Service, 272
United States-Mexico Border, changing,
   4, 6; crossing, 76, 84-85, 134, 301;
   repatriation to, 80, 84-85; settling in
   area, 78; unionization in, 239, 302;
   violence and tension, 39, 42-75,
   76-77, 105, 136, 144

University of Arizona, 331
University of California, Los Angeles
   (UCLA), 331
University of Southern California (USC),
   329

V

Valdez, Luis, 294
Vallejo, Guadalupe, 37-38
Vallejo, Mariano Guadalupe, 37
Vallejo, Platón M.G., 31-32
Valls, John, 173
Varela, María, 332
Varela, Sérvulo, 20
Vasconcelos, José, iv
Vásquez, Tiburcio, 28
Velasco, Carlos, 104
Velásquez, Willie, 337, 383
Vietnam War, 330
Vigne, Luis, 27
Villa, Francisco "Pancho," 43-45, 73
Villalobos, Ramón, 149
Villarreal, Antonio I., 48
Villarreal Zárate, Elías, 167
Visel, Charles P., 80
Viva Kennedy Campaign, 162, 212
Voice, The, 293-294
Volstead Act, 46
voting, 3-4, 39-40, 158, 160-162, 164,
   337-338, 339

W

walkouts, 331-388, Arizona, 331-332;
   California, 329, 353-354, 355, 371;
   Colorado, 360; Texas, 337, 383-384,
   386, 387-388
War, casualties, 330, 350, 374; heroes, 183;
   veterans, 157, 158, 178-184
War on Poverty, 329, 341
War Prohibited Act, 1918, 46
Warren, Henry, 36
Water rights, 272
Webster, Ira, 67
Weinberger, Henry, 47
Welch, Ramón, 221

Wells, Jim, 146, 161
Western Federation of Miners, 217
Westminister v. Méndez, 160, 194-204
Wilson, Henry Lane, 43, 73
Wilson, Woodrow, 43-44
Winter Garden Project, 333-334
Works Public Administration (WPA), 221
World War I, 44, 76-78, 101, 135, 141, 142, 157, 161, 264; draft issue, 77
World War II, 138, 178-184
Wright, F.T., 132

X

Ximénez, Vicente, 162, 325

Y

Yaquis, 56
Yorty, Sam, 350
Young, C.C., 241
Young Citizens for Community Action (YCCA), 329
Ypiña, Emilio, 108

Z

Zavala, Vito, 132
Zoot Suit Riots, 159-160, 161, 187-191

Photographs on the cover appear thanks to the courtesy of the following sources:

Guadalupe School in Austin, Texas, March 12, 1932, Jensen Elliot Collection, Austin History Center; Texas Rangers pose with a Mexican prisoner in 1894, Western History Collection, University of Oklahoma; The National LULAC Convention in Houston, 1937, Houston Metropolitan Research Center, Houston Public Library; Picket line, *San Antonio Express News* Collection, The Institute of Texan Cultures; Man on donkey promoting payment of poll tax in San Antonio, 1925, *The San Antonio Light* Collection, The Institute of Texan Cultures; Mexican miners in Arizona in the early 1900s, Arizona Historical Society Library; Rodolfo "Corky" Gonzales, Western History Department, Denver Public Library; César Chávez with picketers during the grape boycott, Wayne State University; Members of the Ladies LULAC Council, Houston, Texas, 1954, Houston Metropolitan Research Center, Houston Public Library; and An Alianza Hispano Americana parade in Tucson, Arizona, Arizona Historical Society Library.

***

Translations:

With few exceptions, the translations of documents from Spanish to English were done by Gabriela Baeza Ventura, University of Houston.